NONE DARE CALL IT WITCHCRAFT

GARY NORTH

NONE DARE CALL IT
WITCHCRAFT

GARY NORTH

ARLINGTON HOUSE·PUBLISHERS
NEW ROCHELLE, NEW YORK

Copyright ©1976 by Arlington House

All rights reserved. No portion of this book may be reproduced without written permission from the publisher except by a reviewer who may quote brief passages in connection with a review.

Manufactured in the United States of America

Library of Congress Cataloging in Publication Data

North, Gary.
  None dare call it witchcraft.

  Includes bibliographical references.
  1. Occult sciences. 2. Physical research.
I. Title.
BF1411.N66   133   76-12109
ISBN 0-87000-301-1

Contents

Introduction 7
1. Rules of Evidence: Scientific and Religious 11
2. The Biblical Framework of Interpretation 25
3. Paranormal Science since 1960 39
4. The World of a Sorcerer 69
5. Psychics 93
6. Edgar Cayce: Mouthpiece of the Occult 113
7. Demonic Healing 137
8. Magic, Envy, and Foreign Aid 171
9. Escape from Creaturehood 183
Conclusion 209
Epilogue 213
Appendix A 221
Appendix B 225
Appendix C 231
Notes 239

Introduction

On September 20, 1938, a woman was dancing on a crowded dance floor in Chelmsford, England. Without warning, she burst into flames. Not her clothing—her body. Her flesh emitted blue flames, indicating tremendous heat, as she crumpled to the floor. Her escort and others tried to put out the flames, but it was hopeless. Within a few minutes, there was nothing left of her except a few ashes. There was no longer any trace of a human being. Coroner Leslie Beccles announced: "In all my experience, I've never come across any case as mysterious as this."

He would not have been able to make this statement had he been coroner at England's Norfolk Broads the previous July 30. On that day, a woman, her husband, and her children were paddling in a small boat when she suddenly caught fire. She was rapidly reduced to a mound of ashes before the horrified eyes of her family, yet the boat was undamaged and the other occupants were unaffected by the heat.

This, for want of an explanation, is simply classified as spontaneous human combustion, or SHC. It has existed in the medical literature of all European nations for over two hundred years. It has been chronicled in fiction, from Wieland's flaming father in the early section of Charles Brockden Brown's gothic novel, *Wieland*, to Charles Dickens' elimination of Krook in *Bleak House*. Today, almost no medical experts are willing to admit its existence, despite over one hundred cases recorded during the last century. Lester Adelson, pathologist to the coroner of Cuyahoga County, Ohio in the early 1950s, desperately hoped that some logical explanation of SHC would be found, but he knew of no likely candidate. He did define the problem in the March–April 1952 issue of Northwestern University's *Journal of Criminal Law, Criminology and Police Science*: "Spontaneous human combustion is that phenomenon wherein the body takes fire without an outside source of heat and is rapidly reduced to a handful of greasy ashes. Paradoxically, inanimate objects nearby escape relatively unharmed." So much for definitions.

In December 1956, in Honolulu, Mrs. Virginia Caget dashed into the room next to hers in an apartment house that was occupied by a seventy-eight-year-old invalid man, Young Sik Kim. He was on fire in an overstuffed chair. Blue flames shot out of his body, making it impossible for her to approach him. When firemen arrived fifteen minutes later, the victim and his chair no longer existed, except for his undamaged feet, still propped on his wheelchair, unmoved. Had he felt no pain? There are numerous cases in the literature that indicate precisely this.

According to Professor Wilton Krogman, a physical anthropologist at the University of Pennsylvania, it takes eight hours in a crematorium at temperatures of 2,000 degrees Fahrenheit to reduce a body to bones. To turn the bones to ash, temperatures of over 3,000 degrees are required. Krogman has made a study of the records of a hundred modern cases of SHC, and still he has no explanation of how a body can catch fire in this way and how so few objects around it are harmed.

July 1, 1952, St. Petersburg, Florida: Mrs. Mary Reeser, a sixty-seven-year-old widow, was visiting in her room with her neighbor, Mrs. P. M. Carpenter. When she left her that evening, Mrs. Reeser was seated in her armchair by the window, dressed in a rayon nightgown, slippers, and a housecoat, and was smoking a cigarette. The next morning, a Western Union messenger failed to raise her by knocking at her door to deliver a telegram. Concerned about her normally light-sleeping neighbor, Mrs. Carpenter started to open the door. The brass doorknob was hot. She cried out, and two house painters ran to see what was wrong. Together they broke into the house. Although both windows were open, the room was hot. In front of an open window were some ashes: a chair, an end table, and Mrs. Reeser. All that remained of her were a few pieces of charred backbone, a shrunken skull the size of an orange, and a wholly untouched left foot, still in its slipper. Her room was generally unaffected, except for some melted wax candles and melted plastic fixtures. From four feet above the floor was the soot. The clock had stopped at 4:20 A.M., but when plugged into an unmelted wall outlet, it started running again. There were no embers and no smell of smoke. Mrs. Reeser had weighed 175 pounds the night before; now only ten pounds remained.

The FBI was called in. The case received lots of publicity locally. Result: no explanation. Professor Krogman happened to be visiting friends nearby and volunteered to study the case. His conclusion: spontaneous human combustion. But he had never seen a head shrunken by fire. The skull should have exploded, not shrunk. Said Krogman:

Never have I seen a skull so shrunken or a body so completely consumed by heat. This is contrary to normal experience and I regard it as the most amazing thing I've ever seen. As I review it, the short hairs on my neck bristle with vague fear. Were I living in the Middle Ages, I'd mutter something like "black magic!"

Not living in the Middle Ages, he can only mutter "spontaneous human combustion." But what comfort is that? The phenomenon exists. It exists in the twentieth century. People want explanations for phenomena; if they are denied explanations, they prefer to ignore the phenomena. This is why the major news services refuse to pick up stories like the death of Mary Reeser—or did in 1952. In earlier days, when medical men could still hope to find an explanation, the phenomenon of SHC was still discussed and reported.

Adelson wrote only a few months before the Reeser case: "The most noteworthy feature of the entire topic is the prolonged acceptance of these phenomena by educated scientific men when chemistry, physics, and biology should long have effectively relegated them to the status of spontaneous generation, witchcraft, necromancy, and black magic." Spontaneous generation is old hat; spontaneous human combustion, on the other hand, is supposed to say something. But his point is well taken: the phenomenon should indeed be relegated to the realm of witchcraft, necromancy, and black magic.

Black magic? Surely such things are not possible. Black magicians, perhaps, somewhere in tribal societies not yet blessed with television and stereophonic cassettes, but not in the modern world Yet SHC is possible—frighteningly possible. It is the most spectacular of a whole class of impossible yet actual events, which are conveniently described as *paranormal phenomena*. Prior to the mid-1960s, investigations of such phenomena were conducted only by kooks—kooks being defined as those kinds of people who investigate paranormal phenomena. Kooks like William James, Sigmund Freud, and Carl Jung, for example. Kooks like Alfred Russel Wallace, the co-discoverer (with Darwin) of the principle of evolution through random variation and natural selection. Kooks like Sir Oliver Lodge, Sir Arthur Conan Doyle, and the members of the British and American Societies for Psychical Research. And, frankly, a lot of certifiable kooks. But since the mid-1960s, a vast new market for books on the occult and paranormal has developed, and interest in research into the paranormal has been kindled in at least untenured junior faculty members of major universities.

But what of black magic? What of the demonic? Do these worlds really exist? Or are they just catch phrases, like paranormal, extrasensory perception, and spontaneous human combustion—handy classification devices for the presently unknown? Is there any relationship, other than purely psychological or sociological, between the simultaneous rise of interest in the paranormal and the rise of interest in the occult?

The question has validity, especially at temperatures of 3,000 degrees Fahrenheit that do not burn curtains, wheelchairs, and slippers.

1
Rules of Evidence: Scientific and Religious

> Now faith is the substance of things hoped for, the evidence of things not seen.
> *Hebrews 11:1*

So you believe in witches and warlocks, plasmic phenomena, ghosties and ghoulies and things, in James Thurber's immortal phrase, that go bump in the night. Or perhaps you refuse to believe in such oddities. It may even be that you are simply curious about all the commotion, physical or intellectual. And because of your opinions, you have decided to read this book. That this book should even exist in the final quarter of the remarkable twentieth century is itself revelatory of the changes that have come upon us.

Before the mid-1960s, one looked in vain for more than a few scattered new books on occult phenomena. Not that titles were not in print, but they were usually produced by peculiar groups, probably located in either southern California or London, such as the Theosophical Society, the Lucis Trust, and many others. But the typical local bookstore, let alone a campus bookstore, seldom stocked such titles. An owner of a used-book shop might admit to a friend that occult books were a sizable part of his trade, but his friends never asked. There were heavily footnoted anthropological studies of "primitive" magic and witchcraft, written from the perspective of an officially neutral academic observer. There were histories of folklore and magic (often imports from England), and a good number of these titles were reprints of studies produced no later than 1935. Only the stodgy old Mystic Arts Book Club of New Hyde Park, New York actively advertised its hardback University Books titles, and these too were mostly reprints of carefully researched books, though not necessarily skeptical, that had been produced half a century earlier. The dearth of books, especially paperbacks, dealing with occultism, magic, witchcraft, and paranormal science reflected the climate of opinion of the day. There were few buyers of such books in the United States, it was thought (probably correctly), and even fewer writers.

Almost overnight the picture changed. One of the most radical discontinuities ever recorded in peacetime American culture occurred. No one cause and no single zone of American life—indeed, West European life—remained untouched by the multiple dislocations of 1964–70. In music most obviously, but also in clothing, deportment, entertainment in general, sexual roles (especially among the young), theology, church liturgy, academic curricula, politics, economics, change was accelerating at a tremendous rate. To illustrate my point, try to imagine a history of the 1960s that failed to include a section on the Beatles. It would not be too difficult to write a history of the preceding fifty years, decade by decade, without mentioning popular music, except insofar as it was in some way preparatory for the Beatles (Elvis Presley, for example). Their impact, as cultural wedges, was enormous. The climate of opinion was transformed.

The Collapse of Traditional Rationalism

Someone who was not on a university campus throughout the 1960s can scarcely imagine the extent of the change in outlook, especially among students and the younger faculty members. The Vietnam war helped to crystallize the new opposition to traditional political liberalism, but far more was involved than politics. The whole university structure was under fire: administration, tenure, the methodology of the academic disciplines, dormitory life, dating standards, everything. Anyone graduating in 1963 or even 1964 would hardly have recognized his alma mater in 1967.

A pair of articles in the *Saturday Evening Post,* itself a casualty of the 1960s, illustrate the nature of the change. The first one, published in May 1964, announced the following facts concerning the University of California, Berkeley, America's most prestigious state-supported university (second, then as now, only to Harvard in the evaluations of the nation's academic establishment): "The larger campuses, Berkeley especially, are smug in their conviction that they already provide the best university education possible. They believe no important reforms are necessary." The president of the University of California, Clark Kerr, the man who coined that monstrous and absolutely accurate term *multiversity,* was trying to produce quality mass education. "With his talent for achieving a consensus, the chances are that he will succeed. If he fails, the future will look bleak not only for his own university but for all higher education in America." You would be hard pressed to find a more prophetic statement in the annals of popular journalism; Kerr did indeed fail to gain consensus, as did his bureaucratic counterparts on the nation's prestigious campuses. The fabric of education was torn to shreds institutionally, and a decade later the leading educational theorists were still in shock. Ironically, the original article had been called "The Exploding University of California." The author had been speaking of size, but the phrase was really appropriate in another context just one semester later.

The second article, "I Am a U. C. Student: Do Not Fold, Bend or Mutilate," appeared two years later. No longer was Berkeley the smug center of institutional conservatism, the place where "no important reforms are necessary." All that was long gone. "Berkeley is surely the leader. It is the most serious and committed to change. Berkeley is, as they say, 'out of sight.' It is the model of the rebellious enclave within the affluence of mid-century America." Shortly thereafter, Clark Kerr was dimissed by the Board of Regents of the university. He left with his sense of humor, disappearing from the public's hostile eye with this final occupational epitaph: "I am leaving this job just as I entered it: fired with enthusiasm."

Yet this was not the last act for Berkeley. Again it would serve as a model, for after 1970 a new series of weird phenomena appeared: pseudo-Eastern mystics, Jesus (Freaks) People, revived sororities, a shift from hard drugs to marijuana and cheap wine, and an almost total internalization of concern—personal salvation, grade-point average, professional training, grad school. The Old Grad, class of '63, would have been more comfortable in 1973 had he returned to grad school. Only there had been a subtle psychological shift: the optimism of technocratic liberalism, so fundamental to university life from 1945 to 1965, had become schizophrenic. The optimism concerning the benefits of liberal arts training, the possibilities of future employment, the hope of social transformation, and the self-confidence of the earlier era had been smashed by the futility of Cold War liberal rhetoric and the equally futile radical campus protests. Joe College, 1975, is known as a drudge, a grind, a very dull lad. He has strange extracurricular habits and out-of-classroom philosophies. And strangest of all, Joe may well be majoring in some aspect of witchcraft. Which campus do you suppose granted the first bachelor's degree in witchcraft? Of course: Berkeley.

What America and the Western world discovered in the 1964–70 period was the fact that witchcraft and parallel occult phenomena leave their cultural underground and become popular and even influential social factors during times of rapid and unfamiliar social change. They are products of that change initially, and then become contributing causes. This was the case from the first century A.D. through the fourth, as the Roman Empire peaked and then disintegrated. Eastern cults infiltrated the life of Romans throughout the Empire. The great outbreak of witchcraft and witchcraft trials from the fifteenth century through the early eighteenth occurred in a period of historically unparalleled change, especially intellectual change. The Renaissance, not the early Middle Ages (or "Dark Ages"), was the time of magic, and it was the intellectual leadership that dabbled in it. Gauged by the legislation he produced in his years of power, John F. Kennedy may have been an unimpressive President, but in a very real sense, his death closed an intellectual era: from Newton to Kennedy. Ten weeks later the Beatles landed in New York.

Social commentators, historians, and philosophers are always tempted to concentrate on a particular era, usually their own, and then proclaim, *Here* is the watershed Sometimes they are right for the wrong reasons, but usually they are just plain wrong. Nevertheless, I am willing to stick my neck out and say it: Kennedy's death closed an era. The pessimistic implications of original Darwinism and original Freudianism were seen by some scholars from the beginning, but pessimism was not part of the popular culture, including the only slightly less faddish culture of the intellectuals. World War I doubtless shattered much of Europe's optimism, and the advent of the Nazis and fascists shook men's confidence in their present and their past. But victorious America had yet to taste defeat; defeat had not yet produced cynicism and pessimism. The intellectual underground of existential despair was not yet a part of men's outlook; at best, this underground stream was a footnote or two in monographs in philosophy and psychological pathology. Lee Harvey Oswald's bullet made a martyr of the world's primary media hero (a hero sired by the media) and his dynasty of rhetoric; it cut down a man whose programs, like the technocratic liberalism he promulgated, were mostly form without substance. Lyndon Johnson's legislative substance—the culmination of the old Progressive optimism—turned to dust in the mouths of his followers, and the war, the riots, and the deficit-induced price inflation broke the spirit of the age. No one can read the devastating vitriol of David Halberstam's *The Best and the Brightest* (1972) and fail to recognize the end of not only a political era but a state of mind.

On the campus, the new Bible after 1964 was Thomas Kuhn's *The Structure of Scientific Revolutions* (1962). Kuhn, a physicist and historian of science, introduced a thesis that, while not really novel in the humanities, was a blockbuster in the natural sciences. The history of science, he argued, is the history of scientific breakthroughs. Not just new variations on an older theme, not simply a progression upward from fact to fact, testing everything along the path of scientific progress, but real revolutions. In these breakthroughs, the older men in an academic discipline or guild resist the new position. It does not conform to the accepted paradigm, that is, the accepted way of viewing the world. Different questions are supposed to be asked, using different methods of inquiry, looking at different facts, and producing different conclusions. The newcomers, who are very often skilled amateurs, or professionals working in self-imposed (or guild-imposed) isolation, or younger men who find that the old ways of investigating specific phenomena—disturbing phenomena—are no longer sufficient, are the source of the scientific revolution. In short, the old guard is seldom converted; it simply dies off. Science moves in discontinuous leaps: breakthrough, guild battle, retirement or death of the resisters, and a new era of painstaking research and even drudgery—"normal science"—following the new paradigm. In other words, scientists are not neutral investigators, neutrality is a myth, and there is no real standard of truth or universally accepted methods of verification. Epistemological relativism, long understood by the best of the scientists, now filtered down to the undergraduates.

All of this was at least implied in modern, post-Newtonian twentieth-century physics. Social scientists had vaguely known that guilds operate in this fashion, that all truth is really relative. Historians like Carl Becker and Charles A. Beard had been saying so for decades, as had Karl Mannheim, whose *Ideology and Utopia* (1936) had served a few serious scholars as a kind of Bible of relativism. But the old orthodoxy still prevailed in 1963. There might be a nod of the head, a kind of academic genuflection, to the idea of epistemological relativism, and then it was back to the business at hand, namely, transforming the whole world through rationalistic, liberal humanism. Now, however, everyone was reading Kuhn; it was assigned reading in education classes, sociology of knowledge classes, philosophy seminars, and history. Whether the natural scientists, who tend to neglect and even resent inquiries into just how they know what is going on "out there" in the visible world, grasped what Kuhn was saying, is problematical. The undergraduates in sociology did, and sociology, as an academic discipline, will never be the same.[1]

Once the old orthodoxy of rational neutrality and rational investigators was shattered by Kuhn, Vietnam, marijuana, LSD, Eastern philosophy, and all the rest of the cultural acids of the day, the barrier to really strange phenomena was gone. No longer could one argue, *a priori*, that occult phenomena do not exist. Students were experimenting with everything else; they could also experiment with occultism. If anything, the philosophy of mysticism, East and West, blended quite well with many aspects of the cosmology of the occult. The official ideology of the campus had long been Kantian, and Immanuel Kant's philosophy was a philosophy of radical *criticism*.[2] Unfortunately for Kant and his spiritual heirs, the students of the mid-1960s took criticism seriously, turning the intellectual searchlight on Kantian rationalism—a rationalism Kant had deliberately constructed as a final antidote to dogmatism. Yet it was his system that proved to be too dogmatic for certain elements of the cultural revolution. The students had learned their lessons well. Their unwillingness to take seriously parts of the old orthodoxy—the technocratic, optimistic, messianic parts—led a vocal minority into new paths, which in fact are very ancient paths. Clark Kerr had never known what a *real* multiversity is; it was to consume him as thoroughly as the mythical Freudian Oedipus was devoured by his children.

The Dualism of Autonomous Speculation

The seventeenth century was to produce a new worldview: Cartesian rationalism and Newtonian science. Both systems rested on the foundation of applied mathematics. The previous century had brought the startling conclusions of Copernicus and Kepler concerning the heliocentric nature of the solar system. They helped to create interest in mathematics as a tool of comprehension, in opposition to the position of orthodox Aristotelian philosophy that mathematics is not central. In a very real sense, Copernicus and Kepler had returned to Plato, Pythagoras, and the Neoplatonists, who did see mathematics as important.[3] The success of Descartes, who in 1619 experienced an ecstatic illumination informing him that mathematics is the sole key for unlocking nature's secrets, and then of Newton at the end of the century, elevated mathematical logic to a position of preeminence.[4] The capacity of mathematics to provide regularity to certain natural and physical processes convinced many philosophers, most notably Hobbes, that this was a universal tool that could be used to create a science of man and society. Scientism was born; Comte and Marx were its lineal descendants.

Blinded by the dazzling success of Newton, a success vastly greater than the crude measuring devices of his era could record, men hesitated to inquire into the apparent absurdity of Newtonian science. Why should mathematical reasoning, an abstract mental skill, an art, correspond to the mechanical processes of the observed world? Why should such a mind-matter link exist? As Nobel Prize-winning physicist Eugene Wigner put it, such a finding is utterly unreasonable.[5] But the correlation exists. And because it exists, the followers of Descartes and Newton faced a fearful intellectual problem: what becomes of the free will of man in a mathematically deterministic universe? What becomes of the human mind? Is mind simply a ghost in the machine? Does not the very certainty of mathematical logic spell the end of human freedom, since man is undoubtedly a part of this universe?

These questions, or ones analogous to them, have been with man from the beginning. The Greek philosophers grappled with these dualisms—structure vs. change, law vs. chaos, freedom vs. determinism—by means of the so-called form-matter schema. The world was understood as the product of ultimate conflict: abstract metaphysical forms subduing raw, chaotic matter. Another variation had matter imitating form. The ultimate form was monistic in nature, the ultimate One. Out of one came many, that is, diversity. As to which had priority, abstract form or concrete matter, philosophers differed. How the two were linked, or how one was not swallowed up in the other, or how it was possible to compare infinite quantities of raw matter or the necessarily infinite number of abstract forms, no one was sure. The inability of classical philosophers to reconcile this fundamental dualism led to the disintegration of classical culture. Eastern mystery cults spread over the Hellenistic and Roman worlds. Total impersonal Fate battled total impersonal Chance for control of the universe. Astrology flourished, was banned, and still flourished; chaos cults were everywhere. Men could no longer make sense out of their world.

Christianity replaced classicism's fragmented culture. But the lure of Greek philosophical speculation—the logic of the hypothetically autonomous human mind—seemed irresistible to Christian philosophical apologists. They incorporated aspects of Greek wisdom, and therefore Greek dualism, into their defenses of the orthodox faith. The result was intellectual schizophrenia—philosophical syncretism. Thus was born the so-called nature-grace framework. The truths of autonomous human reason, whether Platonic (as in the early Middle Ages), Neoplatonic and mystical (same era), or Aristotelian (late Middle Ages), were understood as autonomous truths. They required the grace of God's revelation to complement and extend them, but they were truths nonetheless. Nature, meaning philosophical speculation, and grace were reconciled. The great synthesis was produced in the mid-1200s by Thomas Aquinas. It did not last a century.

In the fourteenth century, the synthesis was attacked from two sides. William of Ockham and his followers used the famous intellectual razor—the prohibition of useless additional explanations to describe any natural process—to shave grace from the universe. Natural reason is therefore sufficient to understand the world. Grace informs us of nothing indispensable concerning nature and its processes. On the other side, Thomas Bradwardine dismissed reason as a tool for comprehending God's revelation. Personal experience, not endless chains of logical reasoning, is the heart of true religion.

Professor Gordon Leff's assessment of the battle between the two positions not only throws light on the breakdown of the medieval philosophical synthesis, but also reveals a great deal about similar disputes between contemporary scientists and rationalists on the one hand, and religionists and mystics on the other. In fact, the whole question of what constitutes valid evidence for an investigation of the supernatural has not advanced much beyond this fourteenth-century debate. Each side cannot acknowledge the legitimacy of the other's methods of investigation and interpretation. They are *mutually exclusive approaches.* Leff explains:

> The importance of the disputes between Bradwardine and his opponents lies in the change wrought upon scholasticism. Each side, in starting from either faith or reason to the exclusion of the other, made them virtually separate pursuits. Since Ockham and his followers refused to see the supernatural through the natural, they put faith beyond reason's bounds. Because Bradwardine allowed reason no autonomy it lost any validity, and faith became the only law. This meant that, on the one hand, reason, philosophy and science tended to become autonomous disciplines without reference to theology; while, on the other, faith and theology became increasingly a regime for worship, independent of ratiocination. The effect of this break was plain to see: for philosophy and reason it meant the virtual self-sufficiency preached by the Averroists;* it could choose to discuss man in its own terms without much more than a passing reference to God. At the hands of Ockham and his followers, it recognized no more than a nominal obligation to be at the disposal of faith, while in its attention only to practical knowledge it in fact rejected such a role. On the part of theology, the effect of this division was no less far-reaching: through the withdrawal of reason's support, faith came increasingly to rely upon dogmatic assertion and personal experience.[6]

Grace could progressively be ignored in Ockham's rationalism. "To follow the natural laws of the skeptics," argues Leff, "could only mean that grace was questioned, for its existence was too intangible to be asserted." When Ockham asserted the authority of reason, he inevitably pushed God out of rationalism's universe. The voice of authority was unashamedly man's.

The rationalist's hostility to supernaturalism led, understandably, to a reformulation of the old Greek form-matter dualism. Ockham and the nominalists denied any reality to overarching metaphysical forms. Such forms were understood as simply being linguistic conventions. Reality inhered in the particulars. But prob-

---

*Averroes, a twelfth-century Arabic scholar, was a convinced Aristotelian, and his writings were extremely influential in the West during the revival of Aristotle's philosophy. He held a dualistic position with respect to the truths of faith and the truths of reason. Unlike Aquinas, he believed that a philosophical truth can be theologically false, and vice versa. Philosophy is the way of highest truth.

lems beset this perspective. What about nature itself? What binds nature's actions into a coherent unity? Is nature lawless? Is nature a capricious threat to man, a whirling mass of particulars that strikes out randomly to thwart the plans of men? How can men control nature if they have no access to hypothetical forms that themselves impose structure on matter? Man was a slave to nature unless he could find a means of binding down nature to serve his purposes. Nature threatened man's power and therefore man's freedom and autonomy.

The answer of Copernicus, Kepler, Descartes, and the Newtonians was clear enough: man must discover the mathematical laws that somehow are inherent in all of nature's processes. The quest for the knowledge of natural law was a quest for power and freedom. Though Kepler was a pagan worshiper of the sun, as well as an astrologer,[7] and Newton regarded himself as an accomplished student of biblical prophecy, nevertheless their intellectual legacy, at least in retrospect, was the veneration of the quest for natural laws, that is, mathematical laws applicable to an essentially mechanistic universe.

On first glance, this new worldview seemed to provide man with an escape from the tensions of dualism. Instead, the most baffling dualism of all was introduced, the nature-freedom antinomy. If man gains power over nature by subduing all of nature to mechanistically applied laws, then what becomes of man himself? Man is a product of nature. To the extent that we understand nature, we must use law as a guide. But is man simply another effect in an endless chain of cause and effect? Are man's deepest thoughts nothing more than the products of certain chemical reactions in the physical brain? Is man actually determined entirely by the mechanistic laws of nature? Is his sense of freedom and personal moral responsibility a delusion? Can the laws of nature be applied to society, as Hobbes believed, thus enabling a supreme monarch-scientist to construct a political system in which all events would be as predictable as the movement of the stars above? By gaining control over his universe by means of logic, experiment, and mathematics, man simultaneously reduces his own zones of contingency—chance —and increasingly contingency was viewed as the last place of freedom from mechanistic law. Man's quest for freedom through autonomous power turned in upon itself. It led to the enslavement not merely of nature, but also of man himself, who is (so far as he can be known by himself) nothing more than a natural phenomenon.

Descartes' resolution of the antinomy, writes E. A. Burtt, was to hypothesize the existence of an indeterminately huge material world—a giant mathematical machine—which was correlative to another world of unextended, thinking subjects. "But the Cartesian answer," concludes Burtt, "raises an enormous problem, how to account for the interrelation of these diverse entities. If each of the two substances exists in absolute independence of the other, how do motions of extended things produce unextended sensations, and how is it that the clear conceptions or categories of unextended mind are valid of the *res extensa?* How is it that that which is unextended can know, and, knowing, achieve purposes in, an extended universe?"[8] What is the link between mind and matter? Does matter control mind, thus erasing human freedom, or does mind control matter as an independent creative agency, thus denying the fundamental principle of Cartesian science, namely, the universal rule of mechanistic law in all physical extension? Does mechanical law destroy man's freedom, or does man's autonomy—necessarily defined as *outside* the cause-and-effect chain of natural succession—threaten the universal rule of the natural law of cause and effect? The philosophy of autonomous man can provide no answer, yet the question demands an answer.

David Hume, in the middle of the eighteenth century, provided the classic answer of the skeptic: natural law is nothing more than the agreement among men that certain actions follow necessarily from prior actions. Cause and effect, in other words, are nothing but *convention.* The sensation of pain when I thrust my finger into boiling water may have no relation to that water. I may experience pain each time, but experience is not the same as rigorous mechanical law. We simply call certain events effects of prior events, the causes. Nominalism—that is, the denial of the existence of metaphysical forms that order nature—grew to maturity in the philosophy of Hume. Whirl once again became king, despite the fact that men naively think the laws or conventions of their minds relate in some way to a hypothetically lawful universe out there beyond our senses.

Men do not normally choose skepticism, but Hume's arguments seemed to make it impossible to avoid such a choice. Hume's arguments were useful in refuting dogmatic theology, perhaps, but the price of victory was too high. So concluded the man who still stands as *the* philosopher of the modern world, Immanuel Kant. Hume's ideas, Kant once wrote, awoke him from his dogmatic slumbers, but the decade of his conversion to Humean skepticism (1763–72) led him to search for certainty, and certainty clearly was not to be found in the contingent rules of human experience. On that, Hume and Kant were in agreement. First comes dogmatism, then skepticism, and finally, said Kant, truly critical certainty. "Skepticism is thus a resting-place for human reason, where it can reflect upon its dogmatic wanderings and make a survey of the region in which it finds itself, so that for the future it may be able to choose its path with more certainty. But it is no dwelling-place for permanent settlement. Such can be obtained only through perfect certainty in our knowledge, alike of the objects themselves and of the limits within which all our knowledge of objects is enclosed."[9] To find *a priori* certainty, Kant concluded, men must be humble. They must limit their questions to those that can be answered by the combination of sense data (experience) as interpreted by the universal, fixed categories of human thought.

The foundation of the regularity of nature inheres not in nature itself, Kant argued, but in the *a priori* categories of the human mind. Nothing can be known without sense data, but without the categories of human thought to assemble the data into coherent wholes, experience tells us nothing. There is therefore no way of knowing anything beyond our senses *as categorized and ordered* by the concepts of the autonomous mind. "Thus the order and regularity in the appearances, which we entitle *nature,* we ourselves introduce. We could never find them in appearances, had not we ourselves, or the nature of our mind, originally set them there."[10] The human understanding, he concluded, is "the *faculty of rules.*"[11] It is man's autonomous mind that creates what we know as nature. The "stuff out there," that is, the "things in themselves," must be forever unknown and unknowable to us. We can know nature only through our own *a priori* categories of reason. *Man's mind legislates the laws of nature!* "Thus the understanding is something more than a power of formulating rules through comparison of appearances; it is itself the lawgiver of nature. Save through it, nature, that is, synthetic unity of the manifold of appearances according to rules, would not exist at all. . . ."[12] Man is the ultimate creator of his own reality. In this there is certainty of knowledge.

How do we make moral decisions in this world? If the *a priori* categories of logic are universal, in what does our moral freedom consist? Furthermore, how do we know for certain that the "stuff out there" is not personal, active, and independently powerful? God, "things in themselves," morality, the transcendental human ego, freedom, and contingency are assigned to an impotent and forever unknowable realm of *noumenal* reality. The *phenomenal* realm is the only one we can ever know—the world of interpreted sense data. In short, the noumenal realm of freedom and moral choice, as well as the world of God, demons, angels, and "stuff out there," is nothing more than a hypothetical *limiting concept,* that is, an intellectual device to avoid answering the fundamental questions that autonomous human reason is unable to answer.

Cornelius Van Til, a twentieth-century philosopher and theologian, has argued throughout his career that Kant's philosophy is the touchstone of all modern thought. Van Til's analysis is central to the thesis of this book, namely, that the current revival of occultism and witchcraft represents a throwback to the paganism of the pre-Christian world. Furthermore, it is my thesis that *modern secular humanism is not only powerless intellectually to call a halt to the occult revival, but is in fact one of the primary causes of the revival.*

Van Til makes it clear that the epistemological dualism of modern philosophy—rationalism vs. irrationalism—is inherent in *all* forms of autonomous philosophical speculation. From the day that Adam tried to test the word of God concerning his destiny, man has sought some other voice of authority than God. By locating their voice of authority outside God's revelation, both verbal and natural, men create for themselves a series of unsolvable dilemmas. The chief principle of apostate man is his own *autonomy*. Whatever his voice of authority may be, it must never violate the principle of human autonomy. Yet man must have some principle of authority. Van Til's arguments in this regard are vital to any consideration of the rules of scientific evidence:

> First there is the need for authority that grows out of the existence of the endless multiplicity of factual material. Time rolls its ceaseless course. It pours out upon us an endless stream of facts. And the stream is really endless on the non-Christian basis. For those who do not believe that all that happens in time happens because of the plan of God, the activity of time is like to that, or rather is identical with that, of Chance. Thus the ocean of facts has no bottom and no shore. It is this conception of the ultimacy of time and of pure factuality on which modern philosophy, particularly since the days of Kant, has laid such great stress. And it is because of the general recognition of the

ultimacy of chance that rationalism of the sort that Descartes, Spinoza and Leibniz represented, is out of date. It has become customary to speak of post-Kantian philosophy as irrationalistic. It has been said that Kant limited reason so as to make room for faith. Hence there are those who are willing to grant that man's emotions or his will can get in touch with such aspects of reality as are not accessible to the intellect. The intellect, it is said, is not the only, and in religious matters not even the primary, instrument with which men come into contact with what is ultimate in human experience. There is the world of the moral imperative, of aesthetic appreciation, of the religious *a priori* as well as the world of science. There is in short the world of "mystery" into which the prophet or genius of feeling or of will may lead us.

It is of the greatest import to note that the natural man need not in the least object to the kind of authority that is involved in the idea of irrationalism. And that chiefly for two reasons. In the first place the irrationalism of our day is the direct lineal descendant of the rationalism of previous days. The idea of pure chance has been inherent in every form of non-Christian thought in the past. It is the only logical alternative to the position of Christianity, according to which the plan of God is back of all. Both Plato and Aristotle were compelled to make room for it in their maturest thought. The pure "not-being" of the earliest rationalism of Greece was but the suppressed "otherness" of the final philosophy of Plato. So too the idea of pure factuality or pure chance as ultimate is but the idea of "otherness" made explicit. Given the non-Christian assumption with respect to man's autonomy, the idea of chance has equal rights with the idea of logic.

In the second place modern irrationalism has not in the least encroached upon the domain of the intellect as the natural man thinks of it. Irrationalism has merely taken possession of that which the intellect, by its own admission, cannot in any case control. Irrationalism has a secret treaty with rationalism by which the former cedes to the latter so much of its territory as the latter can at any given time find the forces to control. Kant's realm of the noumenal has, as it were, agreed to yield so much of its area to the phenomenal, as the intellect by its newest weapons can manage to keep in control. Moreover, by the same treaty irrationalism has promised to keep out of its own territory any form of authority that might be objectionable to the autonomous intellect. The very idea of pure factuality or chance is the best guarantee that no true authority, such as that of God as the Creator and Judge of men, will ever confront man. If we compare the realm of the phenomenal as it has been ordered by the autonomous intellect to a clearing in a large forest, we may compare the realm of the noumenal to that part of the same forest which has not yet been laid under cultivation by the intellect. The realm of mystery is on this basis simply the realm of that which is not yet known.[13]

The "not yet known" has reasserted itself with a vengeance in modern science and philosophy. Werner Heisenberg's principle of indeterminacy is first cousin to existentialism. The random event in nature, by way of quantum mechanics, is presently intruding into every nook and cranny of man's formerly trustworthy Newtonian universe. Many physicists now teach their fellow physical scientists the wonders of the irrational. And with indeterminacy have come relativism and the loss of faith in wholly objective, totally neutral scientific observation. The rational clearing in the irrational forest, once thought nearly devoid of trees—chance—is blanketed by thick underbrush. Underbrush so tall in places that it covers the majestic trees, so that not even rationalism's sharpest tools can cut them down. The result: increasing despair. The supposedly orderly universe of the nineteenth century is found to be a massive delusion.

To Catch a Ghost

The ranks of the credulous, some of them respected scientists (*before* they began to hunt ghosts), and the ranks of the professional skeptics were fairly clearly drawn in the late-nineteenth century. The rationalists had spent the century trying to squeeze the last traces of God out of the universe, and Darwinism was understood to have accomplished the task. The last traces of "final causation" or ultimate direction to the processes of biological evolution had been replaced with random biological adaptation to randomly changing environments over whatever quantity of time was deemed sufficient to give random change sufficient elbowroom to bring our world into existence. The God of orthodox Christianity had lost His last remaining toehold on the phenomenal realm. From now on, He would have to content Himself with dabbling in the noumenal—a safe enough place for Him, really.

Yet now these ghost hunters and table rappers were allowing something-in-itself to creep across the treaty's boundary markers. While such odd phenomena were believed wholly explainable by rational laws, given enough study, the desire of the spiritualists to relate these odd phenomena to affairs of the noumenal realm —phenomena that have somehow dropped in for a chat from the noumenal—was quite properly understood by the rationalists as violating the post-Kantian secret treaty. The unknown was supposed to stay unknown; any time it becomes known, it is subject to the comprehensive *a priori* laws of the autonomous human mind.

But of course no rationalist ever believed that the unknown was actually invading the realm of the known. What he resented was the obstinacy of the ghost hunters in clinging to their fantasy that there could ever be such an invasion. To acknowledge the possibility of such an invasion was tantamount—indeed, identical—to saying that the only philosophical tool that can be used to keep God locked out of the phenomenal realm actually has a flaw in it. It would have meant that the crack in the wall between the phenomenal realm of scientific, comprehensive knowledge and the unknown (for the moment) might allow God to sneak back in to control the destiny of the universe and to judge it on the final day. If any force has impact, it has to be a phenomenal force, that is, a force that operates by rigorous scientific law, even if we have yet to discover that law. The mutual defense treaty against God was being ignored by the spiritists. Their denial rankled the minds of the Newtonian rationalists.

Van Til has used the following analogy. A fisherman says his net can catch every fish in the sea. His friend is skeptical, but goes along to see. The fisherman tosses his net into the water, pulls in several fish, but several more slip through the net and swim to freedom. "Look there," says his friend. "Your net didn't catch those fish." "Nonsense," replies the fisherman. "Those aren't fish. What my net doesn't catch aren't fish." What those fish were to the fisherman, so are all the bits of evidence of supernatural powers to the cosmologies of the rationalists. No supernatural forces are allowed into the realm of phenomena; the net of scientific observation screens out all noumenal effects, since cause and effect are strictly phenomenal. If there is an effect, it must be phenomenally produced.

In 1882, scholars in Britain who were interested in pursuing "noumenal effects" by means of scientific procedures founded the Society for Psychical Research. Initially, several were avowedly spiritualists, but they gradually left the society. Several members were quite famous as men of science, including William James, Sir Oliver Lodge, Sir William Crookes, Henry Sidgwick (the first president of the SPR), and, much later, Sigmund Freud. Some members, like Frank Podmore, were skeptics who were nonetheless interested in examining the data. But the group was always regarded with suspicion and consternation by orthodox rationalists and scientists. Opponents assumed that such phenomena, being phenomena in the Kantian sense, were simply phenomena. Such data were of little interest as phenomena; only as signs of noumenal or supernatural influence could they have any significance, and that possibility was denied by the very canons of scientific investigation. Thus, even the prestige of Alfred Russel Wallace, the co-discoverer with Darwin of the principle of evolution by means of natural selection, did not impress orthodox scientists, including Darwin himself, when Wallace became a convinced spiritualist. What Professor William Irvine writes of Darwin, he could have written about most rationalistic scientists of the late-nineteenth century: "The supernatural interfered with the aesthetic symmetry of his ideas. The Deity had become an epistemological inconvenience."[14]

One of the last representatives of this naively confident humanism who still writes on the topic of witchcraft with real authority is Rossell Hope Robbins. He was still teaching on university campuses in the late-1960s. His important book, *The Encyclopedia of Witchcraft and Demonology* (1959), announces in no-nonsense terms his presuppositions regarding the witchcraft phenomena of the late Middle Ages: "I have selected what I conclude to be the most significant for the total picture of witchcraft presented here: a colossal fraud and delusion, impossible because the 'crime' of witchcraft was an impossible crime. The present entries could have been doubled or trebled, but the reader would not necessarily be that much richer or wiser." Indeed, when one begins with a religiously held conviction that a particular kind of phenomenon is impossible, every last bit of evidence offered to the contrary will be reinterpreted (or ignored) in order to force it into another mosaic of interpretation—hallucination, torture, self-delusion, desire for notoriety, etc. Robbins is only echoing sixteenth-century skeptics, such as Johann Weyer, a Protestant physician, who blamed the confessions of witches on their confusion. He was not alone in his opinion. Robbins lists several pages of the titles of tracts dealing with witchcraft from the early modern period, and half a dozen were skeptical. Robbins writes in the same tradition of the two great historians of witchcraft in the last century, both totally skeptical: Joseph Hansen and Henry C. Lea. They deny any supernatural reality to the witchcraft phenomena for the same reason that they deny a personal God who manifests Himself in time and space: the natural realm is ours and ours alone, by definition.

At the other end of the spectrum are the totally credulous. Montague Summers is the classic example of a scholarly historian of the occult—witchcraft, vampires, werewolves; he believed almost every word in every document charging these crimes against certain individuals. Looking at the same documents that Lea and

Hansen examined, Summers concluded just the opposite: witchcraft was real, not just as a social pathology, but also as an example of supernatural power. But there have always been other kinds of credulous "searchers" of occult mysteries, and they are all too often taken in either by charlatans or by truly sinister characters, those figures described by the Bible as "having a form of godliness, but denying the power thereof" (II Timothy 3:5). The totally credulous are these people's victims. "For of this sort are they which creep into houses, and lead captive silly women laden with sins, led away with divers lusts, ever learning, and never able to come to the knowledge of the truth" (II Timothy 3:6,7). These are the seance ladies, the yoga ladies, the Mystical Church of Cosmic Vibrations ladies. They are the only too willing victims of the swamis, gurus, mahatmas, healers, mumblers, and holy men, many of whom seem to have been chosen by God in miraculous visions delivered to them near an off-ramp of the Hollywood Freeway.

Conclusion

The increasing quantity and improved quality of the evidence of demonic and paranormal phenomena have become obvious to millions of American and European citizens in the last decade. As younger scholars, themselves the product of the higher education system, penetrate areas once off limits by academic definition, there will be an even larger stream of data. It is unlikely that the data, in and of themselves, will convert present skeptics to full-blown occult believers. A few will experience something like religious conversion, as their interpretative frameworks are overloaded with the new data, and finally one new piece triggers a kind of short-circuiting effect in the rationalist interpretative scheme. But these events are rare. More likely the skeptics, as the torchbearers of a now-dying optimistic, technocratic rationalism, will simply retire or die off. It may take two generations, but the hole in the dike has only grown larger since 1965. What the serious investigator must do now is find an alternative framework to the old skepticism—a new paradigm or interpretative scheme that can handle the supernatural data being released into the modern world.

The proper approach must combine confidence and humility. Confidence in one's basic interpretative framework is mandatory for serious intellectual investigation; it is the first step in any scientific or historical inquiry. At the same time the researcher must be humble. The data can fool him, especially data provided by "true believers," confidence men, and serious but overenthusiastic researchers on the fringes of orthodox science. The data may be of "phenomenal" rather than "noumenal" origin; it may be a question of simply not having enough data or not having discovered some new set of rules that can deal with these perplexing data. But in some cases, the data will truly reflect their supernatural origin. The question facing each man who encounters such data should therefore be: What should I do about my encounter with the supernatural? If he is not a Christian, and therefore not the beneficiary of special protection, the answer is twofold: (1) run; (2) repent and be converted.

2
The Biblical Framework of Interpretation

Such an immense and growing quantity of information is available on occultism, written from so many different viewpoints, that investigators are tempted to give up in despair. How is it possible to assimilate all of this material? Obviously, it is not possible, any more than it is possible to assimilate all the economic data or chemical data or any other kind of data available to a serious researcher. The quest for exhaustive knowledge is illegitimate. Men are creatures with creaturely limitations. That they are not God, with His comprehensive and authoritative knowledge of all factuality, should not disturb men. Yet the ideal of exhaustive knowledge has placed modern scientific man on an endless treadmill, a kind of modern quest for the holy grail (itself a magical image). Man thinks that if he does not know everything exhaustively, he cannot know anything confidently. On the presuppositions of the pretended autonomy of human thought, this is precisely the case. Since any fact in the universe can conceivably influence any other fact, in order to know any fact truly, a man must understand all facts exhaustively.

The Bible teaches man humility, but it also teaches man confidence: humility *before* God and confidence *under* God that the earth can be mastered by man to the glory of God. God, as the creator and sustainer of all facts, provides man with the necessary framework of interpretation that enables him to know facts accurately enough to accomplish his assigned tasks. The key is the interpretative framework rather than the quantity of raw data. Indeed, facts are never "raw"; they are always interpreted facts, since they exist because of and within God's sovereign plan. There is no brute factuality; there is only God-ordained factuality. Therefore, man can have confidence in his intellectual labors if he subordinates his investigative labors to the interpretative framework provided him in biblical revelation. Because of the existence of revelation, man need not know every fact—in this case, facts about occultism—to have accurate knowledge concerning the world. More time spent in study, more facts, better facts, and more attention paid to literary style no doubt would improve people's knowledge of occult phenomena, but as limited creatures we can still have confidence that we sufficiently grasp the topic in spite of the fact that we can never perfectly grasp all phenomena. Not even Satan himself has a perfect grasp of occult phenomena, so we need not despair. Satan should, however.

The most important passages in the Bible concerning occultism are not those that refer to angels, demons, visions, magic, and witchcraft. The truly crucial passages are those that tell us about God and His stance toward the creation, for it is God who is central, not Satan and his host. The universe is *theocentric*. If men would acknowledge this fact and conform their activities to it, there would be no necessity of dwelling on biblical passages dealing with occult phenomena. It is because men consistently suppress their knowledge of the truth that the revelation to man concerning occult phenomena takes on new importance.

An observant student of the occult arts in history begins after a while to detect recurring themes in occult literature. Occultism is the outworking of a series of philosophical and ultimately religious presuppositions about the nature of man, the world, and law. It is a *system,* however disjointed and even self-contradictory the records may be. Like any system of thought and life, it has basic presuppositions. These presuppositions are the heart of the revival of occultism in our era. The miracles, the oddities, the visions, the unexplained—and by post-Kantian philosophy, unexplainable—phenomena get the attention of the newspaper reporters and the thrill-seekers, but oddities, like the poor, have always been with us. The more important problem is: Why have these phenomena reappeared and multiplied so astoundingly in the final third of this supposedly rational century? The answer lies in the *philosophy* of occultism, which is almost a mirror image of biblical revelation, but which is in conformity with contemporary humanism on point after fundamental point. To understand the occult revival, it is mandatory that we understand orthodox Christianity and its presuppositions. It is impossible to understand Christianity without grasping the significance of certain doctrines: creation, the fall, the incarnation, and the final judgment.

Creation

This is the starting point, both philosophically and revelationally. The Bible opens with this announcement: "In the beginning God created the heaven and the earth" (Genesis 1:1). By the fiat and absolutely authoritative command of God's word, all that exists was created but of nothing—*creatio ex nihilo*. Matter-energy was not co-extensive and co-eternal with God, as Aristotle taught (*Physics,* VIII) and as the pagan cosmologies of the ancient world taught. God did not bring the world into existence by struggling with some ultimate chaotic matter in order to produce order. God commanded the light, and there was light (Genesis 1:3). We cannot explain this fiat act, nor need we. Neither can questions concerning origins be answered by the followers of Kant, whose system was created by Kant to call a halt to the asking of such unanswerable questions. Nor can they be answered by the Marxians, since Marx explicitly prohibited the asking of questions concerning origins.[1] All we know is what we are told by the One who was there at the time.

Because God created the universe, there is a permanent, unbridgeable gap between the ultimate being of God and the derivative being of creatures. There is a Creator-creature distinction. Though men are made in the image of God (Genesis 1:27), they do not partake of God's being. They are like God, but they are not of the same substance as God. No other doctrine is more fundamental than this one. Significantly, in every form of occultism this principle is denied, sometimes implicitly and usually explicitly. Satan's old temptation to man hinges on his denial and man's denial of the Creator-creature distinction. "For thou, LORD, art high above all the earth: thou art exalted far above all gods" (Psalm 97:9). He is not some impersonal force, but a sovereign, utterly personal God: "For thus saith the high and lofty One that inhabiteth eternity, whose name is Holy; I dwell in the high and holy place, with him also that is of a contrite and humble spirit, to revive the spirit of the humble and to revive the heart of the contrite ones" (Isaiah 57:15). God is not an evolved man: "For my thoughts are not your thoughts, neither are your ways my ways, saith the LORD. For as the heavens are higher than the earth, so are my ways higher than your ways, and my thoughts than your thoughts" (Isaiah 55:8,9). Close to the man with the contrite heart, yet infinitely removed from the rebellious creature. Here is the God of creation.

Because God created the universe by the power of His word, He also *sustains* it. This is the doctrine of *providence,* the corollary of the doctrine of creation. All things come to pass within the overall plan of God (Isaiah 45:5–12), despite the fact that He is not responsible for sin. This is also a humanly unanswerable antinomy, and the apostle Paul specifically called attention to it and then denied that man, the creature, has any right to raise it (Romans 9:19–22). It is an antinomy in every existing philosophical system, for all systems fragment on the antinomy of free will and predestination, personal responsibility and unbendable cause-and-effect law. The Christian system presents a God who is sovereign and man who is responsible. All other existing systems, as Van Til has demonstrated so well, rest on the presupposition of a chance universe: chance out of chance returning unto chance. But there is no zone of ultimate contingency that can serve man as a "neutral safety zone" for the testing of God's word. There are no zones of existence outside His control. "The king's heart is in the hand of the LORD, as the rivers of water: he turneth it withersoever he will" (Proverbs 21:1). Similarly, "A man's heart deviseth his way: but the LORD directeth his steps" (Proverbs 16:9). The theme of the heavenly potter and his earthly clay—out of which man was created—appears in both the Old and the New Testament. "O house of

Israel, cannot I do with you as this potter? saith the LORD. Behold, as the clay is in the potter's hand, so are ye in mine hand, O house of Israel" (Jeremiah 18:6). It is this image that Paul uses in establishing the doctrine of the sovereignty of God (Romans 9:20, 21).

In direct contrast to the biblical view of man and God, the occult systems, from the magical sects of the East to the Gnostics of the early church period, and from them to today's preachers of cosmic evolution and irresistible karma, are marked by one salient theme: monism. There is no Creator-creature distinction. We are all gods in the making. Out of One has proceeded the many, and back into One are the many traveling. Eastern mystics, philosophical Hegelians, and followers of the overrated Teilhard de Chardin all agree on the reality of ultimate monism. It is such a convenient doctrine, for it denies any eternal separation of God and His creation, and therefore it denies any eternal separation of saved and lost. It denies any ultimate distinction between good and evil, past and present, structure and change.

In the revival of mysticism, which is invariably monistic, whether Eastern or Western, the popular culture has produced many documents that aid the cause, but one of the most successful is Hermann Hesse's pseudo-Eastern book, *Siddhartha*. Published in 1951, it became in the late-1960s a touchstone among members of the counterculture who were still willing and able to read. (For the illiterates, 1973 brought the movie.) Its message: all is one. The last three paragraphs of the book bring this point home graphically. Govinda, Siddhartha's (Buddha's) friend, stares into Siddhartha's face, and he sees a series of pictures in a vision. Lives appear before him, all different but really all the same: an infant, a fish, a murderer, lovers, crocodiles, elephants, oxen, gods, and, of course, Siddhartha's face, blending all of these scenes into a harmonious unity in a peaceful smile. "Govinda bowed low. Incontrollable tears trickled down his old face. He was overwhelmed by a feeling of great love, of the most humble veneration. He bowed low, right down to the ground, in front of the man sitting there motionless, whose smile reminded him of everything that he had ever loved in his life, of everything that had ever been of value and holy in his life."[2] So ends *Siddhartha*. Should we be surprised that it was this book, plus one or two others, that Charles Manson permitted his "Family" to read at the Spahn Ranch, even as they prepared to creep into the night to steal and finally to murder?[3] For in terms of monism, everything is valuable and holy in life or death, for there is no death, as Manson was fond of telling everyone, including the prosecuting attorney at his trial. Monism is the philosophy of nihilism, however disguised it may be.

The other non-Christian philosophy is *dualism*, which holds that good and evil are in eternal tension, and that neither can triumph. It undergirded many of the medieval revolutionary sects that turned, in some instances, to magic and occultism. It argues that God is not sovereign, for He did not actually create all things; the evil god created matter and is sovereign over it. Like monism, this philosophy leads to an attempt to escape the control of matter over the soul, either by radical asceticism or by a radical immersion in perversion (to deny its relevance).

What monism and dualism have in common is the denial of the sovereignty of a personal God, for in neither system is there a Creator-creature distinction. Each leads to rampant immorality, and each leads to a dismissal of earthly affairs and earthly responsibility. The result in each case is moral nihilism.

The Fall

The rebellion of man against the explicit command of God was an *ethical* rebellion. The fall of man was ethical rather than metaphysical. It involved his whole being, body and soul, and the curse of God in response to this rebellion penalized both body and soul, including man's mind. Nevertheless, the fall itself was not a metaphysical "fall from Being." It was not some lack in man's being that prompted his downfall; it was willful rebellion. The curse of God on man involved the creation in which man was now to labor (Genesis 3:15–17); his world would now be one of scarcity. But it was not a flawed environment that was man's downfall, although Adam blamed Eve, Eve blamed the serpent, and they all, by implication, blamed God for their plight. As the fall was *ethical,* so the restoration must be ethical—not a "leap of being" by mystical means, or by environmental manipulation, such as through Marxist revolution.[4]

The restoration of man and the creation is promised (Isaiah 65, 66; Romans 8; I Corinthians 15). This is the work of God in calling His people unto Him (John 17). Restoration is not to be achieved by "secret wisdom" through initiation into "mysteries." The words of Jesus in the Sermon on the Mount forbade secret wisdom to His followers, and thereby forbade mystical secret societies: "Ye are the light of the world. A city that is set on a hill cannot be hid. Neither do men light a candle, and put it under a bushel, but on a candlestick; and it giveth light unto all that are in the house. Let your light so shine before men, that they may see your good works, and glorify your Father which is in heaven" (Matthew 5:14–16). Restoration, both ethical and external, stems from the grace of God—another doctrine anathema both to the modern world and to occult philosophy. Restoration is neither the product of men's "neutral" reason, nor the product of their own unaided, self-initiated works (Ephesians 2:8,9).

The Incarnation

The message of chapter one of the Gospel of John is straightforward: God Himself walked this earth in human flesh during a specific period of human history. He appeared in time and on earth, one person with two natures: perfect humanity and full divinity, but without a confusion of these two natures. The promise given to the people of God is that each man, while retaining his own personality, will be conformed to the image of Jesus Christ on the final day (I Corinthians 15:42–50). In short, redeemed man does not become divine; he finally attains perfect humanity, but not full divinity. The Divine once became a man, and only once. Because of Christ's atoning work on the cross—an act of sacrifice that satisfied God's own standards of justice—some men are to be saved (John 17; Romans 5). But no man can become God. The attempt to become God, or a part of God's being, is wholly illegitimate and constitutes the essence of rebellion. The Creator-creature distinction is everlasting.

The doctrine of incarnation asserts that God took on flesh. The doctrine of monism asserts that out of God flesh and matter appeared, and eventually they must return to (or into) God. Monism implies that God is somehow incomplete. This is the specific teaching of Hegel, for example. We are needed to complete God's being and to restore Him to his pretemporal wholeness. Man is therefore a part of the process of God's salvation. God is saved by man. It is man's efforts to be reunited with God that are crucial in the process of time. The emphasis of monism, while officially theistic, is nonetheless humanistic. A very fine example of just this kind of reasoning is found in a fragment of the writings of Meister Eckhart (1260–1328), a German mystic. Heretical to the core, Eckhart's monism led him into the wildest kinds of philosophical rambling. Yet he was consistent in his presentation of the theology of monism, as the following passage indicates:

> God's divinity comes of my humility, and this may be demonstrated as follows. It is God's peculiar property to give; but he cannot give unless something is prepared to receive his gifts. If, then, I prepare by my humility to receive what he gives, by my humility I make God a giver. Since it is his nature to give, I am merely giving God what is already his own. It is like a rich man who wants to be a giver but must first find a taker, since without a taker he cannot be a giver; for the taker, in taking, makes the rich man a giver. Similarly, if God is to be a giver, he must first find a taker, but no one may be a taker of God's gifts except by his humility. Therefore, if God is to exercise his divine property by his gifts, he well may need my humility; for apart from humility he can give me nothing—without it I am not prepared to receive his gift. That is why it is true that by humility I give divinity to God.[5]

Where this approach to "humility" is present, in either the explicit thinking or the implicit presuppositions of would-be autonomous man, the resistance to occultism is socially and culturally close to zero. While Ph.D.'s in philosophy may not succumb to the temptation of dabbling in the supernatural as a means of climbing up the scale of universal being, the average person who hears such speculation and takes it seriously, especially when it comes from some mystical guru or charismatic leader, will have no intellectual foundation to help him resist. The steps to personal transcendence—the promised "leap of being"—are too frequently only little more than intellectualized magic. The quest for *metaphysical transcendence* rather than ethical transformation and repentance is a major source of the impetus to occultism. Occult exercises are too often the means of the promised self-transcendence.

Final Judgment

The doctrine of the last judgment is clearly a part of the orthodox Christian tradition. The Bible presents it as a time of reward (I Corinthians 3:11–15) and punishment (Luke 12:47, 48). It leads to an eternal separation between saved and lost (Luke 16:19–31). It is a once-for-all event (Revelation 20). In short, "as it is appointed unto men once to die, but after this the judgment: so Christ was once offered to bear the sins of many; and unto them that look for him shall he appear the second time without sin unto salvation" (Hebrews 9:27, 28).

The significance of this doctrine with respect to the philosophy of occultism is its *absolute denial of reincarnation*. Eastern monism, both Hindu and Mahayana Buddhist, as well as most of the Western forms of occult transcendentalism, hold specifically to the doctrine of karma. One's deeds have an inescapable effect on one's destiny in this life and in the next. Endless cycles of birth and death are required for men (or their impersonal souls) in order to shed the effects of matter before they are reintegrated into the One of timeless perfection. It is a theology without grace; men's actions, over vast eons of time, heal their former metaphysical condition. The polluting contact with matter must be washed away by deeds of ascetic withdrawal from or hedonistic immersion in matter. Judgment is temporary, though extended in possibly millions of cycles. Life is in balance, though ultimately it is a progressive balance that leads all living things back into the impersonal perfection of the timeless Void. The judgment on men's evil deeds is impersonal and in the long run—however long the run may be—it must end. The personal judgment of a personal God on men who have but few years of life on earth is denied; the knowledge of it is actively suppressed in the minds of men (Romans 1:18–22). By theorizing on the almost infinite extension of time in which men are "imprisoned," the theologians of karma think they have imprisoned God and His judgment. The motive of all evolutionary thinking, whether Darwinist or karmist, is the same: to escape the wrath of God by pushing the creation and the judgment out of this world and the next. It is also the motive of post-Kantian humanism, including Hegelianism and Marxism.

Prohibitions on Occultism

Because men reject the validity of the preceding biblical doctrines, they are susceptible to occult forces. The people of Israel were protected from occultism by the revelation of God concerning Himself and His relationship to the creation, as well as by His promise of ultimate restoration. But the doctrines alone were not sufficient to preserve the people from the idolatry of the pagan cultures that surrounded them. Explicit prohibitions were placed on citizens of Israel against dabbling in the occult arts. These arts were well known. The most comprehensive prohibition appears in Deuteronomy 18:10–12, but there are numerous other outright prohibitions and warnings against the consequences of occult experimentation:

> Witchcraft (sorcery)—Exodus 22:18
> Necromancy-spiritualism—Leviticus 19:31; 20:6; Deuteronomy 18:11
> Astrology—Isaiah 47:13
> False prophecy

       inaccurate—Deuteronomy 18:20–22; cf. I John 4:1
       idolatrous—Deuteronomy 13:1–3
   Divination—Deuteronomy 18:10
      arrows—Ezekiel 21:21
      livers—Ezekiel 21:21
      images—Ezekiel 21:21
   Fire walking—Deuteronomy 18:10
   Omens—Jeremiah 10:2
   Wizardry (secret knowledge?)—Deuteronomy 18:11
   Charms (snakes)—Jeremiah 8:17
   Enchantment (spells)—Isaiah 47:9–12
   Times* (lucky days?)—Leviticus 19:26

    The term translated "witch" by the King James Version is more accurately rendered "sorcerer." The influence of Walt Disney's witch in the animated movie *Snow White,* while terrifying to young children, is amusing to adults. To a great extent, this is the traditional image of the witch: broomstick, black hat, black cat near at hand. It is as old as the medieval witchcraft trials. Popular culture, since 1965, has updated the witch: she is cute Samantha of "Bewitched" fame, with her middle-class home in middle-class America. (This, by the way, is a far more accurate picture of the modern witch.) She wiggles her nose and—poof —all the morning dishes are washed, dried, and put away. She was immensely popular, even more than her nearest rival, Jeannie, who lived in a bottle in the mid-1960s, cleaning house for an astronaut—the fusion of scientific expertise and magic. So cute, both of them. And so very temporary. By 1970 the public was watching television programs that delved into the evil and powerful side of magic. In 1975, "Kolchak: The Night Stalker" combined the public's taste for private detective shows with its seemingly unquenchable thirst for occult themes. In Kolchak's world, there are killers loose on the streets who possess supernatural powers. Here, at last, is the biblical witch.

    The Hebrew word for sorceress in Exodus 22:18 can be transliterated as *mekashshephah*. The Septuagint, a Greek translation of the Old Testament in the second century B.C., substituted *pharmakeia,* from which we derive our word "pharmacy." The witch of the classical world was an expert in potions. More accurately, he or she was known as a poisoner. Throughout the Middle Ages men were fearful of suspected witches, in part because of this reputation. They could be dangerous.

    The prohibition on occult practices was basic to the preservation of covenantal faithfulness to God. Other gods were false gods, and sacrifice to them was spiritually, even literally, deadly. The worshippers of Moloch (Molech, Milcom) made

---

*Alfred Edersheim, the Jewish convert to Christianity who taught history at Oxford a century ago, refers to a particular kind of Hebrew diviner mentioned in the Talmud, a *meonen,* who foretold lucky or unlucky days. *The Life and Times of Jesus the Messiah,* 2 vols. (Grand Rapids, Mich.: Eerdmans, [1886] 1959), II, 773.

their sons and daughters pass through a fire as a form of sacrifice and testing (II Kings 23:10). Basic to the worship of pagan antiquity was the creation of a divine state that rested on a theology of continuity, that is, the denial of the Creator-creature distinction. The state could take the lives of its children as sacrifice to the god of the state. The prohibitions on occult worship were not only a means of protecting people's lives morally from perverse practices but also a means of restricting the power of a political order theoretically unbounded by the restraint of limited men. Rousas Rushdoony has commented on what he calls the "Moloch state":

> While relatively little is known of Moloch, much more is known of the concept of divine kingship, the king as god, and the god as king, as the divine-human link between heaven and earth. The god-king represented man on a higher scale, man ascended, and the worship of such a god, i.e., of such a *Baal*, was the assertion of the *continuity* of heaven and earth. It was the belief that all being was one being, and the god therefore was an ascended man on that scale of being. The power manifested in the political order was thus a manifestation or apprehension and seizure of divine power. It represented the triumph of a man and of his people. Moloch worship was thus a political religion. . . . Moloch worship was thus state worship. The state was the true and ultimate order, and religion was a department of the state. The state claimed *total jurisdiction* over man; it was therefore entitled to *total sacrifice*.[6]

A revival of occultism in our day, as in the era of the Renaissance, can and must bring with it a revival of the politics of ancient paganism. A state that claims total jurisdiction is demonic. It can provide not law and order, but only order, and that order is man-centered and oppressive. It was this development that the Hebrew prohibitions on occultism were intended to prevent: the rise of the total state. Increasingly, this is what the modern world faces, for both secular, rational humanism and occult humanism deny that there is any voice of authority outside of man who cares for man. Secular humanists may wish to manipulate the world through state power, and occult humanists may wish to manipulate the powers of the "beyond" for their own benefit, but the quest for power leads to the construction of a massive instrument of power. That instrument is the modern state. It is the planning state, the forecasting state, the macroeconomically programmed state. Rushdoony is quite correct:

> The Moloch state simply represents the supreme effort of man to command the future, to predestine the world, and to be as God. Lesser efforts, divination, spirit-questing, magic, and witchcraft, are equally anathema to God. All represent efforts to have the future on other than God's terms, to have a future apart from and in defiance of God. They are assertions that the world is not of God but of brute factuality, and that man can somehow master the world and the future by going directly to the raw materials thereof.[7]

The supposed death or nonexistence of the God of creation is in fact the death of human freedom and human personality.

Angels and Demons

There are about three hundred references in the Bible to "angel," "angels," and about one hundred twenty to "devil," "devils." In contrast, there are some six hundred references to "evil" and perhaps eight hundred to "sin," "sinner," "sinneth" and their variations. The overwhelming emphasis on ethical deviation and rebellion is characteristic of the Bible's message. It does not ignore the operations of supernatural agencies, but the concern of both Testaments is with sin and repentance, not exorcism.

What is an angel? Both the Hebrew and the Greek words that are translated "angel" can also be translated "messenger." There are times when the more conventional usage is preferred, such as in Job 1:14: "And there came a messenger unto Job. . . ." We find instances where the Hebrew word is applied to a prophet (Haggai 1:13; Malachi 3:1) or to a priest (Malachi 2:7). Paul refers to his "thorn in the flesh," which seems to have been a physical ailment—infirmity (II Corinthians 12:9, 10)—as "the messenger [angel] of Satan" (II Corinthians 12:7). These uses of the word, however, would seem to be infrequent. Normally, the term refers to a supernatural being of some kind.

An angel is a spirit, whether a clean one serving as a messenger of God (Hebrews 1:14) or an evil one (I Samuel 18:10; Matthew 8:16). Angels manifest themselves as men on occasion. Joshua was confronted by one whom he took for a man; it turned out to be the captain of the Lord's host (Joshua 5:13, 14). The angels who appeared at the tomb from which Jesus had risen were angels (John 20:12), yet were perceived as men (Luke 24:4). The book of Hebrews warns us: "Let brotherly love continue. Be not forgetful to entertain strangers: for thereby some have entertained angels unawares" (13:1, 2). This was what happened to Lot; angels, seen as men, came to warn him about the impending destruction of Sodom (Genesis 19).

There are multitudes of them. "Ten thousand times ten thousand" is Daniel's phrase (Daniel 7:10), indicating a massive host. The New Testament uses the terms "multitude" (Luke 2:13) and "innumerable" (Hebrews 12:22). One famous Old Testament incident illustrates the invisible company of angels. Elisha's servant, fearful of the army of Syrians that had encompassed the city in which he and his master were staying, was memorably comforted by Elisha: "And he answered, Fear not: for they that be with us are more than they that be with them. And Elisha prayed, and said, Lord, I pray thee, open his eyes, that he may see. And the Lord opened the eyes of the young man; and he saw: and, behold, the mountain was full of horses and chariots of fire round about Elisha. And when they came down to him, Elisha prayed unto the Lord, and said, Smite this people, I pray thee, with blindness. And he smote them with blindness according to the word of Elisha" (II Kings 6:16–18). Blindness among the enemies was also the method of freeing Lot from Sodom (Genesis 19:11). It was not that the angels used their chariots of fire or great numbers to impede the plans of the Syrian army, but that their presence was meant to assure Elisha of his own safety.

One of the difficulties in describing various kinds of angels is that the biblical writers would see them in visions, and they themselves were well aware of the nonliteral nature of some segments of these visions—the candlesticks of the Book of Revelation, for example, or even the great chain that binds Satan (Revelation 20:1). The idea of chains and spirits may make fine reading in Dickens' *Christmas Carol*, but this should not be confused with the spiritual nature of God's bondage of demons. Therefore, Daniel's description of the cherubim—four-faced creatures, part beast and part human, with four wings—may reflect only God's means of revealing the majesty and power of His angels (Ezekiel 10:10–21). John's vision of the seraphim is analogous: four beasts—"like a" lion, calf, man, and eagle, each with six wings—crying "Holy, holy, holy, Lord God Almighty" (Revelation 4:7, 8). When children, or adults for that matter, sing the hymn, "Holy, Holy, Holy," they probably do not spend a lot of time thinking about the original source of the lyrics. These incredible forms could conceivably be the permanent shapes of the various angels, but in the references to their appearances before men (apart from visions), they take less shocking shapes. Obviously, one would be unlikely to entertain these visionary angels unawares.

There are some Old Testament references that indicate that God takes the form of men-angels from time to time. These revelations of Himself are usually called theophanies. We are told that God walked in the garden of Eden (Genesis 3:8), that He appeared in human form before Abraham at Mamre (Genesis 18:1, 2, 22), and that He wrestled through the night with Jacob, afterward providing him with his new name, Israel (Genesis 32:24–28). In the most famous theophany in the Bible, the appearance of God before Moses in a burning bush, Scripture actually states that "the angel of the LORD appeared unto him in a flame of fire out of the midst of a bush" (Exodus 3:2), yet the voice clearly claimed to be God (3:14; cf. Exodus 23:21). Christ specifically stated, "No man hath seen God at any time; the only begotten Son, which is in the bosom of the Father, he hath declared him" (John 1:18). These theophanies would thus seem to have been manifestations of the Second Person of the Trinity—not Jesus Christ as the *incarnate* Son, but preincarnate revelations. The importance that the writer of the Epistle to the Hebrews places on Melchisedec, who was both priest and king of Salem (Genesis 14:18), and who was "without father, without mother, without descent, having neither beginning of days, nor end of life; but made like unto the Son of God; abideth a priest continually" (Hebrews 7:3), should indicate that Melchisedec was a theophany. The centrality of the themes of priesthood and sacrifice in Hebrews —Christ's sacrifice as *the* sacrifice that satisfies God's standards of justice— leaves no doubt as to the importance of Melchisedec for Christian theology. He was no mere man. No ordinary angel is ever compared to the Son of God, either.

The function of angels is multiple. They are messengers of God, although it is unclear how they perform their task in post-Apostolic times. They are eventually to serve as agents of divine judgment (Matthew 13:41, 42; Revelation 6–10). Despite the fact that, in terms of power, men are "a little lower than the angels" (Psalm 8:5), men are nevertheless to serve someday as judges of the angels (I Corinthians 6:3). As creatures, they are fellow servants of God with men (Revelation 19:10), and therefore they are not to be worshiped (Colossians 2:18). It should be clear that since the closing of the biblical canon, angelic demonstrations of power have either been subdued or else attributed by men to other factors, either to natural law or to the direct intervention of God. Demons, frankly, make better copy.

Demons are fallen angels, both ethically and geographically. Christ announced: "I beheld Satan as lightning fall from heaven" (Luke 10:18). The twelfth chapter of Revelation, which is not so difficult a passage as some expositors would make it, affirms that a "dragon" stood before a "woman" about to give birth "for to devour her child as soon as it was born. And she brought forth a man child, who was to rule all nations with a rod of iron: and her child was caught up unto God, and to his throne" (Revelation 12:4b,5). There should be no doubt concerning the identity of a child who was caught up to heaven and to God's throne.

> And there was war in heaven: Michael and his angels fought against the dragon; and the dragon fought and his angels, and prevailed not; neither was their place found any more in heaven. And the great dragon was cast out, that old serpent, called the Devil, and Satan, which deceiveth the whole world: he was cast out into the earth, and his angels were cast out with him. And I heard a loud voice saying in heaven, Now is come salvation, and strength, and the kingdom of our God, and the power of his Christ: for the accuser of our brethren is cast down, which accused them before our God day and night. And they overcame him by the blood of the Lamb, and by the word of their testimony; and they loved not their lives unto death. Therefore rejoice, ye heavens, and ye that dwell in them. Woe to the inhabiters of the earth and of the sea for the devil is come down unto you, having great wrath, because he knoweth that he hath but a short time. [Revelation 12:7–12]

The book of Job indicates the nature of Satan's accusing tongue. After the crucifixion of Christ, that tongue could no longer be wagged before the throne of God. The brethren overcame him, with the cooperation of Michael and the angels, through the blood the the Lamb. This was an historical event. It did not take place in some misty pre-Adamic period, nor did it take place in Old Testament times.* The ethical rebellion did occur, obviously, before the fall of man, although we are never told just when. (My own *guess* is that it was after the sixth day, since God pronounced his blessing upon creation on the sixth day, and Satan is certainly a created being. But this is mere speculation.)

The results of that ethical rebellion have been applied steadily to Satan and his host over time. The religion of Christianity, like that of orthodox Judaism, is a religion that comes to grips with *time*. Understandably, the essence of Satan's religion is a denial of time, for time seals his doom and is an ever-present reminder to him that he has been vanquished and will ultimately suffer total, eternal defeat (Matthew 25:41; Revelation 20:10). Time must either be denied as being real or be extended infinitely in each direction, thereby denying the final judgment. Again

---

*The passage usually cited to show that the event was prior to New Testament times is Isaiah 14:12–15. This interpretation is as old as the early church fathers. But the Hebrew word translated "Lucifer" merely meant "morning star" or "bright star," and its position in a passage dealing with the coming destruction of Babylon indicates that, at best, it is only analogous to Satan's fall. Verse 16 clearly refers to "the man that made the earth to tremble. . . ." Cf. J. A. Alexander, *Commentary on the Prophecies of Isaiah* (Grand Rapids, Mich.: Zondervan, [1865] 1974), pp. 295–98.

and again we find in occult speculation, whether Eastern or Western, ancient or modern, a denial of the reality of *linear, bounded* time—the uniquely Western tradition that was presented in its final form to our civilization in Augustine's *City of God.*

Demons are "unclean spirits" (Matthew 10:1), "evil spirits" (Acts 19:12). They are, in short, unholy spirits. They are rebels who, according to Jude 6, "kept not their first estate, but left their own habitation," and whom God has *now* "reserved in everlasting chains under darkness unto the judgment of the great day." This does not mean, by any stretch of the imagination, that they are impotent today; it simply means that they are more limited now than they were before Christ's era. They no longer can deceive the nations as before, for the gospel is no longer confined to a barren strip of land in Palestine (Revelation 20:3). As followers of Satan, their power today is limited (II Peter 2:4). Hell, prepared for them so long ago (Matthew 25:41), is their abode. And after hell has fulfilled its purpose, the lake of fire will receive them (Revelation 20:10,14).

They are not impotent, however. They have the power to control the actions of ethically rebellious men and to influence or harass the saints of God on earth. This is taught explicitly throughout the New Testament, but especially graphically in the Gospel of Mark: 1:32; 5:1–6; and 16:17. Jesus specifically stated that one of the signs—indeed, *the* sign—of the advent of His kingdom was His ability to cast out demons "by the Spirit [finger] of God" (Matthew 12:28 [Spirit]; Luke 11:20 [finger]). Perhaps the most graphic of all biblical passages dealing with exorcism is in Mark's Gospel:

> And one of the multitude answered and said, Master, I have brought unto thee my son, which hath a dumb spirit; and wheresoever he taketh him, he teareth him: and he foameth, and gnasheth with his teeth, and pineth away: and I spake to thy disciples that they should cast him out; and they could not. He answered him, and saith, O faithless generation, how long shall I be with you? how long shall I suffer you? bring him unto me. And they brought him unto him: and when he saw him, straightway the spirit tare him; and he fell on the ground, and wallowed foaming. And he asked his father, How long is it ago since this came unto him? And he said, Of a child. And ofttimes it hath cast him into the fire, and into the waters, to destroy him: but if thou canst do any thing, have compassion on us, and help us. Jesus said unto him, If thou canst believe, all things are possible to him that believeth. And straightway the father of the child cried out, and said with tears, Lord, I believe; help thou mine unbelief. When Jesus saw that the people came running together, he rebuked the foul spirit, saying unto him, Thou dumb and deaf spirit, I charge thee, come out of him, and enter no more into him. And the spirit cried, and rent him sore, and came out of him: and he was an one dead; insomuch that many said, He is dead. But Jesus took him by the hand, and lifted him up; and he arose. And when he was come into the house, his disciples asked him privately, Why could not we cast him out? And he said unto them, This kind can come forth by nothing, but by prayer and fasting. [Mark 9:17–29]

It took prayer, fasting, and faith in God's healing grace on the part of the father to cure the boy. Even with Jesus commanding the demon, the boy was still injured as it left his body. The disciples had been able to do nothing.

But for a really difficult exorcism, consider the pathetic sons of Sceva: "Then certain of the vagabond Jews, exorcists, took upon them to call over them which had evil spirits the name of the Lord Jesus, saying, We adjure you by Jesus whom Paul preacheth. And there were seven sons of one Sceva, a Jew, and chief of the priests, which did so. And the evil spirit answered and said, Jesus I know, and Paul I know; but who are ye? And the man in whom the evil spirit was leaped on them, and overcame them, and prevailed against them, so that they fled out of that house naked and wounded" (Acts 19:13–16).

Exorcism is no game. It is practiced by the spiritual sons of Sceva, and sometimes the exorcisms seem successful, but the price of these exorcisms is high, if not to the exorcist, then to the one exorcised. As Jesus warned concerning the works of a faith not grounded in Him: "When the unclean spirit is gone out of a man, he walketh through dry places, seeking rest; and finding none, he saith, I will return unto my house whence I came out. And when he cometh, he findeth it swept and garnished. Then goeth he, and taketh to him seven other spirits more wicked than himself; and they enter in, and dwell there: and the last state of that man is worse than the first" (Luke 11:24–26). The illustration was meant to warn men concerning the nature of true faith, but it was based on a concrete example of temporarily successful exorcism.

Conclusion

The testimony of the Bible is that occult phenomena are real. They are the products of acting beings who are normally invisible to man. They possess great power. Their activities are not limited to the manipulation of external phenomena. If anything, their activities in the spiritual, that is, moral and ethical, realm are vastly more important, especially in a Christian or Christian-influenced secular culture that does not acknowledge occult phenomena. While Christians need not fear the visible activities of demons so much as their internal activities, they should nonetheless be aware of the existence of occult phenomena and occult philosophy. To be ignorant is to be unarmed in an era of increasing demonic activity.

3
Paranormal Science Since 1960

We have largely evicted superstition from the physical universe, which used to be the dumping ground of the miraculous. . . . But we have great ground to rejoice that science is now advancing into this domain more rapidly than ever before, and that the last few years have seen more progress than the century that preceded. The mysteries of our psychic being are bound ere long to be cleared up. Every one of these ghostly phenomena will be brought under the domain of law. The present recrudescence here of ancient faiths in the supernatural is very interesting as a psychic atavism, as the last flashing up of old psychoses soon to become extinct.

G. Stanley Hall (1910)

Science no longer holds any absolute truths. Even the discipline of physics, whose laws once went unchallenged, has had to submit to the indignity of an Uncertainty Principle. In this climate of disbelief, we have begun to doubt even fundamental propositions, and the old distinction between natural and supernatural has become meaningless.
I find this tremendously exciting.

Lyall Watson (1973)

The official position of the vast bulk of scientists in the academic world as recently as 1959 was far closer to G. Stanley Hall's presentation of the "facts" than Lyall Watson's. Indeed, the majority of tenured physical and biological scientists today would probably prefer to be categorized as followers of Hall. But the crude confidence of Hall, writing as he was prior to the discovery of the principle of indeterminacy by Werner Heisenberg and the development of quantum mechanics, is decidedly out of style today. While only a tiny handful of scientists would go as far as Watson has gone in his book *Supernature,* they nevertheless would acknowledge the validity of Watson's epistemological position: relativism has invaded physics. The older faculty members may still cling to the literary fashions of nineteenth-century science, but if pressed in a debate, they would have to admit that the theoretical world on which nineteenth-century rationalistic optimism was based is no longer a valid intellectual option. The Newtonian universe may have conformed to mathematical law down to the atom itself, but with the discovery of subatomic particles a revolution was born in the minds of men. The crack in the intellectual dike, while originally no wider than an electron (indeterminate as it was with respect to velocity and location simultaneously), allowed the collapse of the dam of scientific confidence. The world of G. Stanley Hall was engulfed at its foundations, and the structures have begun to slide noticeably.

Yet at bottom the two positions are not that different. If Hall and Watson could be interviewed together, they would regard each other as either superstitious (Hall regarding Watson) or naive (Watson regarding Hall). But both would be firmly committed to a concept of the universe that is open to anything but the God of the Bible. Whatever oddities nature may bring before us to examine, it is always nature that brings them, for nature alone has produced them. Hall would prefer to interpret these oddities within the framework of universal laws—universally comprehensible by the universally rational mind. Watson would prefer to bring a degree of what he would call "mystery" into the universe. The noumenal realm should be given its due, not in the sense that it is somehow personal—no demons or personal God "out there" to mess around with the processes of the phenomenal realm—but in the sense that the random and the ultimately incomprehensible must be acknowledged as basic to the structure of the universe. In this sense, Hall was really pre-Kantian in his perspective. His was the confident world of Descartes, with its mathematical laws comprehending and sustaining everything. Watson is the modern figure, far more self-conscious epistemologically. But both would refuse to give an inch or a proton's worth of influence to any cause itself not produced by the processes of autonomous nature. Hall's approach would be to deny the ultimate "oddness" of any oddity; Watson would affirm the ultimate "oddness" of *all* phenomena; but neither would open his universe to the unnatural.

Watson, however, realizes that Hall's world is too narrow to encompass oddities that must be explained in order to affirm the autonomy of nature, so he has broadened the legitimate definition of the natural: "The supernatural is usually defined as that which is not explicable by the known forces of nature. Supernature knows no bounds. . . . Supernature is nature with all its flavors intact, waiting to be tested. I offer it as a logical extension of the present state of science, as a solution to some of the problems with which traditional science cannot cope, and as an analgesic to modern man."[1] In his definition of what constitutes the science of supernature, Watson sets forth the case for paranormal science.

Although the science of the occult or odd phenomena had been limping along since at least the 1880s, it experienced the beginning of a massive revival about 1960. So massive has this revival been in terms of the *methods* of experimental science that a whole new literature has developed. While the practitioners of paranormal science are still few in number, the impact that this tiny band is having on the way in which the general public views its world is nothing short of astounding. Establishment scientists, most of whom at any stage in history are essentially skilled technicians who pursue incredibly narrow and almost arcane avenues of investigation, are ill-equipped to meet the charges and assertions of these younger and often amateurish scientists of the paranormal. The latter are writing easily understood paperback books for the millions, and the millions are buying them. The average reader is not much interested in bickering footnotes; what he wants is something novel, something to tickle his imagination. Paranormal science fits the bill perfectly. The public is convinced, and not without good reason, that for the affairs of life, including the oddities of life, the razor-sharp intellectual tools of professional scientists are so specialized and precise that they are unfit for anything other than academic hairsplitting. The modern readers of paperback science are only too similar to the residents of Athens in the days of Christ: educated and bored, with a lot of time on their hands. "For all the Athenians and strangers which were there spent their time in nothing else, but either to tell, or to hear some new thing" (Acts 17:21).

Many of the anomalies that Watson presents in his study really do seem to be the products of nature. (Nature in this sense being independent of supernatural secondary causality, though not independent of the *sustaining* hand of a personal God.) God's universe is far more extensive than the canons of nineteenth-century scientific theory. For example, oysters studied by biologist Frank Brown display some amazing properties. Collected by Brown from their home beds in the Long Island Sound off Connecticut, they were able to maintain their patterns of opening and closing with the tides, even when shipped to his laboratory in Evanston, Illinois. But these patterns persisted for only fourteen days. On the fifteenth day, they began to deviate from the original patterns—simultaneously Watson summarizes: "Brown calculated the difference between the old rhythm and the new one and discovered that the oysters now opened up at the time the tide would have flooded Evanston—had the town been on the shore and not perched on the bank of a Great Lake 580 feet above sea level."[2] Furthermore, they persisted in their new rhythm in the dark and under seemingly fixed control conditions. Brown then discovered that their movements generally corresponded to the position of the moon, opening when the moon was directly overhead Evanston. "This was the first piece of scientific evidence to show that even an organism living away from the ocean tides could be influenced by the passage of the moon."[3]

Watson goes on to record other well-known animal responses that are influenced by lunar rhythms: the running (spawning) of the California grunion fish, the movement of a particular variety of worms, and May flies. Even rainfall has been found to be abnormally heavy just after full and new moons, and *Science*, a prestigious establishment periodical, has published the data on this unexplained statistical phenomenon.[4] In addition to lunar rhythms, there are solar rhythms.

We are learning that sun spots may influence some aspects of the earth's weather. They also may influence earthquakes. Changes in human blood serum have been attributed to sun-spot activity.[5] Even the speed of chemical reactions, says Giorgio Piccardi, the director of the Institute for Physical Chemistry in Florence, Italy, is influenced by sun spots. Watson summarizes his experiments with bismuth oxychloride (a colloid), which forms a cloudy precipitate when poured into distilled water. Three times a day he and his assistants carried out this simple test, until they had 200,000 separate results. Sure enough, over a ten-year period they found that the reaction took place more rapidly during sun-spot activity. (Here is a typical test procedure of orthodox science. What is mind-boggling to the average reader, assuming he pays much attention to what he is reading, is not that sun spots have some kind of influence over bismuth oxychloride, but that any highly placed scientist would conduct a decade-long experiment of this nature. What if— perish the thought—the results had been negative? Ten years, a ton of bismuth oxychloride, and a zillion gallons of distilled water—right down the proverbial drain. And the positive nature of the experiment has fascinated only parapsychologists and scientists of the odd, themselves highly suspect in the eyes of orthodox scientists. Finally, there is the question of financing. "Who cares?" is too easy. "Who paid?" is more to the point.)

Watson includes these curious facts in his second chapter. All well and good, but after the long, slow curve comes the fast break: "Astrology is based upon the fundamental premise that celestial phenomena affect life and events here on earth. No scientist, and certainly no biologist familiar with the latest work on weather and natural rhythms, can deny that this premise is proved."[6] We have now leaped from oysters to astrology, for in Watson's universe, both have the same foundation: the premise of celestial-terrestrial relationships. But, to put it bluntly, the moon ain't the North Star, and the stars and galaxies making up the perceived constellations have got nothing to do with the astrological signs of lions and crabs and twins. But Watson thinks that perhaps the French investigator Michel Gauquelin may be onto something. Gauquelin studied the birth signs of famous Frenchmen, and he found a statistical correlation between French scientists and medical men with the astrological sign Mars. Soldiers, it seems, are mostly Jupiters, as are politicians. But what does all this mean? Were the samples too small? Does astrology apply only to *French* soldiers, politicians, and scientists? Have these relationships been eternal? Watson, being an enthusiastic paranormal scientist, categorically states that Gauquelin's work "shows, beyond reasonable doubt, that the position of planets means something—the position, and not the planets themselves. We still have to decide whether the planets are acting directly on us or whether their position is merely symbolic of some much larger cosmic pattern of energy of which they, and we, are just a small part."[7] In short, we are back to Watson's original hypothesis: "Life on earth is united into what amounts to a single superorganism, and . . . this in turn is only part of the cosmic community."[8] *This is the cosmology of traditional monism and mysticism. Everything is One.*

Watson then continues his discussion of traditional, simple-minded astrology, as if this were in some way related scientifically to the observable lunar and solar rhythms of our world. "Supernature knows no bounds." Anything can conceivably be related to anything or everything. In other words, to cite the phrase so dear to the hearts of the occultists and magicians of the so-called rationalistic Renaissance: *As above, so below.* This was the theological and cosmological foundation of all magic and astrology from the beginning. It is Watson's creed. "Matter, mind, and magic are all one in the cosmos," he states.[9]

By taking up the old creeds of Renaissance magic, Watson has placed them into post-Kantian methodological boxes. Randomness has replaced demons in his cosmology, but the goal is still much the same. A new age lies before us, an age of human power:

> So we have arrived at the moment of control with a new and growing consciousness both of the enormity of the task and of the breadth of our own ability to cope with it. In this situation two things stand out above all others: one is that our greatest strength lies in unity with all of Supernature here on earth, and the other is that this unity could give us the impetus we need to transcend the system altogether. Supernature could become something really supernatural.[10]

With this call to power and self-transcendence—metaphysically, a "leap of being"—Watson ends his book and sets before us the most ancient of man's heresies: to be as God. Man shall control his own destiny, ultimately merging with the cosmos in a new evolution. It is this goal that unites Chaldean astrologers, Hindu mystics, the paranormal scientists, the evolutionary philosophers and scientists, and the magicians. To be as God, by means of evolutionary leaps. Above all, it demands the *exercise of power.* Man is a part of a closed universe; there is no higher court of appeal. And as C. S. Lewis has warned, when we hear talk about the possibility of man's taking control of mankind, watch out: some men are about to try to take control of all the others.

Soviet Experiments

If G. Stanley Hall had ever heard about the existence of the book by Sheila Ostrander and Lynn Schroeder, *Psychic Discoveries Behind the Iron Curtain* (1970), he would never have believed a word of it.[11] If Joseph Stalin had ever heard of it, he would have had a copy translated; within six weeks, the book would no longer have been true. The book has become the Bible of paranormal science, although it is written in a journalistic fashion by nonscientists. It went through five printings as a hardback in 1970, and by mid-1974 had gone through ten printings as a paperback. To say that it is a bestseller does not do it justice. Watson cites its reports over and over in his own mass-produced paperback. The book fully deserves its wide circulation, for it tells the story of impossibilities within an impossibility—paranormal studies financed by the most rationalistic political empire in the history of man.

Stalin had prohibited investigations into the occult (although certain forms of telepathy, oddly enough, were not completely banished as scientific facts). Yet within a decade of his death, the Soviet Union's scientific community began to be hit with a series of mini-revivals. Upper-echelon members of the scientific establishment began to examine phenomena that had previously been banned as not only nonexistent but un-Marxist. Here, in the most thoroughly rationalistic and bureaucratized state in man's history, was a scientific guild that was permitting the study of what scientists throughout the world had long called occultism. Yet such studies were being made in the name of Marxism-Leninism, that is, materialism. The Soviets were slowly discovering Supernature. By the late-1960s, scientists in the Iron Curtain nations had become the most heavily subsidized paranormal scientists in the world. Though no scientist would have wanted or dared to admit it, total rationalism was steadily being fused with supernaturalism, that is, the old irrationalism.

What kinds of phenomena are under investigation? Mind over matter (telekinesis), telepathy, and extrasensory perception (the Western phrase given to the unknown and the theoretically impossible). Sight without eyes. Hypnosis-induced reincarnation. Precognition. Bioplasmic bodies (auras). Prophecy and astrology. From the late 1950s, when hardly a word of such research could filter into any official Soviet publication (and that means any legal Soviet publication), to the very early 1960s, old-fashioned scientific orthodoxy reigned supreme. By 1965, as in the United States, the dam had broken. The scientists of the Soviet Union were tentatively being offered a whole new world to explore. Soviet scientists, bit by bit, began to make their peace with the hitherto banned data of the occult. No doubt such a shift in scientific opinion was easier for Soviet scientists than it has been for Americans: the state paid them to change their minds, and in the Soviet Union the discovery of eternal truths inside previously prohibited facts is a familiar process. The revision of encyclopedias in the Soviet Union is literally a way of life.

Telekinesis and telepathy: In 1959, reports hit the USSR (but not the USA) that the U.S. Navy had been experimenting with telepathy. The submarine *Nautilus* had supposedly been trying out ESP techniques (or magic, or not-yet-knownness) as a means of communication between underwater points, something thought to be impossible by presently known scientific techniques. Leopold Vasiliev, a highly respected Soviet physiologist (who had for years been running a highly secret laboratory for parapsychological research), warned fellow scientists that the USSR should not fall behind the USA in the field of paranormal science. He stated himself forthrightly: "The discovery of the energy underlying ESP will be equivalent to the discovery of atomic energy."[12] Like any well-salaried employee of a messianic state, Vasiliev saw his opportunity and he took it. Call attention to the national enemy (the United States), point to a secret new discovery that holds out the promise of almost unlimited power, and make certain that the authorities bankroll it, since it just happens to be one's own area of expertise. In this country, the technique is called "grantsmanship." Vasiliev got what he wanted: access to research money and, perhaps even more important, access to the hitherto closed pages of the academic journals. A special ESP laboratory was established under his direction at Leningrad University.

By far the most prominent human subject of Soviet research into telekinesis—mind over matter—has been "Nelya Mikhailova" (Nina Kulagina), a Leningrad housewife of peasant background. Over forty top Soviet scientists have tested her abilities. After two to four hours of intense concentration, Nelya can perform the following wonders (sometimes): spin a compass needle from several feet away (a terrific talent, especially when you're lost); move various objects around a table—or off; separate the yolk from the white of an egg that is suspended in a saline solution, and then put them back together. All of these activities produce intense physiological reactions in Nelya, including a heart pulsating as fast as 240 beats per minute. A measurable magnetic force field is created by her during these experiments—focused on the object of her concentration. These experiments have been conducted under rigorous test conditions and recorded on film. There are no known explanations.[13]

One of the key signs of occult powers as distinguished from remarkable but natural powers is the *repeatability factor*. Like virtually all psychics, Nelya never knows for certain if her powers are going to appear. Unlike American establishment scientists, who dimly grasp the significance of repeatability, the Soviet scientists who are involved in paranormal scientific research put up with the seemingly random display of these experimental oddities. American scientists dismiss such phenomena as being unreal, which they assuredly are not, or as purely random events needing no explanation, which they certainly do need. But this basic skepticism has kept them away from the dark paths of occult power. The Soviets, demonic to the core in their official materialism, have now embarked on an equally demonic journey into the realms of power that are anything but materialistic. Screwtape, the mythical demon of C. S. Lewis's *Screwtape Letters,* is having his devilish wish come true behind the Iron Curtain. Writing to his nephew, the neophyte demon Wormwood, Screwtape sets forth basic policy:

> Our policy, for the moment, is to conceal ourselves. Of course this has not always been so. We are really faced with a cruel dilemma. When the humans disbelieve in our existence we lose all the pleasing results of direct terrorism, and we make no magicians. On the other hand, when they believe in us, we cannot make them materialists and skeptics. At least, not yet. I have great hopes that we shall learn in due time how to emotionalise and mythologise their science to such an extent that what is, in effect, a belief in us (though not under that name) will creep in while the human mind remains closed to belief in the Enemy. The "Life Force," the worship of sex, and some aspects of Psychoanalysis may here prove useful. If once we can produce our perfect work—the Materialist Magician, the man, not using, but veritably worshipping, what he vaguely calls "Forces" while denying the existence of "spirits"—then the end of the war will be in sight.[14]

It is hardly surprising that outside the Iron Curtain countries, the scientists who are most deeply involved in the study of the paranormal are psychologists: *parapsychologists*. Many of them are deeply Freudian or Jungian. Indeed, Freud himself began investigating psychic phenomena at the end of his career, and Jung built much of his analytic structure around occult themes and powers. But the Soviets are officially materialists; they have no time for such bourgeois theories as found in Freudian psychology, a fact which undoubtedly has made their psychological researches far more concrete. What the Soviets are after, purely and simply, is power.

Take telepathy. Telepathic experimentation never died out in the USSR, but since 1965, there has been a renewed interest in telepathic phenomena. The most famous telepaths in the USSR are Karl Nikolaiev, an actor, and Yuri Kamensky, a biophysicist. They send wireless messages without any form of apparatus. Mental messages, both visual and numerical. Emotional messages, in which one emotional experience is transmitted from one to the other over many miles. Kamensky is the "sender." These experiments are rigidly controlled by scientists who, initially, are often quite skeptical of the whole operation. For example, objects are placed randomly in sealed boxes, and the boxes are then opened randomly by Kamensky. Kamensky then focuses his attention on the contents of the particular box. 1,500 miles away, Nikolaiev records his mental impressions of what the object is. He is correct in an astonishing number of cases. Electrodes attached to Nikolaiev's head recorded the moment of his response to the "message" each time Kamensky "sent" one. By comparing the times in each laboratory, scientists found that Nikolaiev received his messages within a matter of seconds after they had been sent—or at least the responses on the charts indicated a brief delay. These experiments, which were conducted from 1966 on, were fully approved by the Soviet academic guild. Yet the 1956 *Soviet Encyclopedia* had announced: "Telepathy is an antisocial, idealistic fiction about man's supernatural power to perceive phenomena which, considering the time and the place, cannot be perceived."[15]

The most revealing fact about the Nikolaiev-Kamensky researches is the following footnote. The authorities, in characteristically Soviet fashion, had secretly employed a third telepath to monitor the experiments from his apartment. The psychic, Victor Milodan, was able to pick up three of the five images sent by Kamensky on one occasion, and in all five cases knew exactly when the messages had been sent.[16] There are experiments, in the Soviet view, and then there are *the* experiments. (If there are ever enough telepaths running around, the Soviets will pay Western firms a mountain of money—borrowed from the Export-Import Bank at below-market rates, of course—to develop jamming devices for telepathic communications.)

From the 1920s onward, the Soviets had experimented with a combination of telekinesis and telepathy. Vasiliev had been one of these scientists. Dr. K. I. Platonov had demonstrated in the mid-1920s that he could put a dancing woman into a trancelike sleep merely by concentrating on her from across the dance floor. The woman had been involved in a series of experiments in hypnosis conducted by Platonov. Here, in fact, was the very essence of Soviet social theory in action: mind over mind. As the authors remark: "The ability to put people to sleep and wake them up telepathically from a distance of a few yards to over a thousand miles became the most thoroughly tested and perfected contribution of the Soviets to international parapsychology. It is *the* Soviet experiment."[17] Vasiliev found that the ability to transmit telepathic directions to a human receiver is not affected in any known way by any known screening device, including lead capsules and Faraday cages. (This fact of noninterference will be discussed later in relation to the transmission of mental images to a Polaroid camera.) One estimate of the number of people who can be affected by such mental transmissions is four percent.[18] The goal, needless to say, is *control*: the whole man must be put under the domination of the modern scientific state.

In the main, what the Soviets are probably seeking in their exploration of ESP's effect on consciousness is control in a more generalized, everyday, pervasive sense. You hear the word *control* often in the USSR, not as a political concept, but in its comparatively upbeat, scientific meaning. As a Moscow scientist told us, "Science has learned to control outer nature to the great benefit of mankind. Now we are trying to learn the laws governing inner nature. Just as an understanding of outer nature allowed us, for example, to generate electricity to light huge cities, so the ability to control the untapped resources of man should bring equally amazing benefits."[19]

Sight without eyes: There is a phenomenon known throughout the world that baffles every scientist who has ever investigated it—not many, to be sure. Certain individuals who are totally blind, sometimes from birth, have developed the ability to perceive distinctions among colors and even to read letters printed on a page. From time to time, the popular press reports these cases, though usually with considerable skepticism or confusion. An American Pentecostal evangelist, Ronald Coyne, upon removing his glass eye and covering his seeing eye with a handkerchief that is then sealed with adhesive tape, has the ability to read from materials selected by the public. The phenomenon appears to be genuine in his case. He says he is a healer, and in 1969 he healed his way into a Cadillac El Dorado.[20] The public likes a good show, and if an evangelist can mix religion with a visible miracle like eyeless sight, the folks will part with those $20 bills, even if they are relatively poor people.

But in the Soviet Union, the bureaucracy parts with the equivalent of thousand-dollar bills. Rosa Kuleshova, a blind young woman living in the Ural mountain town of Nizhniy Tagil, found in the early 1960s that she could perceive colors in her fingers. The news of her ability spread like wildfire. She was taken to Moscow laboratories to be studied. She performed. She became a celebrity. The great eyeless sight fad was born. Blind students all over the USSR began training themselves, just as Rosa said she had done for six years. Like Rosa, some were found who could perceive lights shined on their hands, color by color. Colors feel differently, apparently. Some learned to read letters. But Rosa's fame destroyed her. She gave demonstrations of her powers, and finally they left her. Over the long run, her power to see with her hands could not be repeated.[21]

Reincarnation by hypnosis: Dr. Vladimir Raikov, a Moscow psychologist, has developed a truly innovative system of art training. He takes zero-talent students, hypnotizes them, tells them in their trances that they are famous artists of the past, and then wakes them. In case after impossible case, they begin to display hitherto unknown artistic capacities. They do not become master artists, but people who had been hard-pressed to draw stick figures have become commercial (pardon the bourgeois phrase) artists. As always, Raikov is searching for the "unknown laws" that govern these artistic transformations that literally create talented people out of average citizens. These techniques have also been used to produce mathematical abilities in otherwise dull students.

If true, the following bit of historical revisionism is a shocker.[22] Raikov claims that Sergei Rachmaninoff had been hypnotized by a Dr. Dahl during a period of depression. For years after the performance in St. Petersburg of his First Symphony, which had received catcalls, he had been unable to compose. Dahl put him under hypnosis, trained him in autosuggestion, and let him loose on his music. The Piano Concerto No. 2 in C Minor was the first result. Rachmaninoff later claimed that whole passages of music would simply come upon him. This phenomenon may be related to the dream-induced musical creations of Wagner and Tchaikovsky.[23]

Hypnosis is hoped to become a tool for the unlocking of hidden talents. The problem is, however, the *source* of such talents. Where, exactly, had they been hidden for so long? And why does hypnosis bring them out? Hypnosis—a phenomenon which has led, time and again, to other manifestations of paranormal powers—is not yet understood by any investigator, yet it is used increasingly by psychologists all over the world. It releases "untapped forces." Indeed, and at times untrapped forces.

Water dowsing: The age-old practice of water dowsing (also metal dowsing, missing-object dowsing, etc.) is being revived in the Soviet Union. Of course, it really never has been absent from either side of the Iron Curtain. There is an American Society of Dowsers which meets annually.[24] The U.S. Army, like the Red Army, employs dowsers for various purposes. In Vietnam, they were used to ferret out underground Viet Cong bunkers.[25] Few and far between are the American municipal water companies that do not (secretly) employ a dowser or two. But in the USSR, scientists are beginning to take them seriously. Men like America's Henry Gross, who once "dowsed" for water on Bermuda from his home in Maine (using a map of Bermuda) and found the only underground fresh-water sources discovered in the island's history, are not ridiculed.[26] (The pendulum, a phenomenon related to dowsing, is also receiving new attention.) Naturally, the phenomenon had to be renamed. Its translation from the Russian is "Biophysical Effects Method." (In France, it is called "radiaesthenia.") Scientists have been able to conclude that this force is not electrical, although physiological changes in the dowsers can be measured when they walk over a so-called dowsing area. (In a series of Swiss experiments, curious scientists discovered that certain plants and trees will not grow in a dowsing zone, nor will mice sleep in one.)

Like American dowsers, Soviet scientists assert that the revolving rods can answer questions concerning the depth of the water or mineral deposits, or the size of the deposits: one revolution equals so many meters, and so forth. Yet all of this is argued in terms of the standards of materialistic science. No magic here

Pavlita boxes: Years ago a Czechoslovakian manager of a textile factory, Robert Pavlita, developed a patent for a new manufacturing process. The royalties made it possible for him to do research that nobody else would finance. He rummaged through hundreds of ancient Czechoslovakian manuscripts, which Czech authorities today refuse to cite directly. Out of designs described in these unnamed manuscripts (alchemical manuscripts, in all likelihood), he came up with designs for dozens of peculiarly shaped metal boxes. Various moving parts rotate in these boxes. There is a problem, however. They are not attached to any known source of power. Pavlita stares at them, and the devices inside the boxes begin to move. He can walk away, and they keep right on rotating. They are receptacles of human energy—tiny generators. Many of them are useless, but some offer intriguing promises. Sealed bottles of dye-filled water are purified in twelve hours by energy radiated by a Pavlita generator. Furthermore, analysis revealed that the actual molecular structure of the now-pure water had been altered: the two hydrogen atoms were spread farther apart.[27]

One generator has operated independently for as long as three days. This one supposedly speeds up plant growth. Another one is psychic. This experiment, by the way, is repeatable. Five ESP cards are laid out in front of the generator's pointer. In another room a "sender" concentrates on a similar set of five cards. Turning up one card at a time, he concentrates. The pointer on the machine slowly points to the comparable card. According to Czech scientists, the machine never misses. Never.

Although films of these generators exist, few Western scientists have been allowed to see them. As of 1970, they were skeptical. But why should Czech state officials pour money into the projects? Was Pavlita nothing more than a hoaxer, trying to fool his American visitors who were going to write a book on psychic discoveries behind the Iron Curtain? In any case, the fact that the authorities openly admit that such generators exist indicates that there is substance to the claims made for them. Not necessarily scientific substance, however.

Pyramid Occultism

If Pavlita's boxes can be dismissed as some sort of elaborate practical joke, what can be done with the discovery of another Czech inventor, Karl Dyrbal? Dyrbal found that by making a scale model of the great Cheops Pyramid, placing a used razor blade one-third of the way to the apex (where the pharaoh's chamber would have been, had there been a scale model of the pharaoh), putting the edges of the blade on an east-west axis, and waiting for a week, the dull blade gets sharp. Placed there every night, it never gets dull. Well, almost never, but a cheaply made Iron Curtain country blade—as all such are—can be used for 240 shaves. The experiment is repeatable to a fault.[28] If you don't think so, write to the president of Gillette. (He knows but won't say.)

The Cheops Pyramid has fascinated both historians and occultists for generations. Herodotus was duly impressed. So are all the rest of us. How could such structures have been built in the middle of a desert? Something like 2.5 million massive blocks of stone, some weighing perhaps twenty tons, each averaging 2.5 tons, were used to build the Cheops structure.[29] There are no traces of carbon on the inner walls. How did the workers and priests light the interiors? What instruments could have been used during the so-called bronze age to form perfectly measured blocks? How did they level the massive site to a deviation of only half an inch? Questions like these go on and on, to the total confusion of the theorists, who are themselves hard pressed to manufacture hypotheses as rapidly as the Egyptians constructed the pyramids.

The pyramids had religious significance architecturally. Like the great tower described in Genesis 11, they were built to be staircases to heaven. The 267th pyramid text of the Fifth and Sixth Dynasties reads: "A staircase to heaven is laid for him [the pharaoh], so that he may mount up to heaven thereby."[30] The theological significance should be obvious: man, by means of his own powers, shall attain divinity, or near divinity. This was explicitly the teaching of Egyptian religion concerning the pharaoh, himself the descendant of the sun god.

Occultists and cultists have, for over a century, devoted great efforts to interpreting the significance of Cheops' dimensions. It seems that in both inches and centimeters, it is possible to see important historical events foretold in the "key" dimensions of the Cheops Pyramid. A whole prophetic literature has grown up around these three-dimensional studies. I choose not to go into detail here, but I can report that prophecies based on these dimensions, if properly interpreted, have achieved extraordinarily high correlation rates, but only so long as the fulfillment of the possible predictions are investigated *retroactively.* (Years ago I read a similar study, written by a pyramid skeptic, of the Washington Monument.)

The most important figure in the revival of pyramid occultism, apart from Dyrbal, is a French occultist, Antoine Bovis. Bovis, after consulting a pendulum, was led to visit the Cheops Pyramid. He was permitted a rare overnight visit. While inside the pyramid, he noticed that animals that had died—rodents, cats—had been placed in trash cans, yet after considerable periods of time these carcasses did not decay. Supposedly he had been told of this phenomenon in a vision or revelation he received while consulting with the pendulum. This feature of the pyramid was apparently confined to pharaoh's chamber, exactly where Dyrbal was later to place his razor blade (after reading about Bovis's discovery). Bovis returned to France, and he constructed a scale model. Sure enough, organic matter is preserved for long periods of time. No refrigeration is needed.[31]

The most striking fact of these reports is the repeatability of the phenomena. Dyrbal had to wait for years for the Czech government to grant him his patent. He had to show that the razor-repairing effect is truly scientific. Dyrbal's theory is incomprehensible: the shape of the pyramid creates certain resonating effects that somehow dehumidify the water molecules in the blades' steel structure. Anyway, in 1959, patent number 91304 on the pyramid was issued. You can buy models throughout the Western world. (If I were you, I wouldn't, as this book will make clear later on.)

More obviously occult psychological effects are produced by the pyramid shape. Some firms make "pyramid tents" that are used for personal meditation. By placing one's head close to the apex (not too hard in a small tent), the meditating mystic sometimes achieves a "higher consciousness."[32] Furthermore, one company now offers a kind of prayer kit (magic kit) built around the pyramid. Prayers or requests are written on certain colored sheets of paper, with colors matching the type of request. The paper is placed inside the pyramid (made of cardboard), and a chant is made over it. After incubating for an unspecified time, the paper is removed and burned, in order to "liberate" the wish. Rewards, according to specifications, are supposed to follow.[33] People who are the products of the rationalistic American public school system are buying these devices.

Some people report tingling sensations in their fingers when they raise them close to the apex inside a pyramid tent. This is strikingly parallel to the tingling sensations in the fingers reported by table-raisers just before the table activates (or is activated). Furthermore, dowsing rods respond to the pyramid shape.

The danger with pyramid occultism, as with so many other forms of occult phenomena, is the simultaneous curiosity and semiscientific nature of the phenomena. After all, a lot of people do shave with blades sharpened, day after day, by these devices. Yet the devices are not normal. They seem safe, yet there is an air of mystery about them. The fruitless quest for accurate prophecies may have kept cultists off the streets for a century, but the recently revived curiosity in pyramid shapes may prove to be another irrational wedge in the door of rational culture. The Egyptian magicians and designers must have known of the occult properties of the pyramid. They certainly knew of its architectural symbolism. But the sorcerer's apprentices of today, blithely sharpening their razor blades or preserving hunks of meat, are too naive. They do not understand the relationship between symbols and demonic power.

Kirlian Photography

One of the most familiar of the doctrines among psychics, theosophists, occultists, and healers is the doctrine of the "aura." This second body, also called the astral body, supposedly surrounds each human being. At death, the astral body departs; ghosts and spirits are often believed to be manifestations of the astral bodies of the dead. It is believed that some gifted or highly trained individuals can experience out-of-body travel—astral projection—by means of the human aura. (In the movie *The Other* the grandmother of a little boy, who himself later becomes a murderer, first trains him in astral projection. Much of the space in Carlos Castaneda's four books on Yaqui Indian sorcery is devoted to astral projection.)

All of this speculation concerning the astral body might have remained confined to curious metaphysical societies had it not been for a Russian technician, Semyon Davidovich Kirlian. In the late 1930s, Kirlian happened to witness a demonstration of a device used in electrotherapy. It emitted a high-frequency spark when its electrode came close to the patient's skin. Kirlian wondered whether it would be possible to photograph the person's skin by means of the light emitted by the spark. He began to experiment with a machine that he constructed. He placed a photographic plate between the electrode and his arm. Sure enough, he got a picture. He also received a serious burn. Undaunted, he continued his experiments.

Eventually he began to produce a series of astounding photographs. They revealed thousands of fiery lights, like miniature flames, shooting from the palms of his hands. Leaves and other types of organic matter also displayed the fireworks, although a cut or dying leaf projected weaker and fewer lights. Early in the 1950s, word about his photographs spread to scientific circles. One visitor brought what appeared to be two identical leaves to be photographed. After struggling throughout the night with picture after picture, Kirlian admitted that he was unable to produce identical pictures; one leaf seemed duller than the other. The visitor, the chairman of a Soviet scientific research institute, was elated. One leaf was known to be diseased, for the plant from which it had been plucked had been deliberately contaminated. Yet no known diagnostic process was then available to warn botanists of the inevitable fate of the plant in question. Kirlian's photograph had diagnosed the illness in advance of any other means available.

One of the fascinating aspects of Kirlian photography is that the experiments are repeatable. Dr. Thelma Moss, an assistant professor at UCLA and a medical psychologist attached to the Neuropsychiatric Institute of that university, has been a leading figure (though few tenured Ph.D.'s are following) in parapsychology, and has used Kirlian photography as a primary tool of her research. Her book, *The Probability of the Impossible* (1974), is perhaps the best written and most intelligent introduction to the field of paranormal science that exists. She has discovered that people under different emotional conditions will produce different Kirlian photos: different colored lights, different intensities, etc. Sickness also affects the results. One professional hypnotist (mesmerist) who employs "magnetic passes" has made such passes over leaves. Subsequent photographs of the "magnetized" leaves reveal brighter beads of light. Even more curious are the photos of the fingertips of a psychic healer and his patient. Prior to the "healing" (or whatever it is), the healer's prints are brighter than after the healing, and the patient's fingertips display the reverse effect. Furthermore, one pathologist at the cross-town University of Southern California has been photographing rats in double-blind studies (the experimenters do not know which are which during the experiments). Tumorous rats produce photographic images that are visibly different from those produced by healthy ones.[34] No one knows why.

Most remarkably, one Soviet surgeon who had studied acupuncture in China in the 1940s examined photographs of hands made with Kirlian techniques. He noticed that certain points of the hand emitted brighter lights. These bright points coincided with the traditional acupuncture points for the hand The surgeon, M. K. Gaikin, returned to Leningrad from his visit with the Kirlians and constructed, with the help of an engineer, a pen-light device that can be used in locating the acupuncture points. This "tobiscope" is now being used by Soviet researchers. Thus, two odd phenomena, the photographs and the ancient techniques of acupuncture, have been linked scientifically.[35] Why such links are possible, or why either phenomenon should exist at all, no one is sure.

What has not been incorporated into the Kirlian system is the occult theory of the astral body. Yet it seems odd that a leaf can be sliced into two sections and, under the Kirlian high-frequency flash of electric light, a "phantom" image of the cut-off section of that leaf appears on the photograph. In any case, the existence of this photographic technique, though still disparaged and/or ignored by most American scientists, has opened up several new avenues of research, and some of them most certainly border on the paranormal. The problem now is to find whether the border line skirts simply the "not yet known" or the truly occult. The links with faith healing indicate the latter, while the link to acupuncture or leaf diagnosis seems to indicate the former. The chief problem is not technological; it is that those doing the research (like Dr. Moss) do not acknowledge the distinction between the occult and the "not yet known." Thus, an insatiably curious public may be subjected in the future to another wedge of the occult into a rationalistic world. The book-buying public, unlike the establishment scientists, is no longer content to wrap each new phenomenon in the swaddling clothes of phenomenal rationalism. The time-honored formula of the scientific guild—to ignore and dismiss anything that seems not to fit the inherited (and steadily weakening) rationalistic methodology—does not impress millions of those who are buying the paperback books. To that extent, they are increasingly at the mercy of the enthusiastic and untenured experimenters—untenured either by their scientific guilds or by the guild of the magicians. The sorcerer's apprentices are now loose in the land.

Talking Plants

The fertility religions of the ancient world, like many of the "primitive" cultures of today, were animistic. It was believed that each field, or each species of plant, or even each individual plant, possessed its own personal spirit. Very often this spirit was understood as being malevolent and had to be placated ritually to ensure agricultural productivity. It has always been the mark of a culture that is essentially the product of Christian orthodoxy, with its trinitarian personalism instead of polytheistic personalism, that animism fades away, at best surviving in the ritual practices of folklore. It may persist in rural areas that have been only marginally influenced by Christian orthodoxy, but generally animism lives a furtive, underground existence in a Christian culture. But where the influence of Christianity recedes, animism is likely to reappear.

The Secret Life of Plants (1973) by Peter Tomkins (a pyramid cultist) and Christopher Bird became an immense bestseller. Over a million paperbacks were issued in the fall of 1974. More than any other book available in English, this one is the cultural wedge for a reviving animism. It dresses up the animist religion in scientific garb, but there can be little doubt that the book's basic premise is animistic. In the final chapter, the authors describe a family of outright mediums (not media, surely) and animists who have converted a dreary section of the Scottish seacoast into a "garden of Eden," in the authors' words. They have used organic gardening techniques, coupled with huge doses of mysticism and spiritualism, to transform the land. One of the "gardeners," who asserts that the spirits gave her the name Divina, "had managed to get into direct contact with the devas or angelic creatures who control the nature spirits that are said by clairvoyants to be everywhere at work nurturing plant life."[36] This perspective, needless to say, is pure animism. "Divina contributed detailed descriptions of the messages she said she received directly from the devas, of which she described whole hierarchies responsible for every fruit and vegetable, for every flower and weed."[37] (In *Silent Spring,* Rachel Carson informed us that our insecticides are killing off the robins, but she neglected to tell us that we may also be interfering with the Intercosmical Association of Devas and Wood Spirits Union.)

It all started, as they say, with Cleve Backster. Back in 1966, Mr. Backster, an internationally famous polygraph (lie detector) expert, hooked up one of his plants to a polygraph device. He noticed that the device recorded significant responses whenever he directed a mental threat toward the plant, such as burning one of its leaves. In a now-famous and frequently cited experiment—frequently cited in paranormal science books, that is—Backster placed brine shrimp on plates, which in turn would dump them into boiling water on a random basis. The machines connected to several plants under control conditions recorded statistically significant responses to the death of brine shrimp—five to one above what random responses would have been. The more limited conclusion would seem to be that plants react to the death of brine shrimp. The more comprehensive conclusion is the one authors of bestselling paranormal science books prefer: plants can read your mind. (*The Secret Life of Plants* and *Supernature* and *Psychic Discoveries Behind the Iron Curtain* all spell trouble for the complacent vegetarians of the world—just the kind of people who might read and believe these books.)[38]

Two other serious sets of tests have been conducted, one set by Pearl Weinberger and Mary Measures at the University of Ottawa, and the other by Mrs. Dorothy Retallack and her instructor at Colorado Women's College (formerly Temple Buell College, formerly Colorado Woman's College). The Ottawa experiments indicated that some seedlings respond to certain audio frequencies (for example, 5,000 cps) by growing more rapidly than would otherwise be statistically normal. Tests are being conducted in a number of laboratories to confirm or refute this thesis.

The Retallack experiments are less rigorous and therefore much more interesting. She has found that some plants—corn, petunias, squash, and marigolds—grow away from loudspeakers that blare hard-rock music, and grow in the direction of speakers playing Bach. They are apparently neutral toward country-western and folk music.[39] (Bluegrass—the music, that is—was not tested. Presumably, the plants, if they have any musical taste at all, will fall over their tendrils trying to get closer to Earl Scruggs.)

The idea of talking and thinking plants is recent, but the notion of sentient plants goes back to the turn of the century. India's great biological scientist, Sir Jagadis Chandra Bose, conducted decades of research into the response of plants to electrical and other stimulations. He found that chloroformed plants could sometimes be transplanted under conditions that are usually fatal to them. By developing extremely sensitive measuring instruments, he discovered that responses characteristic of animal tissues are found in plant tissues.[40] His scholarly papers were suppressed, time after time, by the Royal Society, although the Linnean Society was willing to publish some of them. Too much carbon dioxide, he found, affected plants the way that too much liquor affects men: they swayed, passed out, and finally revived.[41] One instrument, the crescograph, measured incredibly minute growth rates among plants, and Bose claimed that by merely touching a plant it is possible to retard its growth rate in some cases.[42]

In the 1920s, at the time Bose was continuing his researches, Soviet scientist Alexander Gurvitch conducted a series of experiments with the roots of onions. He thought it possible that some form of energy linked onion plants. He built an apparatus that exposed portions of the roots of two onions to each other by means of a glass tube. After three hours of exposure, he said he was able to detect significant increases (twenty-five percent) in the growth rate of the exposed section of the "receiving" onion's root.[43] He tried yeast as a receiver. It increased its growth rate by thirty percent.[44] Several European studies claimed to have duplicated Gurvitch's findings, but the American Academy of Sciences denied finding any change in growth rates. Gurvitch was forgotten.

Half a century later, Soviet scientists revived Gurvitch's discredited theory. At the Insitute of Automation and Electrometry, scientists placed identical tissue cultures into hermetically sealed vessels separated by a wall of glass and then introduced a lethal virus into one chamber. The second colony was unaffected. But when quartz was substituted for glass, the second colony died. Then they used chemical poisons and radiation to kill off a colony. The second colony died. Perhaps ultraviolet rays are the answer, since glass will not carry them. This was Gurvitch's theory. Apparently ultraviolet rays can carry information between cells.[45]

Still, apart from Backster's experiments, plants have not yet been shown to think. They may react in ways that establishment scientists prefer not to admit, but thought is a different kettle of fish—or brine shrimp. *The Secret Life of Plants* spends a chapter on the uncanny career of Luther Burbank, but only in the final paragraphs do the authors reveal that Burbank talked to plants in order to create "a vibration of love." The sources of these revelations are peculiar, however: Manly P. Hall, a Southern California esoteric-mystic philosopher, and Paramhansa Yogananda, the founder of the Self-Realization Fellowship. Even if Burbank did talk to his plants, his successes as a plant breeder are not proof that they answered him. If something *did* answer him, was it a plant?

This is not to say that there is no evidence of some very peculiar events associated with the talking-plant theory. Marcel Vogel, a research chemist, read about Backster's experiments, threw the article away, and then returned to retrieve it a few days later. He decided to begin his own research. He is a genius inventor, having specialized in liquid crystals, magnetics, and computer applications. He has developed several patented concepts. He was teaching an evening training course for IBM. When he introduced some experiments for testing the response of plants, only he among the people in the classroom could duplicate Backster's results. "Vogel wondered why he alone seemed to be successful."

The next few sentences of *Secret Life* give the answer, although the authors seem not to realize this: "As a boy, he had been interested in anything which might explain the workings of the human mind. After dipping into books on magic, spiritualism, and hypnotic technique, he had given stage demonstrations as a teenage hypnotist."[46] Here is the key that unlocks many of the doors in paranormal science: a prior series of experiences by the experimenter or subject in occultism.

Vogel asked a "spiritually gifted friend," Vivian Wiley, to conduct an experiment. Each morning she was to think friendly thoughts toward one plant and no thoughts toward the other. One was told mentally that it would live; the other was ignored. Within a month, the ignored plant was dying. Vogel duplicated this feat with plants of his own. By hooking up philodendrons to various machines, he found that he could produce responses on the machine's recording devices—"in the plant" supposedly—by directing friendly thoughts toward them.

Vogel had discovered early in his career that by "relaxing his mind," he could visualize activities in the behavior of liquid crystals under a microscope that his professional colleagues could not see. He refers to this phenomenon as his "higher sensory awareness."[47] He had trained himself in this state of higher consciousness. Later he became aware of his own unique position in his experiments with plants. Again and again, manifestations of paranormal science are found to be intimately linked to the experimenter—so strongly linked, in fact, that the odd phenomena do not occur when he is not present. As the authors state:

> It became clearer to Vogel that a certain focused state of consciousness on his part seemed to become an integral and balancing part of the circuitry required to monitor his plants. A plant could be awakened from somnolence to sensitivity by his giving up his normally conscious state and focusing a seemingly extra-conscious part of his mind on the exact notion that the plant be happy and feel loved, that it be blessed with healthy growth. In this way, man and plant seemed to interact, and, as a unit, pick up sensations from events, or third parties, which became recordable through the plant. . . . Asked to describe the process in detail, Vogel said that first he quiets the sensory responses of his body organs, then he becomes aware of an energetic relationship between the plant and himself. When a state of balance between the bioelectrical potential of both the plant and himself is achieved, the plant is no longer sensitive to noise, temperature, the normal electrical fields surrounding it, or other plants. It responds only to Vogel, who has effectively tuned himself to it—or perhaps simply hypnotizes it.[48]

Problem: How is anything "simply hypnotized"? Just because the phenomenon of hypnosis is so widespread, scientists and laymen alike tend to dismiss it as another of those daily miracles associated with the mind of man. But to appeal to hypnosis as an explanation for paranormal phenomena is to evade the question of paranormal phenomena, for hypnosis is one of the most intriguing and least explainable of all paranormal phenomena. As has been remarked by students of demonic possession, hypnosis permits men to respond in ways that "primitive" observers would instantly recognize as demonically induced. Furthermore, continued experiments with hypnosis can lead to possession itself. The very principle of hypnosis—subjection to the suggestions of another person, and the implied rejection of responsibility for the subject's actions—is the principle of demonic possession. How, then, does Vogel "hypnotize" his plants? By what kind of power?

Another "plant communicator" is Pierre Paul Sauvin of West Paterson, New Jersey. A confessed medium and a minister of the Psychic Science Temple of Metaphysics (the name tells all!), Sauvin also tinkers with Rube Goldberg plant communication devices. He would call them on his home telephone from a secret phone strapped to his leg (which he also used to communicate from his desk at his job with ITT to various editors, since he was moonlighting as a technical writer). He then monitored their responses. He could communicate with them mentally by putting himself into a light hypnotic trance. He would give himself a light electrical shock at work, and miles away at his home, the plants would respond—or at least the recording equipment to which they were attached would respond. Finally, he put the plants to work. He hooked them up to his garage door opener, and when he approached the door from the outside, he had only to signal them mentally to open it up. This way, the garage was burglarproof, or at least safer. He thinks that a "plant man" could control the flight of an airplane by means of plant communications. (I have this mental impression of being strapped in my seat in a Boeing 747 at 35,000 feet when a recorded voice comes over the loudspeaker: "Welcome aboard. This is your philodendron speaking. My co-pilot this morning is a petunia.") Or plants could be used as screening devices at airports to detect emotionally disturbed people who might be hijackers.[49] (My guess is that if word gets out that plants are flying the planes, the odds are very strong that anyone doing much flying will probably be emotionally disturbed.) Nevertheless, despite all the nonsense, the fact does exist that plants can be used as intermediaries in producing certain electrical-mechanical responses.

Paranormal science does raise questions that should be answered. Unfortunately, establishment science is not equipped even to acknowledge that the data or the questions really exist. If the issues raised by Sir Jagadis C. Bose could not be handled by orthodox science, then the issues raised by Backster, Vogel, and Sauvin are far too difficult.

The key fact of *The Secret Life of Plants* is that the vast bulk of the reported cases of odd plant phenomena have been recorded by occultists, mystics, and others whose "sympathetic attitude" toward both the plants and the experiments made it possible for the peculiar reactions to take place. With the possible exception of Cleve Backster's lie detectors and the experiments with sound, virtually all of the reported experiments are admitted to be repeatable only by those who are "sympathetic." This is a distinct case of borderline science in action. The premise of modern experimental science—repeatability—is violated.

But there is more of the occult than meets the eye of some of the antiestablishment experimenters. The possibility of *animism*—demonic interference in the experiments—is never acknowledged, either by the orthodox scientists (who conveniently dismiss all signs of the abnormal) or the parascientists (who do not want hostile, supernatural forces to intereefere in *their* sympathetic creativity). There is a whole new zone of research for Christian scientists to clarify—disentangling long-ignored patterns of God's creation from the activity of demons. The non-Christian investigators are powerless to sort out facts from theory when demons tinker with the meters.

Psychic Photography

The occult phenomenon of psychic photography is seldom (if ever) discussed in popular photographic magazines, yet the phenomenon has existed for over a century. First encountered by Boston engraver William Mumler in the middle of the nineteenth century, it was pursued rigorously by the British parapsychologist F. W. Warrick in his book, *Experiments in Psychics* (1939). A photograph, sometimes taken by nonpsychic Mumler, but more often taken by or with the cooperation of an occultist, produces strange additions on the negatives. These may merely be streaks of light for which there is no mechanical explanation. There may be what appear to be double-exposed images superimposed on the negative. Perhaps most peculiar of all are "ghost" images, which usually are small reproductions of existing photographs of deceased subjects. Sometimes these images are of famous persons, while other times they are photo reproductions of snapshots of dead relatives of the subject being photographed. These images can appear on films produced by a Polaroid Land camera under test conditions. These weird images can also be found on supposedly unexposed sheets of film that have never been put into a camera. The psychic photographer can actually transfer mental images to sealed, fresh film packs. One of the most proficient of these medium-mentalists is John Myers.

John Myers is a wealthy industrialist who picked up his talent for psychic photography after a visit with Emma Deane, the medium whose work had been basic to Warrick's *Experiments in Psychics*. He has performed his feats of occult skill under numerous conditions, including an appearance on the old *PM East* television show in 1961. Several of his photographs are reprinted in Hans Holzer's book, *Psychic Photography* (1970). Packs of photographic paper are purchased by the experimenter from any store. Myers concentrates his attention on the film for a few minutes, announces that the test is finished, and the film is then developed. Symbols may appear, such as a cross or a tombstone; human faces sometimes appear. Myers is unable to predict in advance just what will appear, but he is aware when the psychic process is finished.

Another successful psychic photographer is Dr. Andrew von Salza, a West Coast physician. In March 1966, he visited the Holzers in New York City, where he took a photograph of Mrs. Holzer, using a Polaroid camera, model 103. Mrs. Holzer's image appeared quite normally, but next to her in the frame was a vague ghostly impression of a painting of Russia's Catherine the Great, suspended in midair. When Holzer had a reproduction of this picture made, it turned out poorly. Nevertheless, he sent a copy to Von Salza. The latter immediately "felt led" to rephotograph the copy. This time he obtained a print with "Catherine" quite clear. He sent back two reproductions of this new picture to Holzer.

To check on this strange procedure, Holzer visited Von Salza in May 1966. The physician repeated the process. He aimed his Polaroid camera at the copy Holzer had sent him, and out of his camera popped another picture of Mrs. Holzer and "Catherine," only this time "Catherine" had extended her arm, as if she were offering a crown to Mrs. Holzer. Unknown to Dr. von Salza at the time, Mrs. Holzer is a sixth-generation descendant of Catherine the Great. (The "Catherine" in the photographs appears as a painting.)

Holzer had met Von Salza a year earlier. He visited the physician's home, along with several other guests, to witness a demonstration. Von Salza set up a Polaroid camera in his living room and photographed the assembled group several times. Each time, the resulting photographs included strange and highly extraneous images. The images appeared above the group. Faces, apparently photographs, of unknown people, plus one each of President Kennedy and John D. Rockefeller, Sr., were suspended above the heads of the guests. Kennedy's image also appeared in another 1966 photograph taken by Von Salza, only this time it was accompanied by an image of Abraham Lincoln. (This one looks suspiciously like a put-up job by the Democratic National Committee, but I am ever the skeptic—of politics, not of ghosts.) Another Von Salza snapshot looks like one of those montage efforts popular in the late 1960s, with dozens of faces, including Marilyn Monroe's and Lee Harvey Oswald's, plastered all over the frame.

Mrs. Florence Sternfels, another medium and clairvoyant, had the ability of going into a trance and imprinting her image—blurred—on an X-ray plate placed inside a shielded box that had been placed beneath her foot. It took about one hour of trance to accomplish this feat. (Frankly, back in 1952 when this event occurred, it would have been much simpler, faster, and clearer to have used a Brownie Hawkeye!) Another series of photographs snapped with black flashbulbs and infrared film show her in a trance. An "ectoplasm" outline of a small dog can be seen emerging from her lower abdomen.

The most famous mental photographer of all, however, is a semialcoholic former elevator operator, Ted Serios. Serios' case was made famous by Dr. Jule Eisenbud, a psychologist and parapsychologist.[50] For years, Eisenbud had despaired of finding psychic phenomena that would be subject to that criterion of criteria in modern science, repeatable experiments. It is the nonrepetitive nature of most paranormal phenomena that plagues those researchers who are trying to bridge the gap between paranormal science and normal science. Either the subjects or the experimenters "somehow" influence the outcome of the experiments —a fact which, in and of itself, ought to cause more intelligent responses from orthodox scientists than the usual cry of "fraud!" Eisenbud himself was highly skeptical when informed of Serios' abilities, even though there had been published material concerning them.

What the scientific community says it wants are some experimental tests like those conducted by J. B. Rhine, formerly of Duke University, or those devised by European parapsychologists. But Eisenbud was well aware of the fact that orthodox scientists, even when allowed to devise such tests and monitor them, invariably assert that some loose end must have been overlooked, and that the experiment was without value. They assert this, it should be mentioned, only when there is positive evidence that paranormal phenomena have been recorded. One of the only truly repeatable paranormal subjects, Pavel Stepanic, the Czech psychic who loves ESP card experiments, has been studied by numerous orthodox scientists, and the startling results have even filtered into the orthodox journals, but it has not been enough to crack the wall of epistemological skepticism. Stepanic once made a sensational run of 2,000 guesses involving cards that were black on one side and white on the other. The cards having been placed in opaque envelopes on a random basis, Stepanic was able to guess which side was up in 1,114 cases. Odds against: one billion to one. He has performed again and again before scientists who devised the tests. No fraud has been unearthed.[51] The guild's reaction is silence.

Eisenbud hoped Ted Serios would be his Pavel Stepanic, only a far more spectacular Stepanic. On several occasions, Serios demonstrated his most peculiar ability. He would work himself up for several hours, usually with a good quantity of liquor, and then pick up a Polaroid camera. Covering the lens with his "gismo"—a tube covered with black tape, which was carefully examined by observers on countless occasions—Serios would trip the shutter. Out would come a picture, usually of some building. But if there was ever a nonrepeatable, Serios was the man. When invited to perform before scientists, sometimes he would go on a binge, or leave town. Other times, especially under the scrutiny of a large group of scientists, he could produce only "whities"—perfectly white frames—which did not impress his witnesses, although obtaining such pictures from a Polaroid with its lens covered is quite impossible. Still, he did perform well on some occasions, as over one hundred photographs in Eisenbud's book demonstrate.

Serios' background is revealing. He had developed his ability under the prodding of an amateur hypnotist during his stint as an elevator operator in Chicago. The hypnotist, also an employee of the hotel, was convinced that hypnotism might give Serios the ability to project his "astral body" in a search for treasure. Serios now claims that a "spirit guide" named "Jean Laffite" met him and took him on several journeys. But "Laffite" made fewer and fewer contacts, became increasingly transparent, and finally told Serios to strike out on his own. Serios told Eisenbud that he did locate a few hiding places of valuables, but too late: someone else was digging them up. Serios' partner then wondered if Serios could "photograph his visions." He bought Serios a roll-film camera to try out. Serios was skeptical, but he did project a few thoughts at it, and when the film was returned, there were images on a few of the frames. Serios then bought himself a Polaroid and began practicing. His images were a bit blurred, but recognizable in many instances.[52]

(Significantly, Pavel Stepanic was also introduced to his ESP abilities—or the abilities were introduced to him—by means of hypnotism. Stepanic is the product of a highly successful trainer of psychics, Dr. Milan Ryzl, who defected to the West in the late 1960s. Hypnotism was Ryzl's primary tool in developing psychics. There is more to hypnotism than meets the eye of modern observers.)

Eisenbud's book has been one of the most popular in the library of parapsychology, and Serios' case is quoted again and again in the literature. Strange as Serios' abilities may be, even stranger are Eisenbud's explanations of them. When he begins to deal with paranormal phenomena, Eisenbud retreats into the language and concepts of Freudian psychology, and the radical humanism of Freud's position colors the entire analysis. The small segment of the academic community that concerns itself with paranormal phenomena from a "rigorously scientific" point of view subjects its methodology to theories even more incredible than the paranormal events it claims to deal with.

What was the source of the mental pictures? Ted's subconscious mind, of course.[53] And why not? What is the subconscious mind, if not the bottomless pit of the unsolved riddles of the mind itself? Being bottomless, it can certainly hold a few psychic pictures produced by Ted Serios. We do not know the mechanism of such tricks, or where to look to uncover it, or how to shield it in some totally rigorous experiment. No known shield can impede the phenomena; whether Ted is inside the Faraday cage or the camera, the pictures still are transmitted. What Freudian psychology tell us, however, is that the source of these phenomena *must* be in Ted's mind. They cannot possibly be demonic, since there is no such thing as the demonic. Demonic beings are the product of sick minds. When a ghost persists, then the psychiatrist's "psychotherapy was not completely successful, and that, as is so often the case, residual conflict material remains to be teased out to the light and worked through;...."[54]

Eisenbud's humanism is common to parapsychology. It is the link to orthodox science. In discussing automatic writing, where relaxed persons holding a pencil produce writings that often are in a foreign language unknown (consciously, of course) to the writer, or sometimes reveal information unknown to the writer, Dr. Thelma Moss, good humanist that she is, explains: "Generally such persons are deluded into the belief that the writing is coming from some outside source, whether divine or demonic, when in all likelihood it is coming from a barely subliminal region of the mind."[55] Parapsychology, by definition, must focus on man alone, asserts Eisenbud. "What is unique about the data of psychical research is that only they suggest that man has in fact within him vast untapped powers that hitherto have been accorded him only in the magic world of the primitive, in the secret fantasies of childhood, and in fairy tales and legend."[56] Parapsychology is *the* legitimate science of man because it ascribes so much *power* to man.

Why, then, should establishment science, itself so thoroughly humanistic, resist the findings of parapsychology? In good Freudian fashion, Eisenbud blames that old standby, the mother-child relationship. Modern scientism, being mechanistic, is a product of men's guilt. Men always hated their mothers. The all-powerful mother, not the father, was the threat to man's autonomy. To suppress guilt feelings, men construct for themselves a universe that eliminates responsibility because it substitutes impersonal, mechanistic forces for human choice. Thus, parapsychology is a threat to scientific orthodoxy.[57] It threatens to dredge up the *personal* side of science, such as the subconscious mind's ability to project images. Man's "dark and sinister side," as Eisenbud calls it, is being brought into view by parapsychology. Man's *mind* has power independent of machines—or at least the subconscious mind does. Orthodox mechanistic science is repelled by such a notion. "It is hardly to be wondered that it automatically sees anything faintly suggestive of the power of thought as superstitious nonsense to be rejected firmly and out of hand."[58]

It seems likely that other reasons are also involved in orthodoxy's rejection of parapsychology, or at least of the data of parapsychology. Scientists see only too clearly that phenomena like these are not explainable in terms of any known view of man, and there is the scent of the supernatural in the air. Furthermore, while there is a mechanistic tradition in all modern science, a point made clear half a century ago in E. A. Burtt's *Metaphysical Foundations of Modern Physical Science,* there has always been a "personalist-indeterminist" strain in scientific orthodoxy. Eisenbud and the other paranormal scientists are trying to enlarge the field of science to include more of the "not yet known," but their colleagues are convinced that *this* kind of "not yet known" is just too close to the demonism that was only too well known three centuries ago. Nevertheless, Eisenbud's summary of the knee-jerk reaction of establishment science to the troubling data of parapsychology is illuminating:

> Science, like a well-behaved compulsive neurotic, is committed to following out blindly a conspiracy of denial and rejection that is bred into its very marrow. As a result anthropologists automatically take it for granted that the stories and legends of the occult they have been collecting these many years from their primitive informants have no basis whatever in fact. Psychiatrists and psychologists, for their part, just as automatically assume that accounts they may hear of alleged telepathic incidents or dreams from their informants must be due to malobservation or purely chance coincidence, and unhesitatingly write off anyone manifesting an interest in the subject as suffering from a regressive need for the miraculous.[59]

But what of Ted Serios? Why should he be able to accomplish these feats of psychic photography, while the rest of us have to rely on light meters, viewfinders, and other physical baggage? Eisenbud has an answer straight out of Kant's *Critique of Pure Reason*—so Kantian that he outdoes Kant himself Extrasensory perception, telepathy, mental photographs, and other such phenomena stem from an excess reservoir of mental power. The bulk of this *mental reservoir of power* is in use on a full-time basis. Where is it used? *It is holding up the universe!*

> Actually the primitive himself had a clue to the mystery in his sense of oneness with nature but, what with his not being an analytically minded fellow, it may not have occurred to him to do the "power auditing" that might have led to the insight I am leading up to. This is, of course, that the latent mental power which all of us possess goes into sustaining—and is thus manifest in—all the natural processes that we see around us, from the growth of the lowliest seed to the movements of the heavenly bodies. It might thus be put down under the heading of "general maintenance." . . . If the curious reader would like to know, however, what would happen if the rest of us were to withdraw our power from the universe at large, all I can suggest is a simple so-

called thought experiment which he can either do for himself or take my word for, as I have done it many times and can tell him exactly what will happen: the universe collapses and in fact vanishes, like the image on a television screen when the current is shut off, putting an end at once to the controversies of the cosmologists, who simply disappear in the general confusion.[60]

Unquestionably, this is as powerful a statement of radical humanism as one is likely to encounter. Both the world of regularity and the world of Ted Serios are the same world, for they are supported by the human mind, although different parts of the mind. "According to this point of view then, the question of what keeps the universe running—the question of who or what is in the back of the Big Store—admits of an answer that is not only sublimely simple but in principle unassailable: just look for the throne behind the power."[61] It is man who sits on that throne. All of post-Kantian science affirms this theory of the universe, but Eisenbud has stated it more forthrightly than most others are willing to do. Man is the creator and sustainer of his universe. And from time to time, certain gifted men dip into the humanistic reservoir of power to perform what many men call magic.

Primitive man's theory makes a lot more sense: demons, not parapsychological power-dipping, are the source of the phenomena.[62]

Precognition

Jeanne Dixon aside, what can be said about scientific studies concerning men's ability to forecast future events? This has been the goal of man for thousands of years. The fact that the Bulgarian government has put their Jeanne Dixon, Vanga Dimitrova, on the state payroll (collecting a fee from her dozens of daily callers) is indicative of the shift of opinion behind the Iron Curtain. Also indicative is the fact that the Czechoslovakian government finances the astrological research of Dr. Eugen Jonas, who claims to be able to forecast by means of a mother's astrological sign when she can conceive, what sex the child will be (ninety-eight percent accuracy claimed), whether the woman is even pregnant, and what sex the now-conceived child is (eighty-seven percent accuracy claimed).[63] But the interest shown by American scientists is far more limited. Nevertheless, some interesting tests have been devised, and some even more interesting results obtained. Some subjects not only guess the present order of cards in a pack, but actually predict the order that will occur *after the deck is shuffled.*

> Perhaps the most ardent of all current psychic research is that which is out to find a new guinea pig for its studies—that is, one other than man. The pioneering work in this area was carried out by French psychologists Pierre Duval and Evelyn Montredon. One mouse at a time was placed in a cage with a wired floor. Electric current was then directed randomly to different sections of the cage in order to deliver a shock whenever the mouse happened to be in the wrong place at the wrong time. When random jumps of some mice were analyzed they were found to have consistently avoided the spot where

the next shock was aimed, despite the fact that there was no consistent pattern to the shocks. . . . But the ultimate along these lines must be the test devised by psychologist Helmut Schmidt for his pet cat. This otherwise quite ordinary curl-up-at-the-hearth-type feline was locked in a cold building with a heat lamp wired to come on intermittently through the night. The number of times the light would switch on was completely randomized by the electrical apparatus, as was the length of time the light would stay on each time it lit. Naturally, the cat wanted the lamp on to provide warmth, and fantastically enough, did seem able to affect its workings. The light repeatedly came on more often and stayed on for longer periods of time when the cat was in the room than when the cat was not present.[64]

Lyall Watson reports on a study by an American mathematician, William Cox, that sought to discover whether people somehow avoid trains that have accidents. He selected a station and took information concerning the number of passengers who rode the train during each of the seven days preceding an accident, as well as the fourteenth, twenty-first, and twenty-eighth days before. The data covered a seven-year period. On days that were marred by an accident, there were always fewer passengers than statistically normal. The difference between the predicted number of passengers, using statistical methods, and the actual number was so great that the odds against it were one hundred to one.[65]

Over and over, the question of the reality of such events hinges on the comparison of chance or random events and those that are supposedly abnormal and therefore evidence of ESP, precognition, or whatever. This is the required methodology of modern science, since modern science rests on the hypothesis of the existence of a world formed by chance and developed by the processes of Darwinian evolution, that is, chance-induced change. Yet in the midst of random change there is stability: the laws of probability. Random changes operate, says modern science, by the fixed laws of probability. These are the test of coherence in any series of events. But the paranormal scientists have found that statistical probability is a one-way street within conventional scientific circles. It is allowed to screen out paranormal phenomena, converting them into random events within a normal distribution. But when these paranormal patterns persist, establishment scientists either blame the experiment's control procedures or, in a last-ditch effort to sweep their universe clear of noumenal influences, appeal to luck—good old lady luck. (You can lead an establishment scientist to a significant deviation, but you can't make him swallow the paranormal camel.) As one commentator summarizes the situation: "All scientific insight rests on some reasonably invariant relationship. The structure of an experiment must be such that when A is done in the lab, B occurs. Psychic research seemed to hypothesize that, when all known factors are controlled, any score deviating from chance would be by definition due to ESP—which continued to mean telepathy to parapsychologists, luck to critics."[66] In short, "Results based solely on odds against chance could simply not be accepted as definitive proof; they had to be confirmed in turn by a repeatable laboratory experiment under controlled conditions which would show that a signal had traveled from one point outside the mind of a human being to some point within. No such experiment had ever been accomplished."[67] Indeed, no such experiment could be devised and still remain paranormal; as soon as some "signal" is discovered, if such a signal exists, then it immediately becomes absorbed into the scientifically normal. This would please most parapsychologists, but not all of them. In any case, the mind-matter link is so insecure in modern philosophy and modern psychology that any such rigorous demand placed upon the methodology of parapsychology is wholly hypocritical, since hypothesized links in psychology are equally unproven and probably unprovable. The relationship between "stimulus" and "response" is still as baffling and divisive an issue among scientists as it was a century ago.

Conclusion

What we have in the division between paranormal and normal science is not a failure to communicate. What we have is not a semantic problem. What we have is a religious debate that is based upon fundamentally opposed presuppositions concerning the nature of reality and man's place in it. When orthodox scientists keep appealing to statistics, they always mean those statistics which confirm their hypothesis. After all, if their view of reality is correct, then statistical results *must* conform to it, since the laws of statistics are by definition controlled by the reality principle, that is, the logic of the phenomenal world. Thus, concludes Wayne Sage: "As intriguing as such findings may be, however, the fact remains that after 40 years of such work, nothing has been 'proven.' Statistics for deviations from a theoretical probability can always be rejected out of hand, and generally are by the scientific community at large. In the words of Rhine himself: 'To say that it [parapsychology] is properly a branch of psychology . . . is to idealize psychology. There is no field of science that now recognizes, even as a possibility, the kind of reality to which the evidence of parapsychology offers support.'"[68] And if the secular parapsychologist suspects that anyone is using his research's findings to support any truly occult or demonic source of the "causes" of the paranormal responses, he too will line up behind the banner of Kantian science to keep such nonsense out of *his* universe.

That Sage should quote J. B. Rhine is not surprising. It was J. B. Rhine more than anyone else who created the academic subdiscipline of parapsychology. In the early 1930s, this young psychologist shocked the academic world with his findings, and that world has not yet forgiven him. From the mid-1930s to the mid-1960s, Rhine conducted his research at Duke University. He now heads his own Foundation for Research into the Nature of Man.

For decades the academic guild has cried fraud whenever a new finding emerged from Rhine's lab, but Rhine patiently went about tightening the controls and producing more paranormal results. It was never enough. "Other psychologists began to demand tighter controls, often tighter than they themselves were using in their own labs."[69] The response of the guild to Rhine's stimuli have been predictable. After four decades of findings, about ten percent believe in parapsychology, ten percent reject it outright, and eighty percent still prefer to suspend judgment and avoid conflict. The statistics have not changed significantly since the 1930s.[70] It is not a question of tests and controls and footnotes; it is a conflict over presuppositions, a debate as to how one legitimately *interprets* the results. There is only one way for the parapsychologists to triumph: win the younger men and wait for the older establishment men to die off. Concludes Sage:

> In the final analysis, perhaps we were wrong to think that ESP ever would, or could be proved to exist. . . . Which is to say that perhaps with ESP, as with religion and the occult, either you believe it or you don't—which is to say that whether or not ESP is now or ever has been or ever will be proved depends on what one is prepared to accept as proof. What parapsychology has given us during its relatively short life is only data to worry over in the manner of Caesar worrying over the ides of March. It is within the nature of such predictions that when they prove accurate, we know no more about how our soothsayers knew—or whether they knew—than we did before they spoke. That which is supernatural requires belief, not proof, simply because it is supernatural. And if we have run short on beliefs these days, it seems we might just as profitably search out new ones with our more traditional divining rods and Ouija boards as with statistical analyses. At least divining rods and Ouija boards are known to work—a certain small percentage of the time.[71]

Sage is trying to stay within the standards of contemporary science's post-Heisenberg relativism. That relativism is constantly being subjected to new pressures from the findings of paranormal science. Rhine's successor at Duke, Helmut Schmidt (whose cat seems to be able to control the random flashing of light bulbs), has devised several experiments that are so radically random in their foundations that any deviation has to indicate the presence of psychic phenomena. Professor Schmidt is a physicist, not a psychologist, and he has turned to atomic physics to demonstrate "psi" phenomena. Subjects were asked to predict which of four lamps would flash next, and out of over 63,000 trials, their results were so positive that the odds against chance occurrence were two billion to one.[72]

In another experiment, Schmidt built a random number generator that was hooked to a display panel. The generator produced random sequences of two numbers that were determined "by a simple quantum process (the decay of radioactive strontium-90 nuclei)." A circle of lights would flash either clockwise or counterclockwise. Subjects had to predict which way the lights would flash. In 256 runs of 128 jumps in the lights, fifteen subjects scored hits on a thousand-to-one level of probability.[73] These experiments, according to Arthur Koestler, have made far more impact on orthodox scientists than Rhine's card-guessing studies ever did. His apparatus has removed their ability to charge fraud. His reports have been published in conservative establishment scientific journals. With the acceptance of the American Society of Parapsychology into membership by the American Academy for the Advancement of Science, the mid-1970s witnessed a major breakthrough.

Nevertheless, parapsychology, and especially the branch experimenting with psychokinesis (mind over matter), is still on the fringes of orthodox science. Telepathy is one thing; mind over matter is another. Extrasensory *perception* may find a way into orthodoxy by sliding through the tiny cracks of Werner Heisenberg's uncertainty principle. But this principle works only in subatomic physics. The law of large numbers is supposed to cancel out the randomness of nature. The deviations have to cancel out, orthodoxy asserts. Koestler writes:

> I am unaware of any serious attempt at a physicalistic explanation of how a mental effort could influence the motions of rolling dice. . . . You cannot influence the progress of a macroscopic body like a rolling die, by microphysical particles or wavicles of imaginary mass. Thus the law of large numbers, which lends such authority to the evidence for ESP, is at the same time the main obstacle to any physicalistic explanation of PK.[74]

Orthodox science is at an apparent dead end. The subatomic holes of randomness through which ESP has crept into the thinking of a minority of orthodox scientists is simply not large enough to allow PK.* If PK is to be demonstrated, then the law of large numbers must be overthrown, yet it is this law that supports the "ESP-ness" of billion-to-one deviations from randomness in long series of experiments. To paraphrase a recent television advertisement, what's a parapsychologist to do?

What they do is to go right on investigating, steadily beating down the foundations of modern rationalism. Science, the most majestic edifice ever built by the philosophy of hypothetically autonomous man and his lawful mind, is being chipped away by men like Schmidt and Rhine—all in the name of a "broader" science, a "new, improved science." Orthodox scientists, unlike parapsychologists, know what is involved. They instinctively grasp the enormous threat posed by paranormal "science." Something more than mere Heisenberg indeterminism is invading the halls of rationalism. Something sinister and threatening to the very presuppositions of Western rationalism lies behind those dice-throwing experiments. In horror, the majority of orthodox scientists turn their backs on the data, preferring to ignore unpleasant facts or denounce them after a cursory examination of the data. But such efforts seldom last more than a generation. The younger men know this. Parapsychologists are laying siege to Western science in the name of open-mindedness.

What is happening is quite simple: demons are beginning to affect the experiments.

---

*Psychokinesis, or "mind over matter."

4
The World of a Sorcerer

> I've told you already, only a crackpot would undertake the task of becoming a man of knowledge of his own accord. A sober-headed man has to be tricked into doing it.
>
> Don Juan

During the summer of 1960, a graduate student in anthropology at UCLA, Carlos Castaneda, was investigating the use and effects of psychedelic plants. The general public knew very little about such substances in 1960, apart from marijuana and hard drugs. Information on mescaline and other plant derivatives was usually confined to little-read monographs like J. S. Slotkin's *The Peyote Religion* (1956). From time to time the news media picked up a story, but not often.

Probably the most publicized early incident in Southern California took place in the fall of 1958, when a University of Redlands freshman, Richard Lanham, walked into his dorm room to find his roommate sitting on the edge of the top bunk. The student fell forward to the floor. Lanham called for assistance; the young man was found to be dead. He had been experimenting with psychedelic substances. The university, a Baptist institution, was embarrassed and promptly put a blackout on all further information on the strange death, including a prohibition on Lanham's speaking with the press.

Incidents like these were temporarily sensational, but they were not sufficient to catch the public's notoriously short attention span. This was the period when Timothy Leary, an untenured psychology professor at Harvard, was conducting experiments quietly on the effects of psychedelic drugs, but news of this work had not yet hit East Coast sophisticates, let alone denizens of the primitive West Coast. A few people may have read Aldous Huxley's *Doors of Perception* (1954), the account of his own limited mescaline experiments, but it all seemed too esoteric—the pastime of the idle educated. The LSD counterculture was half a decade away.

Castaneda knew something about the use of peyote in the religious practices of the Indian tribes of the American Southwest. In a town close to the Mexican border, he managed to obtain an introduction to an elderly Yaqui Indian who called himself Don Juan. For some reason—a very specific reason, the old man confessed years later—he took an interest in Castaneda. He allowed him to visit him at his house in the desert. As it turned out, Don Juan was a *brujo*—a sorcerer. The old man had been drawn to Castaneda because he said it had been revealed to him that the young man would make an excellent initiate into the secret wisdom. The revelation was quite correct; Castaneda has written four provocative books telling of his dozen years of off-and-on initiation:

> *The Teachings of Don Juan: A Yaqui Way of Knowledge* (1968)
> *A Separate Reality: Further Conversations with Don Juan* (1971)
> *Journey to Ixtlan: The Lessons of Don Juan* (1972)
> *Tales of Power* (1974)

Unless Castaneda is exposed as a total fraud—and his first book got through the editorial screening process of the University of California Press—these books are likely to become classics. As primary-source documents of the mind and world of the primitive sorcerer, they are incomparable.

The popularity of these books has been enormous. Between the time that Castaneda first began his studies of the old man and the time of publication, an intellectual revolution occurred in both the academic world and the public at large. His books are now gobbled up; two different sets of paperbacks exist. Every book is a bestseller. Yet they are difficult to classify. They are written in the form of a series of conversations and flashbacks. Castaneda is a superb storyteller. The reconstruction of the conversations is imaginative, although Castaneda's copious note-taking became a source of amusement for Don Juan and another sorcerer, Don Genaro. In fact, they were convinced that this fixation on writing was itself useful in Castaneda's initiation: writing, as a distinctly rational form of activity, would serve as a sort of talisman to shield him from the magic-charged universe into which he was to enter. Time and again, when demonic forces came close, Don Juan insisted that he write and keep on writing. It is likely, then, that the basic perspective of the old sorcerer is preserved intact in the four volumes.

The popularity of these books also raises another question. Did the reading public suddenly find itself sympathetic to an ancient world-and-life view, or is that ancient perspective fundamentally modern anyway, involving no great shift of perspective on the part of the readers? Castaneda's description of Don Juan's perception of reality is no doubt colored by his own modern education, but in the later books, as Castaneda's perspective is more and more that of Don Juan, the books become more explicitly epistemological in tone. The Yaqui way of knowing is really only revealed in the fourth book, *Tales of Power*. The earlier studies were more along the lines of a UCLA graduate student's interpretation of a Yaqui way of knowing. Yet in the final volume, when Castaneda's initiation is completed, Don Juan's mind is revealed for what it is: dualistic to the core and strangely modern in its primitive animism. The dualism between rationalism and irrationalism, phenomenal and noumenal, undergirds Don Juan's epistemology. But the break with modernism comes with his doctrine of the two beings that inhabit the human body, the *tonal* and the *nagual*, which correspond to the rational and the irrational in man's mind. It is not simply that man's mind is dualistic, Don Juan finally reveals; the secret of Yaqui sorcery is that there really are two separate *beings* involved. Strangely enough, this was the theme of another extremely popular book and film, Thomas Tryon's *The Other*, a ghost story about a murderous little boy who had mastered occult techniques quite similar to those presented by Castaneda in his fourth volume.

The world of the sorcerer is radically different from the world of the pre-1965 Western rationalist. As the West has continued to abandon the moral and religious foundations of its rationalistic heritage—a personal God of order who has created a lawful universe that reflects His orderly nature and who has made men in His image with rational minds corresponding to the laws of nature—we have found ourselves confronted with a new paradigm of the world. Forces and possibilities that had once been rejected as preposterous by Western rationalists are now given consideration by a growing number of scholars and a very wide popular audience. Don Juan, a very ancient man living in a very ancient universe, was able to convert young Castaneda from the inherited rationalism of the university. In doing so, he found a man with a distinctly Western skill, namely, the ability to write, who could offer Don Juan's interpretation of his animistic universe as a possible alternative to the West's view. The revival of interest in sorcery made possible the presentation of the world of the sorcerer. We cannot have the magician's power apart from the magician's universe.

The Quest for Power

As Castaneda was to learn only in later years, the use of psychedelic drugs was a device used by Don Juan to disrupt the young man's perception of reality. This was fundamental in the process of initiation. The transfer of power to Castaneda could not be accomplished apart from shattering his Western view of reality. Drugs were the vehicle. Don Juan admitted that on several occasions he had lied to Castaneda, including the time he insisted that drugs were necessary to cross the barrier into the sorcerer's world. Drugs were not absolutely necessary to this transition, but they were certainly an efficient tool in promoting the initial breakthrough. The key was the attainment of a new perception, or as Castaneda calls it, the attainment of *states of nonordinary reality*. It could also be termed altered consciousness or higher consciousness. Yet very early in his training, Don Juan informed him that these states are not to be sought after for their own sake. The ultimate goal is always *power*; knowledge, whether ordinary or occult, is simply a means to power. But the magician's power must be sought through altered consciousness. This is the heart and soul of witchcraft. "Don Juan believed the states of nonordinary reality to be the only form of pragmatic learning and the only means of acquiring power. He conveyed the impression that other parts of his teachings were incidental to the acquisition of power. This point of view permeated Don Juan's attitude toward everything not directly connected with the states of nonordinary reality."[1] Knowledge for its own sake is a product of Western rationalism; the old sorcerer would have none of it. "Power rests on the kind of knowledge one holds," he insisted. "What is the sense of knowing things that are useless?"[2]

This concern with power is one of the important links between the mind of the sorcerer and the mind of the Western rationalist. C. S. Lewis's novel *That Hideous Strength* rests on the possibility of collaboration between modernism and magic, since both are power-hungry by nature. Lewis observed that the great age of magic was unleashed, not by the medieval world, but by the rationalistic Renaissance. There was relatively little magic during the Middle Ages. "For the wise men of old the cardinal problem had been how to conform the soul to reality, and the solution had been knowledge, self-discipline, and virtue. For magic and applied science alike the problem is how to subdue reality to the wishes of men: the solution is a technique; and both, in the practice of this technique, are ready to do things hitherto regarded as disgusting and impious—such as digging up and mutilating the dead."[3] This speculation was confirmed conclusively by Miss Frances Yates' book, *Giordano Bruno and the Hermetic Tradition* (1964), an exhaustive study of a rationalist-magician during the Renaissance. The Renaissance was animistic at heart.

Whenever the question of power is raised, another problem immediately asserts itself: Who is controlling what? C. S. Lewis faced this problem more forthrightly than Don Juan did. When man begins to take control of nature, with nature regarded as a means to human ends, "Nature turns out to be a power exercised by some men over other men with Nature as its instrument."[4] When it comes to power, "Man is as much the patient or subject as the possessor, since he is the target both for bombs and for propaganda."[5] If man is seen as nothing more than a product of evolutionary natural forces, then the means by which nature is controlled must simultaneously pose a threat to the freedom of other men. Men seek power over nature in order to assert their freedom from nature's caprices, yet in doing so they see their own freedom from other men and institutions slipping away. This is the so-called nature-freedom antinomy, and it is one of the crucial problems, philosophically and politically, of the modern world. Lewis writes:

> Man's conquest of Nature, if the dreams of some scientific planners are realized, means the rule of a few hundreds of men over billions upon billions of men. There neither is

nor can be any simple increase of power on Man's side. Each new power won *by* man is a power *over* man as well. Each advance leaves him weaker as well as stronger. In every victory, besides being the general who triumphs, he is also the prisoner who follows the triumphal car.[6]

In short, "For the power of Man to make himself what he pleases means, as we have seen, the power of some men to make other men what *they* please."[7] But what or who controls the scientific planners? This is the crucial question regarding the exercise of power, whether magical or technocratic. If all is ultimately technique (in science) or ritual (in magic), there can be neither ethical good nor ethical evil. There can only be successful or unsuccessful manipulations. If vast evolutionary forces control our thought processes, then Nature, with a capital N, reasserts its domination over mankind through the power of materialistically determined scientists. But if men are not determined, then the transmission belt of scientific technique is slashed.

Don Juan sensed the dilemma of power. Power, he said, is personal. "It commands you and yet it obeys you."[8] Or, with respect to human choice: "When we think we decide, all we're doing is acknowledging that something beyond our understanding has set up the frame of our so-called decision, and all we do is to acquiesce."[9] But in what does the magician acquiesce? He has no answer, any more than the scientist in his self-proclaimed intellectual autonomy has an answer. Given the presuppositions of modern science, Lewis finds the only answer open to the consistent scientist:

> Nature, untrammeled by values, rules the Conditioners and, through them, all humanity. Man's conquest of Nature turns out, in the moment of its consummation, to be Nature's conquest of Man. Every victory we seemed to win has led us, step by step, to this conclusion. All Nature's apparent reverses have been but tactical withdrawals. We thought we were beating her back when she was luring us on. What looked to us like hands held up in surrender was really the opening of arms to enfold us forever.[10]

Lewis is quite correct: "The wresting of powers *from* Nature is also the surrendering of things *to* Nature. . . . It is the magician's bargain: give up our soul, get power in return."[11]

The triumph of Western rationalism came from the faith that men of the seventeenth and eighteenth centuries had in a lawful universe. The source of this faith was the Christian doctrine of creation. The earth was to be subdued to the glory of God, not as a foreign and impersonal thing, as Professor Lynn White has erroneously maintained, but as a part of God's own handiwork for which men are held responsible.[12] The doctrine of creation, when coupled with the doctrines of the cultural mandate and of Christian stewardship, led to the idea of applied science and technology. The secularization of this vision, with man established as the sovereign over nature, no doubt shifted the older perspective, but the idea of law was equally crucial. Man was to accomplish his dominion through the discovery of physical laws. But Darwin's breakthrough shattered the confidence in orderly law. Random variation became lord of the universe. Man was placed in a desperate situation; failure to compete successfully meant literal extinction. The quest for power was no longer the pastime of idle philosophers; it was a biological imperative. Man is either the powerless pawn in the meaningless cosmic processes, or else he is the next stage in the evolutionary process, the one who will direct the path of evolution by means of that great (and utterly inexplainable) discontinuity of nature, the human mind. Somehow, man's brain leaped the boundaries of evolution's most fundamental premise, continuous, uniformitarian change, and now it must take over from random variation and natural selection as the new lord of the universe.

The doctrine of evolution, like all anti-biblical religious sytems, requires the self-transcendence of man. Impersonal random natural selection miraculously provided man, the evolutionary product, with a brain vastly more powerful than his stone-age body needed. He has therefore transcended the evolutionary laws that created him. He must now transcend evolution's impersonal determinism by chance selection; he must now find the techniques—the *power*—to become the new god of the universe. Nothing must be left to chance in this battle against chance. Out of chance evolved everything, including the opposite of chance, human purpose. Now human purpose must not be allowed to be swallowed back into chance's great belly. Man must become the great magician, pulling purpose and order out of chance's universe.

The popularity of Castaneda's books should not be too surprising. Don Juan, the primitive sorcerer, communicates well with the skeptics of modern culture, for he shares the central vision of modern thought: the quest for magical power. He offers men a new evolution.

A World of Death

Again and again during his initiation, Don Juan warned Castaneda of the nameless threats that inhabit the desert and valleys that surround them. Ritual is as important for the initiate as technique for the bomb defuser. It is a life-and-death affair. Water is a threat to Castaneda; demons live there. The desert is a threat; demons live there. A local woman is a threat; she is a scheming sorceress (he later admitted that this story was untrue); it was a means of scaring Castaneda into further initiatory activities. A whole host of oppressive beings inhabits the world of the sorcerer, and the initiate knows too little to protect himself.

Castaneda had originally been interested in discovering facts about psychedelic plants. Don Juan introduces him to "the little smoke." A smoking mixture will reveal to him Don Juan's "ally." The old man warns him of the care that must be exercised in handling the special pipe into which the mixture—itself specially prepared ritually over the period of a year—must be placed. "The pipe will feel the strain of being handled by someone else; and if one of us makes a mistake there won't be any way to prevent the pipe from bursting open by its own force, or escaping from our hands to shatter, even if it falls on a pile of straw. If that ever happens, it would mean the end of us both. Particularly of me. The smoke would turn against me in unbelievable ways."[13] Whether the old man really believed this is questionable; he lied to Castaneda constantly in the stages of initiation. But he never ceased to stress the importance of ritual, and it is likely that he really saw death around them almost as often as he said he saw it.

He did not fear the smoke as such. He feared the ally. The allies never are referred to as demons, but are seen as separate beings, not impersonal forces. They take animal shapes at times, but they also take human shapes. As the final volume states, Castaneda's ally was in the shape of a huge moth. These are the sources of special wisdom and therefore unique power. These creatures must be placated. The quest of the warrior is the quest for union with an ally—a lifetime union. It is this that Castaneda claims to have attained, in the final pages of *Tales of Power*.

Don Juan's ally, the little smoke, is a stickler for ritual. The old man had to care for the pipe, keep it from the gaze of unenlightened parties, and the man who uses it must lead a hard, quiet life. The gift of the smoke is a new vision of the world, or what the Gnostics of premedieval days would have called a new gnosis. This was the quest of Renaissance mystics, alchemists, magicians, and illuminati.[14] "Everything is terrifying and confusing at the outset, but every new puff makes things more precise. And suddenly the world opens up anew! Unimaginable! When this happens the smoke has become one's ally and will resolve any question by allowing one to enter into inconceivable worlds."[15]

On the one hand, ritual observance is crucial. The general principle is as follows: ". . . we must follow certain steps, because it is in the steps where man finds strength. Without them we are nothing."[16] Again: "You must be infinitely careful. When one is dealing with power, one has to be perfect. Mistakes are deadly here."[17] On the other hand, human routines are to be shunned. An entire chapter of *Journey to Ixtlan* is titled "Disrupting the Routines of Life." The true hunter is "free, fluid, unpredictable."[18] In dealing with the personal sources of gnosis and power, rituals must be precise. In dealing with the affairs of life, there must be no routines. As he says elsewhere, there must not even be a personal history. There must be *total atomism of the personality*: one man, alone, in a hostile universe. The hunter must be unpredictable, for he is also the hunted. "All of us behave like the prey we are after. That, of course, also makes us prey for something or someone else. Now, the concern of a hunter, who knows all this, is to stop being a prey himself."[19]

This is the universe of the magical manipulator. All the world is like an enormous container of nitroglycerine. It must be handled with ritually exact care when it is being manipulated, and at all other times, the magician must be devious, fluid, totally unpredictable, in order to escape the manipulations of others. This is the animists' world, where living, malevolent beings strike out and trap the ritually negligent. Perfection is a matter of precise ritual. The magician must content himself with subduing only minute portions of his world on a piecemeal basis; the world is something to be escaped from rather than brought into total conformity on a universal basis. In order to subdue portions of the world, the magician must link himself to mysterious powers that threaten his very existence.

This perspective is almost a mirror image of the Judeo-Christian heritage. Ethics, not ritual, is primary in Christian theology. The prophet Micah warned Israel against the lure of ritualism:

> Wherewith shall I come before the LORD, and bow myself before the high God? shall I come before him with burnt offerings, with calves of a year old? Will the LORD be pleased with thousands of rams, or with ten thousands of rivers of oil? shall I give my firstborn for my transgression, the fruit of my body for the sin of my soul? He hath shewed thee, O man, what is good; and what doth the LORD require of thee, but to do justly, and to love mercy, and to walk humbly with thy God? [Micah 6:6–8]

The biblical cosmology requires humility before God and power over the created realm. Routines are tools of man's conquest over a recalcitrant nature: routines of occupation, education, experimentation, all involving the overarching routines of time. By this vision, Western civilization spread throughout Europe and conquered the animistic cultures of the magicians. The animist elevates ritual before multiple gods over against the daily routines of life, and the result is cultural impotence and stagnation. The Christian elevates routine over ritual, and the stronger that impulse is (in Protestant cultures as opposed to Roman Catholic ones, in Roman Catholic cultures as opposed to primitive ones), the more thorough the transformation of culture and the advent of ideas of progress and external development.

Don Juan emphasizes the necessity of ritual because the world that he inhabits is potentially infused with personal power, and death lurks everywhere. Page after page of Castaneda's books is filled with the old man's observations that death is very near, at times even actively stalking them. The awareness of death is an avenue to power. The knowledge of their own helplessness before animistic forces is the way men build up their own magical potency. Not humility before a personal God, but constant wakefulness and wariness amidst animistic forces. A world of imminent destruction must replace the world of daily routines if the initiate is to be successful in his quest for power. This was the message of Don Juan's own teacher, and the old man passes it along to Castaneda:

> My benefactor said that when a man embarks on the paths of sorcery he becomes aware, in a gradual manner, that ordinary life has been forever left behind; that knowledge is indeed a frightening affair; that the means of the ordinary world are no longer a buffer for him; and that he must adopt a new way of life if he is going to survive. The first thing he ought to do, at that point, is to want to become a warrior, a very important step and decision. The frightening nature of knowledge leaves one no alternative but to become a warrior.
>
> By the time knowledge becomes a frightening affair the man also realizes that death is the irreplaceable partner that sits next to him on the mat. Every bit of knowledge that becomes power has death as its central force. Death lends the ultimate touch, and whatever is touched by death indeed becomes power.
>
> A man who follows the paths of sorcery is confronted with imminent annihilation every turn of the way, and unavoidably he becomes keenly aware of his death. Without the awareness of death he would be only an ordinary man involved in ordinary acts. He

would lack the necessary potency, the necessary concentration that transforms one's ordinary time on earth into magical power.[20]

It is obvious that no man can live in constant fear of death, and Don Juan did not advise Castaneda to enter a life of worry. But some other emotion had to be substituted for fear. The next step in the path toward magical power is *total detachment*. "The idea of imminent death, instead of becoming an obsession, becomes an indifference. . . . Detach yourself from everything."[21] Understandably, a man detached in this manner is not bound by earthly conventions.

It is at this point that Don Juan displays another of the important intellectual and philosophical premises he shares with modern man. *Don Juan is an existentialist.*[22] I think it likely a student could pass off the following quote as if it were part of a formerly unpublished letter from Martin Heidegger:

> Only the idea of death makes a man sufficiently detached so he is incapable of abandoning himself to anything. Only the idea of death makes a man sufficiently detached so he can't deny himself anything. A man of that sort, however, does not crave, for he has acquired a silent lust for life and for all things of life. He knows his death is stalking him and won't give him time to cling to anything, so he tries, without craving, all of everything.
>
> A detached man, who knows he has no possibility of fencing off his death, has only one thing to back himself with: the power of his decisions. He has to be, so to speak, the master of his choices. He must fully understand that his choice is his responsibility and once he makes it there is no longer time for regrets or recriminations. His decisions are final, simply because his death does not permit him time to cling to anything.[23]

Castaneda may be inserting bits and pieces of Western philosophy into the old man's mouth, but the basic themes are repeated over and over in various contexts. The themes of death and detachment, coupled with total affection for earthly life, pervade his teaching. At the end of the fourth volume, Castaneda quotes the old man: "This earth, this world. For a warrior there can be no greater love."[24] This same perspective undergirds the widely publicized Church of Satan in San Francisco, run by Anton LaVey: "Life is the great indulgence—death, the great abstinence. Therefore, make the most of life—HERE AND NOW!"[25] Don Juan's philosophy is simple enough, and it is exceedingly modern: "Life in itself is sufficent, self-explanatory and complete."[26]

Total detachment is supposed to give a man a lust for life. A universe in which death lurks—death that literally stalks a man—is supposed to promote the philosophy of life. Life is everything, yet it is nothing. This is the vital attitude that Don Juan calls "controlled folly." "But we must know first that our acts are useless and yet we must proceed as if we didn't know it. That's a sorcerer's controlled folly."[27] This perspective must be used with everyone else at all times. The sorcerer is an actor; he does not let those around him know that he thinks that they are irrelevant. "Once a man learns to *see* he finds himself alone in the world with nothing but folly."[28] In short, "everything I do in regard to myself and my fellow man is folly, because nothing matters."[29] The *modernism* of Don Juan's outlook is striking. A meaningless universe must be dealt with in terms of a philosophy of ultimate meaninglessness and the concomitant quest for power. For in a meaningless world, nothing counts except personal power. "But you want to find the meaning of life," he taunts his pupil. "A warrior doesn't care about meanings."[30] In such a world there can be neither true nor false: "An average man cares that things are either true or false, but a warrior doesn't."[31] The warrior acts the same in either case.

This is a philosophy of death parading as a philosophy of life. It professes indifference and clings to life tenaciously. It denies that anything matters, yet concludes that power matters greatly. By asserting the total autonomy of detached man, it turns into a philosophy of *action*—a kind of pseudo-fascism. Then again, it is equally a defense of passivity or *inaction:*

> For me nothing matters, but perhaps for you everything will. You should know by now that a man of knowledge lives by acting, not by thinking about acting, nor by thinking about what he will think when he has finished acting. . . . Nothing being more important than anything else, a man of knowledge chooses any act, and acts it out as if it matters to him. His controlled folly makes him say that what he does matters and makes him act as if it did, and yet he knows that it doesn't; so when he fulfills his acts he retreats in peace, and whether his acts were good or bad, or worked or didn't, is in no way part of his concern.[32]

As he puts it toward the end of Castaneda's training, controlled folly embraces "the possibility of acting without believing, without expecting rewards—acting just for the hell of it."[33] This is the goal of the man of knowledge—the man who has achieved gnosis.

Yet the old man cannot really believe his own philosophy. It leads him to equate man and animals. We and the snakes are on a par, he says.[34] But when he describes the death of his mother at the hands of Mexican soliders, he says: "They killed her for no reason at all. It doesn't make any difference that she died that way, not really, and yet for me it does. I cannot tell myself why, though; it just does."[35] There are still traces of human sympathy left in the man. Some of his actor's makeup has rubbed off, and there is still a human being underneath. Yet he is unable to make sense of his feelings of the injustice of the murder. To make sense of any act implies—demands—that there is sense in this world, and that is the premise that his philosophy of life explicitly rejects.

Though all things are meaningless, there is one standard by which all events are measured, by which all things are tested, *death:* "Death is the only wise adviser that we have."[36] Nevertheless, adopting the language of a Zen monk, Don Juan announces: "Death is a whorl. . . . Death is the face of the ally; death is a shiny cloud over the horizon; death is the whisper of Mescalito [the Peyote god] in your ears; . . . death is me talking; death is you and your writing pad; death is nothing. Nothing! It is here yet it isn't here at all."[37] This kind of philosophical mishmash is supposed to be rare wisdom. The old Indian is correct: "To be a sorcerer is a terrible burden."[38] Especially philosophically.

Prisoners of Power

The apostle Paul, writing to the church at Rome, warned them of the inescapability of service in the world. The question is never to serve or not to serve; it is always *whom* to serve. "Know ye not," Paul asks, "that to whom ye yield yourselves servants to obey, his servants ye are to whom ye obey; whether of sin unto death, or of obedience unto righteousness?" (Romans 6:16). Don Juan's discussion of power demonstrates how clearly he understands this principle. On the one hand, union with a demonic ally gives the sorcerer power: "From then on you can summon your ally at will and make him do anything you want."[39] These allies are supposedly neutral forces, "neither good nor evil, but are put to use by the sorcerers for whatever purpose they see fit."[40] Yet on the other hand, he warns Castaneda against becoming a "slave to the devil's weed" (jimsonweed), for "it will never let you go." The weed is the means of obtaining revelations from the female spirit that is associated with it. "She will cut you off from everything else. You will have to spend your life grooming her as an ally. She is possessive. Once she dominates you, there is only one way to go—her way."[41]

Don Juan's references to the "protectors" of some friends and relatives—Jesus Christ, the Virgin Mary, Our Lady of Guadalupe—indicate his contempt for their lack of visible power. But they also indicate how frivolous was his relatives' worship of these occasional church visitors. He contrasts their worship of the traditional Mexican deities with the worship demanded by Mescalito, the god of peyote. "If they were real protectors they would force you to listen," he argues. "If Mescalito becomes your protector you will have to listen whether you like it or not, because you can see him and you must take heed of what he says. He will make you approach him with respect. Not the way you fellows are accustomed to approach your protectors."[42] Power demands respect.

The problem with power is always the same: the user is simultaneously subjected to it. The man who wields the scientific power of the modern world must have a theory of the transmission of power. If causes have effects, then by becoming an intermediary cause a man must admit that his decisions are also effects of prior causes. If he denies that he is necessarily determined, then he must also deny his own power to determine certain effects. Similarly, if a magician uses the power of an ally or demon to produce certain effects, he inevitably places himself under the power of the ally. At the very least, he is subjected to a rigorous series of rituals that must be used when calling forth occult power. To command power—any power—is to acknowledge the sovereignty of the source of that power, whether God, demons, natural law, random variation, or whatever. Men will serve that which they believe to be sovereign.

At the very end of his training, Castaneda is warned of his new responsibilities by his teacher: "The fate of all of us here has been to know that we are the prisoners of power. No one knows why us in particular, but what a great fortune."[43] Simply and less enthusiastically put, "We are dregs in the hands of those forces."[44] Ghosts, spirits, mysterious forces: these are the gods of the world of the sorcerer.[45]

Since the attainment of the gnosis was basic to the the attainment of power, and power involved Castaneda in a new and fearful world, what kinds of power did he actually see or experience that would seem to have made the bargain worthwhile? As a result of the various drugs, he did achieve several nonrational experiences, a few of them terrifying. Learning how to enter into these states of "higher consciousness" apart from the use of drugs, and apparently without hypnosis, also went with his training. But these visions and nonordinary perceptions were more the price paid for power than a benefit. If power was crucial, what signs of power were revealed? The books list a very few examples:

1. The ability to see in the dark on certain occasions.[46]
2. Limited powers of divination—"second sight"—through the combined use of jimsonweed and lizard familiars.[47]
3. Possibly astral projection; it may have been a dream.[48]
4. Mind reading; Don Juan seemed to possess this ability, though Castaneda may have related certain events during one of his hallucinatory dreams.[49]
5. Teleportation; two actual cases are related. It is attributed to a local sorceress, and Castaneda says that he saw her do it. He and Don Juan also experienced it.[50]
6. Floating, flying, defying gravity.[51]
7. Feats of strength—a claim of Don Juan concerning his earlier days of sorcery.[52]
8. Some prestidigitation tricks that may truly have been feats of mind over matter.[53]

When one considers that Castaneda's readers have hacked through four volumes of material to glean these few items of occult power, it would seem that the appeal of these books lies not in their tales of power, but in their presentation of a world of nonrational perceptions. Castaneda is a spinner of first-rate ghost stories. If he has in fact become a practicing *brujo*, then he may prefer to tell us very little, but it seems more likely that his intention is to convey a vision of another conceptual world. He is telling us about occult "knowledge"—magical gnosis—which is essentially antirational. Christ posed the question concerning the price a man would pay for his soul. If he were to gain the whole world, he could not redeem it (Mark 8:36, 37). Castaneda was tricked, according to Don Juan, into leaving the common world of the West in order to enter the sorcerer's world of imminent destruction. The old man is quite correct: no sober-minded man would want to become a "man of knowledge" without having been tricked into it.

Shattered Reality

The gnosis of the primitive sorcerer is an intensely and consistently antirational cosmology. Castaneda's summary of this perspective is to the point: "In fact, the reality of the world we know is so taken for granted that the basic premise of sorcery, that our reality is merely one of many descriptions, could hardly be taken as a serious proposition."[54] But after 1964, a growing segment of the student population, as well as of the American book-buying public, began to take the proposition quite seriously. The acids of philosophical relativism had finally eroded the confidence that intelligent people once had in the distinctly absolutist worldview of nineteenth-century philosophical mechanism.

Don Juan's vision rested on a philosophical premise: all is not what it appears to our reason. The Western process of intellectual rationalization of the perceived world is explicitly rejected. "But to be a sorcerer in your case means that you have to overcome stubbornness and the need for rational explanations, which stand in your way."[55] Again: "We men and all the other luminous beings on earth are perceivers. That is our bubble, the bubble of perception. Our mistake is to believe that the only perception worthy of acknowledgment is what goes through our *reason*. Sorcerers believe that *reason* is only one center and that it shouldn't take so much for granted."[56] What the old man is attacking is the assumed sufficiency of phenomenal knowledge. He forces Castaneda to look at the noumenal side of perception; and unlike Kant, who simply used the noumenal realm as a silent backdrop or limiting concept to deal with the problem of philosophical contradictions in human thought, Don Juan really believes that the noumenal realm is accessible. Not accessible to reason, however, but accessible to the *nagual*: the actually existing magical half of man's dualistic existence. The *nagual* is the occult double. It is also known in Western occultism as the *Doppelgänger*. But he did not reveal this secret to Castaneda until the end of his initiation. The earlier volumes present Don Juan's thought in the tradition of Western philosophical dualism. Castaneda quotes the old man as saying:

> "The world is a mystery. This, what you're looking at, is not all there is to it. There is much more to the world, so much more, in fact, that it is endless. So when you're trying to figure it out, all you're really doing is trying to make the world familiar. You and I are right here, in the world that you call real, simply because we both know it. You don't know the world of power, therefore you cannot make it into a familiar scene."[57]

In short, "the world is incomprehensible," Don Juan asserts. "We won't ever understand it; we won't ever unravel its secrets. Thus we must treat it as it is, a sheer mystery."[58] This is the heart of the sorcerer's conception of the world. The world is fundamentally mysterious.

Western reason in the Newtonian sense is anathema. Man's ability to understand reality is futile. By emphasizing the impotence of rationalism, and by pointing to the mysterious conception of the world as the fundamental one—the most sophisticated, the wisest—the old man steadily breaks down Castaneda's worldview. This is the goal of the initiation. "The warrior lowers his head to no one, but at the same time, he doesn't permit anyone to lower his head to him. The beggar, on the other hand, falls to his knees at the drop of a hat and scrapes the floor for anyone he deems to be higher; but at the same time, he demands that someone lower than him scrape the floor for him."[59] Then the old man drives home his point: "You like the humbleness of a beggar.... You bow your head to reason." What the reader watches for four volumes is the destruction of Castaneda's reason. He admits it in the final volume: "My rational structure was falling apart."[60] This had been the old man's goal. "You're chained!" Don Juan had shouted at him very early in his training. "You're chained to your reason."[61]

In the earlier stages of his training, Castaneda had been given an explanation of the relationship between the human will and reason in distinctly Western terminology. Reason has its limits. The *will* is the link between men and the world.[62] We perceive the world in the combined activity of reason and will. The human will shapes our perception of the world; it is an active perceiving. This is the sorcerer's secret ability. "When we perceive the world with our will we know that it is not as 'out there' or as 'real' as we think."[63] In language similar to that of Professor Eisenbud, Don Juan argues for a conception of man as the sustainer of the world: "We talk about our world. In fact we maintain our world with our internal talk.... We renew it, we kindle it with life, we uphold it with our internal talk."[64] Don Juan is not using figures of speech; he accepts the potency of men as sustainers of the world. "For instance, our rings of power, yours and mine, are hooked right now on the *doing* in this room. We are making this room. Our rings of power are spinning this room into being at this very moment."[65]

Castaneda, in his more simplistic rationalism, rejected this hypothesis initially, but had he been more familiar with Kant's *Critique of Pure Reason,* he might have recognized Don Juan's line of reasoning. Though he did not speak of "rings of power," Kant certainly would have seen the sophistication of the old sorcerer's argument, although he preferred to focus his attention on the human understanding rather than the noumenal side of man. It was Kant, after all, who had asserted that "the understanding is something more than a power of formulating rules through comparison of appearances; it is itself the lawgiver of nature. Save through it, nature, that is, synthetic unity of the manifold of appearances according to the rules, would not exist at all...."[66] The old sorcerer saw what Castaneda's simplistic nineteenth-century rationalism did not prepare him to see, but what humanistic philosophers have maintained for two hundred years: "The world is such-and-such or so-and-so only because we tell ourselves that that is the way it is. If we would stop telling ourselves that the world is so-and-so, the world would stop being so-and-so."[67]

The goal, then, is to "stop the world," to alter our perception of the world. "To change our idea of the world is the crux of sorcery," he tells Castaneda. "And stopping the internal dialogue is the only way to accomplish it. The rest is just padding."[68] The rest—drugs, bodily exercises, secrecy, special foods—is mere padding. *The goal is a higher consciousness.* At last, he reveals the sorcerer's secret:

> "We, the luminous beings, are born with two rings of power, but we use only one to create the world. That ring, which is hooked very soon after we are born, is *reason,* and

its companion is *talking*. Between the two they concoct and maintain the world.

"So, in essence, the world that your *reason* wants to sustain is the world created by a description and its dogmatic and inviolable rules, which the *reason* learns to accept and defend.

"The secret of the luminous beings [living beings] is that they have another ring of power which is never used, the *will*. The trick of the sorcerer is the same trick of the average man. Both have a description; one, the average man, upholds it with his *reason*; the other, the sorcerer, upholds it with his *will*. Both descriptions have their rules and the rules are perceivable, but the advantage of the sorcerer is that *will* is more engulfing than *reason*.

"The suggestion that I want to make at this point is that from now on you should let yourself perceive whether the description is upheld by your *reason* or your *will*. I feel that is the only way for you to use your daily world as a challenge and a vehicle to accumulate enough personal power to get to the totality of yourself."[69]

The true prestidigitation of the sorcerer is intellectual and philosophical. It is the same trick employed by the humanist. From a position which insists that man is no better than an animal, that it is a crime to think of oneself as superior to the animals, we come to man as the sustainer of the universe, man as the total being. What matters to a warrior "is arriving at the totality of oneself."[70] Man is the focus. Man is central once again. It is the same sleight-of-brain trick that modern evolutionists indulge in: man, the product of chance, the product of slime, somehow becomes man the mind-endowed discontinuous leap in the continuous evolutionary chain. Man-the-director-of-evolutionary-processes somehow emerges from man-the-developed-amoeba. It is the lure of Satan: to be as God.

Man is dualistic. He is composed of reason (the *tonal*) and will (the *nagual*). It is man who rules, not God. "God is an item of our personal *tonal* and of the *tonal* of the times. The *tonal* is, as I've already said, everything we think the world is composed of, including God, of course. God has no more importance other than being a part of the *tonal* of our time."[71] Spoken like a true professor of freshman courses in logic. God is simply a part of the climate of opinion.

So far, this old sorcerer has proven himself to be a very hip old man. He could sail through a sophomore class in ethics without cracking a book. A bit of relativism, a strong dose of philosophical dualism, a few swipes with the "climate of opinion" paint brush, and the quest for the totality of man. Not to mention a large chunk of existentialism. The Don Juan of Castaneda's books in many ways is a modern figure. If anything, it is Castaneda, the old-fashioned nineteenth-century mechanist, who sounds like an epistemological fuddy-duddy.

Nevertheless, the modernism of Don Juan is deceptive, for beneath the slogans so dear to the modern climate of opinion lies an ancient faith. Don Juan does not simply see man as epistemologically dualistic; man is *actually* a dualistic construct. There are two sides to man, literally. The *tonal* and the *nagual*—reason and will—occupy man's body in a special way. Yaqui dualism is complete. *There are two creatures that exist in man.* It is the training of the sorcerer that enables the *nagual*—pure will—to capture the body of a man when the *tonal* is asleep. Astral projection somehow involves the use of a single personality and two bodies. Or else one body is an imitation: it is not clear from the explanations of the old man. But he believes that sometimes we are watching one "Don Juan" and sometimes the other. This is the occult doctrine of the *Doppelgänger,* or double. The *nagual* can soar to unseen realms, defy gravity, or see the sleeping *tonal.*[72] If the *tonal* should touch the *nagual*—if a man should touch his double—it means death.[73] The *tonal* maintains order. The *nagual* provides the sorcerer with his power.

> Let's say that a warrior learns to tune his *will,* to direct it to a pinpoint, to focus it wherever he wants. It is as if his *will,* which comes from the midsection of his body, is one single luminous fiber, a fiber that he can direct at any conceivable place. That fiber is the road to the *nagual.* Or I could also say that the warrior sinks into the *nagual* through that single fiber.[74]

Christ informed his followers that rivers of living water can flow out of men's bellies—a distinctly ethical analogy (John 7:38). Don Juan understands the belly as the source of the fibers of power and the entrance place of death—a kind of Achilles' chink in man's armor. Spirits and demons can penetrate the belly. It is also the source of rays of light so strong that they can supposedly support the body, propelling it aloft.[75]

What does it all mean? The sorcerer sees the world as a multiple reality held together by the rational side of man. In this, he agrees essentially with all post-Kantian logic. But man is also multiple. When Don Genaro and Don Juan threw Castaneda from a cliff, he did not die in the fall. Instead, he experienced wholly new sensations. He felt his clothes fall off, then his body seemed to fall off, leaving only his head. Then he was nothing but a pebblelike residue—awareness itself. All of a sudden, he found himself back on the ledge of the cliff. They told him they had pulled him back. They tossed him again.

> I again had the sensations of being tossed, spinning, and falling down at a tremendous speed. Then I exploded. I disintegrated. Something in me gave out; it released something I had kept locked up all my life. I was thoroughly aware then that my secret reservoir had been tapped and that it poured out unrestrainedly. There was no longer the sweet unity I call "me." There was nothing and yet that nothing was filled.... I was a myriad of selves which were all "me," a colony of separate units that had a special allegiance to one another and would join unavoidably to form one single awareness, my human awareness.[76]

When he came back to normal, he felt a loss. "I longed for the 'unknown' where my awareness was not unified."[77] He had experienced a form of pseudo-transcendence. He had attained a higher consciousness. His own multiple reality had entered into new realities of perception. He longed to attain other perceptions like this one. As the book ends, he apparently recaptures the state of altered consciousness.

What is man in this perspective? He is simply a cluster of perceptions held together by we know not what. "At death, however, they sink deeply and move independently as if they had never been a unit."[78] Man is dispersed to "the vastness."[79] There is no threat of judgment, for there is no guilt, "because to isolate one's acts as being mean, or ugly, or evil was to place an unwarranted importance on the self," as Castaneda summarizes Don Juan's teaching.[80] There is no second death. These words are no doubt as comforting to the minds of modern men as they were to Indian mystics a thousand years ago. When it comes to questions concerning final judgment, man—the creator and sustainer of the rational universe—is not to worry, for to worry about such questions is to place "unwarranted importance" on his insignificant self. Strategically professed humility is the escape hatch of ancient as well as modern man.

One, says Don Juan, "can arrive at the totality of oneself only when one fully understands that the world is merely a view, regardless of whether that view belongs to an ordinary man or to a sorcerer."[81] Such a world is indeterminate, and an indeterminate universe does not hand out final judgments. The appeal of such a cosmology to modern man should be obvious. Man the perceiver-creator is safe. The perceived unity of the world is an illusion—a convenient illusion, as well as an inexplicable one—so there are no ultimate questions worth asking. Since man constructs his universe, he is not answerable to anyone else. Don Juan, an "uneducated" Indian of the Southwest, has the same view of the world and man's role in it that Immanuel Kant struggled to attain by means of rigorous logic. Man makes up the rules and serves as the game's only umpire.

> The *tonal* makes the world only in a manner of speaking. It cannot create or change anything, and yet it makes the world because its function is to judge and assess, and witness. I say that the *tonal* makes the world because it witnesses and assesses it according to *tonal* rules. In a very strange manner the *tonal* is a creator that doesn't create a thing. In other words, the *tonal* makes up the rules by which it apprehends the world. So, in a manner of speaking, it creates the world.[82]

Kant never said it any better; in fact, he never said it as well. There is no world-in-itself but only a description of the world that men learn to visualize and take for granted.[83] The only judgment that matters to man is man's own judgement. Which sounds very reassuring, except for one minor point. What are all those shadows in the night, and why do they seek to kill unwary men?

Timeless Dreaming

For the sorcerer, dreams are a source of power.[84] For the sorcerer's apprentice, they are a means of internal discipline in the initiation process. "Think of it as something entertaining. Imagine all the inconceivable things you could accomplish. A man's hunting power has almost no limits in his *dreaming*."[85] Don Genaro, the sorcerer who served as Castaneda's "benefactor" (Don Juan was only his instructor), later told Castaneda that "the double begins in *dreaming*."[86] This is the means by which the self manifests itself as the *nagual*. As the discipline continues, this second personality can take over, the Indians believe, thereby dreaming the self. It becomes impossible to know for sure at any given time whether one is perceiving the world as the *nagual* or the *tonal*. Sometimes a man dreams his double, and sometimes the double dreams the man.[87] "No one knows how it happens," reveals Don Juan. Truer words were never spoken. Nevertheless, the escape of the *nagual* as a second being is made possible by these special dreams.

This is the doctrine of "magical time."[88] It is the *nagual's* time: beyond time, independent of time. When in the *tonal's* time, men are not to be irrational; when in the *nagual's* time, men are not to be rational.[89] When an untrained man faces the *nagual*, his *tonal* may die; *he* may die. The sorcerer must discipline his rational side not to collapse in the face of control by the irrational. Don Juan offers this crucial bit of instruction: "The goal of a warrior's training then is not to teach him to hex or to charm, but to prepare his *tonal* not to crap out. A most difficult accomplishment."[90] But apart from a man's entrance to this magical time, he cannot become a sorcerer. Sorcerers are beyond the limits of time. Castaneda's description of his training is significant:

> In my experience with Don Juan I had noticed that in such states [of altered consciousness] one is incapable of keeping a consistent mental record of the passage of time. There had never been an enduring order, in matters of passage of time, in all the states of nonordinary reality I had experienced, and my conclusion was that if I kept myself alert a moment would come when I would lose my order of sequential time. As if, for example, I were looking at a mountain at a given moment, and then in my next moment of awareness I found myself looking at a valley in the opposite direction, but without remembering having turned around.[91]

He very properly suspected hypnosis as the cause of his altered perceptions. But hypnosis really cannot explain anything. It is the deus ex machina used by scholars to avoid explanations.

Access to such magical timelessness involves self-transcendence. "Do you know that you can extend yourself forever in any of the directions I have pointed to?" asked Don Juan. "Do you know that one moment can be eternity? This is not a riddle; it's a fact, but only if you mount that moment and use it to take the totality of yourself forever in any direction."[92] This, of course, is the *nagual's* time. It is, in the words of the title of Castaneda's second book, a separate reality. "For the *nagual* there is no land, or air, or water. . . . So the *nagual* glides, or flies, or does whatever it may do, in *nagual's* time, and that has nothing to do with *tonal's* time. The two things don't jibe."[93] The goal is the *abolition of time*. "'There's no future!' he exclaimed cuttingly. 'The future is only a way of talking. For a sorcerer there is only the here and now.'"[94] Everything that points to time or history, including personal history, is to be ruthlessly abolished: "Don Juan explained that by the time a warrior had conquered 'dreaming' and 'seeing' and had developed a double, he must have also succeeded in erasing personal history, self-importance, and routines."[95] Don Juan had told him early in his training that personl history must be dropped. Explaining his own past— a contradictory use of that which must be abolished—the old man had revealed: "One day I found out that personal history was no longer necessary for me and, like drinking, I dropped it."[96] Castaneda was told that it would be the same with him:

> But there is no way to go back to Los Angeles. What you left there is lost forever. By then, of course, you will be a sorcerer, but that's no help; at a time like that what's important to all of us is the fact that everything we love or hate or wish for has been left behind. Yet the feelings in a man do not die or change, and the sorcerer starts on his way back home knowing that he will never reach it, knowing that no power on earth, not even his death, will deliver him to the place, the things, the people he loved.[97]

The sociological premise of sorcery is *radical atomism*. The sorcerer is cut off from all social institutions, all sense of history, all sense that one thing is any more important than another—except for the quest for power. With respect to the world and the flesh, it is possible to say: "Everything is equal and therefore unimportant."[98] But one had better not say this about the devil; the philosophy of pure relativism, or "controlled folly," does not apply to the agents of his satanic majesty: "My ally and Mescalito are not on a par with us human beings. My controlled folly applies only to myself and to the acts I perform while in the company of my fellow men."[99]

Over and over in primitive cultures, and now in contemporary occult groups, the abolition of time and the attainment of altered states of consciousness are seen as central operations. They are the fundamental goals of human action. Mircea Eliade, the comparative anthropologist, has placed this theme of timelessness at the center of his numerous brilliant studies of primitive religion. The shaman's quest for the "time before time"—the time of precreation and the creation of the world—is part of his training. Culturally and ritually, the abolition of time is symbolized in chaos festivals like Carnival, Mardi Gras, Macumba, and the ancient Saturnalia. The transcendence of time is to be achieved ritually by the temporary abolition of all standards of rights and wrong. Ritual evil enables man to breathe new life into a dying world. Law is deadening; ritual violations of law are the source of new life.[100] It is *power from below*, as Rousas Rushdoony has called it.*

Primitive cultures have no concern with earthly time. The dream time is central. The future is now. Because of their lack of concern for the future, they are lower-class cultures. They do not place a high value on saving economic growth, or progress. They are intensely present-oriented. This is true of the aborigines of Australia, some of whose magical beliefs are similar to Don Juan's.[101] It is true of various African tribes. It is true of the culture that produced Don Juan. The focus on timelessness requires the abolition of daily routines, normal perceptions, and law. It is the death of culture.

In this regard, perhaps the most important teaching of Don Juan concerns Castaneda's rationalism. The culture of the West is still essentially rationalistic, both intellectually and as to routine. Industrial civilization could not function

*See Appendix A.

efficiently apart from the existence of clocks. This world of conventional routines is the barrier against the sorcerer's world of shadows and death. After experimenting with psychedelic plants, seeing visions of monsters, wrestling with the peyote god, and generally immersing himself in the world of the occult, Castaneda is warned by the old man that he is now totally vulnerable to the dark forces of the wilderness. "You have lost your shields," Don Juan tells him. "What shields? What are you talking about?" replies Castaneda. The answer is straightforward:

> Well, look around. People are busy doing that which people do. Those are their shields. Whenever a sorcerer has an encounter with any of those inexplicable and unbending forces we have talked about, his gap opens, making him more susceptible to his death than he ordinarily is; I've told you that we die through that gap, therefore if it is open one should have his will ready to fill it; that is, if one is a warrior. If one is not a warrior, like yourself, then one has no other recourse but to use the activities of daily life to take one's mind away from the fright of the encounter and thus to allow one's gap to close. . . . At this time in your life, however, you can no longer use those shields as effectively as an average man. You know too much about those forces and now you are finally at the brink of feeling and acting as a warrior. Your old shields are no longer safe.[102]

When danger approaches, Castaneda is told to write. Take notes, write, concentrate: here is his old rationalistic activity, and it is a very Western activity. His notebook will act as his shield. It is the only one he has left. His mind has been shattered by what he has seen, whether in visions or in the phenomenal world. He has left the world of Western rationalism, and he is in danger of destruction by real beings that wield tremendous power.

Western man is progressively losing his shields. Since 1965, loss of faith in traditional nineteenth-century philosophical mechanism has been obvious. People are steadily learning about the paranormal universe around them, even as Elisha's servant learned to see the angelic host around him (II Kings 6:16–18). An Associated Press story released in May 1974 is symptomatic, and the reaction of establishment scientists, clinging desperately to the world of simplistic nineteenth-century thinkers, is typical—and futile:

> NEW YORK—The scientific elite were somewhat taken aback on being informed that amid all the modern technological advances, a new, national study shows people are believing more and more in the active reality of the devil.
> When told of it, participants in a recent meeting in San Francisco of the American Assn. for the Advancement of Science "were absolutely shocked," says Clyde Nunn, a social researcher who reported the findings to them.
> "It didn't fit their presuppositions," he adds. "It was mind-blowing for them."
> He said the fact that Americans are increasingly convinced of the devil's existence runs counter to the scientific community's general assumption of "progressively increasing rationalism as an automatic evolutionary process."
> Most scientists "want to believe that society has become so rationalized that it has moved out of the nonrational world," he said. But he added that the newly gathered data reveal an opposite trend at work.
> The new study, made by the Center for Policy Research here, found that in nine years

the number of people believing in the certainty of the devil has risen from 37 to 48 per cent of the population, with another 20 per cent considering his existence probable.

ALTOGETHER 68 PER CENT is either sure about it or thinks it likely.

Nunn, the center's senior research associate, linked the upsurge in such belief to "times of great stress, when things seem to be falling apart, when there is great uncertainty in society and limited resources to cope with it.

"It's apparently an attempt to make sense of a world of ambiguities and to explain the evil in it," he said in an interview. He said it also made for an atmosphere vulnerable to demagogic promises to hunt out the devil's instruments.

It has the potentiality of "some new round of witch hunting," said Nunn, a University of Nebraska sociology professor before joining the center, which aims to search out trends so social policy can be shaped to deal with them.

The new study, involving a scientifically selected cross section of 3,546 people, was made last spring. Consequently, the results don't reflect the recent movie-stirred interest in demonology but derive from other conditions.

Nunn said the study, by using identically phrased questions as a parallel survey in 1964, provides the first comparative measurement of shifts in intensity of beliefs about the supernatural.

While the major change was the sharp 11 per cent upturn in those considering the devil's existence "completely true," the 68 per cent total either certain or partly so also rose by 3 per cent.

IN REGARD TO GOD, HOWEVER, absolute certainty about His existence dropped 8 per cent, from 77 to 69 per cent, although another 25 per cent believed in God with some reservations.

Only 6 per cent registered no belief, but the disbelief was 3 per cent higher than before.

"Whatever advantage God has had over the devil in the polls of the past, the devil now appears to be getting his due," said Nunn, a Kentuckian who has a master's degree in religion from the Southern Baptist Theological Seminary in Louisville and a doctorate in sociology from the University of North Carolina.

He said the rising certainty of the devil's activity—along with the slight drop in certainty about God—suggests people have difficulty seeing any good purpose or reason in events and consider the balance of "good versus evil to be tipped in the direction of evil."

The study also brought out that those convinced of the devil's reality are much more likely than others to feel that threatening forces are at work in modern life, and that things are likely to get worse.

Faith in God is slipping, but faith in demons is increasing. We are back to Screwtape's letter to Wormwood: the materialists are beginning to believe in demons but not in God. This is the very heart of the demonic cause. The culture that indulges itself in demonic experimentation faces the loss of its shields.

Conclusion

What are we to make of Castaneda's books? Are they works of fiction? One reviewer concluded that whether or not these events took place is irrelevant: "What difference does it make whether one *believes* in astrology or I Ching or sorcery? As though a vote in some cosmic ballot is going to establish its truth or utility. The real issue is what it says, whether the disturbance it causes in the normal ways of knowing will lead to more imaginative ways."[103] No doubt about it: our shields are down. If Don Juan is correct, it makes all the difference in the world whether people believe in astrology or sorcery. It made all the difference to Castaneda's training and his safety during that training. The question concerning the actual historicity of Don Juan may not be crucial; what is crucial is whether the universe conveyed in the writings of Castaneda is true or not.

If these are works of pure fiction, totally unrelated to any concrete historical individuals named Don Juan and Don Genaro, then Castaneda is one of the great writers of fiction in our era. But if he is a writer of fiction, he is also a master of folklore—the greatest that UCLA has ever produced. His reconstruction of the sorcerer's image of this world is striking in its power and its correlation with what we know of other primitive beliefs. As we might paraphrase that old slogan, if Don Juan did not exist, it has certainly been useful to invent him. The teachings of Don Juan ring true. The reader has entered the mental universe of a primitive sorcerer. What we have found is a startling modern thinker.

Did Castaneda really experience these events? I think he did. Were these events historical events, that is, events that could have been photographed or recorded on tape (neither medium was permitted Castaneda in his research)? Some, but not all. He suspected hypnosis.[104] Furthermore, after having experienced a particular nonordinary experience, the disappearance and reappearance of his car, he was told by Don Juan that Don Genaro had not really moved his car from "the world of ordinary men," but that he had "simply forced you to look at the world as sorcerers do, and your car was not in that world. Genaro wanted to soften your certainty."[105] The *nagual*'s time is not the *tonal*'s time.

This is not to say that such events were absolutely impossible. If Satan could transport himself and Christ to the top of the temple, then the Christian who takes the Bible seriously cannot safely say that teleportation by occult means is categorically impossible. But the ability of men to distinguish fact from fiction is limited. The apostle Peter, upon his miraculous release from prison, was convinced that what was happening to him was in fact some sort of vision. Only when he was outside the city's gate was he sure that an historical event had taken place (Acts 12:9–11). The apostle Paul's description of one man's heavenly vision (no doubt his own) is open to this same confusion: he did not know whether he was in the body or out of it (II Corinthians 12:2). Don Juan admitted that Castaneda's body was in the bushes during his first experiments with astral projection.[106] Nevertheless, the reality of the vision may have been historically important. Did he have the ability in his trance to witness, that is, divine, real historical events at a distance? The old man thought so, Castaneda thinks so, and accounts of other people's out-of-body experiences indicate that on occasion such visions do correspond to actual events at a distance.

Primitive fire-walkers really do walk across coals that are measurably hot. They can be photographed performing this feat. It cannot be explained alone by hypnotism. It cannot be explained at all by the accepted canons of modern science.

Sometimes these events are real. Yet sometimes they are not. Ronald Rose, an anthropologist interested in the kinds of psychic abilities studied by J. B. Rhine, spent many months with several tribes of aborigines. One of the stories told to him concerned the belief that magicians had the ability to produce "clever ropes" —long, slimy cords—out of their mouths. Natives insisted that they had seen these sorcerers climb up these ropes into the air. Rose was given a demonstration. The native lay down on his back, reached into his mouth, and then pulled his hand out as if he were pulling something. "Did you see the cord?" he asked. One of the other natives insisted that he had. But Rose saw nothing. When he told the magician that he had not seen it, he was assured that he would see it the next time. The motions were repeated, but this time he drew out a thin line of saliva. The other native saw it as a cord; Rose saw nothing. He believes that the other native was reporting honestly what he thought he saw. Explanation: hypnosis.[107] Of course, there is always the problem of who was being hypnotized. Presumably, Rose's observations were correct. Presumably. Western men presume a great deal, given their epistemological relativism.

Don Juan offers us a philosophy conforming to many of the most cherished tenets of the modern world: power, relativism, antirationalism, existentialism, higher consciousness, self-transcendence, autonomy. As an interpreter, Castaneda has struck a responsive chord in the hearts of hundreds of thousands of readers. Most everyone likes a good ghost story, and Castaneda throws in enough philosophical justification to convince his readers and reviewers that these tales of power have redeeming social value. He offers the world of the sorcerer as a legitimate alternative to the doubt-filled culture of the modern world.

The world of the sorcerer and the world of the self-proclaimed autonomous scientist are not that far apart. Miss Yates, concluding her fine study of Renaissance magic, remarks the nature of the differences between these two universes: "The basic difference between the attitude of the magician to the world and the attitude of the scientist to the world is that the former wants to draw the world into himself, whilst the scientist does just the opposite, he externalises and impersonalises the world by a movement of will in an entirely opposite direction. . . ."[108]

Don Juan, like his Renaissance cousins, provides Castaneda with the training necessary to internalize the world so thoroughly that Castaneda is no longer able to distinguish between his perceptions of the external world and the distortions of his pseudo-transcended mind. But, then again, the self-professed autonomous scientist can be no more confident of his own observations, given the relativism of his own epistemological presuppositions. Castaneda, following Don Juan, is simply more willing to follow the call of the voices and visions of the *nagual*.

5
Psychics

> If there arise among you a prophet, or a dreamer of dreams, and giveth thee a sign or a wonder, and the sign or the wonder come to pass, whereof he spake unto thee, saying, Let us go after other gods, which thou hast not known, and let us serve them; thou shalt not hearken unto the words of that prophet, or that dreamer of dreams: for the LORD your God proveth you, to know whether ye love the LORD your God with all your heart and with all your soul.
>
> Deuteronomy 13:1–3

David Hoy is a psychic. Given his publicly demonstrated abilities, he is *the* psychic—the most baffling mind reader, prognosticator, and diviner practicing his talents anywhere in the world today. He performs without mysterious atmosphere, esoteric wisdom, Eastern philosophy, vibrations, or anything else. His special gift, if one could call it a gift, is instant revelation. Not revelation about God or the universe, but revelation about the more mundane affairs of life, such as where someone has lost her false teeth. As *Newsweek* reported: "It was phone-in time on radio station KCMO in Kansas City. 'Mr. Hoy,' lisped a woman caller, 'my false teeth are missing. Can you figure out where they are?' David Hoy, KCMO's guest expert in extrasensory perception, needed only a few seconds to decipher what he calls his 'ESP flash.' 'Your dog got them and put them under the stove,' he confidently informed her. 'Would you go check and see?' She did and found her bridge just where Hoy said it was."[1]

Incredible? Routine for Hoy and for several other practitioners of radio ESP. Hoy is the one who first developed the call-in ESP format, and it is Hoy who best typifies the fully modern, no-nonsense entertainer on the ESP circuit. Several nights a week, he goes on live radio and takes phone calls from listeners. There are no restrictions on the kinds of questions asked: lost objects, missing persons, job opportunities, future events, identifying thieves, solving family squabbles, and almost anything else that curious callers can devise to thwart or tap his proclaimed powers. He claims that his answers are correct about eighty per cent of the time, which is the top limit ever claimed by serious psychics. In 1974, over thirty stations carried his broadcasts. An example of his skills is provided by John Godwin, author of a book on Hoy:

> In some instances David himself isn't sure of the meaning of his perceptions, though the other party catches them instantly. In November, 1972, a Cincinnati man called KMOX and wanted to know who had broken into his tool shed and made off with his new lawnmower.
> "Hm," David mused, "all I see is a battered old Volkswagen, painted with psychedelic designs and flowers. Does that make any sense to you?"
> "It sure does," said the man grimly. "Thank you."
> David learned the full story from a letter he received two weeks later. The psychedelic VW belonged to the man's teen-age nephew, a full-fledged juvenile delinquent. He had gone over to the boy's home and although he didn't find his lawnmower there, he discovered several other items from his tool shed. The young man finally confessed that he had sold the mower the same day he stole it.[2]

Reporters who have investigated Hoy's powers have been aided by the existence of tapes of the radio shows, as well as by a large collection of letters to Hoy from people who have obtained information through the radio broadcasts or through written contact with Hoy. (He receives about 10,000 letters each month.) Thousands of replies, each date-stamped and marked with the address of the sender, are in his files. Doubtless many people are skeptical about Hoy's claims, but thousands have acknowledged that his ESP revelations on highly specific subjects have been remarkably accurate.

As for telephone calls, there is almost no way that they could be faked. For one thing, radio stations are not eager to be involved in any broadcasting frauds analogous to those that rocked the television networks in the mid-1950s. Professional broadcasters do not want to find themselves stuck with another Charles Van Doren with inside information to specially prepared questions. The stations have to take precautions with men like Hoy. Technologically, there is little possibility that Hoy could be using plants in his telephone audience. (By plants, I mean people, not plants.) The telephone lines jam up whenever he goes on the air. The law of large numbers—so dear to the hearts of scientific investigators—takes over, keeping any given phone call purely random. A letter in his files from Northwest Bell Telephone informed him that on August 10, 1973, some one hundred thousand phone calls came into the station in a half-hour period. The telephone company contacted the station and asked that Hoy limit calls each night to phones whose numbers ended in a specific digit, and he complied with the request. The letter ends: "Although the increasing popularity of the show may necessitate stronger measures in the future, it appears that the control procedures were instituted just in time" (letter dated August 17, 1973).[3]

Hoy's ability to predict the future is uncanny. He avoids the typically vague prophecies of the fortune-cookie variety. His most famous documented example was given on radio station KDKA of Pittsburgh (the nation's oldest commercial station) on Halloween night 1967. "Within sixty days a bridge spanning the Ohio River will collapse with tremendous loss of life. It will be brought out, after the collapse, that eighteen months before, a heavily laden barge going upriver had hit a major pylon of the bridge, backed up, and gone on without reporting the accident." On December 15, thirty-seven days later, the Silver Bridge—linking West Virginia and Ohio south of Pittsburgh—collapsed during the peak hours of the Christmas shopping rush. A dozen people died. A subsequent investigation revealed that the cause of the disaster had been an unreported ramming of the bridge supports by a barge proceeding upriver.[4]

David Hoy was born into a Southern Baptist household, attended Bob Jones University, the independent fundamentalist school in South Carolina, and later graduated from Southern Seminary in Louisville. He then became a missionary to Brazil. From his days at Bob Jones, he had occasionally received flashes of precognition. He had predicted his father's death on the morning that he died, hundreds of miles away (March 10, 1952). Later, when he was working at Calvary Baptist Church in New York, he met a young pianist who was then studying at Juilliard School of Music, Van Cliburn. Cliburn was deeply into the occult: astrology, numerology, and the tarot. He tried to interest Hoy in such matters, but Hoy responded negatively. Hoy was convinced that spiritualist phenomena were just that: phenomena. It was all gadgetry and dexterity, mixed in with a lot of mumbo jumbo and showmanship, he believed. He himself was quite skilled at "magic"—prestidigitation—which he had learned from his Baptist minister father. Yet he was curious about psychic and similar phenomena, and his interest continued through seminary. He continued to receive precognitions—so often, in fact, that the seminary's authorities had to forbid any further prophecies, since the local newspaper was reporting that a seminarian had been predicting local events. He agreed to cease.

During his time on the mission field in Brazil, he attended a voodoo ceremony out of curiosity. He kept returning to the all-night sessions of dancing, rhythms, and ecstatic outpourings. He was fascinated by the glowing coals that were placed on the bodies of ecstatic worshipers, leaving no scars and producing no pain. He saw the priestess pick up a scorpion with her mouth without being stung; he watched her tell the color of a cloth placed in her hand while she was bandaged around the eyes. Once she even hexed him mildly. She asked him to hold out his hand, fingers stiff and spread apart, and after she opened her own hand and touched his, palm to palm, he was unable to clench his fist. His fingers were frozen. Finally, she touched his hand again, and his muscles relaxed. On one occasion, he explained to her that he was a Christian missionary, and she replied:

"You no belong to them. You belong to us."[5] She proved a prophetess; not long thereafter, Hoy left the ministry. He returned to the stage as a "magician."

The flashes of information continued. He would devise elaborate acts of "mind reading," only to find that on occasion he did not actually need the signals of the accomplice in the audience. Pick a word, he would tell a companion. He could tell him the word. He wrote a book, published by Doubleday in 1965, *Psychic and Other ESP Party Games,* in which he encouraged his readers to develop their latent psychic skills. Yet this was before his own remarkable development as a psychic. The flashes of information kept coming. In 1967, he predicted that President Johnson would not run again the following year, and this prophecy was confirmed by a *Louisville Courier-Journal* reporter. He predicted in 1966 that Jackie Kennedy would marry a Greek shipping magnate. Time and again, his prophecies came true.

Hoy began to tour college campuses with a serious ESP act (or so he claims) in 1966, at the beginning of the great epistemological earthquake that threw open the door to every kind of new idea in the academy. Naturally, college administrations and self-conscious department chairmen fought against Hoy's appearances, but students welcomed him. The accepted truths of the establishment, as certified by tenured Harvard, Princeton, Yale, and Berkeley faculty members, were being thrown out in every department by the students, as the hostility to the war in Vietnam—itself a product of messianic liberalism—overflowed into every area of liberal domination on the campus, which meant, basically, everything except the department of engineering. The students of 1965–70 were like the Athenians of St. Paul's day, who "spent their time in nothing else, but either to tell, or to hear some new thing" (Acts 17:21b). Hoy marched into the campuses of America, predicting the outcome of forthcoming athletic events, finding lost books, pointing out the dormitory thieves (not by name, but by the location of the stolen goods, which were sometimes in a particular student's locker), reading minds, and generally disrupting every established theory of what the human mind is capable of accomplishing. The students loved it.

Knowledge is power. People generally seek knowledge, especially technical knowledge, in order to gain control. Hoy acknowledges that his type of mental power works two ways. He says that he can control the thoughts and actions of others. He worries about this, he says, which is understandable, since it is his contention (as it is with most professional psychics) that everyone has latent psychic abilities, and that it just takes time and practice to bring these powers into action. Author Godwin wanted a demonstration. Hoy gave him a good one. Hoy asked him to go into the next room and bring him a vase of flowers.

> We were sitting in the downstairs living room of the Hoy home in Paducah. The adjoining room was the dining room, which lay in darkness. I opened the door and walked in. The room was almost pitch black. I groped my way to the table, banging my shin against a chair en route. I felt over the table top until I touched the vase, nearly knocking it over. Then I picked it up and brought it back.
>
> I handed David the vase and rubbed my sore shin. "Now what?" I asked.
>
> In answer he handed me a slip of paper. On it was written:

"You will not switch on the light in the dining room."

I spent the next hour or so trying to figure out why I hadn't switched on the light. I knew where the switch was, and by all the rules of logic and common sense my first action should have been to turn it on. Yet I didn't. The thought never occurred to me.[6]

It is possible, of course, that Hoy had noticed that he did not switch on the light and hastily scribbled down the note before Godwin returned. But why would he have selected this particular experiment? How many possible combinations of activities by Godwin would have allowed Hoy to single out one of them—clearly peculiar—to scribble down? Godwin was convinced.

Mind over mind: we come to one of the central impulses in all systems of magic, witchcraft, and occultism. The desire to take control over another's will is a dominant theme of all forms of messianic humanism. The psychologist's use of brain implants on animals, or drugs to control their actions; the hypnotist's use of a totally unknown force to bring out secrets or to control the personality; the brainwashing techniques of the Communists; the psychodramatic techniques and sensitivity training of therapists and social revolutionaries—all are part of the same basic motivation, namely, to be as God. Men wish to invade the personality centers of their fellows, taking away the power and responsibility of someone else's human actions. Many of those reformers who castigate the use of Madison Avenue advertising techniques to sell laundry products are willing to use Madison Avenue in political campaigns or for moving a recalcitrant public along "progressive" paths. Religious revivals are terrible, these reformers believe, because people are manipulated by exploiting preachers; but sensitivity training is wonderful, because it breaks down stultifying personality barriers to total intimacy.

Hoy admits that his techniques of mind over mind can be used commercially. In fact, he made a lot of money by applying his techniques to a certain product line of men's hairdressing. He designed a kind of "power of positive thinking" training course for salesmen—in this case, barbers—in which they learned to direct their thoughts to the customer. "This product will make you look terrific. This product will increase your self-confidence." The barber was to visualize the product as used by the customer. The company taught Hoy's twenty-one-page typewritten course for six months to its 4,500 barbers. By the end of the period, sales were up seventy percent.[7]

Those familiar with the so-called science-of-mind movement will recognize the origins of Hoy's techniques. It is fundamentally a religious response to the world. Bryan R. Wilson, an Oxford sociologist specializing in comparative religion, argues that there are eight basic types of supernaturalist responses to the world: one type accepts things as they are (orthodoxy, in his terminology), and the seven others are concerned with changing the world. His catalogue: conversionist, revolutionist, introversionist, manipulationist, thaumaturgist, reformist, and reconstructionist.[8] (As reasonably close-fitting examples of each, we could list: fundamentalist, Marxist, Mennonite, science-of-mind proponent, primitive magician, social gospeler, and puritan.) Hoy is obviously a *manipulationist*. His approach is very much like the approach of "Reverend Ike," the former fundamentalist black preacher who is now a science-of-mind, "God-is-within-you" proponent. He has worked the manipulationist psychology (or metapsychology) into the language of the ghetto. He drives a $90,000 pink Rolls-Royce and encourages his followers to try to do the same. His philosophy is straightforward: "We are not interested in Pie in the Sky bye and bye. We want our pie now, with ice cream on it, and a cherry on top."[9] Anyone who has seen Reverend Ike on television will instantly recognize Hoy's technique, outlined in lesson four of his Roffler products training manual: the stylist (read: expensive barber) is supposed to *feel* the prediction of increased sales . . . the touch of crisp new dollar bills in his hands . . . the motion of the new car he will be driving . . . his sense of personal greatness.[10] Napoleon Hill's *Think and Grow Rich* is a similar handbook; so are the writings of the multimillionaire insurance entrepreneur, W. Clement Stone.

The difference between David Hoy and the other manipulationists is that he frankly acknowledges that the name of this game is mind over mind. He does not appeal to gods within us; he does not use the jargon of the psychologist; he does not propose this system of salesmanship as a program of self-transcendence. He simply says that with sufficient concentration, the person who has developed these powers can get other people to do what he wants them to do. Hoy realizes the danger of sinister men who would make use of these techniques, but he is convinced that these powers are in everyone anyway, and sooner or later the word will get out.

Remember that bit of historical paradox that was repeated everywhere in 1964: Lincoln was elected in 1860; Kennedy was elected in 1960; both had seven letters in their last names; both were slain on Friday and in the presence of their wives; etc.? That, according to Hoy, was Hoy's gift to the American Historical Association. The world is filled with paradoxes, coincidences, and mysterious, unexplainable forces. There is free will, Hoy says, but there is also *destiny*. Or, as Godwin titles the chapter, there is "the Finger of Fate."

For those who do not recognize this philosophy, it is the same interpretation of the world that dominated the Roman Empire and that led to its collapse. Professor Charles Cochrane, in his crucial book *Christianity and Classical Culture* (1944), writes: "The acceptance of such beliefs involved a picture of nature in terms either of sheer fortuity or (alternatively) of inexorable fate. By so doing, it helped to provoke an increasingly frantic passion for some means of escape. This passion was to find expression in various types of supernaturalism, in which East and West joined hands to produce the most grotesque cosmologies as a basis for ethical systems not less grotesque."[11] Gnosticism was the characteristic form of this philosophical crisis—the crisis of total impersonal chance vs. total impersonal fate (destiny). The breakdown of classical philosophy undermined classical culture, leaving the field to Christianity, which proposed a wholly new cosmology, namely, *cosmic personalism*, in which all things come to pass because the creator God has a universal plan of history. It was the philosophy of Augustine, argues Cochrane, that provided a concept of personalistic history that could undergird a new civilization.

David Hoy is very mod, in both dress and language. He does not attempt to build an overarching theoretical structure to explain or justify his abilities. He can cover the field with the letters *ESP* and everyone is happy. But the fact of the matter is that Hoy does have a philosophy, however vague it may appear. It is the same philosophy that caused magic and occultism to flourish at the end of the Roman Empire. A world of blind destiny must be mastered, thereby making it conform to man's goals, man's dreams, and man's nightmares. It is man who rules this universe of cosmic impersonalism. It is man's mind that is the capstone—not the narrow definition of mind given to us by eighteenth- or nineteenth-century rationalists, but man's mind, the master of the cosmos. The mysterious *synchronicities* (to use Carl Jung's term) of the universe serve as avenues for man's mysterious sovereignty over the universe (including over other men). The powers of occultism need not be accompanied by tappings, philosophies of reincarnation, or creeping ectoplasm. Twentieth-century humanism serves occultism quite well.

Gerard Croiset

On January 6, 1957, a Dutch psychic, Gerard Croiset, met with W. H. C. Tenhaeff, a professor of parapsychology at the University of Utrecht, along with biologist L. H. Bretschneider and physicist J. A. Smit. Croiset was handed a seating plan for a meeting to be held twenty-six days later. The room to be used for the meeting would contain thirty-six chairs. The guest list had already been made up. Croiset was asked to select a chair. He chose chair number nine. He was then asked to describe the person who would sit there. He spoke into a tape recorder and gave a dozen specific facts about the person, plus some additional material relating to four of the twelve general features. Some of the facts were:

1. She is a middle-aged woman. She is interested in child care.
2. Between 1928 and 1930, she was around a circus in the town of Scheveningen.
3. As a child, she lived in a cheese-making district.
4. There was a fire on a farm in her childhood.
5. Three boys came to mind. One is working in British territory.
6. She has been looking at a picture of a maharaja.

After the recording was finished, this session ended. On February 1, two packs of cards, each numbered one to thirty, were selected by the experimenters (but not by Croiset). As the meeting was about to begin, both sealed packs were opened independently. From one set a card was placed on each chair; cards from the other were distributed randomly to the guests in another room. The guests went in and sat on chairs bearing the number corresponding to their cards. They were instructed not to touch any other chair. Once seated, they awaited Croiset, who entered a few minutes later. The tape was played back to the audience. The lady seated in chair number nine admitted that several of Croiset's observations did apply to her:

1. She was forty-two and interested in child care.

2. Her father used to take her to the circus in Scheveningen.
3. She had visited farms; butter was the main product (not a solid hit).
4. She had been looking at a photo of an Indian yogi a few days earlier.

Another direct hit concerned her interest in opera, specifically the opera *Falstaff*. Croiset had felt strongly that this particular opera was the first one she had ever seen. She admitted that it had been the first. She had fallen in love with the tenor. Furthermore, Croiset had predicted that on February 1, the lady would take her daughter to the dentist. The lady admitted that she had taken her daughter to the dentist that afternoon.[12]

Once again Croiset had performed his now-famous chair test, an experiment that has been repeated in many countries under many different conditions. Again and again, his predictions have come true with startling accuracy. Like many psychics (or paragnosts, as Professor Tenhaeff prefers to call them), Croiset hates the ESP card experiments. But the chair test contains many of the same elements of randomness that the Zener card experiments contain, and the results are far more impressive to anyone who is not a total captive of the methodology of authoritative randomness. Sometimes the chair is selected by that ultimate of randomness, a Geiger counter. Other times, the biblically traditional method of choice by lot is used. Sometimes Croiset receives no impressions whatsoever; on those occasions, the chair winds up empty. He can see the individual's past and sometimes the future. Prior to a test before a group of intellectuals in Hilversum in October 1953, Croiset informed Professor Tenhaeff: "The person who will sit in that chair was away for a few weeks in another country. I see him walking in a large city. His shoelaces are loose. He leans forward to tie them. As he does so, I see a gentleman walking behind him who bumps into him." A direct hit. The person seated in the chair said that he had been visiting London, and this very incident had occurred.[13]

Croiset is perhaps the most famous psychic in Western Europe. Television specials have been made about him. One was shown in the United States in the mid-1960s. (I remember watching it.) Most Hollanders seem to have heard about him. He performs services for detectives in solving crimes, especially crimes involving missing children. Less well known is the fact that he performs psychic healings for a fee.[14] He is a gifted *psychometrist*, that is, he works with objects that belong or did belong to an individual about whom he is giving the reading. (That other famous Dutch psychic, Peter Hurkos, is also a psychometrist.) He says that he "sees" pictures associated with the owner of the object—sometimes incredibly detailed pictures.

In April 1963, a young boy, Wimpji Slee, disappeared. The boy's uncle contacted Croiset. Croiset told him that the boy had drowned in a particular canal. Dragging the canal for the body proved useless, however. Four days later, the body was found floating in the canal at precisely the spot designated by Croiset.[15]

A similar case had taken place in May 1960. Another young boy, Toontje

Thooner, had been missing for several days when a local resident contacted Croiset. Professor Tenhaeff happened to be with Croiset at the time, and he switched on the tape recorder (which he begs Croiset to use in every case, but which Croiset uses only sporadically), recording the conversation on Croiset's end of the phone. Croiset's biographer reports on the contents of that tape:

> "Is the playground where the child was last seen in a new suburb? [*Yes.*] When you leave it at the left, is there some open ground? [*Yes.*] When you follow the border of this open ground, do you reach a canal? [*Yes.*] Is this canal 200 to 500 metres from the playground? [*Yes.*]
> Croiset paused, and then inquired, "Are you a member of the child's family?"
> "No. I'm a neighbour," was the reply.
> "Well," sighed the sensitive, "I can then tell you that the outlook isn't good. In about three days, the child's body will be found in the canal I mentioned, close to a bridge and near a bucket of zinc."
> Three days later I checked up. Unhappily enough, the police of Eindhoven had just found the child's body next to one of the piers of the bridge over the canal near a bucket of zinc...."[16]

These are documented cases. Dutch police departments have used Croiset and other psychics working with Professor Tenhaeff on many difficult cases. Police officials are seldom willing to resort to such aid unless they regard it as indispensable, since psychic methods of detection are hardly what fellow law-enforcement agents would call professional. This may not be the kind of evidence that impresses scientific investigators of the paranormal, but generally scientists are so hostile to such phenomena that they are willing only to accept negative findings. Police departments do not continue to use potentially embarrassing assistants in order to produce negative findings.

What is the source of Croiset's abilities? He claims that they are gifts from God. But there is a curious side to these abilities. They come upon him while he is in a state of altered consciousness—"lowered consciousness," as his biographer puts it. He obtains visual images of the person or event. With other psychics, this state of altered consciousness may resemble a trance; with Croiset, it is barely noticeable by an outsider.[17] Sometimes these visions are intensely religious, and he places great importance on them. One of them is crucial for an understanding of the source of his powers, because it indicates the link between psychic visions and magic.

> In one of these visionary states, at the age of thirty, there appeared to him a host of angels in a blaze of golden light. He also "saw" two guardians holding trumpets. The next day these guardians again appeared to him, standing by a curtain which was slightly pulled aside. Through the opening a stage was visible and a man clad in oriental dress, wearing a turban with a splendid diadem, stepped forward. Suddenly, Croiset saw that the Oriental's face began *to show his own features*
> "To Croiset, the Oriental symbolized a paranormally gifted superman," explains Dr. Tenhaeff. "Croiset's vision meant to him the promise that, in the future, he would accomplish great things as a Magus—the more so because the Oriental's face started to

show his own features. Croiset felt that he was receiving the call from a Higher Power."[18]

It is not uncommon for people who exhibit psychic powers to have developed them at a very early age. Sometimes an adult trains the child in occult practices. (The grandmother of the little boy in Thomas Tryon's novel, *The Other,* has had real-life counterparts for thousands of years; Tryon based his novel on universal themes in folklore and actual historical practice.) In other instances, moody children, especially teenage children, seem to come upon their powers suddenly. Gerard Croiset fits neither of these categories. In his book on Croiset, Pollack fails to mention anything about the man's childhood, but in a 1964 article in *True* magazine, he does provide some basic information. Croiset's parents were Jewish theater people, always on the road. He had no home life. At the age of eight he was placed in a foster home. He was to go through six sets of foster parents over the next five years, until he finally ran away at the age of thirteen.

Croiset had been an introverted child who lived in a world of his own fantasies. He was a prodigious daydreamer. He was sickly as well, and suffered from rickets. When he spoke of imaginary playmates and imaginary places, people no doubt thought him a trifle immature. When he began to describe people and places he had never seen, and describe them accurately, adults grew concerned for his sanity. He began to predict events on the basis of his fantasies, and they would occasionally turn out to be true. "These daydreams which Gerard didn't understand, together with his telepathic relations with people, were the first signs of his paranormal abilities," wrote Pollack.[19]

Unlike David Hoy, Croiset had little education. He had failed at several occupations by the time he was out of his teens. In 1935, he suffered a nervous breakdown at the age of twenty-six. He joined a spiritualist group at one point, but quit shortly thereafter. He says that he does not believe in spiritualist explanations for odd phenomena. It was only as his reputation grew as a psychometrist (object-handling psychic), from 1937 to 1940, that he began to believe that he had something unique to offer the world.

Croiset's abilities may be questioned by professional skeptics, but police departments throughout Europe are not so skeptical, and families who have been helped in locating lost children or lost property are not skeptical. The chair tests have also added to his reputation. He has become a prophet in his own time. To know in advance when and where a body will float to the surface of a canal is a startling sort of knowledge. There is little doubt that the man's talents are highly unusual.

Modern scientists, unable to fit such phenomena into the categories of pure rationalism, have preferred to ignore him completely. That is the safe approach; it is also the dishonest approach. But at least it had one healthy byproduct: until the shattering of faith in orthodox science, which began after 1964, professional skepticism had kept the Croiset-type phenomena from spreading into the mass media. Skepticism served as a barrier to truth, but it also served as a barrier to the highly personal and deeply hostile demonic threat to man and culture. As a result, for many years Croiset had few imitators with access to popular culture, at least in the United States. The problem today, however, is that skepticism is no longer an effective barrier, and once the public has concluded that mere denial of such powers is not a valid critique, that same public is left without a guide as to what, in fact, the sources of such power really are. Modern science had but one defense, skepticism, and that defense no longer convinces millions of readers.

Peter Hurkos

If Croiset's abilities came as a result of an overactive imagination, or if his overactive imagination came as a result of his discovery of his powers, these powers were nevertheless developed gradually. Not so with Pieter Cornelius van der Hurk. His paranormal psychic abilities came almost in an instant. As a young man, he had assisted his father as a house painter. In July 1941, he was painting the outside of a building four stories up. He slipped and fell to the earth, breaking his shoulder and suffering a concussion. When he awoke, he found that he had "another mind." He could not remember many facts about his past, but he could remember facts about other people's lives. Furthermore, he had other arcane abilities: psychometry, astral projection, visions, and, most significantly, *voices*. More accurately, a single voice that spoke to him about secret things. As he was to say years later, "I felt I had no mind of my own."[20]

Multimillionaire C. V. Wood, Jr., president of McCulloch Oil Corporation and the developer of Arizona's Lake Havasu, is co-founder of an organization called Mind Science Foundation. He has been associated with numerous research projects into psychic abilities. He writes: "Within the Mind Science Foundation we have studied many persons who have had certain psychic abilities, and in almost all cases the ability developed after either experiencing a fall or being hit on the head, or after having an extremely high fever."[21] Why this should be the case no one knows for certain, and orthodox scientists are hardly likely to explore the topic. (At best, they might say that people who think they are psychic are suffering from physically induced mental disorders.) Hurkos's mind(s) may be disordered, but it (they) cannot be said to be powerless.

During his stay in the hospital, Hurkos demonstrated his new abilities on several occasions. At first he inspired fear. It was wartime, Holland was under Nazi domination, and Hurkos seemed to know things that only a spy should be aware of. This suspicion almost cost him his life. Then, when he convinced the physicians that he was no spy, they thought he was mad. Finally, by revealing some very personal and embarrassing facts to one of the physicians concerning his extramarital affair, Hurkos received a confused sort of respect.[22] But he was as confused as the professionals about his powers. Walking the streets of The Hague one night, he stopped in a cemetery to rest. He asserts that he began to hear voices—voices of the dead, he says. He ran home, but he could still hear them. His "gift," which he quite correctly regards as a curse, was to bring him under bondage to these voices for the next three decades, at least. As his biographer writes:

Whatever it was he had about cemeteries didn't go away. Peter gets some of his strongest vibrations at gravesites and from clothing or objects that have belonged to dead people, especially when he works on murder cases. If the body is buried in the ground, he is usually taken to the gravesite. "But I don't like to go in cemeteries," he says. "Not that I'm afraid, but if I walk in a cemetery for half an hour I'm completely exhausted, as tired as if I worked fourteen days. Even when it is cold, I am sweating like hell when I go in a cemetery. Because I get the vibrations, and then comes the mental picture and then the voices."[23]

One of the more familiar words of the "youth culture" of the 1960s was *vibrations*. Good vibrations, bad vibrations, no vibrations: these terms were supposed to convey information about the setting or person involved. The Beach Boys had a big hit record, "Good Vibrations," during this period. (Later on, Dennis Wilson, a member of the group, befriended a bearded hippie guru named Charles Manson and his many followers, who proceeded to eat his food, steal his wardrobe, borrow and then smash up his uninsured $21,000 car. Mr. Wilson finally interpreted these events as being of the bad-vibration variety, having cost him an estimated $100,000. After weeks of such nonsense, Wilson finally asked the group to leave—but not before recording one of Manson's songs as the flip side of a Beach Boys' hit single, however. The song, prophetically, was titled "Cease to Exist," which Wilson prudently changed to "Cease to Resist.")[24] Peter Hurkos (who himself later worked on the Manson case—successfully, says his biographer; disastrously, says Manson prosecutor Vincent Bugliosi)[25] is a man who lives in a world of vibrations. So do countless others inside the world of the occult: vibrations are everywhere and everything. He gets vibrations from the objects he investigates. Sometimes, they are "bad vibrations." But they are vibrations.[26]

Hurkos does not regard himself as a psychic healer or any other kind of healer. This is to his advantage, given the attitude of physicians and state medical boards toward uncertified competition. But on one occasion, witnessed by several people, he performed an act of miraculous healing on himself. (Fortunately, he forgot to charge himself a fee, thus keeping inside the law.) He is unable to explain the following; he simply thought to himself, "I don't want to be in a hospital." (You don't have to be a psychic to figure *that* out.)

If Peter Hurkos could heal nobody else, at least apparently he could heal himself. Even Henry Belk, though no longer friend or believer, still swears by this incident. It happened on the evening of May 17, 1958, in Belk's New York apartment. A group of Belk's friends and business associates had gathered there for a sociable evening. Peter was there, too. At some point during the evening, Peter tripped over something and fell, twisting his leg so badly that, according to Belk, "One of the bones broke clear out of his skin. There was blood all over the place."

While Peter cried out in pain, some of the men lifted him onto a bed. As Belk tells the story, Peter bowed his head as though in prayer, "And before our very eyes, the bone went back into place and the torn skin healed and became smooth. I was there. I actually saw the bone stick out and go in." Belk himself told me. Those are his words verbatim from my notes. He also told essentially the same story to Jess Stearn (*The Door to the Future*) and played him a taped recording of that memorable night, with testimonials from the other eyewitnesses.[27]

Hurkos is most famous, like Croiset, for his investigations of criminal cases. He has worked on many of them, with varying degrees of success. One police officer who believes in Hurkos is police chief Robert White of the Palm Springs police department. Hurkos had helped his department locate the body of a missing youth, Stephen Gallagher. In December 1968, he told them where to search for the body; the following September, they located it very close to the location described by Hurkos. Even more eerie, however, was the way in which Hurkos presented the information. Chief White reconstructs that original meeting:

> "I heard a lot about Peter Hurkos," said Chief White. "I knew of his reputation on the Boston Strangler case, and I was interested in meeting him. While he was in my office he asked whether we had any complicated cases we were trying to solve. I told him yes, as a matter of fact we had several. I asked Captain Richard Harries to bring in some of the folders of unsolved cases. He brought in several.
> "Peter Hurkos laid his hand on the top folder, which happened to be the Gallagher case, and began verbally telling us almost verbatim what was in the report. Both my captain and I were amazed. We had never seen Peter Hurkos before. He had no way of knowing what was in the folder. The case was a year old, and it hadn't been in the news recently. Yet Peter began telling us about it exactly as though he were seeing through that folder.
> "He said it was the case of a missing boy. He named the correct number of persons involved—three. He identified the vehicle they were driving. He told us there had been a little 'party' and there were lots of narcotics involved. This also was correct. The three boys had been off on a little 'trip' on LSD."[28]

Hurkos is able to perform before large groups. He is a professional psychic. His gifts are not limited to dark halls and seances filled with credulous people. He can do his work on television as well as on a Las Vegas stage. In August 1969, he appeared on the "David Frost Show." Columnist Leonard Lyons handed him a sealed box and asked him to identify its contents. Not even Frost knew what was inside. His biographer writes:

> Peter began rubbing his hands over the box. His reading, as many will remember, went something like this:
> "I see wires, yes . . . wires and hooks . . . steel hooks shaped like this [moving his arm in an arc]. . . . Oh, my God, terrible. What this man did to this world, it is too terrible. He's a genius but a bad man for what he did to the world. Yes, wires and hooks. . . . Wait, I see now, It's a telephone. I see a telephone. We must pray for this man's soul."
> When the box was opened, there it was—a telephone. Not the kind of telephone familiar to most of us, to be sure, but nonetheless a telephone and a very special one.
> It was Hitler's telephone, the one he had had in his mountain villa at Berchtesgaden.[29]

How does Hurkos do it? He answers: "I tell only what I see and hear, what the voice tells me." What voice? "The voice that came back with my other mind."[30] His "other mind" came with the blow on his head. It has never left. At other times, he sees pictures along with, or in place of, the mysterious voice. The voice and psychic pictures: *these are the same phenomena described by Carlos Casta-*

neda, phenomena that he encountered during his experiments with divination by means of lizards.[31] The Yaqui sorcerer uses "familiars"—animals associated with demonic power, at least under ritual conditions—in the same way that Western witches have traditionally been linked to special animals. But in Hurkos's case, there are no animals involved, only the voice and the visions. Nevertheless, the basic goal in both psychic phenomena and occult divination is the same: *access to secret knowledge*. In other words, the basic urge is *gnostic*: salvation through knowledge, especially secret knowledge.

The voice gives Hurkos advice. "I never painted before my fall," said Hurkos. "Only house painting. Then a few years ago I start painting. Somebody said, 'Paint. Paint what you saw.' And I am painting." His biographer asked, "Who was the somebody who told you to start painting?" Hurkos gave a two-word answer: "The voice."[32] The voice not only gives information about the external world—past, present, and future—but also instructs in the arts. It sounds very much like the techniques used by Soviet hypnotist Vladimir Raikov, who is able to "reincarnate" great masters of painting in the minds of his subjects, thus producing competent artists in a few sessions.[33] There is power here. Power to give information and power to direct and control personal development. That power is *personal*: being to being.

The doors of perception swing both ways.

There are problems associated with voices. Take the case of one Robert F. Roy, a self-professed "student and disciple of demonology," accused burglar, arsonist, and murderer. He admitted the murder of a mother of nine children. Police in Camden County, New Jersey, said he informed them that an inner spirit seemed to be telling him "to kill an elderly female." He led them to a hidden recess in a wall of the Berlin Hotel, where he was living, and produced a twelve-gauge shotgun, which he said was the murder weapon. The woman had indeed been cut down by a shotgun blast.[34] There is no guarantee that the voices, whatever they are, are reliable, factually or ethically. Yet psychic after psychic relies upon some form of spirit voice to guide him in his mystical revelations.

Jeanne Dixon

"As I touched her hand I saw the death symbol over her. It was high above the ground. I saw life on the ground around her, and thus knew that if she would keep her feet on the ground she could elude danger. It was a sort of inner voice that said, 'Six weeks.' This voice comes to me frequently, and I always listen to it."[35] Jeanne Dixon, like Peter Hurkos, receives messages from a voice. These voices get around.

Mrs. Dixon is undoubtedly the most prominent American psychic of our time. Ruth Montgomery's bestselling introduction to her powers, *A Gift of Prophecy* (1965), was almost prophetically timed to coincide with the initial detonation of the occult explosion. It appealed directly to the literary tastes of those who take seriously the in-depth articles of the *Ladies Home Journal*. Unlike Peter Hurkos, who feels burdened by his talent, Jeanne Dixon (as interpreted by Ruth Montgomery) seems to revel in her gift. Being a prophet may not be easy, the book informs us, but it certainly is spiritually rewarding, and it certainly can make a person the envy of her neighbors. The underlying message of the book is that while everyone is not equally gifted—contrary to David Hoy—it certainly is nice for those who are, especially those who Do a Lot of Good with their gift.

Undoubtedly, Mrs. Dixon has performed some important services for people. She calls ambulances for people who have not yet had a heart attack, but who will in a few minutes. She tells people to see a doctor quickly because they have a serious and previously undiagnosed disease. She keeps people from flying on airplanes that are about to crash. She warns people about business deals that are not going to work out. The book is filled with firsthand testimonials of the beneficiaries of such prophecies. All in all, she makes psychic powers look like a true gift from God, just as Croiset and Mrs. Dixon maintain. Why object to prophecies of this nature?

The biblical quotation that introduces this chapter provides one answer. It is not the *accuracy* of the prophecies concerning the events that is crucial; it is the *philosophy and theology* that undergird the prophecies. Furthermore, the apparent benefits conferred on both the prophet and the recipients of the advance information (provided the recipient does *exactly* what the prophet has instructed) almost guarantee that some readers will imitate the techniques of the prophet, and that others will somehow feel cheated that no such gift has been bestowed on them. The market for materials about or by Mrs. Dixon indicates just how curious the public is. The sales for example, of the Dell Purse Book titles that deal with the development of prophetic skills—*The Book of Omens: Your Guide to Good Luck; Numerology; Palmistry; Develop Your ESP*—indicate how widespread the imitation factor is. The titles, as they say, tell all.

Mrs. Dixon was first informed of her powers by a gypsy. It sounds like a plot in some Hollywood B film of the 1940s, but she insists it is the truth. When she was eight years old, her mother took her to see a gypsy woman in Northern California, close to their home, and the woman said that the young girl had a unique palm. (Eastern mystic types apparently have said the same thing about her, for what it is worth.) The woman told them that when the girl grew up, she would have special powers. Then she went into her covered-wagon home and produced a crystal ball, which she gave to young Jeanne Pinckert. (Her brother is Ernie Pinckert, who became an All-American football player.) Almost immediately she received visual messages in it, including one saying the old gypsy would scald her hand in a cooking accident. Sure enough, it happened. (Crystal balls in the hands of psychics seem to be good for a long life of "I told you so's," not generally regarded as a sure way to win friends and influence people, as Cassandra's biographer, a Greek by the name of Homer, informed us a few years back.)

The use of quartz crystals by Yaqui sorcerers and aboriginal magicians is a curious parallel. Special properties are supposed to be associated with crystals. They permit the focusing of power as well as the inducing of visions. But crystal gazing has a separate history. It has been practiced by psychics and magicians,

East and West, for thousands of years. Lewis Spence, in his *Encyclopedia of Occultism* (1920), reports that in ancient times an elaborate ritual preparation was used by diviners, but that in modern times scryers (gazers) have dropped much of the ceremonial tradition. He argues that the object of the crystal ball has always been to induce hypnosis. The problem with this theory, as Nandor Fodor points out in his *Encyclopedia of Psychic Science* (1934), is that hypnotic symptoms are rarely found in crystal gazers. He writes:

> The most arresting question, of course, is whether the pictures are ever objective. In many experiences this appears to be the case. There are instances in which the pictures grow larger under a magnifying glass, may be reflected in a mirror and may be seen by several persons. Sometimes they have even been photographed. It is very likely that in these cases the vision is due to spirit-operators. The pictures are built up as a means of communication just as messages may be given in the crystal in writing. The fact that in some cases the messages are spelt out backward points to a conscious effort on the operator's part to furnish proof of the exclusion of the medium's subconscious mind [p. 74].

This is not to say that in all cases the pictures inside the crystal are objective; in the majority of cases, such as with Mrs. Dixon's visions, they are not. But there are sufficient documented cases of several people seeing the same vision, including actual photographs, that would indicate the validity of Fodor's central thesis: *the source of the vision is an outside being or beings.* In Mrs. Dixon's case, the most likely candidate is the mysterious voice.

She asserts that she can peer into her crystal and see future events as clearly "as if she were watching a T.V. screen."[36] Sometimes the channels come in a bit fuzzy, however, as when she forecasted that the Soviets would beat us to the moon.[37] (Perhaps this particular revelation was from the voice or in a general run-of-the-mill vision, in which she places less trust.) But at other times, she is uncannily accurate.

Jeanne Dixon's world, like Hurkos's, is filled with vibrations. It is not just a catchy phrase with psychics. In fact, it became a catchword in the late 1960s only when the language of the occult was transmitted by the counterculture to the general population. The literature of occultism reveals a continuing theme: the whole universe is composed of vibrations. Donald Hatch Andrews, a professor of chemistry, has attempted to fuse this religious perspective with modern, post-Heisenberg physics, and concluded that the universe is not so much a huge machine as an enormous melody. He thinks that "the universe is composed not of matter but of music."[38] It is not surprising that his book was published not by a scientific publishing house but by Unity Books, an organ of a prominent science-of-mind type of organization.[39]

Mrs. Dixon finds that vibrations can reveal many things about a person's life. She once diagnosed the health of a friend of Ruth Montgomery's. "Ruth, I have picked up your friend's vibrations. She was suffering some pain in the intestinal region a few minutes ago, which I believe is a chronic condition caused from nervous strain."[40] Her diagnosis proved completely accurate. But vibrations come not only from people, but also from objects, especially her old pack of playing cards, also a gift of the mysterious gypsy:

> "The sweet old gypsy gave me those cards when I was eight years old, and because she blessed them they carry good vibrations. I don't know a single thing about telling fortunes with cards. I simply have a person hold them so that I can pick up his vibrations. It sometimes helps me to pull out his channels."[41]

Houses also give off vibrations. These can sometimes be significant. "The moment that I walked into that Nineteenth Street house I seemed to feel God putting his arms around me. I knew it was for me. All the vibrations were right."[42] Even the future gives off vibrations, which is why they can be used for prophetic purposes. Mrs. Dixon said throughout 1948 that Truman would beat Dewey, and a week before the election, she announced once again that Truman would be the victor. She went down to campaign headquarters to give a donation the Saturday before the election, and she said to a friend who was working there, "Madeline, everyone thinks I'm crazy. [Not because she liked to peer into crystal balls, you understand, which for Washington is not all that weird, but because she was predicting a Truman victory, a prediction involving the essence of craziness as defined by Washington, namely, arguing against the polls.] Let's try it again with the cards, to see if I still get the same vibrations."[43] She did, and Truman won.

Crystal balls, cards, vibrations, voices, visions: what is left? *Astrology.* She claims that she never uses astrology. Not that she thinks it is nonsense. Quite the contrary; she was taught the art, she says, in her teens by a Jesuit priest (a fact that will be readily accepted by all Dominicans). The problem with astrology, according to her, is that it takes too much time.[44] There are more efficient ways of divining the future. Instead of constructing complex astrological charts, Mrs. Dixon has found a short cut, vibrationally speaking:

> In reading for Miss Nichols and other strangers, Jeanne almost invariably asks their birthday. "I do that for the rising and setting signs," she explains, "because it helps in my meditation to see which direction they're going. I don't ask for the minute of their birth, because I don't want to be influenced by what their horoscope charts would say. I just like to know their rising and setting signs, so that I can pick up their correct vibrations."[45]

Jeanne Dixon is, if nothing else, a vibrant woman. How is it that a crystal-gazing, card-consulting, vision-receiving wife of a divorced man could be regarded by everyone, including the Roman Catholic Church, as an orthodox and upright member of that ancient institution? Simple: in the heart of her theology is the humanistic god of ecumenism. This is the god of modern Protestantism and modern Catholicism. It is part and parcel of the humanist culture of our day. It is a basic theme of all theosophist, occult, and science-of-mind cults. Most of these cults believe that a single universal religion is the solution to man's problems and the foundation of a messianic one-world political order. Whether by means of the dry rationalism of university training or the irrationalism of mystical visions, modern humanists have frequently come to the conclusion that man—the best representative of divinity, or else the highest being in a universe devoid of divinity —must be united politically and spiritually. This perspective is the very essence of humanism, and it has been dominant since the time of the Enlightenment. As Rousas Rushdoony writes:

> Humanity is the true god of the Enlightenment and of French Revolutionary thought. In all religious faiths one of the inevitable requirements of logical thought asserts itself in a demand for *the unity of the Godhead.* Hence, since humanity is the god, there can be no division in this godhead, humanity. Since Enlightenment philosophy was monistic, this means an intolerance of differences as being unessential.[46]

In short, he concludes: "The goal is not communion but uniformity."

Bearing this fact in mind, consider Mrs. Dixon's vision of February 5, 1962. She "saw" Queen Nefertiti and her husband, the pharaoh, just outside her window. She saw a pyramid, too. They were carrying an infant from whom rays of light emitted. The queen walked away and was stabbed in the back. The child became an adult. A cross above his head expanded until it was worshiped by everyone. The task of unraveling this vision would have baffled the diviners of Babylon. (A Ph.D. candidate in psychology—Freudian, of course—might have produced his dissertation from it.) But Mrs. Dixon has laid the mystery to rest:

> "A child, born somewhere in the Middle East shortly after 7 A.M. (EST) on February 5, 1962, will revolutionize the world. Before the close of the century he will bring together all mankind in one all-embracing faith. This will be the foundation of a new Christianity, with every sect and creed united through this man who will walk among the people to spread the wisdom of the Almighty Power."[47]

If this sounds a trifle messianic to you, you are not alone. Ruth Montgomery's book ends on a hopeful note: "Mankind, Jeanne Dixon has said, will begin to feel the great force of this man about 1980, and his power 'will grow mightily' until 1999, when there will be 'peace on earth to all men of good will.'"[48] For those who are not of good will, as defined by the creedless creed of ecumenical humanism, times will undoubtedly be tough.

Another favorite doctrine of occult humanism is the idea of the "spark of divinity" in each man. It is most highly developed as a system of belief in Hinduism, with the doctrine of *karma* (reincarnation) of each soul in a progressive evolution back into the formless, monistic divinity from which all diversity (illusion) originally came. But Mrs. Dixon has succeeded in fusing this humanistic creed with pre-1965 Democratic Party politics—no mean feat:

> This is the true meaning of President Kennedy's life and death: that through his martyrdom he would light an eternal flame to remind peoples of the world of God's eternal flame in each of us. During John Kennedy's brief period in the public spotlight, he was able to kindle in the hearts of men an awareness that there is more to life than the narrow pursuit of personal gain. Because his life on this earth was cut short in its prime, it was possible for him to become an eternal symbol of youth, vitality, culture,

and intellect. This was not of his doing but of God's. Like the courteous Washington policeman on the street corner, who radiates good vibrations to all passers-by, and like each of us who tries to develop the talents that were entrusted to us, President Kennedy was simply an instrument of God's will. Through him God has demonstrated that within each of us burns this eternal flame; that our greatness lies not in the size of our bank accounts but in our faith and our development of divinely granted talents.[49]

Any resemblance between John Fitzgerald Kennedy, the consummate political pragmatist-millionaire, whose family has undeviatingly sought political power for its members over four decades, and the man of Mrs. Dixon's eulogy, is purely coincidental. Any resemblance between the God of the Bible and the ecumenical god of Mrs. Dixon is less than coincidental. It is nonexistent.

Conclusion

The facts of psychic power are available for serious students of the question. Too many cases, documented by too many eyewitnesses, now exist for the professional skeptics to continue to discount, ignore, disparage, or explain them away by means of scientific rationalism. The positivist's universe never existed; the faith in that universe is now coming apart at the seams. Somehow ESP must be accounted for, not just mind reading but psychokinesis, precognition, and memories of past existence (*someone else's* past existence, not the psychic's). Croiset says a body will float to the surface of a canal in a particular place on a certain day in the future, and it does. Jeanne Dixon predicts a specific event, and it happens. These are not fortune-cookie prophets mouthing vague generalities, but producers of concrete statements. You will find your false teeth under the kitchen sink, says David Hoy, and the caller does. You will not turn on the light, thinks Hoy, and Godwin doesn't.

Yet with few exceptions, there is more to the psychic's universe than just the ability to see the future or direct thoughts in externally verifiable ways. There are voices. There are odd bits of theology and cosmology that reappear, generation after generation: reincarnation, one-world religion, the divine spark in every person, the "secret doctrines" of the great teachers. The psychics' abilities are not in accord with the humanistic science of the past three centuries, yet they are invariably in accord with the *philosophic* humanism that supposedly created modern science. Should faith in Newtonian science be eroded, what is to prevent a new fusion: messianic humanism and the occult powers of the psychic?

Is it so surprising to find that the Soviet Union should be experimenting with psychics in order to find the "laws" that undergird these most disturbing, yet most promising, impossible phenomena? The messianic state seeks power, and psychics possess power, the power of occult knowledge. The opposition of the modern humanistic culture to occult power has been methodological, not moral. When the methodology shifts, as it has clearly begun to shift, what moral restraint will be present to call a halt to mind readers, mind controllers, and humanistic prophets of the coming one-world order?

6
Edgar Cayce:
Mouthpiece of the Occult

> And as it is appointed unto men once to die, but after this the judgment: so Christ was once offered to bear the sins of many; and unto them that look for him shall he appear the second time without sin unto salvation.
>
> Hebrews 9:27, 28

I first heard of Edgar Cayce [KAY-see] in the spring of 1964. His son, Hugh Lynn Cayce, was promoting his newly published book about his father's work, *Venture Inward*. He was appearing on Long John Nebel's midnight-to-dawn radio show, which originated on New York's WOR. Beamed all over the East Coast, Long John's program drew millions of listeners. A former carnival barker, Nebel opened the microphones to every sort of occultist, fundamentalist, libertarian, renegade medical practitioner, and fringe-group member imaginable. There was only one requirement: they had to tell interesting stories—five hours' worth. Many of them did. No story was more intriguing than that of Edgar Cayce.

From 1901 until his death in 1945, Edgar Cayce won a following of faithful believers and less faithful financial contributors as a result of a unique occult facility. By putting himself into a trance, and by assigning a "control" agent to ask him questions, he could diagnose people's physical illnesses. Not only diagnose them, but prescribe remedies, many of them completely unorthodox and seemingly unrelated to the illness, that were found helpful and very often completely successful. He would simply loosen his tie, take off his shoes, lie down on a couch, and go into his trance state. The control agent would then give him the name and address of the person to be diagnosed. Then would come the familiar words: "Yes, we have the body." The diagnosis would then begin. A secretary would record the diagnosis and recommendations, and these notes would then be put into Cayce's permanent files. By the time of his death, the Cayce foundation, the Association for Research and Enlightenment (A.R.E.), had almost nine thousand of these medical "readings," as they were called. The files also contained letters from patients that had been sent in unsolicited, plus others that had come in as a result of follow-ups made by the A.R.E. Cayce's followers claim, with considerable justification, that this is the largest body of paranormal documentation relating to methods of healing that has ever been assembled. The A.R.E. has opened these files to qualified researchers, which again is a rare occurrence within most occult circles. They do not regard Cayce's talents as occult, however; they see him as a man who possessed certain visionary skills that we all supposedly possess.

An amazing story, if true. An amazing story even if false, because Cayce gave his "readings" for over four decades, received considerable (though sporadic) attention by the press, was investigated by medical and university officials, and was never convicted of fraud. He made almost no money at his trade, built no impressive institution, received criticism from skeptics, wrote no books, made no speeches on the lecture circuit, conducted no seances, and in general devoted his entire life to a seemingly lost cause. He was arrested once, in 1931, on the charge of fortune-telling, but it was dismissed. He was never sued by one of his patients (clients?), and he returned the small fees charged for the readings in later years upon request. What, in short, was in it for him? He said that his work had to go on. If it was a fraud, why could he not impart his "skill" to his son? If it was not a fraud, how can we explain what he did?

Psychic healing is an ancient tradition, especially in so-called primitive cultures. Psychic diagnosis and prescriptions are not common in modern societies. They are unheard of. Yet the press took only sporadic interest in his work, although millions of people knew of it. In the early 1900s, the story was picked up by newspapers in the South. In 1910, Cayce received national coverage, including from the *New York Times*. Yet for the remainder of his life, newsmen simply stayed away from or forgot about him.

There were books by his followers. *There Is a River* (1942), by Thomas Sugrue, sold well if not spectacularly, and Gina Cerminara's *Many Mansions* (1950) received some attention. For the most part, however, the Cayce story was buried. Hugh Lynn's book was superbly timed; it hit the market about the time that the Beatles hit New York and shortly before riots hit Berkeley. The occult revival created a market, and in 1967 Jess Stearn filled it, or at least gave every impression of having filled it. *Edgar Cayce—The Sleeping Prophet* was hardly a sleeper. Released in January, it had gone through eight hardback printings by July. The next year Bantam published a paperback version, and by 1975 it was into its fifteenth printing. That, by any standard, is a bestseller. Yet it was only the beginning. The A.R.E. began issuing books based on Cayce's life and readings, and there are at least twenty titles in print, plus another book by Cayce and a reissue of a second by Sugrue. Millions upon millions of copies of these books have been sold. There are even Edgar Cayce study groups—the final test of a true movement-cult—operating around the country. A brief advertisement for an Edgar Cayce study group appeared in the Long Beach (Calif.) *Pennysaver* (a local throwaway advertiser) only recently—three decades after his death. The occult revival, fittingly, created the whole Cayce movement. Without it, he would be remembered only by a handful of relatives, both of Cayce and of his patients, plus a few occult researchers. Cayce's supporters may try vainly to argue that Cayce's talents had nothing to do with the occult, but the movement has everything to do with it.

History

Edgar Cayce was born in Hopkinsville, Kentucky, in 1877. He had his first vision at the age of six, according to one biographer.[1] His grandfather had been a dowser or, more properly, a water-witcher, and his grandmother told young Cayce that the old gentleman had also been able to make tables and chairs move without touching them, although he had only performed these feats in front of her.[2] His dowsing abilities had been well known, however. His father's only seemingly occult ability was his highly undesirable attraction to snakes. They followed him out of the fields, wrapped themselves around his hat when he would set it down, and generally made life unpleasant for him. He never liked snakes. He finally had to move away from the farm into the town to avoid them.[3] Other than that, his son later explained to Harvard psychologist Hugo Munsterberg, he was completely normal. (Munsterberg, in 1910, arrived to expose Cayce as a fraud; he left convinced that Cayce possessed some sort of legitimate, though unheard-of, abilities.) *Normal:* that was one term that had never fit young Edgar.

As a child, he claimed to be able to see "little people"—companions in the fields. Unlike most children, Cayce never doubted that he had. At the age of thirteen—the age most frequently associated with poltergeist activity—he was reading the Bible through for the twelfth time. Not a good student, he was at least faithful in this activity. He experienced a vision of a lady with wings. She asked him what he wanted, and he said he wanted to be of service to people. (Part of the appeal of the Cayce story to a lot of people is that he was a perpetual do-gooder. He always seemed so sincere.) She granted him his wish, he later said.[4] This incident cannot be dismissed lightly; the next day Cayce demonstrated a most remarkable ability. He was a poor student. His teacher, who happened to be his uncle, had told his father that the boy was hopeless, and his father, like so many fathers before him, was determined to beat a little knowledge into his son. He began to drill him on his spelling lesson. Edgar's mind went blank, as always. The father grew furious, striking the boy. Edgar later recounted that at this point he heard the lady's voice: "If you can sleep a little, we can help you." He asked his father's permission to doze for five minutes. Granted. He put his spelling book behind his head, dozed off for five minutes, and when his father returned, he knew every word in the book, including the page number and the line on which the word appeared.

He brought home his geography book, slept on it, and the next day had it completely memorized. He did this with every school book he had. His teacher could hardly believe it. His father was disturbed; this was too spooky. Yet he was proud of his son. (Some of Cayce's classmates, when interviewed several decades later, still recalled how they had resented his effortless learning technique.)[5] Just before his son's graduation from school (from the seventh grade, according to Hugh Lynn Cayce; from the sixth, according to legend)[6], his father had bragged to former Congressman Jim MacKenzie that his son could memorize anything by sleeping on it. MacKenzie was understandably skeptical. A test was proposed by MacKenzie. Years before, he had delivered a speech favoring repeal of the tax on quinine. He had become known as "Quinine Jim" in the House. He was on his way to Peru as American ambassador, and Peru was the major source of quinine. Therefore, said the congressman, have Edgar sleep on a copy of this famous speech. His father went one better, or so he thought: he would read it to his son while he was asleep. He did, twice, and two evenings later, Edgar delivered the hour-and-a-half oration to the students and parents of the graduating class, to the delight of Quinine Jim and, presumably, the utter boredom of the audience.[7]

The story is marred by the fact that his graduation came in 1892, when he was fifteen years old. If he had developed this ability at age thirteen, why had he not progressed more rapidly? Hugh Lynn Cayce repeats on several occasions that his father's ability in this regard later faded, forcing him out of school early.[8] But years later, Edgar memorized the entire catalogue of a book and stationery store, astounding the owner and customers.[9] The less obvious reason for his apparent failure to go on was the level of achievement common to sixth-grade dropouts. Take a look at the sixth McGuffey reader. Poetry by Shakespeare, Dryden, Whittier, Poe, Tennyson, and others; essays by Edmund Burke, Macaulay, Samuel Johnson, Oliver Goldsmith, Patrick Henry, Daniel Webster. Can you imagine assigning Blackstone's essay on the origin of property to the typical product of today's government high school, let alone a sixth grader? How about William Pitt's answer to Robert Walpole? College freshmen in most of the "better" state universities would have trouble with the sixth McGuffey reader. Furthermore, after the grammar school education of the 1880s and 1890s, sheer memorization would not have been sufficient to get a young man through. The curriculum involved higher mathematics, rhetoric, foreign languages, and the liberal arts. Not what the average farm boy needed. Edgar quit. But he was not soon forgotten by his classmates.

In the spring of 1900, he developed a hoarse throat. It steadily became a whisper. Out of desperation, he became a silent apprentice to a photographer; he could no longer sell books and stationery supplies. A traveling hypnotist visited town and heard about the young man's plight. He guaranteed to restore his voice for $200. When hypnotized, his voice returned; as soon as he came out of the trance, his whisper reappeared. After several attempts, the hypnotist gave up. But another local amateur hypnotist and amateur osteopath, Al Layne, remembered an incident from Cayce's youth. He had been hit on the head by a baseball. Dazed, the boy became feverish and then delirious. Yet out of his delirium, he had told his parents to apply a poultice to his neck. They did, and he recovered quickly. He had no memory of his diagnosis afterward. Layne put Cayce into a trance and then asked him to diagnose his problem. Immediately, the fateful words came forth: "Yes, we can see the body."[10] The voice diagnosed the problem as insufficient circulation. Layne gave a suggestion that the body cure itself. Cayce's neck grew pink, then bright red. Twenty minutes later, it became normal again. Layne told Cayce to wake up, and when he did, his voice had returned.

This was the beginning, not only of Cayce's diagnostic ministry, but also of a lifetime of trouble with his voice. His biographers seldom refer to the fact that throughout the remainder of his life—forty-five years—Cayce had recurring voice failures. He was completely dependent upon his trance state and its circulation stimulation to return his waking voice to normal.[11] No one could give a physiological reason for the loss of his voice. Those familiar with demon possession would immediately recognize the cause: occult bondage. Cayce could not abandon the physical "readings" once they had begun. He was trapped.

Layne, the hypnotist, immediately saw possibilities for himself and Cayce. He could put Cayce under, question him concerning the ailments of others, get a prescription, and then mail the prescription to the "patient." Cayce was initially suspicious, both of his talent and of Layne's proposition. Layne asked him to diagnose his own illness, and when he followed Cayce's advice, he said that he felt much better. Cayce gave in, but he refused to accept any payment for his services. Layne, however, had no qualms about fees.

In 1902, Cayce moved to Bowling Green. His voice plagued him. Layne had to come up every few weeks to treat him. Then Layne came more often, bringing cases. In the summer of 1902, Cayce received the crucial telephone call of the healing stage of his career. C. H. Dietrich, a former superintendent of schools in Hopkinsville, was desperate. His five-year-old daughter had been ill for several years; now she was suffering as many as twenty convulsions a day. She could no longer speak. The physicians, several from out-of-state clinics, had given up on her. Could Cayce help? Cayce got on the train and returned to Hopkinsville. Eight years later, Dietrich had the following statement notarized:

> March 1st, 1902, she was taken to Dr. Hoppe, of Cincinnati, Ohio, who made a most thorough examination. He pronounced her a perfect specimen physically, except for the brain affection, concerning which he stated that only nine cases of this particular type were reported in medical records, and every one of these had proved fatal. He told us nothing could be done, except to give her good care, as her case was hopeless and she would die soon in one of these attacks.
>
> At this period our attention was called to Mr. Edgar Cayce, who was asked to diagnose her case. By auto-suggestion he went into a sleep and diagnosed her case as one of congestion at the base of the brain, stating also minor details. He outlined to Dr. A. C. Layne, now of Griffin, Ga., how to proceed to cure her. Dr. Layne treated her accordingly, every day for three weeks, using Mr. Cayce occasionally to follow up the

treatment, as results developed. Her mind began to clear up about the eighth day and within three months she was in perfect health, and is so to this day.[12]

The trance voice informed them that the girl had suffered a fall from a carriage three years earlier. Sure enough, her mother remembered the incident. Layne was told how to adjust her spine. Once her mind had cleared, she advanced rapidly intellectually until she was a normal child of her age. By having achieved a major success with a prominent, educated citizen, Cayce established a precedent that led to other cases and other successes.

The readings continued. A man in New York heard of the work, wrote to Layne, and asked him to have his "associate" diagnose his case. Cayce did, from hundreds of miles away, and without any statement in advance of the man's symptoms. He had prescribed something called clarawater to the man, only there was no such product listed. Cayce was put under again and the voice came up with the formula. Yet at no time could Cayce remember any of this.[13] His voice would give remarkably detailed anatomical descriptions, and they were sometimes confirmed by physicians, yet Cayce read nothing other than the Bible and simple Sunday school literature. He had not received training in anatomy by sleeping on his grammar school textbooks, however advanced they would seem in today's educational context.

In 1902, Cayce also developed a game for adults that he called "Pit." People liked it, so he sent a sample to Parker Bros. He received their thanks, several free sets, and a letter stating that the game had been copyrighted by them and that it would henceforth be illegal for him to produce it. So much for Edgar Cayce, businessman.[14]

Word finally got out to the press about Cayce's diagnoses. This was in 1903.[15] The medical authorities immediately moved in on Al Layne, who agreed to quit practicing until he graduated from a school of osteopathy. Cayce's voice again departed. Now, however, he had learned that he could put himself into a trance, and with a "control" agent, he could still have himself temporarily cured. A local physician agreed to act as an assistant, but was surprised when Cayce's chest turned red, then returned to normal, and upon awakening, his voice was normal.[16]

Cayce worked with some young physicians in Bowling Green, then returned to Hopkinsville, where he teamed up with a doctor of homeopathy, Wesley Ketchum, who quietly used Cayce to diagnose a hundred cases over the years. It was Dietrich's testimonial in behalf of Cayce that helped to reduce his initial skepticism. But the occult nature of Cayce's power became increasingly blatant. On one occasion, he had prescribed something called "balsam of sulphur." Years later, Ketchum described the scene:

> One day, there were a couple of doctors and druggists in Cayce's [photographic] studio on a complicated case, for which Cayce had prescribed balsam of sulphur. They began scratching their heads. Nobody had ever heard of it. One of the druggists, an elderly man named Gaither, was convinced there was no such thing. They pored over a copy of the dispensatory, listing all available therapeutic drugs. There was no balsam of sulphur. Then, in the attic, they stumbled across an old defunct catalogue, put out fifty years before. They dusted it off, opened it, and there found balsam of sulphur.[17]

Even more eerie was his prescription "oil of smoke." Again, no catalogue listed it. No one had heard of it. They took another reading. The name of a Louisville drugstore was given. Ketchum wired the store for a bottle. The reply: never heard of it. "We took a third reading. This time a shelf in the back of the Louisville drugstore was named. There, behind another preparation—which was named—would be found a bottle of 'Oil of Smoke,' so the reading said. I wired the information to the manager of the Louisville store. He wired back, 'Found it.' The bottle arrived in a few days. It was old. The label was faded. The company that put it up had gone out of business. But it was just what he said it was, 'Oil of Smoke.'!" This story was related to Professor Munsterberg, or so Sugrue reports.[18] It is unlikely that Ketchum would make himself appear to be a fool in front of a Harvard professor. Cayce did possess astounding powers. Or, to put it more accurately, astounding powers possessed Cayce.

Ketchum related some of the Cayce stories to a convention of homeopathic physicians at a 1910 convention. He was asked to put his thoughts down on paper by Dr. Krauss, who then read it before a Boston meeting of the American Association for Clinical Research. The *New York Times* picked up the story and ran it on October 9, 1910. This was before the days of the "new journalism" or "interpretative journalism"; hence, it was run as a straight news story. Other papers picked up the story from the *Times* (some things never change), and an army of reporters descended on Hopkinsville.[19] Local physicians began crying for Ketchum's scalp, but he backed them down successfully. It was the first and last time that Cayce was to receive national attention from the media. Only with the publication of Sugrue's book in 1942 did the nation have the opportunity to hear the story of Edgar Cayce during his lifetime.

Cayce finally broke with Ketchum over the question of his using his readings to do a bit of gambling with fees paid into a supposed hospital fund. He moved to Selma, Alabama, for a time. He tried to find oil by means of his trance; again, to raise money for a hospital. None was found. He worked as a photographer. He taught Sunday school in the Christian Church. He became a prominent leader in Alabama's Christian Endeavor organization. And all the while, he continued to give his readings on people's ailments. Finally, in 1923, there came a distinct break in his thirteen-year-old pattern. In that year, Cayce became a philosophical occultist. The second stage of his career, by far the more enduring, began.

The Occult Readings

In 1923, a supposedly wealthy Dayton, Ohio, printer, Arthur Lammers, visited the Cayces in Selma. He had heard of Cayce's paranormal powers and had decided that Cayce could answer many questions concerning the philosophy of life—occult philosophy. He asked Cayce for a reading, but not a physical reading. He wanted an astrological reading. Furthermore, he wanted it in Dayton. He asked Cayce to drop everything and come to Dayton. Cayce did precisely that. The Sunday school teacher traveled to Dayton to provide an astrological reading—name, date of birth, location of birth—for a devotee of mystery religions. It was so very easy. At the end of the horoscope reading, the trance voice announced: "He was once a monk." Those five words sealed Cayce's fate, and may have sealed the fate of millions of his modern followers. A new world, totally hypothetical, and historically compelling, opened up behind his closed eyes: the world of reincarnation.[20]

Lammers wanted to pursue this new avenue. When was he a monk? Had he lived many lives? His was the first of what came to be known as the "life readings." Lammers' money ran out before he could get his questions answered to his satisfaction—a problem which seemed to plague all of Cayce's well-heeled and temporary devotees—but the pattern was established. Of the 14,249 readings still on file with the A.R.E., 2,500 of them are life readings. Bridey Murphey stuff. Taylor Caldwell stuff. Not just a stream of old ladies of both sexes asking, "Who am I?" but, "Who was I?"

At first, Cayce rejected the whole idea of reincarnation. He was convinced that the Bible rejected the concept. He was absolutely correct. But slowly and steadily he changed his beliefs. He began to apply twisted interpretations to biblical passages (but never to Hebrews 9:27, 28) in order to discover reincarnation. As one of his long-time followers put it: "The active membership of the A.R.E., as it is usually called, is made up of people of all religious faiths and many nationalities, including foreign countries. Strangely, they all seem to be able to reconcile their faiths with the philosophy emerging from Cayce readings."[21] Cayce set the pattern. The fact is that these people have one religion, the Cayce religion. They ignore the teachings of their secondary, official religious memberships.

The importance of his self-conversion, if that is really the accurate way to describe the relationship between his conscious mind and the messages that proceeded from his trance-induced voice, cannot be overstressed. One follower hit the nail on the head when she wrote: "Had his physical readings not been proven accurate and useful in all the years he had been giving them, he probably would have turned from this new development in his psychic work and never given another reading of any kind."[22] Cayce knew his Bible. He had asked himself and his wife for many years whether his work was of God or the devil. Since his philosophy after 1923 denied the existence of the biblical devil, his followers ignore this crucial question. Yet they all know that he once asked it. He concluded, using the argument of pragmatic humanism, that if good is accomplished, a work must be from God.[23] Healing people's sick bodies is obviously good. For thirteen years he had been doing just that. The voice had never lied before. Always before, he explained to Lammers, the voice had confined itself to healing. Nothing was ever said about reincarnation. He had always believed in the Christian view of life: ". . . souls born into the earth, to live a while, die, and be judged." He had *always* believed this. Yet he had watched the force he had been given for many years. "It hasn't ever done evil, and it won't let me do it. . . . But what you've been telling me today, and what the readings have been saying, is foreign to all I've believed and been taught, and all I have taught others, all my life. If ever the Devil was going to play a trick on me, this would be it."[24] This is Sugrue's reconstruction of that initial discussion, as Cayce and his wife must have related it. They saw this encounter as the watershed in their lives, and so do the historians of the movement. Cayce laid it on the line, and then abandoned his previous religious commitment. The voice he could never remember took precedence over the Bible he had read through so many times. He was never to return to orthodoxy.

Reincarnation was only the beginning. About thirty percent of the life readings dealt with the lost continent of Atlantis, that secular and occult version of Noah's flood.[25] A recently published paperback, *Edgar Cayce on Atlantis*, contains the choicest of these visionary historical tidbits. Jess Stearn devotes chapter thirteen of his bestseller to Atlantis. We even had a chronology of Atlantis and its West Coast precursor, Lemuria (the West Coast always gets there first!):

  1,000,000–800,000 B.C.—Early Lemurian development.
  500,000 B.C.—Lemuria inundated by water, peoples scattered.
  400,000–300,000 B.C.—Lemuria inhabited and civilization advanced.
  250,000 B.C.—Second Lemurian catastrophe, possibly by fire.
  200,000 B.C.—Early Atlantean culture emerged.
  80,000 B.C.—First Atlantean disturbance. Final Lemurian submergence.
  28,000 B.C.—Second Atlantean disturbance. Recorded biblically as the Great Flood.
  10,700 B.C.—Final destruction and sinking of Atlantis.
  10,390 B.C.—Completion of The Great Pyramid in Egypt by the priests Ra-Ta and Hermes.[26]

Where is Atlantis? Cayce followers find hints in the record that would point to Bimini. Cayce prophesied a great series of cataclysmic geological upheavals for the period 1958–98. *Edgar Cayce on Prophecy* is filled with specific prophecies, so far completely erroneous, relating to these upheavals. Jess Stearn, as late as 1967, somehow took Cayce's rambling prophecies quite seriously. Part of Atlantis will reappear soon, he said in 1940. Atlantis had broken into five islands. One of them was called Poseidia. (Why anyone bothered to name a handful of islands as they were breaking up is a mystery.) In any case, a June 1940 reading was quite specific: "And Poseidia will be among the first portions of Atlantis to rise again. Expect it in sixty-eight and sixty-nine. Not so far away."[27] Not so far away in 1940, but just far enough away so that nobody was likely to be able to challenge the prophet in his lifetime. His geological predictions were equally specific and equally accurate. Yet Stearn saw fit to devote chapters three to five to earthquake predictions, plus chapter thirteen to Atlantis. But more pathetic than this, some poor Cayce convert apparently has professional credentials as a geologist and is devoting his career to a search for Atlantis. He serves as the official apologist for the geological portion of the Cayce readings. His name is not given by Stearn (a sign of Stearn's charity), but Stearn reverently refers to him as "the Geologist." The Geologist fully expects to see the fulfillment of Cayce's prophecies that, among other earth-shaking events, parts of the West Coast will break up and slide into the sea, probably in the later porton of the 1958–98 period.[28] Japan will also slide into the sea.[29] The earth's axis will tilt.[30] The Great Lakes will empty into the Gulf of Mexico.[31] In 1932, he predicted a great catastrophe for 1936, which would involve a shaking of world powers, both politically and geologically.[32] In retrospect, it is not clear whether this prophecy referred to the invasion by Italy of Ethiopia, the candidacy of Alf Landon, or the Spanish Civil War. From Hitler's point of view, of course, it was Jesse Owens' four gold medals.

Two of the criteria of demon possession used by the Roman Catholic church are: 1) the ability of a man to gain access to information not otherwise attainable by normal means, and 2) the ability to speak in foreign languages without prior instruction. Cayce's career exhibited both traits. The medical diagnoses certainly can be categorized as information unnaturally obtained. Stearn reports that he spoke in French, Italian, Spanish, German, teutonic German, and several unknown tongues.[33] Doris Agee says that he spoke an even two dozen languages at various times.[34] It seems clear enough that his trance states were abnormal. (The third criterion used by Catholics is the demonstration of superhuman strength, which Cayce never exhibited.) His philosophical and cosmological speculations indicate that his trance states were demonic.

Cosmology

What do witches believe in? First of all, we believe that each person has the ability to develop magical powers within himself. We seek ancient wisdom through psychic forces, and know that each individual has a personal link with the Godhead. Secondly, we believe in reincarnation, the survival of the spirit after death; it is essential to our faith.[35]

So writes Sybil Leek, Britain's most famous self-proclaimed witch. The divinity of man, his access to supernatural power, ancient wisdom, psychic revelation, reincarnation—these, in a nutshell, are the creedal position of the Cayce movement. Our thanks to Miss Leek for pinpointing the origin of this statement of faith, or, if not the ultimate origin, at least the competing organizational claims to its use.

The divine-human link is asserted in Cayce's theory of *pantheism-monism*. The doctrine of evolution is basic to Cayce's theory of *reincarnation-karma*. The source of manipulative power over nature, he taught, is man's control over specific *vibrations*. The theoretical foundation of his system of *humanism*—the deification of man. It is significant that these beliefs are shared by most, if not all, of the more prominent occult-theosophist-mental healing cults. Where such ideas are prominent, witchcraft casts its dark shadow over the organization or movement in question. Witchcraft, as Miss Leek correctly argues, is not simply magical spells or specific rituals, however important ceremonial magic is to witchcraft. Witchcraft is, above all, a way of life undergirded by a specific philosophy. This is why the overwhelming number of books dealing with witchcraft and occultism only skim the surface; they do not deal with the heart of witchcraft, namely, its world-and-life view. The rituals of occultism vary far more than the presuppositions that provide the philosophical and emotional support for the various rituals. The heart of witchcraft is not "bell, book, and candle"; the heart of witchcraft is its humanism.

Monism

"Wherever the Law of One has been taught, there truth has lived."[36] All is ultimately One. This doctrine is fundamental to mysticism, both Eastern and Western. God, man, and the universe are fundamentally one. The Creator-creature distinction, so crucial to orthodox Judaism and Christianity, is specifically denied. The so-called spark of divinity in each man supposedly leads all men back into oneness with God. One "life reading" announced: "The body, the mind, the soul are one within the physical forces; for the body is indeed the temple of the living God. In each entity there is that portion which is a part of the Universal Force, and that which lives on. All must co-ordinate and cooperate."[37] God is *impersonal;* only man is truly personal. This is another central theme of monist systems. Man is the personal agent of the impersonal God. "For in the measures ye mete to others—in worshipfulness or in hate, in consideration or in disregard—ye actually mete thy material activities in relationship to Creative Forces, God."[38]

There are many passages in these readings that would appear to be orthodox; their content is not. The essence of Cayce's cosmology is simple: "While individuals differ, let the first principle be the starting point. ALL is One!"[39] It is the same cosmology that underpins Hermann Hesse's *Siddhartha,* Charles Manson's favorite novel. Man, in this scheme, becomes the co-creator with God, a co-sovereign of the universe, for man partakes of the very being of God. This is the humanism of the ancient pagan kingdoms, and it blends well with the godless humanism of the twentieth century that, by denying God, raises man's position to that of co-creator with the impersonal laws of evolution—the humanist's substitute for providence. Cayce's voice stated:

> As has been indicated by some, ye are part and parcel of a Universal Consciousness, or God. And thus (part) of all that is within, the Universal Consciousness, or Universal Awareness: as the stars, the planets, the Sun and the Moon.
> Do ye rule them or do they rule thee? They were made for thine own use, as an individual. Yea, that is the part (they play), the thought which thy Maker, thy Father-God, thinks of thee. For ye are as a corpuscle in the body of God; thus a co-creator with Him, in what ye think and in what ye do.[40]

A few *ye's* and *thee's* and *thy's* do not orthodoxy make. Those people who associate the seventeenth-century grammar of the King James Bible with the content of the Bible are apt to be misled by such revelations. No doubt, that is why the Cayce readings often (though not always) used such stilted phrases. Cayce incorporated the philosophy of the readings into his own Sunday school lessons, but he was careful to update the language. *The Edgar Cayce Reader* presents his own interpretations of the voice messages that he could not remember, but which were taken down by his secretary. He became a *pantheist:* "Life isn't a bit different today from what it was a million years ago. Life is one. God is Life—whether in the oyster, the tree, or in us. Life is God and a manifestation of Him."[41] Yet men, in this karma-directed life are not yet one with God, despite the fact that all life is a manifestation of God's being. A reading revealed that "there has been given to each soul that privilege, that choice, of being one with the Creative Forces."[42] Man was once a part of God, was separated from God, still is a manifestation of God, and is slowly—ever so slowly—returning to be in God once again. The process of evolutionary karma gives all souls not only second chances, but an infinite number of chances, to work off the effects of transgression. Given enough time and reincarnations, men can pay off their debts—debts owed not to an omnipotent, personal God, but to the karmic laws.

In Cayce's theology, God is identified with Universal Forces, also called Universal Awareness. Ultimately, however, God is identified with man's own "higher consciousness," a concept common to virtually all occult groups. In Cayce's readings, as in some of the other cults, this is referred to as the "I AM" consciousness. "Let yourself enter into deep meditation so that the I AM consciousness may make you more aware of how the purpose of this experience may be applicable in your life now. This is highly to be desired."[43] This is the search for the *deity within.* "It is not, then, to be a calling upon, a depending upon, a seeking for, that which is without, outside of self; but rather the attuning of self to the divine within, which is a universal, or the universal, consciousness. . . ."[44] Because man can venture inward, he can tap the infinite powers of the universe. The goal, ultimately, is *power.* "What is the power of the soul, then? All that is within the infinite itself! All of that! It is ours!"[45] Hugh Lynn Cayce, summarizing the essence of his father's religion, points to the internalization of the universe—a mystical quest which leads, in Cornelius Van Til's superb phrase, to the *integration into the void.*

> It seems reasonable that the path of the spiritual quest, the returning to a state of spiritual awareness, must surely at times lead inward, past the dark areas of accumulated guilt and prejudice, fears and frustrations resulting from many false starts, to the lighted areas of the creative or God-mind. Unless we can believe that such areas of the self exist—where we can meet God face to face—we are doomed to a self-created world of confusion and perhaps self-annihilation. . . . This is a venture inward.[46]

Jesus, Karma, and Evolution

Karma, the doctrine of reincarnation, is the *central dogma* of the Cayce movement, just as it is in Sybil Leek's version of witchcraft. Karma is the ancient

Eastern belief that all souls—to the extent that they are personal at all—must live numerous lives, sometimes rising toward God, sometimes falling away from God, but always getting another chance. The good or evil that a man does in each life has an effect on all subsequent lives. The phrase that appeared in many of the readings, and that appears in all of the Cayce books, is the biblical phrase, "You must reap what you sow." Not in a final judgment, as the Bible affirms, but in endless reincarnations. It does not take a genius to understand that this view of man must affirm that *man is fundamentally good*; no evil act, no matter how perverse, can alienate man from God forever. His good deeds can, given a sufficient number of reincarnations, compensate for the evils of all previous lives—a belief denying the biblical view of law affirmed by St. James: "For whosoever shall keep the whole law, and yet offend in one point, he is guilty of all" (James 2:10). The apostle Paul wrote: 'Therefore by the deeds of the law there shall no flesh be justified in his sight . . .'' (Romans 3:20). Only by the perfect fulfilling of the law by Jesus Christ, which he came to fulfill (Matthew 5:17), can men be viewed by God as righteous; Christ died for the sins of many (Romans 5:6–11). To use a crude analogy, one transgression of the law is like a zero. In all schemes of reincarnation, zeros are added up, and positive deeds can register. In the biblical view, zeros are multiplied by the string of deeds: one zero nullifies the entire product. The two systems are antithetical.

Out of One came many. This is the religion of the East. It is Cayce's faith: "In the beginning was the Word, the Word was God, the Word was with God. 'HE MOVED'. Hence, as He moved, Souls, portions of Himself, came into being."[47] This rewriting of the first chapter of the Gospel of John is a mirror image of that gospel. Souls did not come out of a God who moved; they came from a God who *spoke*. His fiat creation was by the power of His word. Not so in Eastern systems of thought, and the Creator-creature distinction is blurred. Therefore, the process of souls over time is back into the One. Cayce's trance readings are the revelations of the East.

The revelations are peculiar, even by Eastern standards. They affirmed a very strange story of the origin of men. There were two separate waves of souls. The first wave was "thought forms" that tried to imitate God's creation. These were the "Sons of Man." (They were not, of course; they turn out to be the fathers of animals and stones.) These thought forms immersed themselves in the earth, in rocks, trees, and animals. They could not escape their own creations, however, so a second wave of souls, the "Sons of God," intervened. They came to rescue their brethren. This wave was led by the Master, who is known to us, in one of his incarnations, as Jesus. They fashioned or evolved human bodies by means of thought forms. Meanwhile, the first wave went on creating, producing monsters: winged, feathered, hoofed, and clawed "men," plus dragons and other weird beasts. But the Master's souls continued to create, and thus the five races of man were formed at one time. This took place about one million B.C.[48]

Later on, Atlantis was formed (300,000 B.C.). The Master took on a human form at this point, 700,000 years after the creation of the five races. He was called Amilius, or Adam. Here is the heart of Cayce's *soteriology*, his doctrine of salvation. The Master, as Amilius-Adam, fell ethically.

Question: When did Jesus become aware that he would be the Saviour of the world?
Answer: When he fell in Eden.[49]

Eden, as later readings seem to imply, was Atlantis. Then the Master began his series of incarnations. He subsequently became, among others: Enoch, Melchizedek, Joseph (son of Jacob and Rachel), Joshua, Zend (father of Zoroaster), Asapha or Alfa (an Egyptian), and finally Jesus.[50] He was incarnated a total of thirty times, which the voice affirmed as a very low number to achieve perfection.[51] The Master's real name was Jeshua. He was also Hermes, the builder of the Great Pyramid of Egypt. Amazingly enough, his partner in this important task was the priest RaTa, who was an early incarnation of . . . Edgar Cayce![52]

The identification of Jesus with Hermes is extremely significant in occult circles. The Egyptian god Thoth was identified as Hermes by the Greeks, also referred to as Hermes Trismegistus (thrice great). The importance ascribed to Hermes Trismegistus by early medieval magicians, astrologers, and occultists cannot be overstressed. The development of Renaissance magic around the legends of Hermes has been studied exhaustively by Frances Yates. Hermes was understood as the real founder of the magical arts. Miss Yates makes a shrewd observation concerning the "cult of Egypt" in the second century, when the legend of Hermes originated. It fits the Cayce cult quite well:

> The men of the second century were thoroughly imbued with the idea (which the Renaissance imbibed from them) that what is old is pure and holy, that the earliest thinkers walked more closely with the gods than the busy rationalists, their successors. Hence the strong revival of Pythagoreanism in this age. They also had the impression that what is remote and far distant is more holy; hence their cult of the "barbarians," of Indian gymnosophists, Persian magi, Chaldean astrologers, whose approach to knowledge was felt to be more religious than that of the Greeks. In the melting-pot of the Empire, in which all religions were tolerated, there was ample opportunity for making acquaintance with oriental cults. Above all, it was the Egyptians who were revered in this age. . . . The belief that Egypt was the original home of all knowledge, that the great Greek philosophers had visited it and conversed with Egyptian priests, had long been current, and, in the mood of the second century, the ancient and mysterious religion of Egypt, the supposed profound knowledge of its priests, their ascetic way of life, the religious magic which they were thought to perform in the subterranean chambers of their temples, offered immense attractions.[53]

That Hermes-Jesus and RaTa-Cayce had once worked together on that greatest of all magical and occult projects, the Great Pyramid, no doubt sent a wave of anticipation down the spines of Cayce's followers. Here was Cayce, RaTa reincarnate, launching yet another work of mysterious power and mysterious knowledge. They would be a part of it. Hugh Lynn Cayce may not have accepted the mumbo-jumbo of reincarnation, preferring instead to see the venture inward as a psychological operation, but his followers seem not to have been equally sophisticated. The stories of the reincarnations, especially concerning Jeshua-Jesus, are referred to in numerous Cayce-related volumes.

The Master, Jesus, was a man. Until the very end of his reincarnation cycles,

Jesus was a fallen man. When he went into the wilderness, he went "to meet that which had been His undoing in the beginning."[54] What we have in the life of Jesus of Nazareth, therefore, is a fine ethical *example*: "In that the man, Jesus, manifested in the world the Oneness of His will with the Father, He becomes—from man's viewpoint—the only, the first begotten of the Father. Thus he is the example to the world, whether Jew, Gentile or any other religious force."[55] Jesus is the humanistic example of the good life, even the final good life which overcomes all our former and imperfect lives.

> Q. What is the significance and meaning of the words "Jesus" and "Christ" as they should be understood and applied?
> A. Jesus is the man—the activity, the mind, the relationships that He bore to others. Yea, he was mindful of friends, He was sociable, He was loving, He was kind, He was gentle. He grew faint. He grew weak, and yet gained that strength which He has promised in becoming the Christ, by fulfilling and overcoming the world. Ye are made strong in body, in mind, in soul and purpose, by that power in Christ. The power, then, is in the Christ. The pattern is Jesus.[56]

There is nothing in these words that could offend the heterodoxy of three generations of Social Gospel preachers, seminary professors, and run-of-the-mill humanists. What is fundamental in Cayce's doctrine of Jesus, which he shares with virtually every other occult group now popular with the young, is not Jesus the God-man whose death satisfied the justice of a personal, holy God, but, rather, the *Christ-Consciousness*, which is available to every man. The Protestant idea that every man, regenerated by Christ, serves as prophet, priest, and king, because Christ was the ultimate prophet, priest and king, is twisted in the philosophies of the occult groups into the idea that every man is his own Jesus, his own savior.

> Q. 16 The problem which concerns the proper symbols, or similes, for the Master, the Christ. Should Jesus be described as the Soul who first went through the cycle of earthly lives to attain perfection including perfection in the planetary lives also?
> A. 16 He should be. This is as the man [he was], see?
>
> Q. 17 Should this be described as a voluntary mission [on the part of] One who was already perfected and returned to God, having accomplished His oneness in other planes and systems?
> A. 17 Correct.
>
> Q. 18 Should the Christ-Consciousness be described as the awareness within each soul, imprinted in pattern on the mind and waiting to be awakened by the will, of the soul's oneness with God?
> A. 18 Correct. That's the idea exactly.[57]

When asked the meaning of *resurrection* from the dead, the voice replied that it meant *reincarnation*, "which is what the word meant in those days."[58] Since all men are reincarnated, all men are continually resurrected. There is a doctrine of atonement in the Cayce readings, and it involved the shedding of blood for the unjust.[59] But he who died was only a man—a perfect man, of course, but a man. It was a man who fully restored himself to God. The example of Jesus is clearly the example of self-atonement and personal self-sacrifice. Jesus "is an example for Man and only as a man, for He lived only as a man. He died only as a man."[60] If Jesus was a savior, then each man must also be a savior. "Each and every soul must be the Savior of some other soul, to even comprehend the purpose of the entrance of the Son into the earth."[61] This is the salvation of humanism—the soteriology of Satan.

Cayce gave 2,500 of these "life readings" throughout his career. People were fascinated with the information regarding their supposed past lives. An amazing number of the ones recorded in the Cayce books were lives of people who had some connection to the ministry of Jesus. One that fills up many pages in *Edgar Cayce's Story of Jesus* concerns a woman, Judy, who in a former life was Josie, the teacher of Jesus. It seems that Jesus was an Essene, a sect about which very little is known, conveniently for the life readings. The life readings of "Judy" and others reveal that the Essenes were deeply involved in the "secret wisdom of the East": astrology, numerology, kabbala, reincarnation—all the things so dear to middle-aged ladies from Pasadena, former LSD trippers, and dropouts from Berkeley. It was Josie who helped Mary and Joseph flee from Palestine and go to Egypt. Predictably, the readings revealed that Jesus was initiated into the secrets of Egypt. (The way the stories have been getting out for 2,500 years, it is amazing that there are any secrets of Egypt left.) She was also there when Jesus studied in Persia and India.[62] (Over and over, the story of Jesus' training in Eastern mysteries comes up in the literature of the higher-consciousness cults.) Jesus may have been a Jew, but his connection to Egypt was crucial: "For as indicated oft by this channel (Cayce), the unification of the teachings of many lands were [*sic*] brought together in Egypt; for that was the center from which there was to be the radial activity of influence of the earth. . . ."[63]

There is not a single shred of evidence that Jesus ever set foot in an Egyptian temple, for his family returned after the death of Herod (Matthew 2:15), who died in 4 B.C. At age twelve, he was in Jerusalem, arguing with the priests (Luke 2:42). How young were boys initiated into supersecret Egyptian mysteries? As for his travels to Persia and India, there is not a word. This legend is the product of the desire of generations of occultists and neo-Gnostics to insert their anti-Christian ideas into religious circles that are at least officially Christian. Yet it is not simply a strategy of men; the voices of the trances affirm this secret tradition over and over. There is a source of this historical tradition, and it is not earthly, any more than Cayce's ability to report on druggists' shelves from a trance condition was earthly.

There is no final judgment. Judas Iscariot is still working out his salvation on earth, the readings informed the Cayce circle. In fact, one of Cayce's clients was the reincarnated Judas, file number 5770, "a fine man today," the voice affirmed.[64] If Judas gets a second chance, anyone seems safe "For the Father has not willed that any soul should perish and is thus mindful that each soul has again —and again—the opportunity for making its paths straight."[65] There need be no final judgment, for there is no ultimate ethical debt:

> Q. What debt do I owe J. M.?
> A. Only that ye build in thine own consciousness. For every soul, as every tub, must stand upon its own self. And the soul that holds resentment owes the soul to whom it is held—much. Hast thou forgiven him the wrong done to thee? Then thou owest naught![66]

What we have, then, is "not a karmic debt *between* but a karmic debt of *self* that may be worked out *between* the associations that exist in the present."[67] This revelation may not be too clear, but it does relieve men of worrying about a final judgment—or would if it were true. Furthermore, the voice affirmed that this karmic debt of self "is true for every soul."[68] Man saves himself, for he can cancel debts owed to other souls by forgiveness, while he cancels his only other debt—the self-owed karmic debt—by working out his salvation through his own labor.

Salvation is therefore an evolutionary process. "Then, karmic forces—if the life application in the experience of an individual entity GROWS to a haven of peace and harmony and understanding; or ye GROW to heaven, rather than going to heaven; ye grow in grace, in understanding."[69]

> Q. Are souls perfect, as created by God in the first? If so, why is there any need of development?
> A. The answer to this may only be found in the evolution of life, in such a way as to be understood by the finite mind. In the first cause or principle all is perfect. That portion of the whole [manifested in the creation of souls] may become a living soul and equal with the Creator. To reach that position, when separated, it must pass through all stages of development, in order that it may be one with the Creator.[70]

This is the theology of ancient Gnosticism. It involves a steady evolution of spirit back into God. Hugh Lynn Cayce, summarizing his father's faith, writes: "Through the guidance of the Christ-Soul the earth has been made a ladder up which souls may return to a consciousness of at-onement with the Creator. Through a series of incarnations in matter in human form the soul can learn to cleanse itself of selfish desires blocking its more perfect understanding and to apply spiritual law in relation to matter. Urges created in the material plane must be met and overcome, or used, in the material plane."[71] This concern with matter, in contrast to ethical rebellion, is characteristic of all Gnostic sects.

Orthodox Christianity teaches that men will have their bodies restored to perfection—material bodies. We shall be like Jesus, the incarnate son of God, in His perfect humanity (I Corinthians 15). Men were made in the image of God; they do not partake of God's divinity. For Gnostics and mystics, perfect humanity, being material, is imperfect. Nothing less than divinity, than reigning co-equal with God and in God, will suffice. Man is, in the final analysis, God. At the end of evolution, he enters the Godhead. Man, by his own labors, creates his own divinity. "In the day ye eat thereof, then your eyes shall be opened, and ye shall be as gods . . ." (Genesis 3:5). Some ideas never lose their glitter in the eyes of those who are not satisfied with the limitations of creaturehood.

The process of salvation, in Cayce's scheme, is one of increasing one's own merit. Each man receives such information as he merits, the voice informed Cayce's stenographer.[72] Thus, it is a system based on the affirmation of autonomous man, the self-savior of his soul. Gina Cerminara, the most straightforwardly anti-Christian, pro-reincarnation of the Cayce writers, summarizes the essence of Cayce's doctrine of salvation. What she writes is applicable to any system of karmic cosmology. Where the doctrine of reincarnation is preached, this perspective, in one form or another, will invariably be present:

> For almost twenty centuries the moral sense of the Western world has been blunted by a theology which teaches the vicarious atonement of sin through Christ, the Son of God. Even skeptics, in the face of the strange events and the tremendous influence that emanated from this man, may concede that Christ was in a sense a Son of God and that —noble and compassionate—he lived and died so that men might be free. But more and more, in the light of the advances of modern physics, people are coming to feel that all life in the universe, down to the minutest power-charged atom, is in essence related to each other life in the universe by virtue of a common sustaining source in one central energy, or God. By this view it seems necessary to conclude that all living things, and all men and women, are the sons of God—like rays from some vast central sun. It can be felt then that perhaps the personality called Jesus was different from us only in that he was closer to the central light than we are.
>
> Moreover, Christ's giving of his life that men might be free is no unique event in history; the study of comparative religions reveals other saviours, among other peoples, who suffered martyrdom and death. In our own Western culture, many idealists have given their lives willingly for humanity's sake, Mazzini, Bolivar, Lincoln, St. Francis, Toussaint L'Ouverture, Semmelweiss, St. Teresa—a hundred names and more can be cited of men and women who lived and died that other human beings might be free. But no one feels that their effort redeems us from effort, or that their sacrifice absolves us of our own personal guilt.
>
> To build these two statements, therefore—that Christ was the Son of God and that he died for man's salvation—into a dogma, has been the great psychological crime not of Christianity but of some of its theologians. It is a psychological crime because it places responsibility for redemption on something external to the self; it makes salvation dependent on belief in the divinity of another person rather than on self-transformation through belief in one's own intrinsic divinity. It violates the sense of justice and psychological verisimilitude because it declares that belief in vicarious atonement is necessary, the penalty for non-belief being everlasting damnation. Twentieth-century minds, trained rigorously in physical and psychological sciences, find it difficult to take such a doctrine seriously.[73]

I have quoted this statement at length, since it is one of the finest statements of what Christianity does hold and why a person with a Ph.D. in psychology, such as Dr. Cerminara, is willing to swallow the Cayce cosmology hook, line, and sinker. *It conforms far better with the humanist thought of the twentieth century!* Parapsychologists are unlikely to believe in either Cayce's karma theories or orthodox Christianity, but if it were a question of one or the other, Cayce would win every time. The humanist's dream of a man-created universe is shared by the trance message-giver Edgar Cayce. Karma is another form of humanism, or better yet, humanism is a modern version of the traditional view of man held by reincarnationists. It is a rival religion. Furthermore, Dr. Cerminara makes clear, it must be believed in, just as Christians claim that Christ must be believed in. He who refuses to believe in the reality of karmic laws must suffer karmic justice: "But whether karma is regarded as a debt or a deficit or a sort of spiritual deficiency, the fact remains that its redemption must be approached in a spirit of willingness rather than of rebellion. To 'deny' its existence partakes more of the nature of rebellion than of acquiescence; for such a 'denial' is expressive of the self-will and desire for convenience of the present personality, rather than the long-term wisdom of the eternal identity."[74] And also like Christianity, for those who believe, there is perfect peace: "In the universe of order and justice and beneficence which the reincarnation principle reveals, there is no need for fear."[75] Hebrews 9:27, 28 says there is a whole eternity to fear. One cannot hold both positions. Each side knows it. Or at least the consistent ones do.

If we are to believe Dr. Cerminara, the doctrine of reincarnation has an important social and political corollary: *the irrelevance of institutional forms.*

> Marriage as an institution is, by the reincarnationist view, less sacrosanct than many people think. If society wishes to make marriage indissoluble, well and good; if not, again well and good. Cosmic law will not be thwarted by either system—if man fails to meet an obligation in one existence, he will irrevocably be called to task in another. The outer forms which man sets up are almost as arbitrary and almost as unimportant as the rules he devises for gin rummy. In the last analysis it matters very little what rules are set up for any game, because through the forms and conventions of all of them it is skill and honesty in playing which are their intrinsic value.[76]

On the one hand, this is *radically antinomian*. It denies that there is any form of social order that is dictated by the limits and needs of mankind. But this is consistent with the humanism of karma: man is ultimately limitless. Therefore, by becoming radically antinomian, the reincarnationist opens up the possibility of *radical authoritarianism*. There is no ethical principle, no higher law, to which men can appeal except social convention. Men must conform, in a Dewey-like fashion, to the rules of society. The Moloch state, as Rushdoony has called it, is set free from the restraining features of godly law. Men are left defenseless to play the institutional games of the totalitarian regime. The worst, as Hayek has said, will tend to get on top of such a coercive state system.[77]

Cayce's movement has proven to be quietistic and retreatist, waiting for Atlantis and California earthquakes. They wait for China to become the new cradle of Christianity, as predicted.[78] (Unfortunately, China did not turn democratic in 1968, as predicted.)[79] They wait for the Soviet Union to change its present leadership, for a prophecy told them that "out of Russia comes again the hope of the world."[80] Not from Bolshevism, but from a reawakening of freedom: Russia's future will be crucial. So they wait, and hope, and study the great prophecies. And the A.R.E. collects its royalties and continues its training in ESP techniques, one of the gateways to "higher consciousness" or "Christ consciousness."

Vibrations

An occult corollary to the doctrine of karma is the theory that life is essentially a series of universal vibrations. As mentioned in a previous chapter, the use of the term *vibrations* by the counterculture was no accident. The sources of the phrase are the many groups that are in, or on the fringes of, the occult underground. Everything is a vibration. One Cayce reading revealed: "The human body is made up of electronic vibrations, with each atom and element of the body, each organ and organism, having its electronic unit of vibration necessary for the sustenance of, and equilibrium in, that particular organism."[81] There is no fundamental difference between the realm of spirit and the realm of matter. "For things spiritual and things material are but the same conditions of the same element, raised to different vibrations. For all force is one force."[82]

The emphasis on the healing ministry of Edgar Cayce is obvious in the literature, although it is subordinate to the emphasis on his philosophy-cosmology. Healing is an activity of vibrations. "Life in its expression in a human body is of an electrical nature. The vibrations from low electrical forces, rather than the high vibrations, produce life-flowing effects."[83] Even more specifically, the color green "is the healing vibration."[84]

Vibrations relate to the human aura. The idea that each man possesses an aura is common to the occult tradition. The attempt by occultists to link the aura to the radiations revealed by Kirlian photography is an example of the relationship between paranormal scientific research and occultism. Cayce asserted that he could see auras around people—not in his trances, but during the normal daily activities. (Castaneda and Don Juan maintain the same thing.) This ability that Cayce said he had is mentioned by several of his followers.[85] He was supposedly able to diagnose people's moods by the color of their auras, indicating that the supposed phenomenon is not constant, but reflective of the human personality. These auras are visualized vibrations.[86]

Nevertheless, the most important teaching connected to the vibration theory is that *God is a vibration.* Understanding this fact, the trance voice informed its listeners, is the key to one's personal salvation. This is the soteriology of vibrations.

> For without passing through each and every stage of development, there is not the correct vibration to become one with the Father. . . . Then in the many stages of development throughout the Universe or in the great system of the Universal Forces, each stage of development is made manifest through the flesh—which is the testing portion of the Universal Vibration. In this manner, then, and for this reason, all are made manifest in flesh and there is the development through aeons of time and space, called Eternity.[87]

Vibrations, in short are the key to evolution. They are also related to astrological influences: "Each planetary influence vibrates at a different rate of vibration. An entity entering that influence enters that vibration: [it is] not necessary that he change, but it is the grace of God that he may! It is part of the Universal Consciousness, the Universal Law."[88] Nevertheless, it is not the planets that determine life; it is the *will of man*. The voice was very specific on that point: "But let it be understood here, no action of any planet or any of the phases of the sun, moon, or any of the heavenly bodies surpass the rule of man's individual will power. . . ."[89] God, the Great Vibration, is secondary at best, probably tertiary and possibly not half so powerful as the color green.

Garbled Messages

One problem faced by all occult mediums is that the messages from "the other side" are often incoherent. It is as if the wisdom of the spirit world gets short-circuited from time to time, leaving the recipients of this wisdom with the vague feeling that the spirits have been drinking steadily for days. Yet the language is always very profound, totally self-assured. For example:

> First, the continuity of life. There is no time; it is one time; there is no space; it is one space; there is no force; it is one force; other than all force in its various phases and applications of force are the emanations of men's endeavors in a material world to exemplify an ideal of a concept of the creative energy, or God, of which the individual is such a part that the thoughts even of the individual may become crimes or miracles, for thoughts are deeds and applied in the sense that these are in accord with those principles as given. That [which] one applies will be applied again and again until that oneness, time, space, force, or the own individual is one with the whole, not the whole with such a portion of the whole as to be equal with the whole.[90]

Got that? If so, then perhaps you are ready for the voice's answer to a question concerning the Sons of the Highest in Atlantis and the second coming of souls to earth:

> There was, with the will of that as came into being through the correct channels, of that as created by the Creator, that of the continuing of the souls in its projection and projection—see? While in that as was of the offspring, of that as pushed itself into form to satisfy, gratify, that of the desire of that known as carnal forces of the senses, of those created, there continued to be the war one with another and there were then— from the other sources (worlds) the continuing entering of those that would make for the keeping of the balance, as of the first purpose of the Creative Forces, as it magnifies itself in that given sphere of activity, of that that had been given the ability to create with its own activity—see?[91]

Frankly, I am perfectly willing to admit that I do *not* see. It is way, way beyond my powers of comprehension. When one worker asked the sleeping Cayce in 1932, "How can the language used in the readings be made clearer, more concise and more direct?" the voice was concise and direct: "Be able to understand it better."[92] Doris Agee nevertheless gives us hope: "Just as you found when you first encountered Shakespeare or Chaucer, familiarity with the particular 'shape' of the language will make you more comfortable with it."[93] I never did get used to Chaucer's 600-year-old English, but at least there are translators and commentators for Chaucer. So far, at least, Cayce's 1932 English is without a translator for a considerable portion of his revelations. Only it is not a translation problem.

Conclusion

Edgar Cayce was a man who saw auras, he said; read people's minds, he said; received visions and revelations throughout his life, he said; and was not an occultist, he said. He did go into something like 25,000 trances over the years, and the records of over 15,000 of them are still available for inspection by researchers. He has been the subject of dozens of books. There seems to be no serious evidence available that he faked the trances; if he did, the motive is obscure. Some of his prophecies and diagnoses—of a minutely detailed kind—did turn out as he has said. These served as the bedrock for the construction of a humanistic, occult cosmology: reincarnation, vibrations, evolution, monism, pantheism, etheric planes of existence, and so forth. What is central to the Cayce movement is his *cosmology*, not the "signs and wonders" that served as the magical validation of the later philosophy.

Max Weber, the great German sociologist, defined charismatic authority as that possessed by some unique personality because of certain magical qualities or demonstrations—the Bible's signs and wonders—"by virtue of which he is treated as endowed with supernatural, superhuman, or at least specifically exceptional powers. . . ."[94] Because of these powers or qualities, he is considered a leader. His rule is characterized by hostility to all other forms of authority, whether bureaucratic [rational] or traditional. He comes with the words, "You have heard it said . . . but I say unto you. . . ." To a very great extent, this classification applies to Cayce. He possessed the unique abilities, and once he had established a small following, primarily confined to his family and close friends, he was then able to take the traditional language of Christian orthodoxy—"you have heard it said"—and transform the meaning into the commonplace, but seemingly revolutionary, interpretations of Gnostic mysticism—"but I say unto you." Given the enormous popularity of Cayce-related materials, it would seem that as a charismatic prophet, he was quite successful.

The reasons why the movement has spread are varied. First, it is basic to the post-1964 times: antiestablishment, inquisitive, curious about the unexplained, interested in new avenues of power, desperate to establish new forms of community. Yet at the same time, Cayce's philosophy is thoroughly at one with the underlying presuppositions of modern thought: relativistic, man-centered, hostile to Christian dogma, universalist, messianic. His is a system of *process* philosophy, so deeply ingrained in Western thought since Darwin.

> Now is Truth such a thing that those who have been followers of Mohammed have *all of the truth*? Have those who have been the followers of Moses, the law-givers, all of

the truth? Or hasn't it been, rather, a growth in our individual lives; and what may be truth for one individual may not, in the experience of another individual, answer at all? Does that make the other any less true for the other individual?. . . Then if this be true, it is possible that truth is a changeable thing—is a growth.[95]

Truth is totally man-centered, "the essence with which an individual builds faith, hope and trust." It is, in "theologian" Paul Tillich's popular phrase, an "ultimate concern." Man constructs his own truth, his own God: "[W]hat you hold before yourself, to create that image you worship—that is what will develop you always upward, and will continue to enable you to know truth."[96] Cayce then came to a doctrine of truth and God that is essentially Hegelian-fascist-Marxist:

> Truth, then, being a growing thing; truth, being a thing that will develop you; is a something that is *entirely in action!* That's what God is! For in every *movement* that has ever been, there has been a continual upward development—upward toward that which is Truth. . . . What is prayer but simply attuning yourself to that which you are seeking assistance through? That's all prayer is—the attunement to that very same thing; and *that becomes Truth when it becomes an action.* When it goes into action, to you it becomes Truth. . . . You go on whichever way your standard is set.[97]

Whether Hegel is writing of the movement of the dialectic, or Marx of the unity of theory and practice, or Mussolini of the necessity of a life of pure action, the evolutionary thrust leads to total, uncompromising *relativism.* No wonder Cayce's cosmology—on the surface so archaic—could have attracted so many modern followers. It holds out that most ancient of modern heresies: the desire to worship oneself as God. Man, made in the image of God, wishes to worship an image rather than the Creator. The first commandment prohibits this practice, but Cayce asks, "Why not?"

> Why not? Because if you make an image, it becomes your God. But if you have for your God that which is within your own individual self—you yourself being a portion of the Creator—you will continue to build upward, to it![98]

Or downward, downward—into the fiery void.

Edgar Cayce's writings, and the writings about him, reflect a striking continuity of thought, from Gnostic speculations in the century following Christ to the present. He was not a profound man. He did not build a large organization. But he left a huge body of written materials, so vital in this day of footnotes and verification. As a representative of occultist philosophy, he is far more personal and believable than a Madame Blavatsky, more readable than Alice Bailey and the publications of her Lucis Trust. He shares most of the central ideas of the rival Gnostic groups, but his work seems so humane, and his modesty was so remarkable, that the average middle-class humanist can hardly resist "the sleeping prophet." They do not recognize the source of his revelations. It all seems so curious; at worst it seems innocuous.

The Cayce movement is indeed a curiosity. It is not innocuous. Ideas do have consequences.

7
Demonic Healing

> Thou shalt not bow down to their gods, nor serve them, nor do after their works: but thou shalt utterly overthrow them, and quite break down their images. And ye shall serve the LORD your God, and he shall bless thy bread, and thy water; and I will take sickness away from the midst of thee.
>
> *Exodus 23:24, 25*

There is probably no educational guild more outspoken in its claim to a technical monopoly than modern medicine, and none more confident in its claims than American medicine. The idea that alternative forms of healing exist is immediately treated as the promotion of quacks—*quack* being defined as anyone who claims to be able to accomplish healing apart from the techniques and presuppositions of modern medicine. While the overwhelming number of sicknesses are treated outside the office of a physician—home remedies, self-diagnosis and cure, chiropractic, and the old favorite, two aspirins and plenty of rest—there is little doubt that most modern Americans believe that healing is accomplished by means that are scientifically explainable in principle, if not in fact at the present. (No one knows exactly how an aspirin relieves a headache.) This is the every essence of modern intellectualism. Max Weber, the great German scholar, set forth the basic principles of the modern worldview in 1918:

> Scientific progress is a fraction, the most important fraction, of the process of intel-

lectualization which we have been undergoing for thousands of years and which nowadays is usually judged in such an extremely negative way. [The antirationalistic themes of the post-1965 counterculture were in vogue half a century earlier.—G.N.] Let us first clarify what this intellectualist rationalization, created by science and by scientifically oriented technology, means practically.

Does it mean that we, today, for instance, everyone sitting in this hall, have a greater knowledge of the conditions of life under which we exist than has an American Indian or a Hottentot? Hardly. Unless he is a physicist, one who rides on the streetcar has no idea how the car happened to get into motion. And he does not need to know. He is satisfied that he may "count" on the behavior of the streetcar, and he orients his conduct according to this expectation; but he knows nothing about what it takes to produce such a car so that it can move. The savage knows incomparably more about his tools. . . . The increasing intellectualization and rationalization do *not*, therefore, indicate an increased and general knowledge of the conditions under which one lives.

It means something else, namely, the knowledge or belief that if one but wished one *could* learn it at any time. Hence, it means that principally there are no mysterious incalculable forces that come into play, but rather that one can, in principle, master all things by calculation. This means that the world is disenchanted. One need no longer have recourse to magical means in order to master or implore the spirits, as did the savage, for whom such mysterious powers existed. Technical means and calculations perform the service. This above all is what intellectualization means.[1]

The disenchantment of the world: here is one of Weber's most powerful and influential themes. Unquestionably, the development of modern, Western thought, especially since 1660, has promoted this process of disenchantment. The average man believes in God, but he also believes in technology and science, and he looks to these for answers to problems of physical pain and biological affliction. The escape from pain is perhaps the most revered development of the modern world. Ask anyone what scientific advance over the last century he would least be willing to abandon forever, and if the list includes anesthetics, it will be checked off more readily than any other. Yet the use of anesthetics is primarily surgical; modern man believes in cutting. Four centuries ago, only elitist scientists and occultists believed such a thing (and both drew upon the illegal services of graverobbers). But the cutting today must be guided by rational, scientific knowledge.

"It should not be surprising that Edgar Cayce's feats of trance-induced medical diagnosis and prescription are dismissed out of hand by professional medical men. Such practices must be invalid, by definition. Not only are they unsubstantiated claims made by unprofessional occultists and mystics, but the claims are, by their very nature, unverifiable by the *only* accepted criteria of validation: the investigative techniques of rationalization. Such claims *must* result from fraud, self-delusion, madness, or ignorance of valid testing procedures. Interestingly enough, this same set of explanations was used by Reginald Scot to deny the occult power of the social phenomenon of witchcraft. He wrote his *Discoverie of Witchcraft* back in 1584, and the same old rationalistic arguments are still in current use by his intellectual heirs.

Nevertheless, in the field of nonrationalistic healing, or paranormal healing, or, most accurately, demonic healing, Cayce was remarkable only within the confines of urbanized America. He left more records than anyone else—a peculiarly Western concern. But in terms of volume of healings, rapidity of diagnosis, and the rationalistically impossible nature of the cures, no one in man's recorded history has ever approached Brazil's Jose Arigo.

Arigo

The story of Arigo is now known by millions of people outside Brazil. The *Reader's Digest*, which has a larger circulation worldwide than any other magazine, included a condensed version of John G. Fuller's *Arigo: Surgeon of the Rusty Knife* (1974) in its March 1975 issue. Fuller's study of flying saucers, *Incident at Exeter*, was one of the important books of the mid-1960s that helped to revive public interest in this aspect of the paranormal. His new book is even more startling. It chronicles the life of Jose Pedro de Freitas, who was known from his youth as Arigo (jovial country bumpkin), a Brazilian peasant who possessed incomparable powers of healing. During the two-decade period, 1950–70, Arigo treated as many as *two million* patients; the number may have been less, but only because some may have returned more than once. He saw over three hundred patients per day, five days a week, for almost twenty years. He ran them through his "clinic" for about six hours a day. He spent only about one minute on each patient: diagnosis, treatment, and/or written prescription. If St. Paul could claim historical justification for the resurrection of Christ because Christ was seen by over five hundred people (I Corinthians 15:6) and also defend himself and his account of the resurrection in a court of law by arguing that "this thing was not done in a corner" (Acts 26:26b), then the fact that two million people saw Arigo at work should be very solid evidence. When the Brazilian authorities began an investigation of his healing ministry in order to convict him of that crime of crimes —practicing medicine without a license—they could find no one to testify that he had injured anyone or defrauded him of his money. They finally could convict him only by using the testimony of supporters that he had healed them, since this admission proved that he was indeed practicing medicine, and had no license. When no complaints out of two million possible clients can be ferreted out by the authorities, it seems safe to say that Arigo had a most remarkable practice. If he were in the United States today, he might well be the only medical practitioner who might be profitably insurable by the insurance companies against malpractice suits at rates that anyone could reasonably afford.

The volume of patients is only the tip of the implausible iceberg. His method of operation was to take a simple pocketknife, jab it into the body of the patient (usually his eye), twist it around violently, reach in and pull out the growth or whatever, seal up the flesh in a matter of seconds without stitches, and send the patient on his way. And most implausible by the standards of modern medicine, he accepted no pay. ("The story *has* to be false, then," the skeptic will say.) There was no pain for the patients, no fear, little bleeding (if there was, he could command it to stop), and no scarring. This process was recorded on movie film on numerous occasions, witnessed by physicians at close range, run and rerun in slow motion. No one ever detected a single sign of fraud, manipulation, or sleight of hand. On occasion, he would leave the knife stuck in a person's eye while he turned around to pick up tweezers or another implement, returning to his jabbing and twisting a few moments later. This was hardly a repeatable stunt, yet physicians witnessed it on many occasions. (We are still waiting for the Amazing Randi to offer to duplicate it on the "Johnny Carson Show" in front of a team of M.D.s. No doubt he will claim that he could do it, but he is busy doing stage work in Cincinnati.)

Like so many of the faith healers and miracle workers, he had not been a good student. Several of his brothers had gone on to higher education, but after dropping out of third grade, Arigo returned to the family farm. From his earliest years, he had experienced flashes of eerie light and hallucinations, but they were relatively infrequent and he refused to discuss them. Also like so many occultists who display paranormal powers, he would hear a voice that spoke in a strange language.[2] He grew up where he finally died, in a small town about 250 miles north of Rio, Congonhas do Campo. He married in 1943 at the age of twenty-five.

In his early working days as an adult, he labored as a miner, walking to the mine seven miles each way. He became a union organizer and then its president. The union struck, was compelled by the authorities to return to work, and that ended Arigo's years in the mines. When he resigned his presidency, he opened a restaurant, dabbled in real estate, and sold used cars. His visions increased, too, primarily in dreams. The voice continued to speak to him in these dreams, and he recognized the language as German. He kept dreaming of a hospital operating room.[3]

Finally the voice identified itself. It claimed that it was the spirit of Dr. Adolpho Fritz, a German physician who had died in 1918. He announced that he intended to use Arigo to complete his as yet unfinished work. He did not explain why a Brazilian peasant was necessary to complete the work of a German physician. Arigo awoke from this dream-hallucination and ran screaming into the streets, naked. Friends had to lead him home. Headaches began, and nothing could cure them, including an official church exorcism. Finally he capitulated to "Dr. Fritz," consenting to participate in his work. According to Arigo, the headaches immediately ceased, beginning again only when he later temporarily agreed to discontinue the healings. Like Edgar Cayce, Arigo was possessed; without becoming a healer, he could not avoid the headaches and dreams, just as Cayce could not maintain his voice. Arigo was trapped.

The healings began on a small-scale basis. He would issue verbal commands for them to get well. They were not spectacular, although they gained enough notoriety to draw the warnings of the Roman Catholic church to cease them. He put up a sign: "IN THIS HOUSE, WE ARE ALL CATHOLICS. SPIRITISM IS A THING OF THE DEVIL."[4] The headaches returned, along with daytime blackouts. He was in desperation.

At this point, in 1950, a unique event took place. Senator Bittencourt, a prolabor union politician, swung through Arigo's district in search of votes for the presidential candidate, Getulio Vargas. Arigo still controlled the union's loyalty, and he promised to support Bittencourt. The senator invited Arigo and other miners to attend a rally in nearby Belo Horizonte. Both he and Arigo spent the night in a hotel in Belo Horizonte.

The senator had recently been informed that he was suffering from cancer of the lung. He was told that he required immediate surgery and that he should go to the United States for treatment. He intended to do just that as soon as the campaign was over. That night, as he lay on his bed, Arigo entered his room. He seemed to be in a trance. He was carrying a razor. Bittencourt blacked out. When he awoke the next morning, his pajama top was slashed, blood was on both his chest and his pajama top, and there was a neat incision on his rib cage. He got up, staggered to his closet to get dressed. He was in a state of shock. He went to Arigo and told him what he had seen. Then Arigo went into a state of shock. He had no memory of such a thing. He helped the senator to a taxi, got into his jeep, and drove home.[5]

The senator went to his physician. When X rayed, he learned that all traces of the cancer were gone.[6] This was a miracle. He began to tell people what had happened. He spoke of it in his political speeches. Arigo became an instant celebrity known throughout Brazil. The sick and wounded began streaming to his door. For the next two decades, they continued to come.

Brazil was the perfect place for a man of Arigo's talents. As Professor Bryan Wilson writes, "perhaps there is no society with so rich a profusion of thaumaturgical cults as Brazil. . . ."[7] Elements of African tribal healing magic were imported with the slaves centuries ago. Catholicism, while officially hostile to magical practices, tended to absorb and modify the aboriginal healing traditions. The ancient practices continued. "Tribal deities and deities associated with fixed location," writes Wilson, "necessarily lost significance or acquired new functions among detribalized slaves. The integrative functions of religion for tribal groups were now no longer relevant, but the therapeutic and psychic functions of traditional religion, the practice of thaumaturgy in putting individuals into contact with ancient and traditional sources of power and reassurance, acquired new appeal."[8]

The primary forms of occult healing in Brazil are associated with one of three groups: umbanda, quimbanda, and kardecism. Umbanda is an outgrowth of macumba, an African-originated religion of spirit possession. A rudimentary form of spiritualism, Western in origin, fused with macumba to produce umbanda. The umbanda priests seek communication with long-dead saints. Animal sacrifices are rejected. The priests practice occult healing, although they deny that they are involved in black magic. They distinguish their practices from the outright witchcraft of quimbanda. During spirit possession, umbanda priests and participants frequently speak in tongues, the same phenomenon known in Christian Pentecostal circles as glossalalia.[9] Quite frequently, members of the umbanda cult register as Roman Catholics. Umbanda developed as an independent movement in the early 1930s, but it has gained a mass audience only since World War II.

Far more curious than either umbanda or quimbanda is kardecism. Named after

Allan Kardec, a pseudonym of Leon Hyppolyte Denizart Revaill, a French spiritist (1804–69), kardecists believe in a healing system based on guidance from deceased spirits who guide physicians in both consultations and actual operations. Instead of operating on the physical body, however, kardecists operate on the "etheric body," which is suspended a few inches above the physical body. These healer-mediums actually use surgical instruments in these spirit operations. Supposedly, this operation can heal the physical body, too.[10] The same occult technique is used by the British medium George Chapman, although he does not use instruments, only his hands.[11] Well-trained Brazilian physicians who are licensed to practice medicine by the equivalent of the AMA use kardec techniques. They refer to these techniques as "supplements" to normal medical practice. By 1951, about the time that Arigo began his ministry, there were twenty-one kardec associations in Brazil.[12] It is extremely interesting to compare the doctrines of kardecism with those of the Cayce "readings."

> The principal doctrines of Kardecism are: (1) the possibility and ease of communication with spirits; (2) reincarnation; (3) no cause exists without an effect, so that no one can escape the consequences of his acts; (4) the plurality of inhabited worlds, each of which represents a stage of spiritual progress; (5) no distinction of natural and supernatural, or of science and religion: there is no grace, and individual progress depends exclusively on personal merit accumulated in earlier incarnations; (6) the principal virtue is charity as exercised toward the dead, the disembodied, and the living; (7) God is an immense distance from men; (8) there are important spirit-guides who help men; (9) Jesus Christ was the greatest incarnated being.[13]

With the exception of the idea that God is at an immense distance from men (Cayce's system was monistic, identifying God and the creation), and the idea of showing charity to the dead, the doctrines are virtually identical. Occult healing in Western settings generally is accompanied by a comprehensive and almost universally accepted cosmology, and Wilson's summary of kardecism is a very useful summary for all of the other groups.

The setting was perfect for Arigo. Almost immediately, spiritists throughout Brazil began to claim Arigo for their own. This was especially true of kardecist leaders. Although Arigo initially dismissed the theory, since he wanted to remain in good standing with the church, by 1968 he openly stated: "All my family are Catholic. I am a spiritist. But I believe that all religions take people to God."[14] By that time, the church and the civil authorities had ceased their efforts to stamp out his ministry.

His earliest spectacular cure which was witnessed by a number of people was of a woman with cancer of the uterus. She was dying, and the priest had administered the last rites. Arigo was a friend of the family and had come to pay his respects. Suddenly, the tingling sensation that accompanied a visit by Dr. Fritz—a sensation common to table-raising, Ouija boards, and seance activity—rushed through his system. In a trance, he rushed to the kitchen, grabbed a knife, and ran back into the room. In front of the dazed family, he pulled down the sheet that covered the woman, thrust the knife into her body, and began to twist and jab, widening the opening. Finally, he reached into the wound, yanking out an enormous tumor, which was the size of a small grapefruit. Apart from the blood on the tumor, there was almost no bleeding at all. He returned to the kitchen, dropped the knife and tumor into the sink, and collapsed into a chair. When the family came into the kitchen, he was sobbing.

The physician who had diagnosed the cancer was immediately called to the scene. He found no hemorrhaging. The "patient" said she felt completely relieved. The doctor took the tumor for examination, and the woman subsequently recovered.[15] There was no possible medical explanation for the tumor's removal, her survival, and the disappearance of all traces of cancer. Arigo had performed a miracle, according to the family.

The lines lengthened in front of his door. He would treat people for hours, yet after he was finished, he asserted that he remembered nothing. He wrote long, complicated medical prescriptions in a matter of half a minute, while staring blankly into space. He operated with a pair of scissors, a knife, and perhaps some tweezers. The prescriptions were sometimes for long-forgotten drugs, yet on other occasions they were so new that they were not yet imported into Brazil. The best pharmaceutical firms were used.[16] This later was an important point raised by his defense lawyer in opposition to the charge brought against Arigo of witchcraft. As his biographer writes: "In order to prove witchcraft, it was necessary to prove that a defendant had personally distributed concoctions of roots and herbs. This was clearly a thing Arigo never did."[17] Yet these weird prescriptions, often of abnormally high dosages, did not work when any other physician imitated them. They worked for Arigo and his immediate patients, but not for anyone else.

Carlos Paranhos da Costa Cruz was a dentist in Belo Horizonte, had his office in the same building as the British consul, H. V. Walter. He reported the story of one of Arigo's operations to Walter, who was to become a frequent observer at Arigo's "clinic." Sonja, Cruz's sister-in-law, had cancer of the liver. This, at least, was the diagnosis of several physicians, including her own father. She was deemed inoperable. In desperation, she, Cruz, and her father journeyed to Congonhas do Campo. She got in line, and when she came to Arigo, he asked no questions. He told them she had a tumor on her liver. He insisted on performing an operation. The description of what followed is nothing short of fantastic:

> Within minutes, Sonja was placed on newspapers on the floor of Arigo's small room. Arigo brought some cotton and several instruments, including scissors and knives. He selected a penknife and made an incision. Both Cruz and his father-in-law knew that it was impossible to cut into the liver without massive hemorrhaging, and neither could explain why they permitted this to be done, or why they stood by passively as Arigo cut into the patient with an unsterilized knife and no anesthesia. Perhaps, they thought later, it was because this was the last chance: all else had been given up.
>
> They watched for the blood to spurt out, but only a thin trickle slid from the sides of the wound. Then, Cruz claimed, an even stranger thing happened. Arigo inserted the scissors deep into the wound, removed his hand, and the scissors seemed to move by themselves. Cruz turned to look at his father-in-law, who nodded and exchanged glances. Later, they were to compare notes and confirm, at least to themselves, what

they had seen. In moments, Arigo removed the scissors, reached into the wound, and pulled out a tumorous growth. With a showmanlike flourish, he slapped the tumor into Cruz's hand. Then he took the cotton and wiped it along the incision. When he was finished, the edges of the wound adhered together without stitches and Arigo momentarily placed a crucifix on it. Then he told Sonja to rise, which she was able to do. She was weak and shaky, but felt no pain.[18]

The biopsy of the tumor confirmed that the growth was cancerous. The liver regenerated itself—it is the one major organ that can do this—and the woman lived. Neither Cruz nor his physician father-in-law had any rational explanation for what they had seen. Obviously not; there is no rational explanation, that is, an explanation in terms of laws known to men or conceivably knowable to men. What they had seen was a denial of what Weber described as Western rationalization. It could not happen, rationally speaking. Only it did happen.

Prominent patients now joined the long lines of hopeful visitors. They waited for hours in line; it was first come, first served. (I wonder if "patient" refers to what people have to be in order to get into a physician's inner offices. No other profession has patients rather than clients, only those in the healing profession.) President Kubitschek, the builder of that majestic political pyramid, Brasilia, sent both his daughter and his pilot to visit Arigo, and both were cured. The head of his security police also was treated, and if Arigo was a fraud, this would have been a predictably harsh culmination of his career. Investigating physicians, who were willing to put their reputations on the line, publicly announced that the operations, while unexplainable, were successful: few scars, tissues removed skillfully, valid diagnoses.[19] Operating on Mrs. Maria Silveiro, in the presence of a visiting physician, Dr. Ladeira Margues of Rio, Arigo removed a piece of tissue thirty-one inches long and fifteen inches wide from her ovaries. Dr. Margues later described the incision:

> Arigo was taking hold of one half of the scissors. Then we [he and a safely anonymous physician friend] began to see the other side of the scissors start to move alone. It was as if another hand had taken hold of the free handle and was beginning to make clear motions, causing the scissors to snip and cut. The sound of metals and tissues being cut was obvious. In moments, "Dr. Fritz" removed the scissors. When he saw bleeding begin, he ceased what he was doing, and said: "Lord, let there be no more blood." There was no further hemorrhage, as the operation went on.[20]

The possession of Arigo by a demon should be clear to anyone who takes seriously the biblical doctrine that it is appointed once for man to die and after this, the judgment. It was not a floating soul of a dead physician. Physicians do not have the power to perform the kind of surgery Arigo performed, not even dead Prussian physicians. The ability of Arigo to halt the flow of blood—an ability demonstrated on numerous occasions—is not medical; it is supernatural. But the claims of the wife of Czar Nicholas II of Russia concerning the similar abilities of Rasputin with respect to the young Czarevitch, Alexie, become much more plausible in light of Arigo's skills. The charges of Rasputin's opponents, that he was sinister and even satanic, also seem more believable.

Arigo never signed any of the prescriptions that he was seen to write with lightning speed. Yet the local druggist did a land-office business in filling the complicated prescriptions. The author does not explain the intricacies of Brazilian law respecting medical prescriptions, but since the druggist was never shut down, it appears that the practice was legal. Then again, maybe there were other ways of skinning the bureaucratic cat.

In 1963, Arigo was visited by a pair of investigators into the paranormal, Henry Belk and Henry (Andrija) Puharich, M.D. Both are well known within occult and paranormal circles. Two of Puharich's books, *The Sacred Mushroom* and *Uri*, have created considerable controversy, especially the latter. The word had filtered back to the United States that a Brazilian peasant was performing impossible feats. They had come to test these abilities. Jorge Rizzini, who had previously photographed color moving pictures of Arigo's operations, joined them. His own wife had been cured of arthritis, and his daughter had been cured of leukemia. (Fuller's book reports on several astonishing cures of leukemia by Arigo's prescriptions.)

Arigo welcomed them. Almost immediately, he performed an operation. It was to leave Belk and Puharich totally dumbfounded. He picked up a four-inch paring knife, plunged it into an elderly man's eye socket, and began to scrape. The patient made no sign of being in pain. He also was not afraid. Arigo had Puharich place his finger on the eyelid in order to feel the blade beneath. Puharich confirmed that it was under the flesh. This, Arigo explained, was one of his methods of diagnosis. When he removed the knife, it had pus on it. There had been no bleeding and no scar remained. Total time elapsed: one minute.[21]

At 11 A.M. he left his "clinic" to go to his job as a receptionist in the local social security office. This was his sole source of income, other than his wife's sewing. The job took four hours a day. The Brazilian government obviously had its employees on the dole.[22]

Puharich had developed a nonmalignant growth just under the skin of his right elbow. It was called a lipoma. He knew that it normally took twenty minutes to remove one, under ideal conditions. He decided to test Arigo. Arigo agreed. With Rizzini manning the movie camera, Puharich stepped up for his operation. A feeling of calm came over him. Arigo had him look away. He rubbed the knife over the elbow for a few seconds—Puharich estimated about half a minute—and then slapped the moist growth in Puharich's hand. The films revealed later that the whole operation had taken *five seconds*. It was medically impossible. Then, with his traditional medical care, he wiped the knife on his shirt and went on to the next patient. Yet no infection appeared in Puharich's arm. He took his lipoma back to New York.[23]

Anyone might have been baffled by what he saw, day after day, in Arigo's "clinic." A peasant healer who could write complicated prescriptions and speak with a German accent. Knives in people's eyes. Instant diagnoses. Hundreds of patients streaming through the lines each day. Yet Belk and Puharich took all these events in stride, or at least in staggering progression. What they could not grasp was Arigo's straightforward explanation of his talents.

The very fact that Arigo claimed to be "incorporated" by the spirit of a deceased German physician was enough to turn off most of the scientists who might be otherwise interested. This bothered Puharich and Belk too, and strained their own credulity. It was incredible enough to accept the documented empirical evidence, without having to consider a concept so foreign to the practical mind that it might shut off intelligent inquiry before it started. And yet this strange claim of spirit "possession" could not be ignored or buried, since Arigo insisted it was not only an integral part of his work, but was the entire essence of his skills and powers. Far from enhancing an explanation of what Arigo did and how he was able to do it, this was a stumbling block. A scientist who stood up before a meeting of a professional organization and began with a statement about Arigo and "Dr. Fritz" would be likely to be laughed off the podium.[24]

This is an extremely revealing fact. Modern science cannot handle the facts of paranormal science. Each of the major researchers will go so far into these studies of the scientifically impossible, convincing himself, step by step, that he is only investigating the statistically improbable. Dr. Thelma Moss calls her book *The Probability of the Impossible*, which she tries to make acceptable by dealing with these scientifically impossible facts in terms of the "as yet unknown." What Dr. Moss and her professional kinsmen will not face is the fact that there is a demonic realm of life—not just a metaphor of evil, but demonic activity in the realm of Kantian phenomena, that is, the denial of Kant's neat cleavage between the unknown and the scientifically known. Puharich's account of Uri Geller is so totally improbable that one wonders why, apart from the expectation of enormous profit, any respectability-seeking publisher would have touched it. Messages from intergalactic robot ships, self-destructing cassette tapes, and on and on: Puharich could put his name on *Uri*, yet he feared, back in 1963 anyway, to consider the possibility that spirit possession is a fact of life. Anything might be true, except that. Let spirits of dead men into your universe, and the idea of a God who acts in history gets much too close for comfort. Let demons in, and you cannot protect yourself any longer without allowing God in, too—and that, above all, is what secular man dares not contemplate.

In the spring of 1957, Arigo was convicted of practicing medicine without a license. Both the Roman Catholic church and the medical association were behind the prosecution. He was put on probation, and in May 1958, President Kubitschek pardoned him.[25] Throughout 1961, 1962, and 1963, the authorities once again began to build a case against him, now that Kubitschek was out of office and barred by the Brazilian constitution from holding the top office again. This time, however, the authorities also were planning to try him for witchcraft, a far more serious crime. Arigo had to be very careful. He knew that his visitors were collecting data that could be used against him, if only by subpoena. Nevertheless, he consented to have the photographs and movies taken. He hoped to have a full-scale investigation by scientists of his powers.

Belk and Puharich, as paranormal researchers, wanted more data. They were still operating under the delusion that if you can just gather enough examples of impossible events, orthodox scientists will accept their reality and reformulate their concepts of what is and is not possible. But all you should expect is that numerous impossible events are only marginally more difficult to dismiss than a single impossible event. It becomes a matter of rejecting a large sample of events as being either statistically insignificant (which is almost always the case, given the nonrepeatability of most occult phenomena) or insignificant because of a statistical fluke. The scientists will send the researcher back to tighten his controls and/or increase his sample until signs of the paranormal disappear. Only then will the orthodox scientist accept the verdict of the experiments. *The conflict is at bottom religious.* The orthodox scientist stands at the edge of a bottomless pit, daring the paranormal scientist to present another fact that cannot be explained by means of orthodox categories. Then he shovels it over his back and calls for more facts. But Puharich, like all paranormal researchers, cannot grasp this fact. After all, they themselves have found the evidence compelling—up to a point. Not "over the line" into the occult, but compelling to an extent great enough to get them laughed off any orthodox podium. Once they have the facts, they try to explain them. They simply cannot do this, given their commitment to the standards of scientific investigation and correlation. But they try. They reach for explanations like Dr. Jule Eisenbud's psychoanalytic explanation of Ted Serios' mental photography. They press on, undaunted by skepticism, though not unaffected by it. They cease asking questions that are too embarrassing—the absolutely crucial questions, in other words. As Fuller writes:

> Puharich himself had already challenged Arigo with his own lipoma operation. On the surface, this would be reasonably good evidence, if not proof, of the worthiness of further study of Arigo. So were the films. But these still would not be enough for the exacting requirements of scientific-journal publication, which demands, in addition to prolific footnote references of past practices and observations, some pragmatic frame of reference on which a theory could be built and accepted. It had taken centuries for acupuncture to be even considered worthy of scientific study. Arigo's practices went so far beyond acupuncture that they almost soared out of sight.[26]

Fuller's reference to acupuncture is quite appropriate, though totally misleading. It had not taken centuries for acupuncture to be taken seriously by the American medical profession. It is still not taken seriously by most members, and those who have begun to consider the possibility that acupuncture might have some anesthetic effects were converted in a few months, not centuries. For centuries, the whole idea was rejected out of hand. Then came President Nixon's repudiation of a quarter-century of foreign policy toward Communist China. Ping-pong diplomacy was born in 1971–72; Nixon visited Red China, and he took along the usual contingent of reporters, all of whom seemed hypnotized by the clean streets of Peking. The atrocious, hysterical, preposterous "art form" of anti-imperialist "ballet," invented by Mao's wife, was hailed as being deeply significant, though of course alien to Western taste. All things Chinese—Red Chinese—were up for reconsideration. After all, if this progressive, rationalistic, Marxist democracy still used acupuncture, then acupuncture must be progressive, rationalistic, and democratic. Then *New York Times* columnist James Reston suffered from an attack of appendicitis, and the Chinese physicians used acupuncture as the anesthetic. Reston felt no pain, survived, and began to sing the praises of this ancient medical practice. That, and that alone, converted a small minority of American physicians, not a careful investigation of centuries of accumulated data on acupuncture. *We are dealing with religious conversion when we deal with the acceptance by former orthodox rationalists of some facet of paranormal science.* The impetus in the case of acupuncture was the religion of democracy, as interpreted by the *New York Times*.

Unfortunately for Arigo, he was not a physician in Red China. His story did not fit the editorial policies of the *New York Times*. When he was sent to jail in 1964, James Reston failed to drop in for an instant diagnosis and lightning-fast operation. It would have been better for the free world if Arigo, rather than the Red Chinese, had received the credit for curing Reston. Arigo's demons did not possess ballistic missiles and a messianic ideology of Communist domination. Arigo's demons had not slaughtered thirty million people. Arigo's demons did not play ping-pong.

When Puharich returned to the United States after his first visit to see Arigo in action, he began a series of experiments that are only too typical of the pathetic attempted fusion of demonic possession and orthodox scientific inquiry—as if the two were not totally antithetical in both theory and practice. He felt compelled to continue true research. Not acknowledging the demonic nature of Arigo's healing abilities, Puharich and Dr. Luis Cortes of the New York University School of Medicine attempted to imitate Arigo's techniques. First, they took rats as their victims. "Using painstaking care, Cortes held a rat firmly while Puharich tried to insert a small knife under the lid and up toward the sinus cavities. They found that it was literally impossible to do this on a conscious, unanesthetized rat unless its head was held in a vicelike grip."[27] Surprise, surprise! Rats simply do not like to have knives stuck into their eyes. But rats are not people, as even a fairly large percentage of experimental psychologists know. What would people think of having a physician stick knives into their eyes? Fortunately, a subject was eagerly awaiting just such an experiment. A young laboratory assistant, fascinated with the stories she had heard about Arigo, insisted that they try Arigo's trick on her. Neither of them wanted to try this, the author writes, but "she kept on insisting. . . ."[28] Cortes took a small knife and began to insert it into her eye. It went in only a fraction of an inch under her eyelid, when the girl signaled that she could not stand the pain. "The experience convinced all three that they were dealing with an extraordinary case in Arigo that would be a mammoth challenge to science."[29] Puharich and Cortes caught on fast. After rigorous experimentation like this, they proved, at least to themselves, that normally it hurts someone when you poke a knife into his eye, at least in a statistically significant number of cases, if the sample is large enough. Paranormal science marches on!

The scientific investigating techniques that are affirmed as exclusively valid by the cosmologists of human autonomy and neutral observation are impotent to handle the manifestations of the demonic. The questions that must be asked regarding the origins of such occult phenomena are denied from the start as being legitimate questions. Thomas Kuhn's enormously influential book, *The Structure of Scientific Revolutions*, explains why it is that apparently rational men such as Puharich would perform such meaningless and irrational experiments as probing the eyes of rats and a laboratory assistant in order to demonstrate the obvious:

> Effective research scarcely begins before a scientific community thinks it has acquired firm answers to questions like the following: What are the fundamental entities of which the universe is composed? How do these interact with each other and with the senses? What question may legitimately be asked about such entities and what techniques employed in seeking solutions? At least in the mature sciences, answers (or full substitutes for answers) to questions like these are firmly embodied in the educational initiation that prepares and licenses the student for professional practice. Because that education is both rigorous and rigid, these answers come to exert a deep hold on the scientific mind.[30]

A strong element of *arbitrariness* is inevitably involved in scientific research, Kuhn concludes. Conventional science thinks it knows what the universe is really like, at least insofar as it can be known at all. Conventional science, therefore, "often suppresses fundamental novelties because they are necessarily subversive of its basic commitments." Kuhn is convinced, however, that this suppression of the novel cannot go on very long. Men like Puharich who are involved in paranormal science are doing their best to undermine orthodoxy as it now stands, thereby creating a scientific revolution. But to accomplish this goal, *they dare not depart from formally established procedures.* They are attempting to use the investigative tools of orthodox science as wedges (or crowbars) to break open the hard shell of establishment orthodoxy.

The overwhelming problem with this approach is in the very nature of the tools they are using, including the assumptions about the universe that are accepted by all supposedly reasonable participants in scientific research. If the subject studied does not, by its very nature, fall within the post-Kantian laws of science, what good are the operating assumptions of post-Kantian science in determining what factors are involved in the observed phenomena? Orthodox scientists conclude that there must be some flaw in the observational capacities of paranormal researchers. They are being tricked by sleight-of-hand artists. They have not studied enough cases. The cases are not repeatable. The anomalies are a product of the inherent randomness of the universe. The researchers are liars and involved in a massive conspiracy against their colleagues. The researchers are mad. The paranormal researchers reply that the orthodox leaders are blinded by prejudice, are unwilling to examine the facts, suppress evidence, lie about paranormal researchers, and are too stodgy and wrapped up in pre-1965 concepts of what constitutes the possible to be accurate judges. Notwithstanding, both groups claim allegiance to the increasingly shaky canons of post-Kantian rationalism. Yet it is precisely this—the operating presuppositional foundation of all modern science—that is being undermined by the realization that men like Arigo do exist, and that neither orthodox medicine nor paranormal science can make any sense out of the facts. The hard reality of the facts is like a knife jabbing its way into the eyes of the scientists. The orthodox scientists act like Arigo's patients: they seem unaware of what is taking place. The paranormal scientists understand that what is happening is impossible, but they also claim that there is no discomfort involved. They are self-deluded. Arigo's knife is cutting away the public's faith in the world of the scientists. The public is coming to believe that scientific rationalism cannot account for the miraculous events that are being reported in book after paperback book, and even in that establishment organ of conventional wisdom, the *Reader's Digest*. The public, feeling no pressure to publish in respectable scientific journals, and not having gone through the mind-directing program of scientific initiation, sees that Arigo's knife is cutting out the heart of science's most cherished presupposition: that the rational, categorizing mind of man can give an account, at least in principle, assuming sufficient facts are available, of any known phenomenon. The key word, of course, is "known." *If science is unable to explain it, it is not known.* The public, slowly but surely, is becoming aware that orthodox science is involved in a sleight-of-hand trick far more comprehensive than anything dreamed of by peasant healers. Peasant healers sometimes fake miracles; orthodox scientists who face the fact of the demonic are constantly faking nonmiracles. "Give us time; we can explain this," they say, paraphrasing the Amazing Randi's challenge: "Give me time, and I can duplicate this." Then, like Randi, orthodox scientists scurry away, hoping that both the unexplained phenomena and the public's memory of their challenge will somehow fade away.

Arigo was again convicted of practicing medicine without a license in 1964. This time he was sent to jail. Predictably, he began healing prisoners. The public kept coming to him, and the jailers looked the other way. He even was given a key to allow him to come and go when he wished. The worldwide effects of the occult revival were making themselves felt in Brazil in 1964–65. The Roman Catholic church, like a growing minority of formerly orthodox scientists, was involved in a holding operation called "redefinition." If an occult practice could not be stamped out, or at least suppressed enough to keep the public from making it into a fad, it was redefined as "parapsychological" in nature. Parapsychology was seen more and more as a legitimate subdivision of scientific investigation, thereby sanctioning the observation of occult abilities. Somehow, by calling demonic possession "parapsychological behavior," the church's leadership hoped to justify its retreat from the fray. This was neutralizing the old hostility to witchcraft.[31] In Arigo's case, the authorities were growing tired of trying to suppress him. He had become one of Brazil's half a dozen most widely recognized citizens. He was front-page news, year after year. He had treated people from every station in life. He was paroled in June 1965, after spending seven months in jail.

The following summer, Puharich led a well-equipped team back to Congonhas do Campo. They watched, charted, and recorded events for three days, involving about a thousand patients. With a tape recorder, they took down each of Arigo's 965 diagnoses. Then they checked to see if the patient had brought along his own physician's written diagnosis. In 545 cases, they had. Of these 545, Arigo had made diagnoses in accord with the physicians' in 518 cases, a ninety-six percent score. The researchers, being men of good faith, assumed that in the twenty-seven discrepancies, the physician was correct and Arigo was wrong. These diagnoses, remember, took about thirty seconds each. Movies were made of the operations. More photographs were taken.[32] Still, they needed more data. Always more data were required. Paranormal scientists are forever fearful of the standard charge: insufficient observations to permit statistically significant correlations. If one instance of a knife being poked into someone's eye does not convince the orthodox scientist, then perhaps 500 instances will. If he thinks you have faked one set of films, possibly 500 sets will convince him.

Another expedition would be needed. This time, the questions to be asked would be restricted even more—so restricted, in fact, as to be virtually irrelevant in making any sense out of the observed data: "Paramount in the plans was the study of those aspects of Arigo's work which could be explained and related to accepted modern medical theory and practice. . . . The 'voice' that told Arigo his amazingly correct diagnoses would be considered, but the statistics on the actual diagnoses and treatment would come first."[33] As for the kardecist explanation of Arigo's nonmiracles, that he was a vessel for a God-given energy, or higher form of energy, it could be ignored completely. "These concepts were interesting, but utterly useless for the medical researchers, who needed more statistical information on the hard, observable facts. It is one thing to be convinced by direct observation. It is another to articulate the facts in a form acceptable to the editors of a scientific journal, who must have precedents and previously documented material to fall back on."[34] It is, in fact, the old "egg before the chicken, chicken before the egg" routine: no precedents can be set without access to the journals, but the journals require precedents. The thousands upon thousands of cases of impossible events compiled by Charles Fort and his followers have never crept into respectable journals. The idea of these journals is to *keep out disturbing precedents*. One can never be sure just where a precedent may lead, so editors handle them very carefully. Anyone who doubts that outright suppression goes on should read Alfred de Grazia's *The Velikovsky Affair* (1966), which demonstrates how faculty members of major universities, including Harvard, pressured Velikovsky's publisher, Macmillan, into dropping his books. They did not get back into print until 1965—in the midst of the occult revival. Unlike Arigo's knives in the eye, the knives of the scientific guild, delivered very often from behind, can maim and kill a man's reputation, sometimes affecting his ability to get an academic job, especially if he is not yet tenured.

It was Arigo's dream to establish a hospital. This had been Edgar Cayce's dream, too. This was why he had hope in the investigations of these North American scientists. He did not understand that they were basically pariahs in their profession for even daring to promote his story back home. When the team returned in 1968 to make more films, gather more statistics, and play the data game again, it was driven out by the press, which had received reports on the clandestine visit of the North Americans. Nothing fills a paranormal scientist's heart with greater fear than the attention of journalists prior to the full and final report, written in the discipline's jargon, addressed to one's skeptical colleagues.

In an academic world where the mere writing of a *textbook* may tarnish a man's reputation, as Kuhn reveals, a summary by a journalist of a "major breakthrough" is nothing short of suicidal.[35] The team left when the reporters appeared. Arigo was not going to get his hospital.

Why did he want a hospital? This is the anomaly. What would a hospital have provided for him? He could treat 300 patients a day. No one else in the world had his talents, so there was no possibility of the division of labor, which is one of the primary functions of a hospital's medical staff. He could perform feats of surgery that no medical team could even imitate. His powers were vastly beyond those ever dreamed of by a medical technician. Indeed, the very nature of his ministry was a denial of the need for medical technicians. What need was there for a hospital? What need did a demon-possessed peasant who cured men with a rusty knife in a filthy room have for a hospital, the product of centuries of slowly improving medical techniques? What need did he have for sanitary conditions, teams of researchers, diagnostic equipment, anesthetics, or any other product of Western technology and theoretical science?

This is the central *social* implication of the conflict between Western science and primitive healing. It is not that Western techniques, being rational, are therefore the only successful avenues of medical treatment. That may be what the orthodox scientists think, but what they think and what happens in the world are very often two entirely different processes. It is not that peasants are too stupid, generation after generation, to recognize the difference between staying sick and getting well. It is not that the monopoly of Western rationalism really is what it claims to be: solely efficacious. What is at stake is the idea of *progress*. It is a fact that only by means of Western science has a centuries-long period of constant improvement of skills, equipment, and treatment been maintained. Scientific progress, which was originally grounded on the Christian ideas of providence, progress, and the subduing of the earth to the glory of a preeminently rational and personal God, was exponentially increased by the social and intellectual aftermath of the Reformation.[36] The idea that men can increase their control over nature by an ever-increasing division of labor, including intellectual labor, is at the heart of Western progress. Simple men, with only average or slightly above-average intelligence, can perform almost miraculous feats through the use of painstakingly devised techniques and equipment. The "uncharismatic" plodders who are the troops of any scientific organization steadily advance certain aspects of the discipline. Scientific progress is not simply the product of centuries of such plodding—a continuous addition of minute improvements—but it certainly is aided by such narrow but progressive additions of human knowledge. Teams of researchers are able to participate in a systematic, cost-effective program of investigation. It is only through such increments to knowledge, coupled with occasional breakthroughs by "scientific revolutionaries" like Newton and Einstein, that the West has achieved universal dominance through science and technology. And science and technology would not have been possible without the capital produced by thrift, intelligent investing, and continual economic progress.

Systematic testing, trial-and-error investigations, double-blind experiments, widespread publication (however controlled) of results in over a hundred thousand scientific periodicals in the world, and all the other features of incremental and progressive scientific advancement are not possible in a culture dominated by an occasional charismatic magician-leader and his association of enchanted priests, shamans, and visionaries. The whole society becomes dependent on a tiny handful of religious healers, whose powers stem from unpredictable and hostile occult forces. The rule of terror is prominent. There is no hope of progress culturally; there is only the *ad hoc* healing of physical ailments. Short-term healing of specific ailments is as much as anyone can hope for. If the charismatic healer dies, or loses his gift, the society cannot escape from its illnesses. By *personalizing* the techniques of healing, primitive societies have in principle abandoned the idea of medical, economic, or any other kind of progress through more impersonal organizations of human talent.

Arigo worked in unsanitary conditions. Why not? His magic worked. No ideal of Western cleanliness was present in his peasant surroundings, nor was he expected to conform to Western standards of sanitation. He did not use his prestige to promote voluntary local programs of personal and community sanitation. His teaching did not include cause-and-effect doctrines of the nature of good health. "Dr. Fritz" was the source of health, not public sanitation.

Arigo was incomparable, but he died in January 1971. What did he leave behind? What healing is accomplished today by his legend? Who relieves human suffering now? He only established the tradition of spirit possession that much more firmly in the minds of both Brazilian peasants and upper-class products of Western education in Brazil. He gave the Kardec movement new impetus. By 1960, some 680,000 spiritualists were recorded in Brazil.[37] The knife is gone; the spiritism remains.

Demonic healing is the denial of progress, the denial of widespread public health, the denial of cause and effect, not because it is invariably and necessarily fraudulent, but because it is externally, visibly, miraculously successful in a "statistically significant number of cases." The curse of demonic healing is not that it never really works, except in cases of psychosomatic illness—and all healings that do take place, say orthodox scientists, by definition were psychosomatic in origin—but that it so often relieves the visible symptoms of sickness. The primitive peasants who go to these healers, not being trained in modern universities, have no *a priori* incentive to shut their eyes to the obvious manifestations of healing. They permit themselves to accept what their eyes can see, unlike Western scientists. They are therefore willing to place their bodies under the control of the agents of demons and demons themselves. The epistemological protection of autonomous Western science is not present.

Christians must understand the nature of a society like Brazil. It may be able to telescope its progression from primitive religion to Western science and religious skepticism to post-1965 paranormal science and parapsychological fascination. It may be able to skip the rationalist phase. Skeptical rationalism may never get a strong enough foothold, even among the intellectual elite, to secularize the culture. This fact is extremely important, for it has made it very difficult for Christian evangelism by denominations that have a puritan-like commitment to education and rational techniques. Long-term economic growth is made far less likely; mass inflation will be the substitute. The foundations of progress are simply not present, for the primary foundations are matters of faith and attitude.[38] The only Western churches that have access to these people are those that hold very similar conceptions of the universe. Writes Wilson:

> In Brazil and elsewhere in Latin America the appeal of Pentecostalism, which in America and Europe we should regard as a conversionist movement, may have much less to do with the specific elements which have been significant in its spread in Protestant societies, and more to do with those thaumaturgical aspects which are a part of its inheritance. Thus we find that in missionary activity . . . the ostensible configuration of doctrine, organization, and practice that is offered, is not accepted as a whole: certain elements are more readily embraced than others. In cultures with strong indigenous religious traditions it is entirely expectable that the appeal of any missionary denomination which includes thaumaturgical elements should be precisely these, rather than other features of its teachings, activities, or organization.[39]

In short, it is very difficult to deliver societies in occult bondage by means of evangelism that is based on similar manifestations of occult healing. The Protestant ethic, which was firmly grounded in a deemphasis on charismatic signs and wonders, and placed great emphasis on self-discipline, education, thrift, and material uplift, cannot be implanted readily in the hearts and minds of the newly "converted" population. Those in bondage may stay in bondage, or at best may not experience the fruits of total redemption from occult power.

The Philippine Healers

Arigo was unrivaled as a demonic healer. His powers were utterly baffling, the least disputed, the most consistent, and the most widely witnessed of any healer on record. Yet what Arigo did for two decades in Brazil differs only in degree from what other demonic healers in primitive cultures have performed for centuries. When we examine the healing arts of another widely publicized group of peasant spiritists, the Philippine wonder healers, we find the same basic patterns, both theologically and methodologically. Their abilities have been challenged more successfully, since some instances of fakery have been detected, and far fewer people have been treated by any one of these men. Nevertheless, in the aggregate, a large number of films, photographs, and firsthand accounts have been assembled that demonstrate that successful operations are being performed that are impossible to explain by known biological and physical principles.

One of the earliest "psychic" healers in the Philippines whose work was observed and reported by American visitors is Brother Eleuterio Terte. *Fate*, a popular magazine of occult and "Fortean" anomalies which is modeled along the lines of *Pageant* and *Coronet*, ran an April 1960 article that dealt with Terte's powers. Two moving-picture producers recorded several of his bare-handed operations. His techniques were analogous to Arigo's, although they were far more explicitly religious in nature. He uses a female medium in a trance state to add to his power; she, rather than Terte, is visibly entranced. J. Bernard Ricks, a clairvoyant and self-professed medium, journeyed to Terte's tiny village in 1963 to see him in action, and his report appeared in *Fate* the same year. The editors of the magazine decided to include this essay in a compilation published in 1965, *The Strange and the Unknown,* an anthology gleaned from the pages of *Fate.*

According to Ricks, villagers in the little town of 400 formed a choir to sing hymns before each operation, supposedly in order "to stir up the vibrations." After the hymns, Terte recited the Lord's prayer and went to work. A middle-aged man who claimed to be suffering from a blood clot was seated on the operating table. Terte's hand began to massage the man's chest area. Within ten seconds, according to Ricks, a small, black object began to appear on the chest, actually coming out through the chest. Yet there was no opening visible to Ricks, who was standing on the other side of the operating table. The clot fell into Terte's hands. Ricks said it was the size of his thumb. The man stated that he had felt nothing.

The next patient had an acute case of appendicitis. The choir sang for a while, then stopped; Terte said his prayer, and commenced. He washed his hands and the patient's body with rubbing alcohol—the only condescension to Western standards of cleanliness—and began to massage the man's abdomen. A one-inch hole appeared. A few seconds later, the appendix rose up through the small opening. Terte lifted the organ and placed it in Ricks' hand. There was almost no sign of blood. By pressing on the opening with his hand, Terte closed the wound. A few seconds later, Ricks reported, there was no sign that there had ever been an opening.

Ricks watched the third operation from a distance of a few inches. Terte made an incision on the back of a patient and drew out long strands of foul-smelling flesh. As always, the patient felt no pain.

This phenomenon of internal organs or objects located inside the body passing through the flesh, even apart from openings larger than the pores, is relatively common with primitive forms of demonic healing. Ronald Rose, in his study of Australian aborigines, records a conversation he had with one native concerning an alleged healing. Rose is convinced that such operations involve trickery:

> When the old Birri full-blood from Bowen (Queensland), Harry Monsell, told me about seeing a doctor suck a stone about the size of a hen's egg from the body of a woman who was suffering from abdominal pains, I put it to him that the doctor had deceived them.
>
> "Oh, no," he said firmly. "That same old doctor I saw once fix up a man who had a chest pain. He said the man had got a porcupine [echidna or spiny anteater] spike in him. The doctor sang a song, and I saw with my own eyes the quill come out of the body of the man."
>
> "Do you mean that it seemed to come directly out of his flesh?"
>
> "Yes."
>
> "Did the doctor perhaps pull it out?"

"No. He just sang and it came up. When it came right out, it fell down onto the ground."

"Was there any blood or any mark where the quill had come out?"

"No, there was no mark. The man got better."[40]

The native could have been telling a tall tale, or he could have been hypnotized, but in the light of the scenes photographed and attested to by numerous Western visitors to Philippine healers, it is more likely that the "old doctor" did remove the quill with a song. What he says he saw is not different in principle (or at least different in its nonconformity to Western science) from what Mrs. Bobbie Gironda, of North Hollywood, California, saw in the Philippines.

Her son had a crippled leg. He had been operated on but still could not walk without crutches. He was nine years old. She took him to Juan Blanche, one of the more prominent healers. Blanche placed a copper coin on the back of his leg, close to the tumor that was causing the trouble. Then he put a piece of oil-soaked cotton on top of the coin. Next he lit the cotton with a match. Placing a glass atop the coin, Blanche put out the flame. He tapped the top (that is, bottom) of the glass, and a circle of blood appeared beneath the rim of the glass. He grabbed the hand of the boy's grandmother, closed it into a fist, and left her forefinger extended. He made a slashing motion above the circle of blood, and a pink slash appeared in the skin, eight inches beneath her forefinger. He then reached in and withdrew a piece of hard tissue. Actually, he removed it part way, allowing them to snap a photograph. Then he pulled it out.[41] After a few more chiropractic-like treatments, the boy's leg was healed, and there are signed statements by American physicians to that effect.[42]

Mrs. Gironda was so impressed that she convinced the Filipino housegirl, Fanny, that she too should visit Blanche to have her red rash cured. Mrs. Gironda's description of what took place follows:

Fanny shyly approached the table. Blanche, after a cursory examination began picking little seedlike objects from her arms, face and neck. I had been busying myself getting the camera loaded but the sound of the things plinking into a bowl partly filled with water caught my attention. At my hard look at the bowl, the helper held it out to me for closer inspection.

"He's got to be a magician!" I thought to myself. "It's the hand quicker than the eye. Where else could these things be coming from?"

The instant my thought was completed, I felt Blanche's eyes on me. He was grinning broadly, as if he had heard my thoughts aloud. Then he spread his hands wide, slowly turning them over, back and front. I was so embarrassed, I wished the floor would open up and let me drop out of sight. Since my skepticism was already in plain sight, I was going to satisfy it. Blanche's helper snickered aloud and the psychic surgeon kept grinning pleasantly as he watched my face stop blushing and determination take its place. I looked Blanche up and down, all sides too, carefully checking for any hidden gimmicks which might contain a reservoir of these magical seeds. His hands and arms were bare and the short-sleeved cotton shirt he wore was too damp to offer any concealment.

I put my nose within four inches of Fanny's arm. Blanche obligingly, and in slow motion, pressed two fingers on either side of a skin pore. The tip of another seed began emerging. His hands were visible at all times and since we were standing hip to hip in that cubbyhole, I felt satisfied no tricks were under way.

Blanche paused for my benefit as the seed was half out, and again, at the three-quarter mark. These things, well over fifty removed, resembled what I would imagine long grain rice with husks would look like. The amazing thing was that they were much larger than the pore from which they were taken. Blanche then simply grasped the seed, with the tips of his fingers, and picked it out of the skin.[43]

Many of the prominent healers are members of the Union Espiritista Cristiana de Filipinas, a self-confessed "Christian" spiritist association. It is explicitly religious in outlook, and members view their powers as stemming from God. They admit quite readily that similar powers can be given to men by evil spirits.[44] They do not accept payment for their healings, just as Arigo did not. Very significantly, the union has officially adopted Allan Kardec's *The Spirits' Book* as one of its official documents. The members believe in reincarnation, karmic law, and the universal salvation of mankind. Professor Guillermo Tolentino, a famous sculptor and leader of the organization, puts forth the standard humanist-spiritist doctrine that all religions lead to God, but his, being eclectic and universalist, is undogmatic and therefore superior. "All religions set up barriers when they say there is no salvation outside their own belief. Without exception, they are all commercialized. Christian Spiritism, on the other hand, sets up no barrier because it embraces mankind as a whole—since all are One in worshipping God in Truth and in Spirit. . . . All, without exception, will be saved through *multiple reincarnations!*"[45] This is kardecism, pure and simple. Remove the doctrine of reincarnation, and it is just another run-of-the-mill brand of humanism. Man saves himself by merit; God does not discriminate on a permanent basis between good and evil; everyone gets a second, third, or infinite number of opportunities in life to reform himself. Man is therefore divine.

Tolentino revealed some of the background of Terte. He discovered his talents in 1948, the same year in which the stream of outsiders began to seek out psychic healers.[46] There were many to choose from. They all had one factor in common besides their healing abilities: none had advanced beyond the fourth grade.[47] By these standards, Edgar Cayce was a postdoctoral candidate. Like Arigo, they had dropped out very early. This is indicative of the inverse relationship between Western rationalism and primitive demonism. Where rationalistic education flourishes, and where it still retains the confidence of the students and faculty members, psychic healing techniques are infrequently manifested. In an age of *confident* rationalism, demonic phenonema are minimized; people refuse to accept the validity of nonrationalistic phenomena. Such phenomena are regarded as mythical. But when the confidence in the monopoly of rationalism weakens, primitive cultures, especially the demonic aspects of primitive cultures, receive new attention from a growing minority of disaffected rationalists. In 1948, the Philippines experienced a spiritist revival. Similarly, the Kardec movement and umbanda became major religious forces only after World War II in Brazil, with Arigo appearing in 1950. By the early 1960s, word about healings in both nations had begun to filter back to the United States, and after 1964 there was a growing flood of interest. (Though this book does not go into the subject, it is also significant that the first widely reported sighting of flying saucers in America was Kenneth Arnold's report of having seen nine flying discs from his private airplane near Mt. Rainier, Washington, which he announced on June 24, 1947, and which was front-page news the next day. It was not the first, nor was it one of the best, of the post-World War II reports on UFOs, but it was the first to gain widespread coverage by the media. The close relationship between UFO hunters and ghost hunters has been growing even closer to a one-to-one ratio since 1965, although the groups are not wholly meshed yet. It is my personal opinion that the UFO phenomena serve as demonic manifestations aimed at the more scientific, materialistic searchers of the abnormal. St. Paul's ability to be all things to all people in order to save some [I Corinthians 9:22] is apparently imitated by Satan.) *The rise of occult humanism is presently offering an alternative to a growing body of formerly materialistic humanists who are losing their faith in materialism, but not in the tenets of humanistic religion.*

Of all the Philippine healers, Tony Agpaoa is by far the most famous—or infamous. The two books written on the subject of psychic healing in the Philippines, one by Harold Sherman and the other by Tom Valentine, deal most heavily with Agpaoa's ministry. He does not belong to the spiritist's organization, and is therefore regarded as a renegade by the members of that group. He also accepts donations to his "research foundation," a practice hotly criticized by the spiritists. Apart from a simple prayer before each operation, his healing techniques show no traces of being religious in nature. But in one crucial respect, Agpaoa's ministry does maintain a basic continuity with the work of Arigo, Terte, and all the rest: the lack of sanitation. These healers have an almost philosophical commitment to unsterile operations.[48] This is not to say that people are actually infected. Indeed, from the reported cases of infection—virtually none—there is far less infection in one of these primitive clinics than in a typical North American hospital, with its staph infections and other horrors. The bodies of those treated are not infected, but what is infected is the attitude of the public toward standards of cleanliness. The lack of sanitation is a visible testimony against the law of cause and effect in the medical realm. The relationship between cleanliness and health is symbolically rejected by these healers. Those peasants who are treated by them remain in a kind of microbiological bondage to their primitive culture. They remain dependent upon the charismatic healers who alone seem to be able to provide efficacious treatment within the framework of the traditional culture to which these people are clinging. These static cultures are kept static, in part, by the very success of these healers. As one Western physician remarked during a television documentary on a group of doctors who use light aircraft to bring Western medicine to African tribes: "I'm always the second doctor called in for consultation."

Agpaoa normally treats thirty to fifty people per day, seven days a week.[49] His absolute maximum was Arigo's average day: 300.[50] His operations generally take as "long" as five minutes, five times as long as Arigo's. His trance state, like

Terte's, affects only his arms and hands.⁵¹ When the power comes upon him, he says, there is a tingling sensation, a phenomenon which is reported as preceding numerous forms of demonic activity.* Then he goes to work.

Occasionally, one of these healers will use a razor blade, but normally they use only their bare hands to enter the body. Juan Blanche, as mentioned earlier, uses the index finger of an onlooker to make the slit in the flesh—eight inches away from the body. Then they enter the cavity of the body with their hands.⁵² Typically, the healer begins by massaging the flesh for a few moments. When it opens, he inserts his hands and makes the necessary "repairs." Sometimes he may use a pair of old scissors to cut the internal organs; other times, most horrifyingly, he simply pulls out the organs—supposedly diseased—by the handful.

Moving pictures and photographs of these operations are now relatively common. Valentine reports that by the early 1970s, there were at least 200 different home movies of various healers in action that circulated in the Chicago area alone.⁵³ Other more professional films have been made over the last fifteen years. Harold Sherman showed one to the late Louis Lomax, who had one of those curiously popular and short-lived "harassment of weirdoes" television programs that were made popular by Joe Pyne (himself a debunker of Agpaoa). Lomax indicated to Sherman before the show that he would not be easy to convince, but a showing before they went on camera of one of Sherman's films of Agpaoa in action shocked Lomax into confused neutrality. The film was shown to the studio audience as it went over the airwaves. People were stunned. Lomax did not adopt the typical attitude of the knowing rationalist while he was on camera, yet he could not wholly escape the intellectual's usual assumption that if a phenomenon is not reported by the *New York Times,* it probably is not true or relevant to the public. He displayed this bias when he responded to a UCLA student from Upper Volta in Africa, who stepped up to the microphone and thanked Sherman for having shown the film. He asserted that he had witnessed numerous bare-handed operations conducted by tribal healers in his own country. Lomax seemed shocked.

> "My dear man!" said Lomax. "If this is true—how come the newspapers of the world have not headlined this great event? That's the same question I might ask Mr. Sherman? If these bare-hand operations are true—why hasn't the world heard about them before now?"
>
> Mr. Guirma's reply was self-contained but potent.
>
> "Your foreign missionaries and medical doctors with your foreign missions have known about these kinds of operations for years—*but apparently they do not consider what our native doctors have been doing of any value to their culture.*"⁵⁴

This answer touches on one aspect of the stone wall of silence encountered by all who would point out that such phenomena exist. The typical Western rationalist, being a materialist, cannot accept the possibility that there are forces that can

---

*Rev. David Ketchen's experiences in table-raising also included this tingling sensation. See Appendix B.

affect the visible, measurable world that do not conform to the laws of that world —laws that are at bottom the laws of the self-proclaimed autonomous reason of man. This is especially true of American physicians, but it is even true of missionaries, including fundamentalist missionaries. Occasionally, missionaries will report home about the existence of demonic activity, but for many years the people back home, especially the ordained pastors, preferred not to believe in such reports. The missionaries stopped sending back such reports, for their financial support was dependent upon the cooperation of the churches back home.

Yet it goes even deeper than this. Western rationalism is at bottom *Darwinian*. All progress is evolutionary. Progress in nature is blind, random, and totally unplanned. It is dependent upon the response of random genetic mutation in existing species to the randomly changing environment. Out of competing randomness comes the order of progress. In human affairs, this same evolutionary perspective persists; indeed, it was assumed even before Darwin published his investigations. Therefore, the *primitive* is primitive because it is *temporally prior*. Not because primitive cultures are perverse, present-oriented, demonic, envious, or whatever, but because they are temporally prior. This is the great sin of primitivism, not the particular characteristics displayed by any given culture. Therefore, that which has come after is, by definition, better—*better* being defined as rationalistic and materialistic. The argument is rigorously circular, as Robert Nisbet has demonstrated so forcefully in his important book, *Social Change and History* (1969). It assumes that what has come later *in the West* is that which is truly progressive. *Later* is therefore defined as whatever the West has done, and *West* means those peculiar aspects of culture that are distinctly rationalistic and materialistic. If progress has not come to one or another culture, it must be because there have been *institutional impediments* to progress, and obviously the belief in the power of tribal medicine men is one such impediment. Therefore, to assist a culture in becoming progressive—to speed up the blocked processes of cultural evolution—it is necessary to convince primitive people that their medicine men do not have occult powers, for to be progressive is to rely totally on human reason and natural laws as defined by human reason. It is not simply that what native doctors can do has no value to Western rational culture; it is that what they claim to do, if accepted even as a possibility, denies the very premises of Western rational culture.

Sherman describes one of Agpaoa's operations that he witnessed personally. He was accompanied by Dr. Hiroshi Motoyama, a professor in religious studies at the University of Tokyo.

> Tony patted the abdomen with the flat of his hand, then held both hands up, fingers extended, to show he had nothing in them.
>
> "I am going to open the body here," he said, and placed the fingers of his right hand against the body, pushing downward. As he did so, it appeared as though the flesh separated and rolled back. Using both hands, he now quickly pulled the body open, widening the "incision." His hands went quickly inside and what appeared to be blood oozed out. Tony looked across at me and smiled. "You think I am not *in* the body?" he said. "Here, put your hand in here beside mine!"

I hesitated.

"Go on—it is all right," he reassured, as he held the wound open.

Dr. Motoyama's face was a study. I had heard that no infections ever resulted but the possible chance of infection crossed my mind. A decision had to be made.

I extended my hand toward the body opening. I felt my fingers go down beside Tony's. I felt blood and tissue of some sort. When I extracted my hand it had turned red in color. Louie [Agpaoa's assistant] handed me a piece of cotton to swab it off.[55]

When Sherman delivered a lecture on what he had seen before the Los Angeles Breakfast Club on April 13, 1966, the large crowd was fascinated. But two weeks later, a physician who had been in attendance demanded that the club's manager repudiate the speech. The facts cited by Sherman, in the eyes of this critic, were nothing short of preposterous, an outrage. In short, demonic healing did not conform to the standards laid down in the nation's medical schools.

In response, Sherman invited the club's manager, the critic, other important members of the club, and any surgeons who wanted to come to see his films of Agpaoa's operations. Then he intelligently covered his flanks. He invited numerous former patients of Philippine healers who lived in Southern California, and Southern California being what it is, a roomful showed up. But he did not announce who they were until after the showing of the movie. Three surgeons, friends of one of the important club members, asked to come and received invitations. Sherman showed the film. Then he announced his little surprise: several carloads of cured patients who had brought before-and-after certificates from licensed physicians concerning the post-Philippine absence of the previously diagnosed medical problems. He offered to let any of the physicians examine any of the patients. The result, as Sherman wisely had guessed, was instant victory; the opposition folded.

> There was an instant stir among the three surgeons up front. Without giving the patients a chance to open their mouths, they got up and walked out, giving no expression of appreciation for the courtesies extended them. It was plainly obvious that they did not wish to face this kind of evidence and testimony. It might be one thing to criticize the picture, to brand it fraudulent, to say that the operations on film were faked —but to have to admit to having met actual patients who had gone to the Philippines with medical records of operations and other ailments, and had returned greatly benefited by psychic surgery was just too much. They did not even want it known that they had been there, I learned later, and one of them had said he would sue if whoever was taking flashlight pictures ever published one with his likeness in it. Brave men.[56]

This is orthodox science in action, or inaction. Fight on your ground where you know you can win; otherwise, remain anonymous and clear out quickly.

Nevertheless, orthodox skepticism is not entirely wasted. Sherman and Valentine report that they had seen several cases of apparent sleight-of-hand manipulations by psychic healers. It is also true that on several occasions, psychic healers refused to appear before Western investigators, or failed to operate when the investigators sought them out. It is almost as if Western rationalists were surrounded by some sort of negative aura that in some way hampers the activities of the demonic control agents. This, in fact, is precisely what old Don Juan told Castaneda: the everyday activities of Westerners serve as shields against the powers of the spirit world.[57] The barrier can seemingly work in an offensive fashion as well as defensively.

All things are fair in love and war, the slogan says. In epistemological confrontations, the rules of war prevail. While the psychic healers would sometimes do a bit of fakery when the flesh was willing but the spirit was weak, their rationalistic opponents were also not above a little sleight of hand. Valentine reports on an experiment he conducted. "With the help of a Filipino-American medical doctor who was in Baguio when we were, I carried out an informal placebo test on a clinic. Two genuine gallstones removed from a living patient were sent to a laboratory, but the clinic was informed that the stones had been removed by psychic surgery. The report came back without detailed analysis, but it carried a flat statement that the stones were not organic."[58] This, as might be suspected, was the invariable answer whenever researchers sent in products of admittedly psychic operations. The specimen might be animal, vegetable, or mineral, but it was never human.

Physicians predictably claim that the only possible healings resulting from psychic surgery are psychosomatic illnesses. ("Take that knife out of his eye, and I'll prove it!") Again, there are indications of just this kind of mental healing, but consider the case of Joseph Ruffner. Ruffner suffered an industrial accident in 1956. He was put on crutches permanently. In 1966 he visited Agpaoa. Here is his description of what took place in 1966:

> I was scared, but I didn't feel any pain. I saw him cut into me with his bare hands and dig something out. I saw it open, I saw it close, and I saw blood. A guy who said he was a doctor asked me if he could put his hand into my wound. I said it was okay by me if it was clean. He put his hand in [what—no washing with soap and water for twenty minutes?], and I could feel it. When he drew it out, it was covered with blood. Then Tony took his hands out, and the wound was instantly healed. He said to me, "Get up and walk." I didn't think I could—you know, after surgery and all—but I did.[59]

He never used crutches after that. Yet upon being X rayed when he returned to the United States, he learned that his bones were still broken. He should not have been able to walk. He could walk, though, and without any pain.[60] If this is psychosomatic healing, it is a very peculiar kind.

Others who had journeyed to the Philippines to be healed by Agpaoa were not equally happy. In fact, several later said that they had not been helped. Some had gone as skeptics and had returned skeptics. Others went in hope, and came back disappointed. Still others had felt better after the treatments. But the later patients tended to give mixed reviews.[61] Tony Agpaoa is no Arigo.

Tony and many of the other healers are expert tooth-pullers. They simply reach in with their bare hands and yank out the tooth, and the patient feels nothing. P. L. Katigbak, the Philippines' general manager of the Detroit-based Parke-Davis Co., and an M.D., visited a tooth specialist, Batangas. (Who says these healers are not following modern medical practice? Now, if Batangas can just persuade the Philippine government to prohibit other psychic healers from pulling teeth without a license. . . .) Katigbak says that "in a split second my tooth was out with no pain. Unbelievable."[62] Yet when confronted with a similar display of psychic healing in the tooth extraction field, in this case a series of extractions made by Agpaoa, Dr. Seymour Wanderman, a friend of Sherman's and one of the great professional skeptics in medical history, simply remarked: "Means nothing. Anyone can do that."[63] He had seen this at close range, peering directly into the patient's mouth. No pain, no resistance from the tooth, just instant removal. Fraud, said Wanderman. No fourth-grade dropout was going to fool Seymour Wanderman, M.D. Agpaoa had even opened up a woman's stomach in front of him, using his bare hands, in front of a movie camera clicking off eighteen frames per second. He offered to let Wanderman stick his hands into the wound. Wanderman refused. Agpaoa then offered him samples of the woman's blood. "No, that's not necessary," said Wanderman.[64] How about the bottle containing the growth that he had just removed. Again, unnecessary. When questioned about his opinion later by Sherman, Wanderman said the whole thing was sleight of hand. How about the blood? "It wasn't real blood." What about the tissue in the bottle? Animal tissue, he said, two or three days old. But what about running clinical tests? "I haven't been trained for years to observe tissue and handle it as I have, not to be able to tell. That growth was not taken from that woman's body." Why did he refuse to put his hand into the wound? "I didn't need to, to know what was going on. I am a trained observer. I was seeing what you did not see."[65] Anyway, that is Sherman's reconstruction of the exchange between them. But Wanderman was in the moving-picture film. He was there. He did not believe.

Why should he have believed? Why should he trust his eyes? Men make mistakes in viewing facts. What should he do, throw out a life's career based on one set of absolute presuppositions, in favor of a twenty-seven-year-old medicine man? What is reality, anyway? Isn't it what our minds say it must be? When Sherman had warned him that he was going to have to put aside all his medical training and view these events as a separate type of phenomenon, he stoutly refused. "I can't put aside a medical background of over fifty years in viewing any operations of whatever kind on the human body. If it is not right, in my judgment, based upon proved and established standards, it is not right, no matter who does it or how it's done."[66] Wanderman was testifying to a *faith* in Western medical techniques. It was his deeply felt religion. It was filled with oughts and ought-nots, like any respectable religion. Western medicine is the product of Western religion, a religion which denied the use of spirits in healing, although it did permit prayer and ritual anointing (James 5:14, 15). That religion had produced religious techniques and standards unparalleled in the recorded history of man. Was he to throw out the standards of Western medicine just because of a sight that, by definition, *had* to be produced by trickery? Was it not preferable to assert what *had* to be true—fraud—rather than to admit that he was not quite sure how it had been accomplished? Isn't it far better to admit that a peasant can fool you rather than to admit that a peasant can have access to powers that dwarf anything a trained physician can do? Why should he abandon his faith in exchange for nagging doubt all the rest of his life—not to mention ridicule by his peers if he should lend support to such *a priori* nonsense? Why, in short, should any Western physician who is not an amateur ghost-chaser abandon his faith in rational medical techniques?

There is only one answer: because what Western physicians are confronting is a real phenomenon. It can be tested. It is, to use an overworked term, the real thing. What is *not* real is the Kantian phenomenal realm—a hypothetically autonomous world that man's mind can comprehend, thereby giving man power over phenomena. But unlike the religion of Christianity, rationalistic materialism cannot successfully deal with such phenomena. Materialists can try to bottle up occult facts, as they did for two centuries, but the genie is out of the bottle. The only defense is an epistemological system that accounts for the phenomena of occult powers, while simultaneously denying their long-run efficacy in comparison with an even more powerful system of thought and practice that employs both spiritual power *and* the power inherent in rational thought. In short, the religion which gave birth to the bastard system known as Western materialism: Christianity. For if Christianity does not win the battle, then we must continue to bury the truth, or return to the primitive, or, worst of all, witness the fusion of technocratic power and occult immoralism. The Wandermans of the world have been unable to bottle up the genie of occult power. Who, then, is prepared to step in where the Wandermans have failed?

What this chapter has described has been referred to as primitive healing. But primitivism is not the monopoly of the underdeveloped nations of the world. *Primitivism is a philosophy of life.* There are now signs that demonic healing has become popular in urban America. The point of entry, it seems, is California.

California Dreaming

At a "festival" put on by the greater Los Angeles chapter of the International Cooperation Council (your instinctive reaction to the name is no doubt quite correct), called the "New Consciousness Celebration," held on July 28, 1974, several hundred weirdoes and I listened to a day of speeches by yogis, swamis, experimental educators, sufi dancers, and goofy singers, who informed us about the possibilities of higher living and greater power. The highlight of the day came when Rev. Roslyn Winsky appeared—late, it turned out, because her car had broken down. (Bad vibes? Bad plugs?) She is a truly charismatic person, in the Bishop Sheen sense, as well as the Tony Agpaoa sense. Vibrant, confident, Winsky convinces an audience that her story is the truth. She is a psychic healer. Operating from a trance, Reverend Winsky (who appears to be in her early thirties) and her spirit mediums perform such feats, she claims, as rebuilding spinal discs by mental power. She operates on a regular basis, and she trains people in these techniques. She assured us, as they all do, that "anyone can do these things." When we broke off into discussion groups—some things never change—her group session was jammed with enthusiastic people. Next door were the

Chaneys, of Astara fame, more traditional Los Angeles instructors in metaphysics.[67] About a dozen people came by, mostly middle-aged ladies. Healing was clearly where the action was understood to be.

The Reverend Harold G. Plume is regarded by some as being the most powerful medium in central California. This may not mean very much, since California's more sane people—farmers, oil rig workers, country music singers—live and work in central California. One does not even capitalize the *c* in central California, it is so normal. But Reverend Mr. Plume is not normal. He uses the same operating techniques that the Philippine healers use. He sticks his fingers into the body. He is pastor of St. John's First Chapel of Healing, which has lots of prayers, hymns, passing of collection plates, and other spiritual activities. If he did not have spiritual activities, he might be in jail for practicing medicine without a license.

Like Tony Agpaoa, who had visions as a youth, Plume had visions. But he had them at age three, which may be a record of some kind. People would appear to him in his room. He saw the disembodied spirits of the departed. He is now controlled by a Chinese physician who lived 2,500 years ago. His name is Hoo-Fang. Honest. And he does something even Dr. Fritz and Agpaoa's "protector" never tried: he operates right through clothing. Complete modesty prevails in his church; he is British, not some simple barbarian. Things are done properly. Furthermore, he inserts only his fingers whenever possible, not his hands, plus a piece of Kleenex. There is no muss, no fuss, and no blood. Ladies in knit dresses bought in California shops do not appreciate bloody performances.[68] (Agpaoa is unique in this respect; he loves a bloody show.)

The Reality of Hexes

If the power of healing by demonic possession exists, as the external evidence indicates, then a secondary problem appears: the ability to produce illness by these same occult forces. The belief in primitive cultures that certain "holy men," meaning unholy men, have the power to inflict illness and even death is widespread. Western observers almost always regard such beliefs as being totally superstitious, yet the evidence is overwhelmingly on the side of the primitive accounts. The problem with the Western explanation of death from sorcery, namely, that the "victim" commits suicide, against his will, by means of his psychosomatic power, raises the question of the kinds of mental power possessed by primitive people. How does the human mind self-destruct the human body within a few hours or at most a few days? How does it come about that this power of self-destruction is triggered, time after time, by the fear of a particular man's threat to kill the victims?

One incomprehensible example of primitive witchcraft is reported by Valentine. One of the Philippine healers, Mercado, who had been trained by Agpaoa, healed a young woman whom he had diagnosed as a witchcraft victim. She had not been aware of her plight and was horrified. She had only thought that she was ill for some physical reason. Without doubt, her case is the strangest that appears in this book. Valentine describes what he saw:

> Again Mercado worked rapidly on the patient's lower abdomen. The girl was not in pain, but she was evidently upset at the thought of being a witchcraft victim. She covered her face with her arms and sobbed convulsively during the operation. I leaned in for a closer look; my nose was about eighteen inches from the action. Suddenly several large, flat leaves from some tropical plant popped up from the surgical opening like a jack-in-the-box. I stared in blank disbelief as the crowd behind me gasped in unison. Mercado plucked the leaves out of the girl and waved them to the onlookers.
> "Witchcraft," he explained with a toothy grin.
> Kurt Osolsobie's eyebrows were raised—he too was seeing but not understanding. Jack Netchin, standing at the head of the table taking pictures, just shrugged and kept on filming. I picked up a leaf that had missed the wastebasket and examined it closely. It looked and felt like the leaf of a plant. It was spattered with blood and about ten inches long and three inches wide at its widest point. If Mercado had palmed the leaves, they would have been crumpled; that leaf was perfectly smooth. I'd already made routine checks of the sheet and the cotton. Before the girl got off the table, I examined her, with Lolet's help; the waistband of her skirt was tight. Those leaves *had* been inside the girl.
> In Don Wild's film, Marcello Jainar removes about two feet of "plastic wrap" from a patient's abdomen as Tony looks on. The slowest of slow motion cannot detect any sleight of hand. Certainly it's illogical, but the whole phenomenon is illogical.[69]

How can we explain this? Fakery? At eighteen inches, in front of cameras and many witnesses? Yet how could leaves get into a woman's intestinal area? Aborigines in Australia believe that when a hex using a "death bone" is made, a second bone literally enters the victim and kills him, either directly or by the sorcerer's burying the death bone, burning it, or in some way destroying it.[70] Can this be correct? Is this analogous to the Filipino housemaid's rash, which was treated by pulling rice-sized pellets through microscopically small pores? What has a leaf in common with pellets? There is no logical answer, simply because such phenomena are not governed by rational categories. What is more likely than the idea that such items do reside inside men's systems is to assume some form of demonic transformation. The pellets and the leaves are literally materialized, either by the healer's control agent, or by some other occult source of power. In other words, the victim of witchcraft is under spiritual bondage, and this bondage has physical aspects, such as a feeling of illness or discomfort. But these feelings are not those that would be caused if real leaves were inside the body. No Western physician could operate on the victim and discover leaves inside the body, or pellets instead of a rash. The visible signs that are produced when the spirit control agent of the healer works on the bodies of the victims are a means of confirmation to primitive people that the occult is directly involved. The leaves become *tangible symbols of demonic power*, confusing to the Western observer, but understood in principle by the local population. The local tribesman nods in agreement with the healer's diagnosis: yes, it must have been witchcraft. The sight of the abnormal affirms the existence of occult power, thereby increasing men's fear of the local medicine man or village sorcerer who must have produced the hex. Seeing, after all, is believing—unless you are a *Western* observer. For the Westerner, seeing is also believing, but the belief is in sleight of hand by men, not a kind of sleight of hand by demons. But the effect on the tribe is the same, whoever is playing games: continued occult bondage and perpetual fear in a world of unfamiliar laws and hostile forces—intensely personal forces.

Kurt Koch, the Protestant exorcist whose books are filled with case histories of occult bondage, relates a remarkable story of a native pastor in Nigeria, a member of the Izi tribe. He had been suffering from a serious disease of the lungs, and his physicians believed that he was close to death. His X rays indicated that both lungs were filled with blood. He was literally drowning in his own blood. The pastor had asked the local missionary to come and visit him.

> "I sense I am not going to die," he told the missionary. "It seems to me as if this is only an attack of the powers of darkness. Please, will you command these powers to leave me." The missionary, however, hesitated for he was more inclined to believe what the doctors had told him than to believe what his native brother said. But the pastor urged him again. Finally he agreed and he prayed roughly with the words, "Lord Jesus, if my brother here is right, and this is only an attack of the enemy, then deliver him. But forgive me if what I am saying is silly." The missionary then commanded the evil powers to go, although in his heart he doubted if he was doing the right thing. What happened? Suddenly the pastor vomited and brought up a vast amount of blood. The doctor was called immediately, but he said that this was the end. Yet instead of dying, the man began to recover. A few days later he was X rayed again. A miracle had taken place. The massive caverns in his lungs had closed up, and instead of certain death, the native Christian was wonderfully healed by the hand of the Lord.[71]

The missionary's reaction was typically Western. It is hardly surprising. Orthodox Protestant theological seminaries never offer courses in demonic possession. Demons are covered during one week, or even less, in one semester of systematic theology. ("Angels, Fallen.") That men are possessed today, or that missionaries might face problems relating to actual occult power, is (or was in the mid-1960s and earlier) never even considered.

Koch then goes on to say: "Events of this nature are nothing we can copy. God cannot be forced to do the same for all who are suffering in this way. He alone is sovereign. It is he, and not us, who decides who is to be healed and who is not." Understandably, Koch is totally hostile to the full-time faith healers in Christian churches, and their cousins, the independent healers with their tents or their regularly scheduled miracles at the Shrine Auditorium or Sports Arena. God is not a kind of injection that is at the beck and call of flamboyant faith healers. He is not a package of instant healing mix (just add holy water, stir under a spotlight, and pour). The Christian ministry of healing is to be done quietly by prayerful elders in the home or in a hospital (James 5:14, 15). And God's healing is not to be accompanied by three to five collection offerings. (Rev. Gerald Latal, an Orthodox Presbyterian church minister, was asked in the 1940s to co-sponor the appearance of a now-famous healing lady. It was at the beginning of her career. He was skeptical, but he and his elders met with her. She wanted her organization to handle all the mechanics, including the promotion. He asked whether co-sponsoring churches would be given full credit. "All *right!*" she replied to him. "But I'll take the *collections.*" The Reverend Mr. Latal wisely decided not to have anything to do with the project. The lady is still taking those collections.)

Koch makes some telling comments on the ministry of Oral Roberts, who established himself as a faith healer. Today, Roberts' televison programs are modeled along the lines of the more conventional evangelists: a weekly "intimate" get-together, with a small studio audience, plus clean-cut but "upbeat" singers. He has abandoned the mass healings; he just bows his head and prays that God will heal people in the audience. This is valid enough. But in the early 1950s, before he had joined the Methodist church, before he had built a college and recruited a basketball team of NCAA tournament caliber, he was on the sawdust trail. He did not have one-hour travelogue specials on Alaska in full color; he had live broadcasts from his tent. The walking wounded hobbled up to be healed, and he laid hands on them all—or at least those who were screened to come up onto the stage. Koch comments on Roberts' appearance at the World Congress of Evangelism held in Berlin in 1966. Roberts was the leader of a subcommittee.

> There were about 300 delegates present including the Rev. Pagel, the evangelist Leo Janz and myself. Roberts had been speaking on the subject of healing when one of the Americans present asked him, "Mr. Roberts, isn't it true that during your television programs you have sometimes asked the viewers to place a glass of water on the television during the actual broadcast?" After receiving an affirmative answer, his questioner went on, "And isn't it also true that at the end of the programs you have told the viewers to drink the water if they are seeking healing?" Again, in the presence of the 300 or so delegates Oral Roberts replied, "Yes." That was honest of him. But what type of healing is this? Occasionally during similar programs one of the viewers has been asked to place his hand on the television set and with his free hand to either touch or to form a chain with other viewers present. But this is the sort of practice one finds in connection with spiritistic table-lifting, when chains are formed in order to encourage the flow of mediumistic forces.[72]

Roberts admitted publicly that when he was younger, an old Indian once healed him. Koch speculates that this may have been the origin of his healing powers.[73] Transfers of such powers are reported again and again by healing mediums. (Rev. Harold Plume is one example.)

Conclusion

Western rationalism is as one-sided and narrow as any other world-and-life view. Those who hold to its premises have exercised great power over the last two centuries. Much of this power is well deserved. By refining the techniques of science, Western thinkers have made possible a flowering of human culture that is the envy of the primitive, magical world. The whole underdeveloped world wants a piece of our action, but it does not usually want to give up the other aspects of its culture that guarantee continued poverty. By turning its leaders into socialists, materialists, bureaucrats, and rationalists through scholarships to our better universities, we have cut off the leaders from their popular support. Democracy cannot flourish in these nations for many reasons, not the least of which is the undemocratic nature of all bureaucratic rule; and it is bureaucracy, far more than democracy, that has been the West's major organizational export—bureaucracy financed by government-to-government foreign aid and heavy taxation inside the recipient nations. But democracy also cannot flourish where demonism is present. The essence of demonism is an elitist manipulation of the common tribesmen. The means of power are personal asceticism, demon possession, trances, visions, dreams, and total immersion into the occult. *Ritual,* not a study of the regularities of nature, is the law of primitive cultures. The ideology of bureaucracy may be in conformity with some of the aspects of demonism, but democracy is in total opposition. No one but a Western intellectual could have believed that India was democratic, or that its traditions and institutions might permit the limited democracy of the liberal West. Indira Gandhi did not cut down Indian democracy at the roots; there never were any roots, except in the dreams and visions of Western commentators and Indian newspaper editorials. And what is true of India is true of the whole so-called Third World. Where demonism is a part of the culture, democracy cannot take root. Neither can the rationalistic production methods of free-market capitalism.

What is so disturbing today is the growing popularity of the Eastern cosmologies within Western circles, especially among the formally educated young. It is not possible to import Western versions of Eastern philosophy—all nicely sterilized by the professors of Eastern religion on the campuses—without simultaneously opening up one's mind and soul to all the rest of Eastern culture: monism, mysticism, asceticism, irrationalism, and finally magic. The East is coming West. It represents the importation of intellectual and cultural stagnation at best; at worst, it will destroy the very foundations of Western productivity. It is integration into the void.

Everyone wants to "do good." Healing seems to do good. Occult healing seems to do good much more cheaply. Henry Belk, the rich psychic investigator who helped to popularize both Arigo and the Philippine healers, and who is rich because his staunchly Presbyterian father established a cost-effective, economically rational chain of stores, has in classic words described the "benefits" of healing by spirits: "They don't eat, they don't pay taxes, and they supply the labor."[74] At the heart of all magic is the quest for power, but at low cost. Asceticism is personal, not cultural. Economically, it is the philosophy of something for nothing. Westerners who think they can make use of Eastern and primitive healing techniques without the personal ascetism required of the healing adepts will find that the price of their power is far, far higher than they think.

Westerners who do accept the validity of the stories concerning psychic healing may say to themselves: "What a shame that we in the West have closed off ourselves to such wonderful powers." Wonderful indeed; *filled with wonder.* But the same person who is saddened by the absence of occult healing techniques in the West lives in a clean environment and has at his disposal skilled medical diagnosticians operating in terms of the division of labor (meaning physicians can check each other's progress and learn). The Western citizen wants the blessings of both cultures, not realizing that what primitive man has is a *curse*. Now we find men who are out to fuse Western technology and Eastern irrationalism. They are out to build an electric Tibet. They fail to comprehend that in an electric Tibet, not even the machines would be healthy. A Tibetan culture does not accept a Western view of the world in which men can gain access to electrical power, thereby increasing the productivity of all people, not just the demonic elite. We cannot fuse the two cultures; the two cultures are at war.

If your head hurts, take two aspirin and go to bed. Let the Arigos of the world remain where they belong: struggling in the jungles.

8
Magic, Envy, and Foreign Aid

> But it shall come to pass, if thou wilt not hearken unto the voice of the LORD thy God, to observe to do all his commandments and his statutes which I command thee this day; that all these curses shall come upon thee, and overtake thee.
>
> *Deuteronomy 28:15*

One of the characteristic features of the Christian West is its commitment to the concept of linear history. Westerners seldom give the concept much thought. They assume, almost automatically, that no other idea of history could be held by anyone. But the concept of linear history—a unique past, present, and future—is very much the product of religious faith. It was the Hebrew concept of the creation as an unrepeatable event that gave the West its belief in historical time. By affirming the doctrine of creation, Christianity transformed the West—indeed, created the West. It is quite proper, therefore, for Charles N. Cochrane to end his book *Christianity and Classical Culture* (1940) with a chapter on Augustine, and for William C. Bark to begin his book *Origins of the Medieval World* (1958) with a chapter on Augustine. It was Augustine's formulation of linear history in *The City of God* that served to transform the thinking of Western scholars. The concept of cyclical history, held by classical culture and the ancient pagan kingdoms, was overturned by Augustine.[1] His words served as a kind of intellectual touchstone: "The education of the human race, represented by the people of God, has advanced, like that of an individual, through certain epochs, or, as it were, ages, so that it might gradually rise from earthly to heavenly things, and from the visible to the invisible."[2]

The source of the idea of progress is Christianity. The pagan concept of historical development, with its inevitable cycles of growth and decay, did not leave room for long-term progress. But Christianity offered hope to men: by conforming themselves to the image of Christ, men might see progress spiritually. This, in turn, was understood by Protestants, and especially Calvinists, as undergirding the possibility of external, cultural, and economic progress—a literal fulfillment of the promises of Deuteronomy 8 and 28. Thus, with the sixteenth and seventeenth centuries came a new concept of applied Christianity: economic growth.

This is not to say that medieval Catholicism entirely ignored economic growth. In fact, one of the continual problems of the church in the Middle Ages was its constant tendency to grow rich. The legendary productivity of the Benedictine monasteries became a recurring source of embarrassment. Benedictine monks, though they owned no property personally, were energetic, thrifty, and innovative farmers. Over and over, their monastic communities prospered, occasioning cries for reform. The external economic blessings were simultaneously a sign of efficient management and a source of embarrassment. In one sense, the Protestants made every man an industrious monk, and by affirming the legitimacy of private property, the Protestants opened the door to the expansion of riches. Nevertheless, they cautioned against the dangers of wealth, even as Moses had cautioned his listeners in the oft-quoted Deuteronomic passages. The idea of compound growth over time was the product of an explicitly theological interpretation of time.

Primitive Culture

Because Western thinkers operate by some version of the idea of progress, they inevitably think of primitive cultures as those which are *historically prior*. Somehow, they have not been able to "progress" along the linear time model. They have been held back, and the supposedly innate tendencies toward progress that can be found whenever men form communities have not been able to flourish. But this approach to the question of economic or cultural development is fundamentally in error. The existence of what we might call expansionary pressures is in no way automatic. What is normal, that is, historically most common, is for a few members of a culture to be innovative, with the vast majority content with things as they are. There is no confidence in progress; in fact, the whole idea is absolutely foreign. Traditional approaches are assumed to be satisfactory for most problems; social change is therefore not expected, nor even appreciated. Two distinctly Western beliefs are absent: first, the belief in linear history, and second, the belief that reason is capable of unlocking the secrets of nature. Without a future orientation, primitive cultures do not possess an inner dynamic favorable to social advancement. Without a concept of practical reason—the link between the laws of the mind and the laws of nature—these cultures lack the engine of progress.

It is not enough to argue that primitive cultures are historically prior. The reason why they are primitive is that the concept of "historically prior" has no meaning for them, for the concept of "historically future" is meaningless. The remarkable scholarly writings of the cultural anthropologist, Mircea Eliade, have dwelt on this subject at length. Cyclical history (or, as he calls it, the myth of the eternal return) has placed a premium on the escape from the burdens of history. Only through ecstatic release, or ritual chaos, do primitive cultures expect to regain the lost paradise of the age of gold. Magic is central to this quest. Through magic, the holy men of the tribe or community can recreate the conditions of the original creation—an evolutionary creation—thus permitting the community to participate ritually in that original creative act or series of acts. The festivals of Mardi Gras and Carnival are the product of the pagan faith in cleansing chaos and the annual abolition of conventional behavior. The bondage of law, which is itself the product of the degeneration of the ages, is one of the primary targets of ritualistic chaos. The ages of gold, silver, bronze, and now iron (to use Hesiod's traditional outline in his *Works and Days*) have brought with them the increasing bondage of men to law. Lawlessness is therefore a ritual affirmation of a better way of life, a kind of regeneration socially. It is the philosophy of "power from below," in Rushdoony's words.

Pagan cultures deny the doctrines of evolution. They affirm the doctrine of *devolution*. The hope of these men is in some magical *discontinuous event*—a messianic magical savior, a successful revolution, the discovery of a magical formula—that will restore the lost paradise. They see life's problems as metaphysical—the lack of some attribute of being—rather than moral and ethical. The problem of man is therefore not covenantal disobedience to a holy and sovereign God, but a flaw in the creation. Men will restore the lost paradise, not by repentance and godly labor in every area of life, but by the magical exercise of power.

The heart of cultural primitivism is the desire to transcend time, to abolish time's burdens. The Christian idea of slow economic progress that is the product of continual spiritual discipline and conformity to God's ethical laws, is absolutely foreign to the pagan culture. In magical society, there is a distinctly revolutionary impulse, as Eliade notes:

> The wish to abolish time can be seen even more clearly in the "orgy" which takes place, with varying degrees of violence, during the New Year ceremonies. An orgy is also a regression into the "dark," a restoration of the primeval chaos, and as such precedes all creation, every manifestation of ordered form. The fusion of all forms into one single, vast, undifferentiated unity is an exact reproduction of the "total" mode of reality. I pointed out earlier the function and meaning of the orgy, at once sexual and agricultural; at the cosmological level, the "orgy" represents chaos or the ultimate disappearance of limits and, as time goes, the inauguration of the Great Time, of the "eternal moment," or nonduration. The presence of the orgy among the ceremonials shows the *will to abolish the past totally by abolishing all creation.*[3]

The concern is not with ethics but with the limitations of all created being. *The attempt to abolish the limits of creaturehood is the very heart of all demonic religion.* It is this impulse that militates against human progress. The existence of both law and the limits imposed by law is denied. But without law, the tool of progress is denied, for it is by the systematic application of the laws of nature that men subdue the creation, causing it to become fruitful (Genesis 1:28). Magic substitutes meaningless ritual for law, and rituals do not change. Discovery is left to the random event; illumination is understood as ecstatic rather than intellectual. Progress dies.

Subsidizing the Primitive

Western commentators generally and correctly associate magic and primitivism. The explanation, unfortunately, tends to be environmentalistic: these societies still practice magic because they are primitive. The assumption seems to be that the West, by massive doses of foreign aid, the Peace Corps, scholarships for their bright young men to Cambridge, Oxford, or Harvard, plus free public, secular education, can bring these primitive cultures "into the twentieth century." At that point, magical practices will slowly fade away. Yet the analysis is fatally flawed. The reason why these cultures are primitive is that magic, which involves a definite world-and-life view, dominates all of them. The cultures are the product of the religion of magic, not the other way around.

It is not what men possess externally that counts in the long run. What is crucial is the *attitude* toward God and the world that permeates the culture. By failing to recognize this fact, modern foreign-aid administrators have produced one folly after another, and this is as true of the Soviets as the West.[4] *Primitivism is a state of mind, a set of attitudes.* All attempts to overcome cultural backwardness, apart from a prior change of mind by the members of the culture in question, are doomed to failure. P. T. Bauer, a professor of economics at the London School of Economics, has written several important books on economic development, but in his 1972 study, *Dissent on Development,* he lays it on the line. The key to the economic development of a society is the character of the people. What they believe is vastly more significant than what they presently own:

> Examples of significant attitudes, beliefs and modes of conduct unfavourable to material progress include lack of interest in material advance, combined with resignation in the face of poverty; lack of initiative, self-reliance and of a sense of personal responsibility for the economic future of oneself and one's family; high leisure preference, together with a lassitude often found in tropical climates; relatively high prestige of passive or contemplative life compared to active life; the prestige of mysticism and of renunciation of the world compared to acquisition and achievement; acceptance of the idea of a preordained, unchanging and unchangeable universe; emphasis on performance of duties and acceptance of obligations, rather than on achievement of results, or assertion or even a recognition of personal rights; lack of sustained curiosity, experimentation and interest in change; belief in the efficacy of supernatural and occult forces and of their influence over one's destiny; insistence on the unity of the organic universe, and on the need to live with nature rather than conquer it or harness it to man's needs, an attitude of which reluctance to take animal life is a corollary; belief in

perpetual reincarnation, which reduces the significance of effort in the course of the present life; recognized status of beggary, together with a lack of stigma in the acceptance of charity; opposition to women's work outside the household.[5]

Bauer's list, coming after a lifetime of research into the question of economic underdevelopment, must be taken seriously. Obviously, no society is ever totally categorized by such a list, just as each Western, industrial nation will possess certain features found in the list. It is an ideal type, a kind of master model, and not a summary of any given culture. But where a significant number of these features are found in a culture, all the Western foreign aid available will not, in and of itself, succeed in transforming the culture. To believe that money or technical training can bring permanent economic growth is simply to believe in environmentalism.

The list is extremely informative, given the information found in previous chapters of this book. A close look at the so-called counterculture reveals that most of the elements of the backward economic society are part of the world-and-life view of the counterculture. The hippie movement of the 1960s did not begin with magic, seances, occultism, blood sacrifice, and ritual murders. It began with pessimism concerning rational methodology. It began with pessimism concerning the future, at least the Establishment's future. Vegetarianism, Eastern religion, philosophical monism, mysticism, and chemical escape from the rational world were standard tenets of the counterculture. Only toward the end of the decade did the faith in reincarnation, occultism, spirits, and other elements of witchcraft become commonplace. "Tune in, turn on, drop out" was Timothy Leary's antirational slogan, and it rested on a view of life that fundamentally corresponds with Bauer's outline of the underdeveloped society. As to the stigma associated with charity, a generation of the welfare state had eroded the older concepts of full personal responsibility and personal labor. The affluence of the society led young people to believe that wealth is automatic. Begging and outright scrounging became a way of life because of the easy availability of vast wealth in urban trash cans. As God warned the people of Israel, covenantal obedience produces wealth, but wealth brings temptation, the temptation to forget the God whose covenantal law-order made possible the wealth (Deuteronomy 8:6–20).

The occult epidemic threatens the very foundations of Western culture. Middle-class morality is the distant heir of the Puritan work ethic. As such, it has produced abundance. But this historically unprecedented economic prosperity is not a self-sustaining process. It is the product of certain attitudes and presuppositions about the nature of reality. It rests, ultimately, on a religious perception of the world. By introducing a new (and very ancient) set of religious principles—the religion of magic—the counterculture serves as a kind of Pied Piper. Religious transformation will inevitably produce cultural transformation. Western capitalism cannot possibly survive in a society that is committed to the tenets of magic.

Bauer mentions magic as one factor that retards economic development, but the German sociologist Helmut Schoeck has developed this theme in relation to another retarding factor: envy. Schoeck's book, a masterpiece, traces the impact envy has had on thinkers, cultures, and economies. Its thesis is straightforward: envy toward the wealth or achievements of others reduces the ability of individuals to advance themselves economically. Envy is not mere jealousy, as Schoeck defines it. It is not simply one man's desire for another man's possessions. It is a strong resentment against the very existence of another man's wealth or status. It involves the desire to reduce another man's wealth even when this reduction in his wealth in no way improves the position of the envious person. Nowhere is envy more devastating than in so-called primitive cultures.

If a person or a family should get ahead of the accepted tribal minimum per-capita wealth, two very dangerous things may easily occur. First, the offending party may be suspected of being a wizard or witch. Second, he may become fearful of being the object of the envious evil magic of others. As Schoeck writes: "The whole literature on the subject of African sorcery shows the envious man (sorcerer) would like to harm the victim he envies, but only seldom with any expectation of thereby obtaining for himself the asset that he envies—whether this be a possession or a physical quality belonging to the other."[6] Understandably, this envy is present only where there is *close social proximity* between the envious and the envied. It is always regarded as very difficult to bewitch a stranger with any success.[7]

The efficacy of demonic magic is strong in these non-Christian cultures. The fear of magic is pervasive. Thus, the threat of its use against the truly successful man causes men with talents to conceal them from their fellows. Men become secretive about what they own. They prefer to attribute any personal successes to luck or fate, both impersonal.

> *Institutionalized envy* . . . or the ubiquitous fear of it, means that there is little possibility of individual economic achievement and no contact with the outside world through which the community might hope to progress. No one dares to show anything that might lead people to think that he was better off. Innovations are unlikely. Agricultural methods remain traditional and primitive, to the detriment of the whole village, because every deviation from previous practice comes up against the limitations of envy.[8]

Furthermore, Schoeck writes: "It is impossible for several families to pool resources or tools of any kind in a common undertaking. It is almost equally impossible for any one man to adopt a leading role in the interests of the village."[9] While Schoeck does not discuss it, the problem of institutionalized envy and magic for the establishment of republican institutions in primitive cultures is almost overwhelming. Once a chief's link to traditional authority is officially denied by secular educators in a culture, who is to lead? If a man cannot point to a long tradition of authority or his semidivine status as a leader, who is to say who is to lead? Whoever dares to proclaim himself as leader had better be prepared to defend his title not merely at the polling booth, but from envious magic. In a culture in which the authority of traditional rulers has been eroded by Western secularism and Western theories of individualism and democracy, the obvious alternative to traditional authority is military power.

In April 1975, the tiny, poverty-stricken African "nation" of Chad had a military coup. Months later, the news media briefly picked up the story of the deposed leader, Ngarta Tombalbaye, who had been executed by the military. He had imported Haitian witch doctors—one of Haiti's few products that can compete successfully in the international division of labor—and had used Radio Chad to broadcast what were purported to be spirit messages. Men in every station of life were told to return to their tribal villages and participate in initiation rites from Chad's Stone Age past. (Chad's Stone Age, chronologically speaking, ended a couple of centuries ago.) From 1962, when Tombalbaye took control of the government, until his death, Christians who refused to participate in these rites were tortured, murdered, or forced to flee the country. One pastor, Moussa Bopen, opposed the rites for a year, and when he was threatened with execution, asked if he could preach one last sermon. His request was granted. His topic: "The Evils of Idolatry." He was fatally clubbed from behind before he could finish. One European-educated college professor returned home to his village, underwent initiation, and later claimed to have been born free. He wears a suit now (he had worn a loin cloth during his initiation), but sleeps with magical knives under his bed.

What finished the man's rule was his attempted purge of the army. He arrested two high officers and promised to reorganize the army. He was seized and executed shortly thereafter. It was not Western democracy that replaced the rule of the magicians, but military despotism.[10] Similar reports have come from other Third World areas for a decade. The centuries-long, or millennia-long, paralysis produced by demonic power cannot be overcome by Western checks and Western educations. The winners are those who have mastered one aspect of Western technology: weaponry. Military despotism has been the secularized West's major export to the Third World. "General" Amin of Uganda is only the loudest, most flamboyant of the corporals who came to power when the Western colonial administrators gave up and went home. He is the symbol of transported Western administrative techniques—the strange hybrid of tribalism, occultism, and secular technology.

Envy has crucially important implications for a culture's concept of time. Schoeck concludes: "In a culture incapable of any form of competition, time means nothing."[11] Men do not discuss their private plans with each other. Shared goals, except of a traditional nature, are almost absent in magic-dominated societies. "Ubiquitous envy, fear of it and those who harbour it, cuts off such people from any kind of communal action directed toward the future. Every man is for himself, every man is thrown back upon his own resources. All striving, preparation and planning for the future can be undertaken only by socially fragmented, secretive beings."[12] Is it any wonder, then, that primitive cultures stay primitive, despite massive doses of foreign aid, that is, government-to-government aid. Schoeck does not exaggerate when he writes, "As a system of social control, Black Magic is of tremendous importance, because it governs all interpersonal relationships."

Power, Cause, and Effect

"The fundamental aim of all magic is to impose the human will on nature, on man or on the supersensual world in order to master them." With these words, E. M. Butler introduces her book, *Ritual Magic* (1949). The goals, however, are rigorously materialistic: fame, power, fortune, success. Anton Szandor LaVey, the self-ordained (1966) minister of the Church of Satan in San Francisco, is quite open about the goals of Satanism: "Anyone who pretends to be interested in magic or the occult for reasons other than gaining personal power is the worst kind of hypocrite."[13] Further, says LaVey:

> White magic is supposedly utilized only for good or unselfish purposes, and black magic, we are told, is used only for selfish or "evil" reasons. Satanism draws no such dividing line. Magic is magic, be it used to help or hinder. The Satanist, being the modern magician, should have the ability to decide what is just, and then apply the powers of magic to attain his goals.
>
> During white magic ceremonies, the practitioners stand within a pentagram to protect themselves from the "evil" forces which they call upon for help. To the Satanist, it seems a bit two-faced to call on these forces for help, while at the same time protecting yourself from the very powers you have asked for assistance. The Satanist realizes that only by putting himself in league with these forces can he fully and unhypocritically utilize the Powers of Darkness to his best advantage.[14]

In short, concludes LaVey, "Satanism is not a white light religion; it is a religion of the flesh, the mundane, the carnal—all of which are ruled by Satan, the personification of the Left Hand Path."[15]

The Left Hand Path: here is one of the familiar slogans of the occult underground. The Right Hand Path is the path of mystical illumination, higher consciousness, white magic, and philosophical monism. Members of these seemingly innocuous groups constantly warn newcomers against the Left Hand Path, that is, the quest for occult power for selfish ends. LaVey regards all this as hypocrisy: occult power is occult power, so why mix in remnants of Christian morality? It is ultimately the power of man, says LaVey, that Satan symbolizes. "Man, the animal, is the godhead to the Satanist."[16] What's more, "The Satanist realizes that man, and the action and reaction of the universe, is responsible for everything, and doesn't mislead himself into thinking that someone cares."[17] Therefore, he says, men should live consistently with this faith. There are no standards except those forged by each individual Satanist. "Death to the weakling, wealth to the strong!.... I break away from all conventions that do not lead to my earthly success and happiness."[18] The great enemy is a conservatism that is grounded in Christian principles.

> Behold the crucifix; what does it symbolize? Pallid incompetence hanging on a tree. I question all things. As I stand before the festering and varnished facades of your haughtiest moral dogmas, I write thereon in letters of blazing scorn: Lo and behold; all this is fraud.... The chief duty of every new age is to upraise new men to determine its

liberties, to lead it towards material success—to rend the rusty padlocks and chains of dead custom that always prevent healthy expansion. Theories and ideas that may have meant life and hope and freedom for our ancestors may now mean destruction, slavery, and dishonor to us! As environments change, no human ideal standeth sure![19]

The hope of LaVey is that his recommended system of power will produce "healthy expansion." Yet the religion of magic is calculated to destroy the very foundations of social progress. By creating a social system based on fear of other men, magic destroys the possibility of a systematic division of labor. It destroys the concept of linear time, for in a world of flux, especially moral flux, it becomes impossible for men to calculate the difference between good and bad results over time. Moral flux reduces time to chaos; indeed, the very chaos cults of the ancient world and today's primitive cultures acknowledge this fact: moral flux, ritually applied, recreates the eternal moment where time's bounds are broken. Without the ability to distinguish good from evil, men cannot distinguish cause from effect over time. If whirl is king, who can comprehend the kingdom? Science becomes impossible, for the regularities of nature are forever being transcended by the power of the magicians. As Don Juan told Castaneda, without faith in his everyday world and its everyday activities, the occult world of power threatened him day and night. The radical autonomy of the philosophy of Satanism, like the radical autonomy of existentialism and modern philosophy, cannot help but result in cultural impotence and stagnation. It is the death of culture.

Conclusion

The fruits of magic, economically speaking, are not productivity and unlimited wealth, but just the opposite: the erosion of capital, the stagnation or even decline of per-capita wealth, and the end of economic growth. The society of Satan lives off the stolen capital of two thousand years of Christian culture.

The Christian premise is that the fear of God is the beginning of wisdom (Proverbs 1:7), but that those who live in the fear of the Lord need not fear other men (Psalm 27:1). The Satanic premise is that the Lord of heaven need not be feared, but that both Satan and other men are to be feared. This creates a sense of bondage; the creation, rather than the Creator, is feared. The source of *Christian activism* is the knowledge that under God's providence, the faithful servant triumphs, if not during his stay on earth, then at least on the final day of judgment. Thus, the command that the earth be subdued to the glory of God (Genesis 1:28) can be taken seriously. Passivity toward the affairs of life is clearly prohibited. Christian men, as God's delegated superiors over the creation, are required to take positions of leadership. The source of their strength is their faith; the source of their power over earthly affairs is their commitment to the tool of social reconstruction: the revealed law of God.

On the other hand, the Satanist lives in a universe devoid of predictable laws. Ritual rules supreme, but there is always the fear that some minute aspect of ritual will be neglected or transgressed, or that some other magician can master the terms of the prescribed ritual even more efficiently. The source of man's power is therefore in the hands of a created being who is fundamentally hostile to man's desires, basically the liar of liars whose solemn word cannot be trusted, whose tongue is a snare to the unwary. There is a marvelous science-fantasy short story about a young man who was failing his class in mathematics. He then discovered an old book of magic, and decided to master the ritual and summon up a demon. After going through nights of preparation, he drew the protecting hexagram on the floor of his room and called forth the hideous demon whose power he would command. The awful creature appeared, sending terror through him, but he knew that he was protected by the chalk marks on the floor. "I need help with my geometry," he announced. "You certainly do," the demon replied, as he stepped easily across the pentagram.

The spirit of the law has no place in demonic rituals. It is the form that counts, above all. Men are in bondage to the outward forms, in contrast to the biblical perspective that states that God has no need of our sacrifices, but desires justice, mercy, and a humble walk before Him (Micah 6:6–8). Christian men can be confident in the face of the creation precisely because it is the trustworthiness of God that reassures them, not confidence in the ritualistic works of their own hands. This element of trust is what is totally absent from the world of Satanic intervention. The idea of the compact with the Devil is that the ultimate goal is to break it. Mutual distrust is its very foundation. In contrast, the idea of the covenant with God is based on the hope that God will honor it even in the face of our weaknesses (Romans 8:28–31). A society can be constructed on the basis of mutual trust and the fulfilling of contractual (covenantal) obligations precisely because each man sees every obligation as one made under God's ultimate sovereignty and authority. A man's word can be regarded as his bond, not because he is autonomous, but because no man is autonomous.

The implicit humanism of all Satanism—that men shall be as God, knowing [determining] good and evil (Genesis 3:5)—has been made explicit in the writings of LaVey and the man on whose model LaVey is obviously acting, Aleister Crowley. Crowley's important book, *Magick in Theory and Practice*, which was originally written in 1911, has spelled out the Satanic premise: man is God. "For the Gods are the enemies of Man; it is Nature that Man must overcome ere he enter the kingdom. *The true God is man. In man are all things hidden.* Of these the Gods, Nature, Time, all the powers of the universe are rebellious slaves."[20] He then informs his readers that it is in his name that all others should conquer nature. He was no shrinking violet. Yet the result of his faith was a kind of impotence. All money, he admitted, slipped through his fingers. "Every human affection that He had in His heart—and that heart aches for Love as few hearts can ever conceive—was torn and trampled with such infernal ingenuity in His intensifying torture that His endurance is beyond belief." As he says, his children died, his wives drank themselves to death or went mad.[21] In short, his life was a disaster. But he invariably capitalized his name and spoke of himself in the third person, as if he were a god.

Crowley was at least consistent. He knew the origin of his faith, for he spoke of

"Chaos, the All-Father."²² There is no law in the world, no truth, except for his own writings.²³ He had to believe in "Gods," for these are nothing more than the laws of nature, "and thus their 'Wills' are immutable and absolute."²⁴ Yet there is no law, except for his famous dictum: "Do what thou wilt shall be the whole of the law."²⁵ There is no Devil. There are demonic hosts who can serve men.²⁶ These demons are fallible, and they can be manipulated emotionally. Every fact is autonomous; there is no law-order that stands in relation to man.²⁷ Yet the magician is nonetheless sovereign: "For there is no power either of the firmament or of the ether, or of the earth or under the earth, on dry land or in the water, of whirling air or of rushing fire, or any spell or scourge of God which is not obedient to the necessity of the Magician!"²⁸ And to achieve this absolute sovereignty over nature, the magician must submit entirely to the invisible forces of secret intelligence—demonic spirits who are not infallible, as he informs us: "It is equally necessary that the muscles with which he manipulates the apparatus of divination must be entirely independent of any volition of his. He must lend them for the moment to the intelligence whom he is consulting. . . ."²⁹ Chaos, in Crowley's world, is indeed king, the All-Father. His is the world of terror and destruction: "There is a Magical Operation of maximum importance: the Initiation of a New Aeon. When it becomes necessary to utter a Word, the whole Planet must be bathed in blood."³⁰

Should it be surprising that such a moral and spiritual universe is impotent? Should it startle us to find that where the philosophy of magic reigns supreme in men's hearts, they are unable to construct permanent institutional conditions favorable to the full exercise of human creativity? Should men wonder why it is that the Christian West has provided the emotional and legal incentives for men to transform the external realm of nature in order to conform it to the needs and goals of men? Embarked on a quest for autonomous power over nature, the Satanist finds chaos and ultimate impotence. Desiring to create conditions favorable to his own personal goals, the Satanist consumes the spiritual and legal capital of Christian civilization. The world of the Devil is a masochistic universe that is destined to total failure. Yet secularism has eroded the commitment of Western men to such an extent that they believe that foreign aid by government decree will bring demonic societies the blessings of Christian liberty apart from the spiritual foundations, which indicates how demonic the foundations of secular humanism really are. That Western capital should wind up in the treasuries of the Chads of the world is preposterous. To subsidize the demonic systems that have kept most of the world in spiritual darkness and economic poverty is to erode Christian capital that much faster. It is masochism—multi-billion-dollar masochism—yet the practice has gone on for a generation. We think that Western money and Western secular educations can convert savages into modernism. What we see before our eyes is one set of savages, bearing Ph.D's from Harvard and D. Phil's from Oxford, subsidizing the savages in the Third World (who sometimes have degrees from the same universities) with the earnings of less sophisticated men who have been made to feel guilty for their hard-earned prosperity. The politics of guilt and pity, as Rushdoony has called it, is the Devil's tool. It is money down the Devil's fiscal rathole.³¹

9
Escape from Creaturehood

> Therefore if any man be in Christ, he is a new creature: old things are passed away; behold, all things are become new.
>
> *II Corinthians 5:17*

We come now to the heart of this book. By now the reader may be confused. What do all these things mean? Eyeless sight, auras photographed by Kirlian photography, spontaneous human combustion, psychic healing, knives in eyes, water witching, and other improbable facets of human life that the textbooks ignore: there is far too much here for any one person to master. Dozens of books could be written and have been written on these topics, as well as thousands or even hundreds of thousands of books on similar weird events. Yet we must not become like those described by the apostle Paul as "ever learning, and never able to come to the knowledge of the truth" (II Timothy 3:7). There are fascinating aspects about the general subject of the occult, but books about the occult should not be written merely to satisfy the curious or the potential occult practitioner. Men and women should know of the existence of such phenomena in order to avoid them and give competent warnings to those who have not avoided them.

There are many other subjects that might have been covered: exorcism and demonic possession, ghosts, poltergeists, flying saucers, Fortean phenomena (the weird and unexplained), mediumship, Theosophy, spiritualism, secret societies, the history of witchcraft, vampirism, and on and on. But the endless piling up of data cannot convince the rationalist skeptic, and it threatens to overwhelm the average reader. And as we read in the Bible, "of making many books there is no end; and much study is a weariness of the flesh" (Ecclesiastes 12:12).

The thesis of this book is straightforward: there are unexplained events in this world. There are events that cannot, by their very nature, be explained by the standards of nineteenth-century rationalistic science. These events are real phenomena, and few men can simply push them aside by attributing their origin to the random events in a chance-created world. Finally, while some of these facts may be explained sometime in the future by science (Kirlian photography is the most obvious example), the best explanation is that supernatural and highly personal powers are involved. The events are too frequently associated with religious teachings that are at bottom demonic: reincarnation, self-transcendence, radical monism, the deification of man, the worship of evil, and the denial of the Creator-creature distinction.

A corollary of the main thesis is that modern humanism and logically permissible developments of the humanist tradition accord with the premises of Satanism with regard to the definition of man. This is not to say that all humanists are demonists. But it does mean that a commitment to the philosophy of humanism is no longer a shield against the demonic. It does not prevent men from dabbling in the occult or even embracing it. It certainly does not prevent the sons and daughters of the humanists of the 1930s from experimenting with demonic forces as enthusiastically as they experiment with hallucinatory drugs. In fact, such experimentation is consistent with an overall philosophy, inherited from their humanistic parents, of total criticism, antinomian experimentation, and radical skepticism. As Screwtape wrote to Wormwood, when the materialists believe in demons but not in God, the battle is over.[1]

The first principle of humanism, from the Greeks to the Renaissance to the present, is that man is the measure of all things. The Roman poet Terence said it best: "I am a man; and nothing human is foreign to me." This was one of Karl Marx's favorite phrases. It undergirded the philosophy, writings, and practices of the Marquis de Sade. But that which is human can be utterly inhuman. Man as the sole measure is a potentially terrifying guideline.

Why do men turn to the occult? There is no single answer. Different men have different motivations. The quest for power is common to all occultists who call upon the forces of nature, the forces of human intuition, or the demonic forces of the nether realm. But occult experimentation goes beyond the mere quest for power. If men wanted power, and only power, modern technology would provide them with abundant power. Colin Wilson, himself an occultist, has argued that men are trapped in the "triviality of everydayness," to use the phrase of the modern philosopher Martin Heidegger. They have had their minds formed by the focused vision of rationalism, but as a result, men have been cut off from the unseen realms around them.[2] It is a quest more for *meaning* than for power. In a crucial passage, Wilson states: "Religion, mysticism and magic all spring from the same basic 'feeling' about the universe: a sudden feeling of *meaning*...."[3] Magic is therefore the science of the future, not the past. The human mind is about to evolve to a new stage. For a thousand years, the unconscious powers of man were pushed underground by the development of the intellect. "Now the wheel has come full circle; intellect has reached certain limits, and it cannot advance beyond them until it recovers some of the lost powers."[4] Modern philosophy is rigid, narrow, and formal. It has failed in the quest for both meaning and power.

Why should the occult provide meaning? How can it provide power? These questions are seldom even asked by those who write about occultism. Why should the mere existence of personal powers that are outside the range of normal human experience testify to some higher meaning? Why is the world of the savage any more meaningful than that of the physicist? Wilson asserts: "In a sense, the Indians and Peruvians were closer to the truth than modern man, for their intuition of 'unseen forces' kept them wide open to the vistas of meaning that surround us."[5] Those who buy Castaneda's books apparently believe this, but why is it so? Why does the ability to recognize the manifestations of occult power as the products of demonic interference with regular patterns of fixed—or seemingly fixed—law entitle the savage to claim that he senses the true meaning of creation? Don Juan's explanation of the universe is strangely modern, almost Kantian. Familiarity with hallucinatory herbs and occult rituals may well open up one's mind to realms of the creation that Western men have learned to ignore, or in fact have actually overpowered temporarily, but why should there be more meaning associated with this form of perception and power than with the computer or the atomic bomb? Yet there is a growing body of occultists and mystics who are convinced that Wilson is correct and that the realm of the occult is a more meaningful realm.

No socially important movement survives without a philosophy of life and a religious commitment to that philosophy by its adherents. This is as true of the various forms of Satanism, occultism, mysticism, and paranormal phenomenalism as it is of the major religions in man's history. Men want to find both meaning and power in life. If they have abandoned this hope, then they will search for a means of escape. The fact that the major Eastern religions—Buddhism and Hinduism—are marked by magicians and mystics, power-seekers and monistic retreaters, should not surprise us. Those who have sought power and meaning apart from God have at times found power, both rational and occult, but the ultimate hope—that there is meaning in the world apart from that imposed on creation by a sovereign personal God—cannot be achieved. Power does not satisfy, and meaning does not stem from man, the hypothetical measure of all things.

The heart of occultism is its commitment to a universe devoid of an ultimate sovereign. Man may have power, individual men may have power, and demons may have power. Forces of the universe may have power. But there must not be an ultimate form of power that is absolutely sovereign. The universe is chance- or fate-created; it may or may not be illusion; but it is not controlled by providence. The universe may have meaning or it may not; in any case, its meaning or lack of meaning is autonomous.

> The world's a chance-determined thing,
> It's plain enough to see;
> Probably governed by the laws
> Of probability.

The religion of Satan offers self-determination to man, yet it simultaneously promises bondage. To take power over anything in the creation requires a source of power: law, demons, forces, God. Every man is under someone's yoke. The assertion of total autonomy is a fool's dream. There can be no order, no meaning, no existence apart from sovereign authority. But men persist in clinging to their claims of autonomy. When they look at themselves and their world, however, they see that imperfection is overwhelming. They want to escape from the imperfect universe around them if they cannot control it and purify it, yet they themselves are immersed in the creation, imperfect creatures who would not find peace even if they could remake the universe in their own image. *The enemy of autonomous man is the creation itself.* It testifies to a holy God and a judgment to come (Romans 1:18–25).

Orthodox Christianity's response to the human condition is to point to the source of the imperfection: man's ethical rebellion against God. It is a willful suppressing of the truth in unrighteousness that blinds man and condemns him. The curse of the universe was a response by God to man's ethical rebellion, and the promise of external restoration goes with the promise of internal regeneration (Romans 8:18–23). Men must be conformed ethically to the image of God's Son, who was perfectly human, but to achieve this goal, each man requires grace from God (Romans 8:29; Ephesians 2:8, 9). The heart of man's problem, therefore, is man's own heart. The grace of God involves *progressive sanctification*: the step-by-step submission to the laws of God. St. Paul writes: "I press toward the mark for the prize of the high calling of God in Christ Jesus" (Philippians 3:14). The goal is therefore the ultimate (postjudgment) attainment of *perfect humanity*, not the attainment of full divinity. "For our conversation [citizenship] is in heaven; from whence also we look for the Saviour, the Lord Jesus Christ: who shall change our vile body, that it may be fashioned like unto his glorious body, according to the working whereby he is able even to subdue all things unto himself" (Philippians 3:20, 21). The goal is not *metaphysical self-transcendence;* the goal is *ethical maturity.* The fall of man was ethical; the restoration of man is ethical.

This is the Christian view. In contrast to it is the religion of Satan. The Satanic religion, whether occult, evolutionist, Marxist, environmentalist, or any other form of human autonomy, presents man's plight as essentially metaphysical. There was a flaw in the creation. Indeed, some systems (monistic Eastern philosophy) teach that the creation itself was the flaw. The Time before time, the Existence prior to existence, was the golden age. Whatever the form of Satanic philosophy, it sets forth as the goal of man self-regeneration. It may be achieved by ritual, contemplation, asceticism, magic, drugs, lawlessness, revolution, economic planning, or whatever, but the source of the regenerating power is to be found in the creation. Man must transcend himself. He must become a new creature. He must overcome the world. He must do all of these things by means of power that is immanent. In short, the very essence of the Satanic religion is the call to *escape from finitude*. This means the *divinization of man,* and it very often also includes the *abolition of time*. It requires a *higher consciousness*. It requires a *politics of humanistic self-transcendence*.

The Divinization of Man

In the previous chapter, I cited the explicit statements of two modern Satanists, Anton LaVey and Aleister Crowley, that affirm that man alone is sovereign because man alone is divine. Colin Wilson goes one step farther: "It is unnecessary to point out that all the great religions hold the view that the essence of man and the essence of God are one and the same."[6] He is incorrect; neither orthodox Judaism nor orthodox Christianity has ever affirmed such a doctrine, and the absence of just this doctrine made both religions unique in the ancient world. In contrast, as Wilson correctly points out, is the philosophical principle of magic—a principle attributed to the mythical Hermes Trismegistus, the supposed writer of influential occult manuscripts that were revived during the Renaissance: "As above, so below."[7] The microcosm is the same as the macrocosm. As Crowley put it: "There is a single main definition of the object of all magical Ritual. It is the uniting of the Microcosm with the Macrocosm. The Supreme and Complete Ritual is therefore the Invocation of the Holy Guardian Angel; or, in the language of Mysticism, Union with God."[8] Furthermore, wrote Crowley: "This consists of a real identification of the magician and the god. Note that to do this in perfection involves the attainment of a species of Samadhi; and this fact alone suffices to link irrefragably magick with mysticism."[9] Union with God or even identification with God: here is the concept of the divinization of man. It is a denial of the Creator-creature distinction. The fall of man was not the willful ethical rebellion against an absolutely sovereign God, nor shall restoration be the absolutely sovereign gift of a merciful God. Man shall save himself by becoming the saving God.

The alchemists believed in such a self-transcendence. Alchemy was not limited to medieval Europe; it was a phenomenon also common to India, China, Greece, and Islamic culture. It produced a huge and virtually unreadable body of esoteric literature. There is today a scholarly journal, *Ambix*, devoted to alchemy's history. The mental image of the alchemist in the minds of those who have even heard of it is that of a lonely investigator in his secret laboratory, painstakingly searching for the chemical formula that will allow him to turn lead into gold. Textbooks in European history may mention alchemy briefly as the forerunner to modern scientific chemistry. The textbook formula runs something like this: take medieval alchemy, add to it the principles of Cartesian logic and mathematics, sprinkle in a bottle of Enlightenment philosophy, and shake gently for three centuries: out pops modern chemistry. But the textbooks are misleading. It was the Reformation, not the Enlightenment, that produced modern science.[10] More important, it was not the methodology of alchemy that made scientific investigation possible. However secretive scientists may be prior to publishing their findings, the methodology of science is based upon open knowledge, publication, repeatable experiments, the international division of intellectual labor, and the concept of regular law. In contrast, alchemy was above all the knowledge of the secret initiates, and its goal was secret, esoteric knowledge. It was the science of Gnosticism.[11] Its technique was based on the idea that by the endless mixing of the same ingredients—chemical opposites—the chemicals would somehow transcend themselves after a hundred or a thousand identical operations. No one could know in advance when and how this transformation would take place. No one attempting to repeat this process could be assured of success. The discovery of the so-called Philosopher's Stone, which would allow the alchemist to turn lead into gold, was the soul of alchemy. It would enable the alchemist to achieve metaphysical self-transcendence.

The crucial fact to bear in mind is this: alchemy was fundamentally a religious procedure. Eliade, summarizing the findings of the psychologist C. G. Jung, writes:

> The aim of the *opus magnum* was at once the freeing of the human soul and the healing of the cosmos. In this sense alchemy is a continuation of Christianity. In the eyes of the alchemists, observes Jung, Christianity saved man but not nature. It is the alchemist's dream to heal the world in its totality; the Philosopher's Stone is conceived as the *Filius Macrocosmi* who heals the world, whereas, according to the alchemists, Christ is the Saviour of the Microcosm, that is, of man only. The ultimate goal of the *opus* is Cosmic Salvation; for that reason, the *Lapis Philosophorum* is identified with Christ.[12]

Chinese alchemists searched for the "divine cinnabar," or drinkable gold, which would produce eternal life—the elixir of youth, in other words.[13] The Philosopher's Stone was seen as the elixir of immortality.[14] The alchemist was concerned with the transcending of time, and he was therefore the inheritor of ancient paganism, with its ritual attempts to return to the primordial chaos, the Time before time.[15]

Louis Pauwels and Jacques Bergier, the authors of the enormously successful book *The Morning of the Magicians* (1960), believe in alchemy. Their book supposedly heralds a new dawning of an age of alchemy. They, too, agree with Jung about the religious impulse of alchemy.

> For the alchemist, it must never be forgotten that power over matter and energy is only a secondary reality. The real aim of the alchemist's activities, which are perhaps the remains of a very old science belonging to a civilization long extinct, is the transformation of the alchemist himself, his accession to a higher state of consciousness. The material results are only a pledge of the final result, which is spiritual. Everything is oriented towards the transmutation of man himself, towards his deification, his fusion with the divine energy, the fixed center from which all material energies emanate. The alchemist's is that science "with a conscience" of which Rabelais speaks. It is a science which tends to exalt man rather than matter; as Teilhard de Chardin puts it: "The real aim of physics should be to integrate Man as a totality in a coherent representation of the world."[16]

Interestingly enough, they quote Teilhard, whose monistic, evolutionary philosophy was condemned by the Roman Catholic church. He was far more Buddhist or Hindu in his religious perspective than Christian.

Alchemy follows the lead of magic, arguing for the principle that "as above, so below." All being is at bottom one. It is therefore man's task to bridge the gap between his own temporarily limited being and God's eternal being. (The fact that Martin Luther was a supporter of "scientific" alchemy comes as a shock, for his theology rejects the monism that undergirds alchemy.) [17] With its roots in Gnosticism, alchemy was self-consciously committed to the divinization of man.[18] Pauwels and Bergier wax eloquent about the alchemist's quest:

> The "Great Work" is done. The alchemist himself undergoes a transformation which the texts evoke, but which we are unable to describe, having only the vaguest analogies to guide us. This transformation, it seems, would be, as it were, a promise, or foretaste, experienced by a privileged being, of what awaits humanity after attaining the very limits of its knowledge of the earth and its elements: its fusion with the Supreme Being, its concentration on a fixed spiritual goal, and its junction with other centers of intelligence across the cosmic spaces. Gradually, or in a sudden flash of illumination, the alchemist, according to tradition, discovers the meaning of his long labors. The secrets of energy and of matter are revealed to him, and at the same time he glimpses the infinite perspectives of Life. He possesses the key to the mechanics of the Universe. He establishes a new relationship between his own mind, which from now on is *illuminated*, and the Universal Mind eternally deepening its concentration.[19]

The manipulation of metals somehow brings on the sudden flash of illumination, the *higher consciousness*, which is the goal for all occult groups. This key phrase —higher consciousness—serves as a kind of talisman among radical humanist groups. Consciousness-raising within Women's Liberation, the new consciousness of Esalen and the other mystical illuminist organizations, and the drug-induced consciousness—mind expanding—of the counterculture all reach out to the void in search of a new creation. Such a hypothetical "leap of being" is the very essence of Gnosticism. Man is needed to complete the evolutionary development of the Universal Mind, God. Without man, God could not complete His own being. This is not the God of Christianity, but the god of Hegel, as Professor Thomas Molnar has demonstrated so well in his book, *God and the Knowledge of Reality.*

Alchemy, like modern humanism, is based on a Pelagian view of man. (Pelagius earned the wrath of Augustine fifteen centuries ago.) Man is supposedly basically good. The possibility for perfection is always present in life. Man's being is not hopelessly flawed by the effects of ethical rebellion. Given this outlook, the self-transcendence of man becomes a sociological imperative: "At the stage we have reached in scientific research our minds and intelligence will have to surpass themselves and rise to transcendent heights; the human, all-too-human, will no longer suffice."[20] Not only is this leap of being a sociological imperative, but it is also an ethical imperative: "If men have in them the physical possibility of attaining one or other of these states [of higher consciousness], the quest for the best means of doing so ought to be the principal aim of their lives."[21] This transformation is strictly a question of the proper *technique.*

> If my brain is equipped with the necessary machinery—if all this does not belong exclusively to the domain of religion or mythology—if it is not all a question of divine "grace" or "magical initiation" but depends on certain techniques and certain internal and external attitudes capable of setting this machinery in motion—then I am satisfied that my only ambition and most urgent duty ought to be to reach this "awakened state" and attain these heights at which the mind can soar.[22]

The techniques of two thousand five hundred years of alchemy are a standing testimony to men's faith that the "if nots" of the cited passage really *are* nots—that technique is superior to grace in the quest for human self-transcendence.

Like the vast majority of the "higher-consciousness" prophets today, the authors are totally committed to a theory of cosmic evolution. Not Darwin's antiseptic evolution of random mutations and randomly changing environments, but purposeful evolution. We are headed for Teilhard's "omega point," that Hegelian monist resolution point of all progress. A new stage in man's evolutionary process is dawning:

> A revolution is taking place before our eyes—the unexpected remarriage of reason, at the summit of its victories, and intuition. For the really attentive observer the problems facing contemporary intelligence are no longer problems of progress. The concept of progress has been dead for some years now. Today it is a question of a change of state, of a transmutation. From this point of view those concerned with the domain of the interior life and its realities are in step with the pioneering savants who are preparing the birth of a world that will have nothing in common with our present world of laborious transition in which we have to live for just a little while longer.[23]

What these defenders of alchemy are saying is significant. They are focusing their attention not on the everyday labors of the common man, nor on the steady accumulation of scientific knowledge, but on the radically discontinuous event that will bring forth a new world. They have abandoned the idea of cumulative progress, as have so many of the intellectuals of our day, especially the younger men whose careers were closely linked with the occult explosion and Vietnam protests of the post-1965 era. Not progress but mutation. Yet not random mutation, either. *Directed mutation* by a new elite of illuminated ones. Activism toward the world has no meaning for the authors; theirs is an interior world. The next stage of history will stem from the affairs of the psyche or the transcendent states of consciousness—beyond consciousness. The formal activism of the alchemist has once again become internalized and passive. Thus it must always be. If men are not passive before God, they cannot be active toward the world. Only for brief periods of time can they borrow or steal the spiritual capital of future-oriented Christianity. Modern autonomous man has killed the faith in progress, yet he is called upon to create a new world:

> Man can have access to a secret world—*see* the Light, *see* Eternity, comprehend the Laws of Energy, integrate within himself the rhythm of the destiny of the Universe, consciously apprehend the ultimate concentration of forces and, like Teilhard de Chardin, live the incomprehensible life that starts from "Point Omega," in which the whole of creation, at the end of terrestrial time, will find its accomplishment, consumma-

tion and exaltation. Man is capable of anything. His intelligence, equipped from the very beginning, no doubt with a capacity for infinite knowledge, can in certain conditions apprehend the whole mechanism of life. The powers of the human intelligence, if developed to their fullest extent, could probably cope with anything in the whole Universe. But these powers stop short at the point where the intelligence, having reached the end of its mission, senses that there is still "something other" beyond the confines of the Universe. Here it is quite possible for an analogical consciousness to function. There are no models in the Universe of what may exist outside the Universe. The door through which none may pass is the gateway to the Kingdom of Heaven.[24]

In this universe, man can cope with anything it has to offer. Man, in good Kantian fashion, stands reverently at the door to the kingdom of heaven, making sure that nothing over there bothers us over here. If something there gets into man's universe, however, it can be coped with. The mind of man will see to that.

What we are supposedly witnessing is the coming of an elite corps of mutants. Some have come before: Jesus, Confucius, Mohammed. An international secret society of these mutants now exists. Salvation is coming—metaphysical transformation through the techniques of applied mutation. Pauwels and Bergier are optimistic, for they promise Gnostic salvation. Man's very mind is the agent of salvation; salvation comes through knowledge (Socrates' famous dictum):

> We are on the side of the invaders, on the side of the life that is coming, on the side of a changing age and changing ways of thought. Error? Madness? A man's life is only justified by his efforts, however feeble, towards better understanding. And to understand better is to become more attached. The more I understand, the more I love; for everything that is understood is good.[25]

The ideal of exhaustive knowledge is placed before mankind. If mankind or an elite secret society of mutants can attain exhaustive understanding, sin and the effects of sin will be erased from the universe. Man will be lord of creation. Nothing human is foreign to the alchemist, and nothing understood can be evil. This is the ancient Gnostic heresy: salvation by knowledge. The leap of being is ultimately intellectual, not moral. The secret knowledge of the adepts shall redeem mankind and cope with the universe. As Crowley describes the process: "The adept should have realized that his Act of Union with the angel implies (1) the death of his old mind save in so far as his unconscious elements preserve its memory when they absorb it, and (2) the death of his unconscious elements themselves. But their death is rather a going forth to renew their life through love."[26] The mind dies in self-transcendence (as Crowley's seems to have done from time to time); the adept transcends memory, logic, and creaturehood. Beyond human limitations is love. (But *only* beyond human limitations, if Crowley's life is any indication.)

Man becomes God. "By the use of this system," Crowley asserts, "the magician is able ultimately to unify the whole of his knowledge—to transmute, even on the Intellectual Plane, the Many into the One."[27] Crowley knew the language of alchemy. It is the search for exhaustive knowledge that motivates Eliade, too: the triumphant advent of the post-Christian era (and few men can claim the breadth of knowledge that Eliade has).

Now an encounter with the "totally other," whether conscious or unconscious, gives rise to an experience of a religious nature. It is not impossible that our age may go down to posterity as the first to rediscover those "diffuse religious experiences" which were destroyed by the triumph of Christianity. It is equally possible that the attraction of the unconscious and its activities, the interest in myths and symbols, the fascination of the exotic, the primitive, the archaic, and encounters with "others," with all the ambivalent feelings they imply—that all this may one day appear as a new type of religious experience.[28]

What is coming is a *new form of humanism*, according to Eliade. "Now we may anticipate that all these elements are preparing for the growth of a new humanism, which will not be a replica of the old. For what principally concerns us now is to integrate the research of the orientalists, ethnologists, depth psychologists, and historians of religion in order to arrive at a total knowledge of man."[29] Humanism can have encounters with the nonrational "wholly other," (Karl) Barthian style, or with occult "others," LaVey and Crowley style. We are about to arrive at the total knowledge of man, inaugurating a new religious era that will be a new humanistic era. The West is about to be swallowed up in universal world history.[30]

As *The Last Whole Earth Catalog*—the Bible of the counterculture, dropouts, retreatists, dome-building, back-to-nature communalists—puts it in the introduction: "PURPOSE: We *are* as gods and might as well get good at it." This is humanism's religious first principle, and alchemists, magicians, and occultists of all kinds can cooperate on the basis of it.

The Abolition of Time

Time is inexorable, merciless, and linear. This is the Western view of time. The rebellion of man brought forth the burden of time. The day of judgment shall finally remove the burden of time for the godly, and death, the last enemy, shall be overcome (I Corinthians 15:55). Time shall be redeemed.

This view of time clearly involves the belief in a *radically discontinous event*. "Behold, I shew you a mystery; We shall not all sleep, but we shall all be changed, In a moment, in the twinkling of an eye, at the last trump: for the trumpet shall sound, and the dead shall be raised incorruptible, and we shall be changed" (I Corinthians 15:51, 52). But it is an event in which man's actions play no part, ritually or otherwise. Jesus, speaking in His capacity as perfect humanity, admitted that He did not know when the day of judgment would come: "But of that day and hour knoweth no man, not the angels of heaven, but my Father only" (Matthew 24:36). While Christians look forward to that day, the church has never institutionalized or ritualized the day of judgment, except insofar as the symbolism of baptism (for those churches that immerse their members) points to death and resurrection, and the burial formulas, especially for seamen, mention the final day. It is significant that the church has ritualized neither the beginning nor the end, neither creation nor the day of judgment, for God and He alone is sovereign over these two events. Time is totally in the hands of God. It is the means by which His plan is unfolded.

Such a view of linear time is not shared by all peoples of the world. Were it not for the distinctly Western ideologies and Christianity, the primitive countries and the Eastern cultures would not believe in it, and many of them still do not. The burden of time is viewed as a metaphysical condition to be transcended, rather than as a specific response by God to an act of moral rebellion by man. The burden of time can therefore be thrown off, by karmic evolution through innumerable lives, or by communal ritual, or by asceticism. If men can return to the Time before time, actually or ritually, this return symbolizes escape from time. In ritually participating in the creation event—when the god brought form out of the primeval chaos—the community can hope to escape time's bondage in the future. These cultures are therefore backward-looking; in the past is their hope of collective salvation. The future-orientation of the West, as well as the West's commitment to the irreversibility of time, is not present in pagan cultures. Eliade's description of Indian thought indicates the extent of the difference between Western and Eastern approaches to the question of time. When we realize the startling growth of interest in Eastern philosophy and religion among the West's young, Eliade's summary takes on an increased importance.

> According to the Buddha, as indeed in Indian thought as a whole, man's life is doomed to suffering by the very fact that it is lived in Time. Here we touch upon a vast question which could not be summarised in a few pages, but it may be said, as a simplification, that suffering in this world is based upon, and indefinitely prolonged by, *karma*, therefore by the temporal nature of existence. It is the law of *karma* which imposes the innumerable transmigrations, the eternal return to existence and therefore to suffering. To deliver oneself from the karmic law, to rend the veil of Maya [the illusion of existence]—this is equivalent to spiritual "cure." The Buddha is "the king of physicians" and his message is proclaimed as the "new medicine." The philosophies, the ascetic and contemplative techniques and the mystical systems of India are all directed to the same end: to cure man of the pain of existence in Time. It is by "burning up" even the very last germ of a future life that one finally breaks out of the karmic cycle and attains deliverance from Time.[31]

One of the techniques used by Indian mystics to escape time's bondage is an exploration by the mystic of his supposed previous incarnations. In doing so, one "burns up" his karmic residua. Buddha and his contemporary sages practiced this technique and recommended it. The goal is to retrace time backwards to the point of time's origin, "the point where existence first 'burst' into the world and unleashed time. Then one rejoins that paradoxical instant before which Time was not, because nothing had been manifested." Further,

> to re-live one's past lives would also be to understand them and, to a certain degree, "burn up" one's "sins"; that is, the sum of the deeds done in the state of ignorance and capitalised from one life to the next by the law of *karma*. But there is something of even

greater importance: one attains to the beginning of Time and enters the Timeless—the eternal present which preceded the temporal experience inaugurated by the "fall" into human existence. In other words, it is possible, starting from any moment of temporal duration, to exhaust that duration by retracing its course to the source and so come out into the Timeless, into eternity. But that is to transcend the human condition and to regain the non-conditioned state, which preceded the fall into Time and the wheel of existence.[32]

Man's goal, in this perspective, is to transcend all created limits. The existence of such limits, manifested best by the existence of time, is an intolerable burden. Men are to seek the precreation state, which was nonconditioned. This can mean one of two states: either total union with the metaphysical One or total and perfect spiritual autonomy. There have been yogis pursuing each of these goals: the One (fusion with Oneness) or the Many (isolated autonomy).[33]

The primary difference between the Indian view of time and the view of other pagan cultures is that in Indian theory man plays no part in the periodic re-creation of the world. The goal of ritual regeneration of the cosmos, such as we find in the seasonal fertility festivals of most primitive cultures, is not pursued. Instead, the goal is escape from the cosmic cycle.[34] But the means is the same in each case: the attempted return to the Time before time.

The question of time is the question of mortality. Why do men die? By reconstructing the creation events, men hope to explain how death came into the world. But the history of the creation is a sacred history; the concern with these pretime events is soteriological: men want salvation from imperfection, a release from the bondage of mortality. The concern with profane history is reduced accordingly. Written records of the actions of actual men, apart from the tales of heroes and demigods, are not crucially important. It was the coming of Christanity, with its commitment to God's actions in human history, that brought the triumph of the book over the oral tradition, especially the secret oral tradition of the initiated. A people without a written history is a people without a history today.[35] Only by a lifetime of incomparable scholarly labor can a book like Maenchen-Helfen's study of the Huns be produced, and he never did complete it in his lifetime. Huns left no written records; the details concerning them must be derived from artistic fragments and the records of those nations, predominantly Christian, that the Huns invaded.

One of the techniques used by adepts to escape the restraints of time and space is *astral projection*. Castaneda said that he used this technique during his initiation. The book and movie *The Other* has the young occultist-murderer develop his powers through this exercise. Thelma Moss, the UCLA parapsychological researcher, devotes a chapter of her book, *The Probability of the Impossible* (1974), to out-of-body experiences.

Astral projection and reincarnation are taught by the Edgar Cayce movement—Cayce was an astral projectionist, or at least he diagnosed people from great distances and described their surroundings—and by the Church of Scientology. An important part of the initiation of shamans (medicine men) in primitive cultures is the out-of-body experience of flight.[36] In short, however such experiences occur in the perception of the actors, astral projection is a traditional means of transcending both time and space. It is a denial of the binding nature of man's normal faculties. Where it exists, Western concepts of privacy are made most difficult. (Western techniques of spying and electronic communication are a lot more reliable and, in the long run, more of a threat to privacy. Technology has made possible the equivalent power of astral projection, but it has placed such power in the hands of third-level bureaucrats instead of an initiated elite of adepts. The West has democratized, or at least bureaucratized, the out-of-body snooping of the shamans of the world, and has added videotape recordings as well.)

The West is also concerned with reducing the burden of time. The communications revolution, the computer revolution, the data-retrieval networks, the highway, the jet plane, and numerous other features of Western culture have provided men with savings in time undreamed of by the pagan masses. But with a difference: the burden of time has been recognized as ultimately unyielding to the manipulations of men. Each saving of time has a cost; technology can reduce this cost, but it cannot reduce it to zero. The quest for zero-cost reductions in time is demonic. It denies that man faces fundamental limits as a creature. Western man may not be satisfied with running a hundred meters in 9.9 seconds. He admits that he cannot safely predict how low this time restraint will fall. But he affirms what the occultist will not admit: the time it takes a man to travel one hundred meters cannot and will not be reduced to zero. The fact that Western man counts the cost accurately, that is, can calculate the weight of each burden, enables him to reduce the burden through effective planning, discipline, and, above all, capital formation. The socialist or communist, who affirms the religion of the occult—that the constraints of scarcity are not natural, but are man-created—is less rational, cannot calculate economically, and threatens economic productivity whenever he takes over the reins of political power. Socialist economics is the demonic philosophy of "stones into bread."[37] It denies the limits imposed by man's finitude and man's ethically fallen nature. The yogi and the commissar are not so very different after all.

Where present-oriented men dominate, culture degenerates. If the future-orientation of the Christian West is not present in a society, that society will be essentially lower-class and stagnant. Men get what they pay for. If they prefer instant gratification, then they will pay for it at the expense of capital formation and greater future output. Professor Edward Banfield's classic book, *The Unheavenly City* (1970), earned him the wrath of political liberals because he argued forcefully that the Negro ghetto is what it is because of the time-preference, that is, the view of the future, held by the majority of those who live there. One's class position is primarily determined not by income but by one's view of the future. For arguing in this manner, radical students and many of his professorial peers pressured him to leave Harvard University. This kind of thinking was clearly apostate: it argued against the acceptable tenets of liberal environmentalism. It meant, as Banfield specifically said, that apart from a change in the time-preference of those who live in the ghetto, all the wealth redistribution schemes in the world will not lift the ghetto dwellers out of poverty. At best, the redistributed wealth will enable some ghetto residents to move out. He writes:

> At the present-oriented end of the scale, the lower-class individual lives from moment to moment. If he has any awareness of a future, it is of something fixed, fated, beyond his control: things happen *to* him, he does not *make* them happen. Impulse governs his behavior, either because he cannot discipline himself to sacrifice a present for a future satisfaction or because he has no sense of the future. He is therefore radically improvident: whatever he cannot consume immediately he considers valueless. His bodily needs (especially for sex) and his taste for "action" take precedence over everything else—and certainly over any work routine. He works only as he must to stay alive, and drifts from one unskilled job to another, taking no interest in the work.[38]

In the face of a lower-class time perspective, the liberal political remedies have failed, especially welfare programs. In St. Paul, Minnesota, six percent of the city's families absorbed seventy-seven percent of its public assistance, fifty-one percent of its health services, and fifty-six percent of its mental health and correctional casework services.[39] Furthermore, "It is not at all unlikely that cultures (as opposed to individuals) change their time horizons so as to adapt to changes in environment, but any such change must occur very slowly: a certain stability over time is a defining characteristic of culture."[40] He fails to mention religious revival. What we have seen for over a decade in America is religious revival: the higher-class families have seen many of their children converted to the lower-class, present-oriented philosophies of the East. The denial of time's boundaries has economic and cultural consequences. Those consequences are disastrous.

Altered Consciousness

It was in the mid-1960s that hallucinogenic drugs became known as mind-expanding drugs. Somehow, the public was expected to believe that the expansion of the mind produced by these drugs is beneficial. After all, isn't expansion like growth? Isn't it a good thing to have one's perspective broadened? Isn't one of the goals of higher education cultural and intellectual broadening? The doors of perception were to be swung open, and whole new worlds would be available for exploration. The narrow bands of frequencies in which our eyes and ears operate were no longer sufficient; our "vibrations" had to be increased. Our narrow, Western, middle-class blinders had to be ripped from our foreheads by means of new chemical substances. It would be "better living through chemistry" for one and all.

There was a messianic enthusiasm about drugs in the very early stages of the counterculture. The introduction of the Beatles' "Rubber Soul" album was generally regarded as a first step. The "Yeah, Yeah, Yeah" days of wanting to hold hands were gone; the Beatles had entered a new, more creative phase. The source of the new creativity, so the rumor went, was marijuana or some other drug, such as LSD. As a matter of fact, Ringo Starr, the group's drummer, later admitted that they had been "fooling around" with drugs, but that they had stopped. In 1965, the year of "Rubber Soul," the counterculture's euphoria had not yet worn off. I can remember being told in 1966 by one former evangelist for hallucinogenic nirvana that he had once believed that if the President and the Soviet Union's top leaders could have sat down at a conference table after having ingested some LSD, they could have solved the world's problems. But by 1966, he had lost his faith.

By 1970, the word was out on LSD: too dangerous. Yet in the interim, marijuana had become middle-class, taken as seriously by the general public as bathtub gin had been taken in 1930. There were still the equivalent of the "drys" cautioning young people about the marijuana-heroin link, but not even the police were using that line any longer. Timothy Leary reversed himself a few years into the 1970s, repudiating his slogan, "Tune in, turn on, drop out." The counterculture had grown up a bit. It had found jobs scarcer and stereophonic albums more expensive than in 1965. The days of grass and roses were over.

Nevertheless, a profound change had taken place in the West, for the counterculture's influence had been international. There was a new acceptance of altered states of consciousness by a significant minority of the public, especially the intellectuals, the young, and the growing legion of sideline occultists, so that by the early 1970s a lot of people were talking about alternatives to drugs. The Jesus Freaks advised people to "turn on to Jesus." The Hare Krishnas recommended rhythmic chanting. Proponents of the new techniques of biofeedback (alpha-wave machines) had their alternative, in kit form for the less affluent. The Beatles had gone on Transcendental Meditation, or TM (and, since the words are trademarked, as any good business name should be, it is advertised as TM™), and their followers responded by the millions. The Beatles are gone, but TM is going strong. ("Not a religion," the advertising says, just as yoga techniques are only "an old body-building program from India.") Cheap California wines became popular after 1970, although the recession of 1974-75 has led to some bankruptcies in the California wine grape business. Drunkenness, the world's ancient pastime, was back in favor, but now there was a whole series of techniques and substances to supplement man's old standby. Drunkenness might still be regarded as gross though legitimate, but TM, yoga, alpha-wave training, and chanting, while a bit odd, were baptized avant-garde and were officially respectable.

The problem with drunkenness is the problem with pot is the problem with LSD: the deliberate altering of the human consciousness merely for the sake of alteration, or for psychological escape, is a form of cultural and religious rebellion. "And be not drunk with wine," St. Paul writes, "wherein is excess, but be filled with the Spirit" (Ephesians 5:18). Paul could advise Timothy to "use a little wine for thy stomach's sake" (I Timothy 5:23), so he was not issuing a general prohibition on what we might call social drinking. But he did condemn drunkenness. Why? Because drunkenness is the deliberate distortion of a man's perception of God's created reality. It is a denial of the creation to be drunk—the twisting of God's revelation of Himself through his creation. In short, man is forbidden to indulge in the distortion of his mental faculties merely for the sake of escaping normal reality. (This is not to imply that anesthetics are illegitimate, for these make the physician's task easier in operating and increase the likelihood of a man's restoration to health. Health, after all, is normal for a godly, progressive society, that is, normative [Exodus 23:25].)

Each man is personally responsible for his actions. This is the starting point of all human action. Each man is responsible before a sovereign God who has created reality. Each man is therefore responsible within his lawful sphere of influence. From him to whom much is given, much is expected (Luke 12:48). Therefore, for any person to assess accurately his own gifts and responsibilities, he must strive to perceive reality accurately. One of the most important economic developments of all time was the double-entry bookkeeping ledger. It enables men to keep an accurate record of their liabilities and assets. Without a free market that can assess the economic value of scarce resources, there can be no rational economic calculation and therefore no rational economic planning. Unless men are trying to conceal something, they do not deliberately make false entries in their business ledgers. The use of hallucinogenic drugs, yoga techniques of meditation, and other self-transcendence devices is comparable to making deliberately false entries in a ledger. It reduces men's ability to make accurate assessments of their actions in relation to a real external reality.

That yoga techniques are successful in altering men's perception should come as no surprise. The philosophy of Indian monism, like that of Zen Buddhism, is to deny all reality. Reality is an illusion; existence is Maya. The first step at transcending reality is control of the body. Hatha yoga techniques are the outward form of an inner system of philosophy. The goal of yoga is the liberation of man from the illusion of existence, and physical culture is the first step in this "liberation." Mental purification and spiritual awakening come from the manipulation of the body. This, of course, is almost the mirror image of Christianity, which teaches that regeneration precedes the acts of men, for "the natural man receiveth not the things of the Spirit of God" (I Corinthians 2:14). The Christian doctrine of the fall of man is ethical; the Indian one is metaphysical. The Christian responds outwardly to a change in his inward condition; the yogi attempts to change his inward perception of reality—illusion—by manipulating his body. The Indian mystic tries to escape from created reality, and various methods are used: asceticism, libertinism, withdrawal from society, meditation, immersion in work. The goal, however, is the systematic distortion of perception. One of the first things to be distorted, as mentioned earlier, is the sense of time. This is also equally true of the hallucinogenic drugs. Aldous Huxley, in his *Doors of Perception* (1954), comments on his altered sense of time:

> And along with indifference to space there went an even more complete indifference to time.
> "There seems to be plenty of it," was all I would answer, when the investigator asked me to say what I felt about time.
> Plenty of it, but exactly how much was entirely irrelevant. I could, of course, have

looked at my watch; but my watch, I knew, was in another universe. My actual experience had been, was still, of an indefinite duration or alternatively of a perpetual present made up of one continually changing apocalypse.[41]

Plenty of time: for the Eastern mystic, yes; for the Western thinker, no. "Time is money," wrote Ben Franklin. But even more to the point are St. Paul's words, just two sentences before his statement on drunkenness: "See then that ye walk circumspectly, not as fools, but as wise, redeeming [buying back] the time, because the days are evil" (Ephesians 5:15, 16). Time is the one truly unrenewable resource in man's life, but *only in a world of linear time and without reincarnation.*

What Huxley found was meaningful irrelevance. "I looked down by chance, and went on passionately staring by choice, at my own crossed legs. Those folds in the trousers—what a labyrinth of endlessly significant complexity! And the texture of the gray flannel—how rich, how deeply, mysteriously sumptuous "[42] He stared, seemingly for an immensely long time, at a chair.[43] He had the sense of being separate from himself.[44] Yet for all of these mindless experiences, he calls for more of the same—or better. Alcohol and tobacco cannot be prohibited, but they are not safe.

> The universal and ever-present urge to self-transcendence is not to be abolished by slamming the currently popular Doors in the Wall. The only reasonable policy is to open other, better doors in the hope of inducing men and women to exchange their old bad habits for new and less harmful ones. Some of these other, better doors will be social and technological in nature, others religious or psychological, others dietetic, educational, athletic. But the need for frequent chemical vacations from intolerable selfhood and repulsive surroundings will undoubtedly remain."[45]

We need a new, non-habit-forming drug, cheaply synthesizable, less toxic than present ones. "And, on the positive side, it should produce changes in consciousness more interesting, more intrinsically valuable than mere sedation or dreaminess, delusions of omnipotence or release from inhibition."[46]

A well-known fact about the use of LSD is that the user needs someone "straight" in the same room with him, or at least someone who is chained to the perception of reality. Psychologist Paul Stern writes: "Ordinarily one does not trip alone, but needs at least one other person who officially functions as guide or as a sort of safety net."[47] In a philosophical sense, Huxley wants to find a new hallucinogen that can, in and of itself, serve as a rational, "straight" guide. No mere dreaminess for him. We need meaning—the educated, well-read man's kind of meaning. But this desire is absolutely impossible to fulfill. The doors of perception are supposedly autonomous. (No man, biblically speaking, can impose his perception on another man. No man may impose his reality on any other. Each man has to be responsible before God for interpreting reality properly, given his limits as a creature. He must think God's thoughts after Him, but as a creature. No drug can erase this ultimate responsibility.) "In general," writes Stern, "drug users tend to overestimate the stimulus value of hallucinogens. Drugs do not 'cause,' in any meaningful sense of the term, the so-called hallucinogenic experience, as the stylus of our stereo does not 'cause' the music filling our room. To the extent that hallucinogens are effective, they act as catalysts releasing latent images stored in the mind."[48] Huxley hopes for built-in restraints from chemistry. He cannot have them. All he can reasonably hope for is that other users of such drugs, even the "perfect drug," will have pleasant, uplifting, and even educational escapes from reality. It will be like a day in the countryside, assuming the users like and appreciate the countryside. But what if the users like and appreciate mass murder? What if the drug users are the members of Charles Manson's family? Who will serve as the "straight man" in a society of Mansons?

The battle over consciousness is the supreme human battle. Karl Marx called for class consciousness. Women's Liberation groups call for consciousness-raising. R. M. Bucke, in a mediocre turn-of-the-century book that has somehow become a kind of classic, calls for *Cosmic Consciousness* (1901). The Western occultists call for Christ consciousness. The doors of perception are governed by first principles of interpretation, and each religious or ideological group wants its first principles sovereign in regulating other men's conscious (or unconscious) perception.

"The Saviour of man is Cosmic Consciousness—in Paul's language—the Christ."[49] So writes Bucke, who has assembled selections from the more famous historic figures who believed in cosmic consciousness (or who Bucke thinks did). His is another version of monism, as are most of the systems of cosmic consciousness. Like so many late-nineteenth-century illuminists, Bucke believed fervently in evolutionary progress, socialism, and mystical illumination.[50] The goal of cosmic consciousness is self-deification: "Finally the basic fact in cosmic consciousness is implied in its name—that fact is consciousness of the cosmos—this is what is called in the East the 'Brahmic Splendor,' which is in Dante's phrase capable of transhumanizing a man into a god."[51] Clearly, Bucke's own brief experience of cosmic consciousness did nothing to improve his sentence structure. He quotes Walt Whitman: "Divine am I, inside and out."[52] He quotes John Yepes (St. John of the Cross; d. 1591):

> For the soul courageously resolved on passing, interiorly and exteriorly, beyond the limits of its own nature, enters illimitably within the supernatural, which has no measure, but contains all measure immanently within itself. To arrive there is to depart hence, going away, out of oneself, as far as possible from this vile state to that which is the highest of all. Therefore, rising above all that may be known and understood, temporally and spiritually, the soul must earnestly desire to reach that which in this life cannot be known, and which the heart cannot conceive; and, leaving behind all actual and possible taste and feeling of sense and spirit, must desire earnestly to arrive at that which transcends all sense and all feeling. . . . The more the soul strives to become blind and annihilated as to all interior and exterior things, the more it will be filled with faith and love and hope.[53]

This distinctly Eastern view of reality—the void—is a common feature of all monistic systems of mysticism. Van Til calls the process the "integration into the void." With reference to modern psychology, he writes: "The real reason why modern psychology has left no room for responsibility is found in the fact that it has taken the whole of the human personality in all its aspects, self-conscious and sub-conscious, and immersed it in an ultimate metaphysical void. Man cannot be responsible to the void."[54] It should surprise no one to learn that the founders of modern psychology, Freud and Jung, were both keenly interested in occult subjects, that Freud once remarked that he regretted not having devoted more of his life's work to a study of ESP, and that Freud was convinced at one stage of his career that cocaine would be a wonder drug for psychological therapy.[55] Salvation is in the void, beyond the categories of rationality, beyond the pressures of created reality.

The void need not be empty to function as a void. It may not be Buddhist Nirvana—the abolition of all existence—but if it is devoid of structure or meaning, it is a void. The experiences of the so-called higher consciousness remove men from the realms of created reality in which the direct confrontation with structure and meaning are more clear-cut. The observer may train himself to say "chaos" when he examines his surroundings, but no one, other than a lunatic, can convince himself of this for lengthy periods of time. Reality and time are burdens, for they are cursed. Those who are in ethical rebellion feel the weight of reality, and they seek to flee into a more chaotic realm. In chaos and meaninglessness they believe they can escape God, escape their own creaturehood, and escape final judgment. They are wrong, but this is their hope.

Not all Eastern thinkers are committed to the cultivation of states of altered consciousness. One contemporary Zen Buddhist master has written: "An ancient Zen saying has it that to become attached to one's own enlightenment is as much a sickness as to exhibit a maddeningly active ego. Indeed, the profounder the enlightenment, the worse the illness. . . . My own sickness lasted almost ten years."[56] Krishnamurti, a modern Indian religious teacher, has said much the same thing:

> Meditation is not the mere experiencing of something beyond everyday thought and feeling nor is it the pursuit of visions and delights. An immature and squalid little mind can and does have visions of expanding consciousness, and experiences which it recognizes according to its own conditioning. This immaturity may be greatly capable of making itself successful in this world and achieving fame and notoriety. The gurus whom it follows are of the same quality and state. Meditation does not belong to such as these.[57]

One of the significant aspects of Aldous Huxley's life was that he finally abandoned hope in mystical "higher" consciousness at the very end of his life. A week before he died, at a time when he believed that LSD could put a man in touch permanently with the Tibetan Buddhists' "Clear Light of the Void," he realized, as Zaehner puts it, "that this was probably a gross misrepresentation of what was actually happening." While he was under the influence of a sedative, his wife made a tape recording of his discussion. "This whole thing has been very strange because in a way it was very good—but in a way it was absolutely terrifying, showing that when one thinks one's got beyond oneself, one hasn't. . . . I began with this marvellous sense of this cosmic gift, and then ended up with a rueful sense that one can be deceived. . . . It was an insight, but at the same time the most dangerous of errors . . . inasmuch as one was worshipping oneself"[58] (author's italics omitted). There would be no salvation through *soma* drugs in some brave new world, no final creation of an electric Tibet.

Despite these protests, those who have promoted Eastern techniques of mystic illumination have unquestionably gained followers on the basis of a promised entry into "higher" consciousness. Western men want results, they want action, they want bright lights and communion with God. Furthermore, they want these things in no more than three easy lessons. Maturity is not what most of them are after, especially Eastern maturity. Why import a highly disciplined foreign maturity when Christianity at least delivers the compound growth rates? If Zen Buddhism requires hostility to all reality, including altered consciousness, then it is easier to flirt with a less consistent form of consciousness-expanding relativism and world-denial.

A religion like Zen Buddhism is totally elitist. It is not simply that only a few people ever seem to get involved. If that were all there were to it, Americans searching for avant-garde religious commitments would have far less trouble. The intensity of Zen Buddhism's training in total irrationalism *necessarily* limits its members. Abbot Zenkei Shibayama, a modern Zen master, has admitted this: "It may not be difficult to *talk about* this experience of awakening to 'Self-nature' or 'True Self' which we have deep at the bottom of our personalities, but to come to this realization experientially as the fact of one's own actual experience, is not easy at all. It is so very difficult that it cannot be easily attained by ordinary people."[59] In short, "not everyone can be expected to have the training required for the attainment of the exquisite moment of *satori*."[60]

In contrast to these elitist religions, so obviously individualistic as far as the promised blessings are concerned, Christianity has always been a religion of the average man. We must become as little children, Christ said, to enter the kingdom of God (Matthew 18:3). The breadth of membership in an open congregation has inevitably led to the presence of hypocrites, immature beginners, and all sorts of weak characters inside the congregations, but that is the price of open doors. The initiatory secret societies, the narrow membership of ascetic brotherhoods, the elitist access to altered consciousness may appeal to true elitists and the temporary avant-garde hangers-on (before the training takes up too much of their energy), but the exclusion of the broad mass of humanity has confined these movements to groups of monks or subsidized solitary adepts who contemplate their navels as a technique for merging with the meaningless, monistic, divine void. Societies are not constructed on the likes of these. Their productivity is generally minimal, and very often they are subsidized by the "unwashed masses" who are willing to get dirty in order to be productive. But it is this very element of elitism that has caught the attention of the "hipsters, flipsters, and finger-poppin' daddies" (to quote "Lord" Buckley, the 1950s cult figure) and the drifting young who want membership in a group sufficiently weird to shock their liberal parents.

The Politics of Self-Transcendence

Their parents, however, who are equally adrift, refuse to be excluded so easily. They too can wear bell-bottoms (which the U. S. Navy has finally abandoned) and beads, and smoke marijuana. They can also search for cosmic consciousness. And once they find it, they will try to politicize it. This is probably why Southern California is the home of the International Cooperation Council (ICC). The ICC is a clearinghouse for every pseudo-Eastern society, every higher-consciousness club, every association of do-gooding, bead-wearing middle-aged, swami-following ladies in the state. It is the organization that can get members of the Committee on Cosmic Humanism and the Center for the Study of Democratic Institutions to sit down and discuss the nature of the Good Society and the bureauractic World Constitution that will be necessary to impose vegetarian ecstasy upon a thoughtless and underdeveloped world. Its slogan:

> Fostering the Emergence of a New Universal
> Man and Civilization Based on Unity in Diversity
> Among All Peoples

Located at 17819 Roscoe Blvd., Northridge, California (a Los Angeles suburb in the San Fernando Valley), the ICC sponsors annual consciousness celebrations and other activities. It publishes a quarterly magazine, the *Cooperator.* It involves itself in educational activities, supplying any and all schools with materials. Its description of itself sounds quite progressive:

> The International Cooperation Council (ICC) is a non-profit coordinating body of autonomous individuals and groups, each seeking in its own unique way to contribute constructively to the global transformation of our time. Based on the principle of "unity in diversity among all peoples," ICC is an experiment whose goal is to foster the emergence of a new universal man and civilization serving the well-being of all mankind. Utilizing the methods and knowledge of modern science in concert with valid insights of religion, philosophy, and the arts, the creative activities of ICC cover a spectrum from the search into man's inner nature to dynamic social action. More than one hundred twenty-five groups are now cooperating with ICC.[61]

And what groups they are! Here is a partial listing:

> Academy of Parapsychology and Medicine
> Ananda Meditation Retreat
> Aquarian Arcane College
> Association for Humanistic Psychology
> Astara, Inc.
> Astro Consciousness Institute for Self-Enlightenment and Peace
> Avatar Meher Baba Group
> Boston Visionary Cell, The
> Buddhist Publication Society

California Institute for Asian Studies
Center for the Study of Democratic Institutions
Center for the Study of Power
Church of Essential Science
Committee on Cosmic Humanism
Esperanto League for North America
Foundation for Universal Understanding
Inner-Space Interpreters Service
Institute of Human Engineering
International Association of Educators for World Peace
Konko-Kyo Church of Izuo
Love Project, The
Mandala Society, Inc., The
New Age Press, The
Ontological Society
Rosicrucian Fellowship
Servers of the Great Ones
Sivananda Yoga Center
Sri Aurobindo Society
Technocracy, Inc.
Temple of Peace
Temple of Understanding
Theosophical Order of Service
Thomas Jefferson Research Center
United Nations Association
United World
Women's Universal Movement, Inc.
World Family
World Institute Council
World Union
You Institute

This list is taken from the *1974 Directory* (8th annual edition). Hopefully, it provides a general sense of what the ICC is really all about. Southern California is undoubtedly the congregating point in the United States for such groups as these, and it is nice to know that modern man's hunger for community is still alive. The problem for the rest of us is the kind of community these groups have in mind. In the spring-summer 1973 issue of the *Coordinator*, the editorial, "A Model for Mankind," informs us:

> Mankind is indeed being born and we of this time have the great privilege of being present at the creation. We must do everything we can to ensure that the new infant is not misshapen at birth but is well-formed and healthy so that it can have the maximum opportunity for surviving and growing to realize its full potential in the universe.
> Mankind, it should be noted, is an adrogynous being, having both male and female characteristics in one. It will grow both through an increasing complexity-conscious-

ness of each cell and by individual cell multiplication. However, for Mankind to survive and flourish, a cure for the cancer of unlimited population growth must be found. When Mankind is ready to expand outward into space a new phase of growth can start, but that is primarily for coming generations. Our immediate task, in the childhood of Mankind, is to work for a universal consciousness.

This is a very revealing editorial statement. *First*, it displays the sense of drama: we are present at the creation of a new mankind. A great metaphysical event is about to take place: the autonomous self-liberation of Mankind. We are participating in the creation-event, just as pagan chaos festivals are supposed to allow men to do. *Second*, we are to see that the new infant is not misshapen. In other words, man is about to take control of man, or as C. S. Lewis warned, some men are about to take control of all the others. *Third*, the editor refers to society as an androgynous being. The image of the androgyne goes back to pagan religious symbolism. It is one of the most important elements of alchemy, East and West. The unity of opposites will produce the Philosopher's Stone, the transformation of man and nature. Professor Molnar's comments on this symbol are relevant to any discussion of the politics of transcendence:

> In Theosophy, the androgyne figure is the symbol of the union of divine and human nature, and hence of the soul purified in view of ascent to unity in God. The androgyne is thus the archetype of man, symbolizing the end of passion, the final reabsorption of creation. . . . Through androgyny or other forms of Hermetic union the manipulator gains access to magic knowledge and power in order to complete nature's work and to complete it in a shorter time than nature would be able to do it. Paracelsus was among those who assumed that nature has a certain direction not decipherable except by the true knower, and that this direction pointed toward the primordial—undivided—state, toward the reintegration of the heavenly elements in one unity. The task of the Hermetic was to help nature achieve this end.[62]

Fourth, the myth of the population explosion is reaffirmed in order to call into question the legitimacy of one of man's primary means of subduing the earth to the glory of God (Genesis 1:28). Man is not to achieve his goal by means of procreation, but by higher-consciousness techniques and social planning. *Fifth*, we must "work for a universal consciousness." In short, we must deny that there are fundamental distinctions between the saved and the lost, while affirming the universal consciousness of mankind.

The quest for the spiritual unification of mankind is the product of a distinctly religious impulse. Humanity is the God of the Enlightenment and post-Enlightenment humanism. The unity of the Godhead is an inescapable premise of all religious systems, and humanism's deity is man. Mankind must be forced to unite.[63] Yet at the same time, each man's full and absolute autonomy is the presupposition of man's rebellion. Thus, we find in the *Cooperator* a pair of essays, one calling for economic communism and the other for the abolition of all hierarchical bureaucracies and the establishment of "The Horizontal Society," in which all previous guidelines and institutions will be scrapped for a new, fluid, evolutionary set of institutions, and in which "the future need not happen to us; we can make it happen."⁶⁴ In "The Two Forms of Communism," the author criticizes political communism, which is not grounded on morality. The premise of a new, spiritual communism is, of course, that there is no ultimate scarcity of goods and services, but that nature is totally bountiful:

> But communism with a little "c" greatly strengthens Western democracy. The technological resources of the West could be used to eliminate poverty, sickness and suffering to a near-utopian degree if the profit motive and the concept of private property—both of which are based on egotism—were abandoned and replaced with deep concern for human welfare instead of material goals. Eventually, of course, this would lead to the abandonment of money as the basis of our economy, and thereafter it would function on a good-will basis, using barter. In the meantime, every citizen could find his condition immensely improved through the provision of free necessities (food, clothing and shelter) while luxuries such as boats and cars and televisions might be sold at cost—not the inflated cost based on advertising, market research, wholesaler and retailer profit, and stockholder dividends, etc., but the real cost, which would be amazingly low.⁶⁵

There is no curse on nature. Information is free (advertising must go). Capital equipment is free (no stockholder dividends needed). There is no need for an extensive and productive division of labor (no money needed). The planners are omniscient (no market research needed). Cars, boats, clothing, food, and shelter are not "material goals," but are obviously part of the "deep concern for human welfare." Such is the contemplated society in which cosmic consciousness shall reign supreme. This is the rationality of the politics of transcendence.

Predictably, the ICC is trying to take over the curriculum of the California government ("public") school system. Its bulletin, *New Consciousness Education*, explicitly states this as a goal. The reason for selecting the schools is simple: ". . . those participating in schooling are young, and their minds, during the elementary years, are relatively free from prejudice or harmful varieties of stereotypes commonly held by adults."⁶⁶ Of course, the curriculum designed by ICC adults is free from prejudice or harmful varieties of stereotypes commonly held by adults. Besides, the churches are too diverse to organize successfully, and the civil government is too bureaucratic to move rapidly. Furthermore, every nation has a school system. It pays to take over the schools. The ICC gained the support of Assemblyman John Vasconcellos of California, who is the chairman of the Joint Committee on the Master Plan of Higher Education for the state and chairman of the Educational Goals Committee. Vasconcellos is regarded as a bit of a weirdo by his colleagues, but that has not kept him from becoming very influential on the committees for education, where many of the major decisions are made.

My estimation of the ICC's influence is that it has very little. Still, it is another representative of a whole spectrum of occultist, higher-consciousness, humanist organizations that are doing what they can when they can to reconstruct society along the lines of one-world government. To try to find *the* central organization that is somehow directing all of the evil we see around us is futile. Besides, it gives too much credit to the organizational abilities of the Satanic opposition. But with multiple pressures, political and educational, from similarly minded groups like the ICC, voters become confused and their leaders can be swayed by organized, concentrated propaganda.

The Committee for the Future, an ICC-related organization (2325 Porter St., N.W., Washington, D.C. 20008), has actually called for "the Politics of Transcendence." Its *New Worlds Newsletter* promises: "Estimates differ, but most knowledgeable observers agree that humanity has but a few decades—a cosmic blink of the eye—to alter our behavior patterns and to coordinate our basic functions globally." The fusion of evolutionary humanism and evolutionary Eastern mysticism is striking:

> The Politics of Transcendence grows out of new knowledge of the awesome history of our own genesis. With our young, but far-seeing, deep-seeing eyes of science we have caught a first glimpse of our own cosmic origins from a fiery star to our present condition as Mankind in the 1970's A.D. From this "parental perspective" through which we view our own development, we appear to be a continuous, energetic process. Each stage in our evolution—the formation of the solar system, earth, life, animal, human—appears as a natural "discontinuity." This future condition, the future stage, the "next step," is as difficult for us to forecast as it would have been for a macromolecule in the early seas to predict the cell, or for the single cell to imagine the fantasy of animals, or for those animals to foresee humankind.
>
> The perspective of the Politics of Transcendence sees our present problems as dangerous but natural signals of an evolutionary shift which is occurring in every functional system within the body of mankind—economic, environmental, social, political, spiritual. From this perspective we appear to be making a birth-like transition from earth/only, scarcity systems toward universal, abundance systems.
>
> The crucial action we will take during the period of transition will be profoundly affected by our image of our future—our idea of our "next step." If we see ourselves as a failing race, limited to one planet with finite resources, cursed with the original sin of irremediable selfishness, we shall surely fail. But, if we view ourselves as Universal Humanity, at the beginning of our emancipation from the brutalizing struggle for survival out of the animal world, born into a universe of process and pattern which appears conducive to ever-higher more coherent forms of life, if we see ourselves as capable of synthesizing our physical and psychic powers toward the transcendence of time/space . . . why then, no one can predict our future. It is open, wide, far, outward, inward, toward a new dimension of being which now attracts millions to become the active constituency of the Politics of Transcendence.[67]

Conclusion

Man is finite and man is operating under a curse because of his ethical rebellion. The best and the most that man can and should hope for is the eventual abolition of the effects of his rebellion. He can legitimately hope to become perfectly human *after* the day of judgment, when the manifestation of the new heavens and the new earth is made complete. But until then, he must content himself with the working out in daily life of the principles of biblical law. He must content himself with being finite. He must understand that he can never be more than human, although the progressive sanctifying of regenerated men and of the society that they gradually construct is God's down payment (earnest) of the coming day of restoration. In short, man is human, his world is under limits, and finitude is with us forever. The foundation of cosmic restoration is therefore ethical regeneration —the new heart which God promises His people (Jeremiah 31:31-34; Hebrews 8:10, 11; 10:15-17). Our problem as men is not our finitude, for we are created beings. Our problem is moral, for we are rebellious creatures.

The society of Satan promises self-transcendence in every area of life. It calls for a new age, an Aquarian age, a proletarian age, an Aryan age, a millennium of humanistic peace. Men are to transcend all limits, becoming gods, determining good and evil. Men are to stand in judgment over God's word. Men are to build a paradise on earth, but without a blueprint, for in a world of evolutionary process, whirl is king. The universe of humanism is theoretically an open universe—open, that is, to everyone but God. By closing the universe to God, humanistic man opens the door to the Moloch state. Rushdoony's words should stand as a perpetual warning:

> Humanistic law, moreover, is inescapably totalitarian law. Humanism, as a logical development of evolutionary theory, holds fundamentally to a concept of an evolving universe. This is held to be an "open universe," whereas Biblical Christianity, because of its faith in the triune God and His eternal decree, is said to be a faith in a "closed universe." This terminology not only intends to prejudice the case; it reverses reality. The universe of evolution and humanism is a closed universe. There is no law, no appeal, no higher order, beyond and above the universe. Instead of an open window upwards, there is a closed cosmos. There is thus no ultimate law and decree beyond man and the universe. In practice, this means that the positive law of the state is absolute law. The state is the most powerful and most highly organized expression of humanistic man, and the state is the form and expression of humanistic law. Because there is no higher law of God as judge over the universe, over every human order, the law of the state is a closed system of law. There is no appeal beyond it. Man has no "right," no realm of justice, no source of law beyond the state, to which he can appeal against the state. Humanism therefore imprisons man within the closed world of the state and the closed universe of the evolutionary scheme.[68]

We are indeed called to create a politics of transcendence, but not a politics of self-transcendence. We are called to execute godly justice as laid down by God. We are called to work out our salvation with fear and trembling (Philippians 2:12). What we are *not* called to do is to regenerate our world, ourselves, or our institutions. Man is not ultimately creative; he is only subordinately creative. When he attempts to be ultimately creative, man becomes subordinately destructive, bringing death and mayhem to himself and his environment. The society of Satan is therefore doomed to failure in the long run, but it can play havoc with Christian culture in the meantime.

Conclusion

What we have surveyed so far is only the tip of the iceberg, if that. The witchcraft phenomenon has been treated in detail in countless books in recent years: animal sacrifice, covens, human sacrifice, trances, spells, and so forth. What I have attempted to demonstrate is that the philosophy of witchcraft undergirds many movements that are not openly allied with the ancient arts of *wicca*. Occult forces exist that are not generally classified as witchcraft. In the case of Arigo, for example, the authorities could not prove that he prescribed potions or herbs. The Roman Catholic church did attempt to exorcise him, but having failed, the church's authorities steadily reclassified his powers as being simply *parapsychological*, which added an element of legitimacy to his healing. He himself distinguished between those of his patients who were genuinely ill and those who were under some sort of hex. (His vomiting occurred in the latter cases.)

The heart of witchcraft is its quest for occult power. But this quest is supported by a philosophy of life. Man is to become God. Man's powers flow from the beyond, but not a God-controlled beyond. The restraints of biblical law are not acknowledged by practitioners of the occult arts. Some may acknowledge spirits as the source of their power; others, like LaVey, believe that the powers of witchcraft stem directly from man's link to impersonal forces of the universe. But all hold to a view of man as a being wholly autonomous from the God of the Bible. When they speak of God, it is not the God who prohibits occultism and warns men to test both prophets and spirits for their orthodoxy.

There is always a great temptation to investigate occultism for the sake of mere curiosity. It is exciting to be exposed to a world that is denied by one's former teachers. We are all subject to the "secret garden" syndrome, which is why most occult groups are so heavily immersed in mysteries, secret signs, oaths, and other such baggage. The Bible, in contrast, tells men to let their lights shine, not to hide their lights under a basket. Christians are to act like the city on a hill, illuminating all others with the wisdom of God. Secrecy may be a temporary measure in times of widespread persecution, but it is not the standard for the churches. But this lacks the excitement of belonging to a secret inner circle, or a supposed inner circle. The cell system of the Communist Party is efficient, no doubt, in keeping out spies, but it is not the ideal form of organization. One never knows just who is in control of such a cell system, and the structure leads to a kind of moral blindness—a blind following of orders from above and a stifling of those beneath.

Occultism is curious. It is fascinating. But it is not to be studied for its own sake. When the newly freed Israelites were being prepared for entrance into the promised land, which at the time was inhabited by numerous Canaanitic peoples, they were told to "make no mention of the name of other gods, neither let it be heard out of thy mouth" (Exodus 23:13). If there were any budding sociologists of religion in the Israelite camp, their Ph.D. dissertations on the gods of Canaan were thereby cut short. The temptation to delight in ghost stories is always present, and we should take care to guard ourselves from this temptation. Most of the stories are false, but some are true, and it is the true story that can harm men.

We must always ask why we are investigating a topic, whether it be UFO's, Soviet prison camps, psychic healing, or whatever. Horror should not be indulged in for its own sake. The movie *Dracula* is not a horror film, but amusing, almost "camp," as they say. But *The Night of the Living Dead* is truly horrifying, and a person would be wise to avoid it. The same is true of the facts in this book. They are presented in order to instruct, not to invite imitation or endless research into the demonic.

The goal of this book is to present evidence of a set of phenomena that cannot be explained by the canons of Western rationalism. Some of them may be explainable, but not all. And even if there can conceivably be a post-Kantian explanation for a Ted Serios (which I doubt) or an Arigo (which I strongly doubt), this does not mean that the "rational" answer is, in fact, the accurate one. Ockham's razor—that the acceptable answer is always the simplest, that is, the one in closet conformity to the known laws of the universe—was devised by a radical religious skeptic who was self-consciously trying to push the signs of the supernatural out of the universe. Ockham's razor is not a neutral tool, and in times of growing irrationalism, occultism, and demonic activity, it is less and less useful in describing certain kinds of facts. Ockham's razor is best suited for a Christian culture that is not subjected to daily manifestations of occult power. When the rationalist culture that has abandoned the God of the Bible for Ockham's razor—a neutralist, rationalist conception of the autonomous universe—is invaded by the very supernatural, personal forces that rationalism denies, the exclusive use of Ockham's razor is suicidal.

This book is not to be used by men to achieve Screwtape's goal: making materialists believe in demons but not in God. The demonic forces discussed in this book are powerful. We are wise to recall the second half of the first stanza of Martin Luther's hymn, "A Mighty Fortress Is Our God": "For still our ancient foe/Doth seek to work us woe;/His craft and power are great;/And, armed with cruel hate,/On earth is not his equal." That hymn is a reminder of the power of God and His victory over the Devil. Men who really do take its words seriously are not supposed to concentrate on the idea of Satan's power. They are to be reminded of the might of God's fortress. "The prince of darkness grim,/We tremble not for him;/His rage we can endure,/For lo his doom is sure;/One little word shall fell him."

The revival of occultism in our era, and especially since 1965, is not necessarily a sign of the end of the world, the triumph of Satan, the second coming of Christ, or any other apocalyptic event. There have been outbreaks of demonism before. The Roman Empire suffered such a plague after the first century, A. D. There was renewed interest in witchcraft and magic in Western Europe in the late medieval period. The Renaissance was marked by magicians and astrologers, and to a lesser degree, so was the Reformation. We have lived in a Christian era, for modern rationalism has grown up in a culture in which the logic of autonomus man has had restraints from Christian theology, or at least the cultural residue of that theology. In our day, however, the residue has been eroded away to a great extent. We have spent our spiritual capital, and our checks are bouncing. The decay of humanism has let to the revival of occultism. What we are witnessing is *occult revival and cultural disintegration.*

The answer is not terror, retreat, and hopelessness. The answer is a systematic, well-financed, decentralized program of Christian reconstruction. Every area of life must be called back from the rot of humanism and the acids of occultism. Power must be seen as the product of self-confidence *and* a system of laws in conformity to the moral law revealed in the Bible. Confidence of victory is our motivation; biblical law is our tool of conquest. Reason flourishes in a framework of biblical revelation. It dies when it attempts to operate in terms of hypothetical neutrality and autonomy. We see before us the fruits of rationalism running wild. The sons and daughters of twentieth-century rationalism have become, if not occultists, then certainly tolerators of the world of occultism. The thin cord of Western rationalism cannot, apart from Christian values, support the weight of occult forces. If men want power apart from meaning, then they will seek it any way they can. If rationalism works, fine; if occultism works, fine; if a fusion of the two works, fine. But ultimately, we are told, none of this works. Power cannot be attained in the long run by those who seek it and it alone.

We must know the kinds of enemies we face. A traditional rationalist who is tied to his nineteenth-century worldview does not recognize the danger of real, existing, active, personal occult forces. The modern rationalist who worships chance cannot recognize them either. (He may, however, acknowledge that the manifestations of such power cannot be explained, on principle, unlike his nineteenth-century cousin, who believes that anything can be explained, given enough data and an appropriate theory.) We must know that reason has its limits, and he who is "purely rational" is blind to existing forces that can literally kill.

Occult revival and cultural disintegration can be reversed. But they can be reversed only by men who recognize their responsibilities under God to subdue the earth for the glory of God (Genesis 1:28). If those who call themselves Christians continue to ignore the cause of both occult revival and cultural disintegration, namely, the defection of Christians from the battlefields of life—social, intellectual, political, economic, artistic, educational—then the crises will only intensify. We are like stubborn mules; God has to hit us in the head several times before He catches our attention. I, for one, am tired of being hit in the head. I get the picture. It is time to go to work.

Epilogue
The Parable of the White Crow

Once upon a time, in a land very far away, there was a priesthood that was very powerful. It had not always been so powerful. In fact, theirs was a relatively new religion, perhaps two centuries old. But now they ruled the land with an iron grip, for it was they who laid down the truths and dogmas concerning the nature of all reality. And the fundamental dogma, which appeared in every child's catechism and every scholar's preface, was very short: "There are only black crows." All of the collected wisdom of the ages had to conform to this dogma; anyone offering evidence to the contrary was immediately expelled from the priesthood (heresy in the priesthood, understandably, was rare, since an expelled priest was generally incompetent to perform any other profit-making service), or, if the person was not in the priesthood, he was excommunicated. This meant that he would spend his life in outer darkness.

Yet despite the rigid code concerning the impossibility of white crows, reports continued to filter in concerning the alleged discovery of one or more white crows. The newspapers would report on these stories occasionally, or perhaps even a flurry of such reports would be publicized, and then, after the priesthood would issue its mimeographed forms denying the reports as based on insufficient evidence and/or fraud, the newspapers would cease publishing these reports for several years. Then a flurry of new sightings would be reported, newspaper and magazine articles would be printed, and more mimeographed denunciations—

occasionally issued on brittle and yellowed paper, yet strangely identical in wording to the latest rebuttals with their unfaded ink—would be sent out.

Finally, an intelligent young man one day found a wounded white bird while on a trip to distant mountains. He brought it back in a small sack. Then he put it in a sturdy cage in his garage. He brought in several friends, all young priests who had not yet reached the fourth degree (in a system of eighteen levels of initiation), and they all confirmed the young man's suspicion: this was a white crow. Five young priests reported back to their superiors that a white crow had been found. All of them were severely reprimanded, two were defrocked, and all were warned that if they persisted in this heresy harsher discipline would be applied.

Three of them—the ones who were not defrocked—decided to write up the discovery for one of the respected theological journals. The manuscript, heavily cross-referenced to the Scriptures, was rejected. The data involved could not pass the standard tests, the editors stated, and several of the scriptural citations were clearly (and possibly deliberately) taken out of context. The trio sent it to still other theological journals, but the response was the same. The denominational monthly did run a brief column announcing the existence of the three young priests' work, but made no reference, one way or the other, to the actual existence of the white crow in their friend's garage.

Finally, because the young men allowed their manuscript to be published by one of the new heretical journals—which were notably erratic as far as editorial policies were concerned, with articles of uneven quality—the priesthood became alarmed. When cheap, popularly written books began appearing, all based on the young priests' manuscript (plus follow-up studies written by the individual members of the trio), the hierarchy announced that a team of three distinguished priests, all fifteenth degree or higher, had been appointed to examine the claims of the young priests and their friend who owned the alleged white crow.

The official team journeyed to the now-famous garage. They brought all sorts of equipment with them, but no one outside the priesthood, except for the owner, was allowed to view the investigation. However, a summary report was promised to the news media just as soon as the team had made up its collective mind.

The first priest stepped up to the cage and ran his hands over the bars. "This is a shoddy cage, indeed," he said. The young man answered, "Well, it's good enough to hold the white crow, sir. I did employ a few used pieces of metal for the hinges, but otherwise I got everything out of a standard mail-order catalogue." The priest replied, "It's just as I thought: a cage constructed by an amateur. The whole story is amateurish, from start to finish. A person who would employ such an inferior cage as this for a white crow is clearly not to be taken seriously. For accurate crow studies, you need first-rate cages." "But sir," replied the young man, "I could hardly afford one of the approved cages. The only reason I bought the parts for this one and put it together is because I just happened to find a white crow. I had no idea I would find one; I virtually stumbled upon it." Then one of the young priests spoke up: "Besides, we've all seen the cages you have designed for white crows. They *are* sturdy, that I'll grant you. But they are all painted white inside and out, including the glass over the front. The only thing you can see inside is a shadow, and then only if a black crow is inside. If a white crow were in there, you couldn't possibly see it." The older priest, angered by these remarks, shouted: "Since there are only black crows, obviously they are the only ones that could cast a shadow. Your whole line of reasoning is faulty to the core." "And your line of reasoning," replied the young priest quietly, "is totally circular." With that, the older priest began to walk away. "Wait a minute," pleaded the young man. "Aren't you going to look at my white crow?" "No need to," came the reply. "Anyone who uses a cage like yours is not the kind of man who could have found anything as important as a white crow—if such things existed."

The second priest on the investigating team—a seventeenth-degree priest, two degrees higher than the priest who had just walked out—stepped up. "Never mind, young man. I'm willing to examine your crow. Reverend Mr. Caruthers is overly sensitive to cages, as so many of our thirteenth- and fourteenth-degree men are. But I think your cage is good enough for the job at hand. Now, let me look here. . . ." He bent down and peered into the cage. "Why son, that's not a crow. That's a seagull. A normal, everyday white seagull." "But sir," the young man said, a twinge of desperation in his voice, "I found that bird in the mountains. There are no seagulls in the mountains." The priest stopped for a moment, seemed to stare into space, and then said: "I remember, about twenty-five years ago, that I read a study of the migration patterns of seagulls, and while few, very few, of them go near mountains, there are one or two varieties that have, on rare occasions, been seen by reputable witnesses within flying distance of at least low-lying hills. This is apparently one of those cases." "But sir, this bird doesn't look anything like a seagull. That's a crow!" The priest had brightened up considerably by now. "No, son, you're mistaken. I am a specialist in ornithology, and this, I assure you, is a seagull—an oddly shaped one, I will grant you, but a seagull nonetheless." He turned and walked out of the garage.

The third team member stepped up. He didn't say a word to the young man or the younger priests. There was a steely gleam in his eye. He looked in for about three seconds, and then stepped back. "Just what I thought, gentlemen, *just as I thought*." He seemed to spit out the words. "This is a crow, all right. A black crow. You have dyed it white. This is nothing less than outright fraud." The young man was speechless. Two of the three younger priests protested, although the third one just smirked, nodding silently to himself. "We never touched that crow," said one of the young priests. "I did not mean to imply that you did," the priest replied. He was an old man, eighteenth degree, who had achieved this high distinction forty years earlier with a revolutionary study involving horses. "But you have not used the faculties of observation that our God has given you. And you, sir," he said, looking at the young man, "you are going to be excommunicated, if it's the last thing I ever do." The young man was close to tears. "I never dyed the crow, sir. It's white, it's white. You can take it to your laboratory. Test it. It *is* a white crow. I'm an honest man."

"Wait a minute," said the third young priest, who had so far remained silent. "Don't let that crow get out of your sight. First, take it to those reporters outside. Let them look at it. Then we can *all* go with this *gentleman*," he almost sneered the word out, "to several *independent* laboratories to test the source of this bird's color. And we will provide them only with feathers, not the bird."

The old priest was enraged. "Who do you think you are? Are you implying that I would tamper with crucial evidence?" "Frankly," said the younger priest, "ever since you became an expert in crows, defending the old dogma by means of scriptural citations instead of hard research—unlike your early path-breaking research on the left rear hoof of the Apaloosa—I have suspected that you are not above doing just that." The old man glared at him: "I'll have your frock for that statement, young man, and we'll see if you can earn an honest living outside the cloistered halls that have provided you with so much protection." "I'll take that chance," the young priest replied.

"But, sir," interjected the bird's owner, "can't you examine my bird more carefully? He isn't painted, dyed, or anything. Just take a look." The old man yelled, "Look here, I've seen these dyed crows before. Frauds, every one of them. Nothing but a lot of sideshow buncombe, a lot of trickery. Just a means of getting the common people to shell out their hard-earned money." The young man pressed the old priest: "But just because the white crows you examined before were frauds, why do you think mine has to be a fraud?" The old man replied, word by word, giving emphasis to each word as he spat it out: "*Because there are only black crows!*" With that, he turned as if to stomp out. "But what am I to do with the bird?" wailed the young man. "I'll tell you what I would do with it if it were mine," the old man said. "I'd kill it, clean it, burn its feathers, and enjoy a good meal. Then I'd forget about the whole thing."

"That's easy enough for you to say," snapped the young priest. "You've never had to eat crow in your life. Up until now, that is." With that, the old man walked out, slamming the door behind him.

When he got outside, he was met by the two other team members. "What are we going to tell the press? We have to tell them somthing," said the second priest, the one who had said the bird was a seagull. "We'll tell them these people are misinformed, unreliable as witnesses, men without certification," said the first priest. "But that story isn't working any more," said the second priest. "The reporters just don't trust anyone's explanation, unless it has been quoted in the *Times,* and the *Times* refuses to cover these white crow stories. The editor says such tales are undignified." "We'll tell them," said the third and oldest priest, "that there is no substance to any of it—*any* of it! Each of us will go to one or two reporters after the official announcement is made, and offer his own opinion. Since few people read all the papers, the public will believe what it wants to believe—that this white crow business isn't true—but the reader will get a different reason why it isn't true: unqualified observers, seagull, or painted crow. The group explanation will be printed with footnotes, lots of mathematics, and a few easily quoted phrases, which are all the reporters or the readers are interested in, or capable of dealing with, anyway."

"But I tell you, they won't buy it," said the second priest. "Those reporters will want to see the bird. They won't take our word for it." "All right, then," said the leader, "we can tell them the bird is diseased. Anyone going near it will have to be quarantined. In fact, anyone who has been in contact with that bird for over, say"—looking at his wristwatch—"two hours has got to be run through a series of tests to determine whether it is safe for him to mingle in public again." "But what about the bird?" asked the second priest. "Already taken care of," said the first priest, the expert in cage construction. "Those cheap cages have wide spaces between the bars, comparatively speaking. Wide enough, in fact, to toss in a few pellets," he said, patting his priestly robe (which had the traditional secret pocket underneath in which priests in olden days had carried little flasks for medicine and similar liquids—a fashion maintained by the traditionalists within the order). "You mean . . . ?" whispered the third and most experienced investigator, with a grin. "I do, indeed," said the first one. "The bird is as good as dead." "Caruthers," beamed the old priest, "level sixteen is closer than you think."

That afternoon, the authorities were called, and all four of the young men were put under quarantine. The bird had died, and the authorities realized that it must have been infected, as the priests had said. The priests took the body, "for further research," to the order's official lab, where it was immediately incinerated.

That evening, there was a fire in the garage, and the photographs taken by the young owner were destroyed, or so he later said. The team of priests denied that they had been shown any photographs, which was true.

The three young priests were put on trial. Two confessed that they had been hasty in their judgments. The third one—the one who smirked—refused to retract his earlier statements and was defrocked. He later became an editor for one of the small-circulation heretical journals, while working evenings in his home as a proofreader for the "Fabulous Writers Home Study Course, Inc." He still had three copies of the photographs of the white crow, but experts in the theological journals said they were faked, and the negatives had been destroyed in the mysterious garage fire.

The young man, when released from quarantine, went to live in the hills, determined to find another white crow. He never did.

The old priest died, and the church canonized him. The second priest—Reverend Mr. Seagull, as the younger priests called him, among themselves, from that day on—never made level eighteen. He retired and went to live in a community of ornithologists, where he spent the rest of his days trying to discover whether any variety of seagull had actually been found deeper in the mountains than the low-lying hills. He never did. The technician, who believed in rigorous cages, became director of teacher training in the order's seminary, until it finally was closed down for lack of students.

And none of the seven, it can be said, ever felt that he would have been worse off if he had never seen the crow. Odd as it may seem, the four young men never made much of themselves after that. The crow incident had been the high point in each of their lives. The young man died in the mountains a few years later, and the two recanting priests never made it beyond level nine. The defrocked priest committed suicide about ten years later.

Perhaps the story should have ended here, but it does not. The crow, like all crows, was a very smart creature. It had never touched the pellets tossed into its cage. It knew what they were. It did not care, one way or the other, for it knew it was dying. The old priest had been quite correct, though for the wrong reason. The crow had been infected, dangerously infected. And all seven of the men had been both right and wrong. The crow was not a white crow, but neither was it black. The crow was red.

This priesthood, as mentioned in the beginning, was a new development. Thousands of years earlier, an older priesthood, now ridiculed in the official texts of both priests and heretics, had ruled the land. It had known of crows from the beginning. It knew that there are black crows and white crows, but it also taught of red crows. Black crows are common, men were taught, and quite worthy of study. They could be tamed and used for the purposes of men, although they could be mean and sometimes peck a man's eye out. White crows were rare, wonderful birds. They loved men, but did not come near men often, out of respect for man's relationship with black crows. Red crows were the most rare but they hated men. They were not long-lived creatures, for they were infected from birth. But they could infect men, and did so, understanding somehow that their misery could be transferred. The weakest of the crow kingdom, they were very clever. They would fly into the sides of chalky mountains until they resembled the white crows, so beloved of early men. Then they would go to men, infecting them whenever possible. But the priests of the old world had learned of this treachery, and they had made a rule: *Men should, in general, handle only black crows, and then very carefully, so as not to have an eye pecked out.* The rule, when followed, reduced both infection and eye injuries, and the white crows were satisfied to see man's development and hardly ever flew near men, except on moonless nights when men could not see them.

The new priesthood had twisted the older priesthood's dogma, which had been only a corollary in the old faith, and elevated it into the familiar law: There are only black crows. This seemed safe enough. At worst, there were only occasional eye injuries to worry about (although these had been increasing for many years). The new priests had become masters at training black crows. They had studied them, catalogued them, and learned how to breed them. They were experts in black crows, and white crows were either forgotten or shot at on sight. But the only time anyone ever saw a white crow directly was when it was not a white crow at all; it was a red crow in disguise. And those who did not shoot at them to scare them off were very often infected, dying horrible deaths. So men avoided all but black crows, except in the very mountainous areas, where older, forgotten religious cults survived: worshippers and attempted trainers of red crows.

Those few remaining exponents of the older established priesthood still told stories of red and white crows, but even they, for the most part, placed such events in the distant past. After all, their own leaders were usually required to spend several years in the new priesthood's theological seminaries, or at least in their preseminary schools. A few laymen really believed in red crows, and they all knew that white crows preferred to stay in the background most of the time.

So when "white" crows, which were really red crows, began to appear inside cities, neither the new priests nor the older, ignored priests could do much about it. The new priesthood recognized only black crows, and most of the remaining old-fashioned priests recognized red and white crows only on principle, not during the day.

Common people, and even a few priests, began collecting "white" crows, but very quietly. Many of the heretical groups actually tried to train them. They seemed trainable, at least initially. It became a kind of fad to have a few "white" crows around, or at least have a friend who said that he had once seen one. The entertainment people were especially big on "white" crows. So were some of the undergraduates in the seminaries.

And steadily, there were stories of infection. Crazed activities by those who said they owned "white" crows. Dark activities. And madness, always madness. The infection spread, for those who once recognized the danger were embarrassed even to admit that they believed in nonblack crows, and those who believed only in black crows blamed the signs of the epidemic on psychosomatic illness, poverty, or the lack of proper toilet training of society's youngsters. Such speculation did not even slow down the epidemic.

Nothing seemed to slow down the epidemic.

In response to the epidemic, a new priesthood, or perhaps a potential priesthood, began to be formed by young men and amateurs, some of whom were graduates of the approved seminaries, and others who were self-taught. The new priesthood adopted a modified version of the establishment priesthood's dogma: "There are only black crows, but newly discovered red crows, which underneath are actually black crows, throw new light on the heretofore unsuspected breadth of black crow phenomena. But there are only black and pseudo-red black crows. *There are not now, nor have there ever been, pure white crows.*" In short, the new priesthood was content to rub off the white chalk from the red crows, so long as they could then dye the red crows black. And that, as it turned out, suited the red crows far better than white chalk had ever done—chalk being so easily washed off. Now they could become acceptable as *special* black crows.

The epidemic intensified. The only antidote would have been the use of white crows to drive off the red ones, and the only people who believed in white crows were embarrassed about the whole business. Besides, the black-dyed red crows seldom bothered them, for these people knew enough to stay away from red crows. No one else did.

The moral of the story: No crow is completely trainable by man, but red crows, painted white or painted black, can kill you.

APPENDIX A*
Power from Below

Rousas John Rushdoony

One of the basic lusts of fallen man is for power, but, more accurately, his desire is for autonomous power. Man was created by God to exercise dominion over the earth (Gen. 1:26–28) in knowledge, righteousness, and holiness, and basic to that task is the use of godly power. But the use of power in subordination to God and in submission to His word is alien to man in revolt. Man, seeking to be his own god, and to determine good and evil for himself (Gen. 3:5), wants power in independence from and in defiance of God.

Historically and religiously, men have looked to power from above, and, in a variety of religions, men have looked to the gods for power. Non-biblical religious worship, while no less an aspect of man's revolt against God, was still marked by a belief in a higher realm of spirits and powers whose aid it was held to be wise to seek. These higher beings could be allies of men, if properly approached. Temples of pagan antiquity were not places of worship, corporate or private, but places for transactions with the gods. The favor and help of these higher powers were sought in a particular venture, activity, or area of personal concern. If the insurance, protection, or help of the particular god or temple proved unsatisfactory, the individual took his business elsewhere and bought security or insurance at another temple or shrine. In all these cults of antiquity, and of various cultures to the historical present, the reality of a higher world of beings was assumed. It was believed, of course, that these higher beings were only different in degree from

---

*The appendices reproduced in this book first appeared in *The Journal of Christian Reconstruction*, I (Winter, 1974). Reprinted by permission of *The Journal of Christian Reconstruction*, P.O. Box 158, Valecito, California 95251.

men, and that a continuity existed between men and the gods. As against the biblical doctrine of the uncreated Being of God, and the created nature of man and the universe, pagan religions held to the great chain of being doctrine. All being is one being, the differences being one of degrees between the gods and men, and between men and all other creatures. The idea of continuity militated against worship in anything resembling the biblical sense. All the same, this higher world, however different in nature from the biblical view, was held to be real.

The culmination of modern philosophy, beginning in Descartes and coming to focus in Kant and Hegel, led to Darwin and the doctrine of evolution. This doctrine had deep roots in pagan antiquity and the belief in the great chain of being and was a logical development of it. It did, however, militate against any higher world. Both the old pagan doctrine and the biblical faith were ruled out. Man was held to be alone in a meaningless universe which was a product of blind chance. There was no sentient power, no mind or purpose beyond and above man, only blind and evolving energies and forces.

Power from above was thus eliminated from the universe, in both its Christian and its pagan versions. Moreover, in looking at *the power in man,* it became apparent that mind, in terms of evolution, had to be ruled as a shallow-rooted late comer. The older and more basic forces in man lay below the surface, and Freud located them, as did others, in the unconscious, in the subterranean within man. There followed what Dr. Cornelius Van Til has described as integration downward into the void: man was re-interpreted in terms of the child, the child in terms of primitive man, primitive man in terms of a mythological animal past, and so on. Culture began to seek vitality in the subterranean, in what lay below modern, civilized man. Primitivism in the arts became synonymous with vitality. A jungle beat in music with an abandonment of reason became a symbol of power, and, in every area, the downward quest for power was held to be the only means of escape from sterility and impotence. The perverted, lawless, primitive, and chaotic became equated with power.

All of this was a relentless development of the logic of the modern myth. *Power from above* having been denied as a myth, modern man became involved in a *desperate search for power from below.* The earlier means of this quest of power from below was psychoanalytic, psychiatric, and artistic. It also became political, and a new breed of leaders from below began to dominate the twentieth century—Lenin, Stalin, Hitler, Mussolini, and their paler counterparts in the democracies. Democracy itself was an enthronement of power from below: *vox populi, vox dei.*

The quest, however, soon took occultist directions. The human scene failed to manifest sufficient power. The source of power being the subterranean, modern man, by definition concluding that God and "the above" are dead, felt that what lies below must indeed be very powerful. The result has been the rise of magic, witchcraft, Satanism, and related interests.

Satanism is not new, and its past history is an ugly one, but the new Satanism is the most vicious yet, and potentially the most dangerous. The biblical Satan is a creature who seeks to be god and is fully aware of the existence of God (James 2:19). His program is a reasoned one: *First,* man is to be his own god, determining good and evil for himself (Gen. 3:5). *Second,* man should be freed from all testing and judgments and given cradle to grave security. If man needs bread, the stones should be made bread (Matt. 4:3). *Third,* faith should be totally unnecessary; man should be able to walk by sight and God should prove all things for man's benefit (Matt. 4:6). *Fourth,* rightness is an attribute of the creature, and the creature should be worshipped and served rather than God (Matt. 4:8–9).

The new image of Satan is a product of Darwin and Freud. *First,* he is not a creature made by God but a dark force evolved out of chaos and essentially is chaos. There was never thus any higher status for Satan, but a totally subterranean one, a creature of chaos, not of God. *Second,* the new image of Satan is of a totally mindless, irrational, perverse being whose existence is total terror to the rational in man. The new Satan is the utter contradiction of reason, whereas the biblical Satan is an example of fallen and totally depraved reason. It should not surprise us that some of the new Satanists lose their reason and become themselves mindless. *Third,* because no power exists above by definition, total power is held to exist below, and the result is a growing evidence that there is a strong tendency to believe in the omnipresence and even omnipotence of Satan. Satan is held to be everywhere, operative in all situations, and hence to be reckoned with at all times. It is surprising how far this idea has infiltrated the churches. Too few churchmen remember that Satan, like themselves, is a creature, capable only of a local appearance, i.e., able to be in only one place at a time. Only God is omnipresent and omnipotent.

Power from below, whether feared or courted, is thus very much a part of modern man's faith. That power can reside in inanimate nature, as in the stars, and hence the revival of interest in astrology. It can reside in magic and witchcraft, or in other related practices, but, in any case, it is *power from below.*

The result of such a faith can only lead, as it already has, to a greater faith in raw and primitive violence as against reason. We can only expect, until this faith is shattered, a steady intensification of violence, crime, and revolution. *Power from below* means that normal sexuality is regarded as sterile and inhibited, and violence, rape, and perversion are thus regarded as raw and true power in the sexual realm.

It also means a greater stress on mindless religion, as witness the so-called charismatic movement, an emphasis on mindless experience as power. The charismatic who learns to babble insanely in what is no tongue at all has no answer therein to moral and intellectual problems, but he "witnesses" eloquently to others of the feeling of "power in the Spirit," power which is in essence a cultivation of what is mindless and subterranean.

In the world of films, television, novels, student riots, and political revolutions, power is held to come from below. The answer to all problems is violence. Problems are all held to be solvable if only enough violence and mindless force are applied. In the world of television, killings and brutal beatings solve all problems, and in the world of the revolutionist, the same great faith in the healing force of violence, power from below, is in evidence.

The world thus is in crisis. *Power from below* is a faith which insures the triumph of mindlessness and violence. No calls for law and order can stem this intense faith of the new pagans. The so-called religious revivals of recent years have only been a part of the same ugly faith. Instead of "turning on" with narcotics, the call is for "turning on" with Jesus. Instead of the narcotic "trip," the "trip" with Jesus and the "great Trip" (the Rapture) are offered, so that religion is made a part of the same tradition as the pagan creed, and mindlessness is not challenged.

Only a full-orbed and intelligent orthodoxy, stressing the sovereign and triune God, the doctrine of creation, and the sovereign grace of God in salvation, can do justice to the fact of *power from above*. Anything short of God's total claims is a deception.

APPENDIX B
Table Raising:
Introduction to the Occult

David R. Ketchen

In the little Ontario (Canada) village where I grew up, nobody ever thought very much about the devil. In the Presbyterian Church, which we attended religiously, he was never mentioned. Indeed, life was so sunny that we were never aware at all of the Prince of Darkness.

In those pre-television days, people still knew how to entertain themselves. Our activities were as varied as our own ingenuity would permit. It was one of our closest friends, the local lady undertaker (women's libbers please take note), who introduced us to the intriguing pastime of table raising.

At the time we were quite unaware of the history of such phenomena or their attendant dangers. We had never heard of the Fox sisters; Ouija boards had not yet flooded the market; the spiritist activities of Mackenzie King, the recent Canadian Prime Minister, were not then so widely known as they are now. Anyway, we were Tories and would not have been at all surprised at any nonsense in which the Liberals might have indulged. Thus, we tripped blindly into the realm of the occult, oblivious to the obvious.

"Getting the table up" was always an exciting prospect for a young teenager. It involved a number of preparatory procedures, none of which was probably necessary to the final outcome, but served to emphasize the mystery of what we were doing. First of all, the table itself was selected with care. It was our understanding of the rules of the game that a wooden table rather than a metal one must be used.

The folding card table we used had metal corners, but apparently that was a minor infraction, for we were nearly always successful. The table was placed in the north corner of two outside walls. If there were openings in the corner it would not work. A rug or heavy blanket on the floor helped to keep the table from slipping. Five people sat around the two exposed sides, placed their palms down on the table top, and linked their fingers to form a chain along the two sides. Then began a period of waiting which might last from a few minutes to half an hour.

We followed none of the other procedures which one might expect in this type of endeavor. The room was not darkened as is customary for seance-like activities, nor did we ever concentrate specifically on what we were doing. In fact, the conversation during this preliminary period of waiting usually consisted of a great deal of jovial bantering about what apparent idiots we were, and speculation as to what the neighbors' reaction might be if they came in and caught us.

After some time one of the group was sure to remark on the curious tingling sensation in his fingers, as though a weak electrical current were passing from hand to hand about the table. Kurt Koch, the German theologian whose labors have largely been in the field of the occult, has noted and documented this phenomenon (*Christian Counselling and Occultism,* pp. 44, 121ff.). This was the signal that the table was prepared to rise, and then began a short period of earnest pleading with the table to "Rise, table, rise." If the table was reluctant to cooperate, we would add some flattering adjectives: "Up, table, *pretty* table, *nice* table," much as one might cajole a timid kitten out of a tree. Skeptical novices had to be encouraged to join in these fervent pleas, which they would usually do, albeit reluctantly and in embarrassed whispers. Whereupon, to mingled glee and astonishment, the two table legs along one of the walls would rise about eighteen inches from the floor, thus tilting the table into the laps of those sitting along the opposite side. If those sitting along the adjacent side were newcomers to the game there were invariably snorts of disgust as they accused the others of pulling the table towards them, thus causing the tilt. This would indeed have been possible and to a novice would certainly seem probable. If our protestations of innocence went unheeded, it was a simple procedure to tell the table to go down and come up the the other way. The skeptics were effectively silenced when the table bounced up towards *them,* making it appear that *they* were pulling it. Of course, some refused to be convinced. I still remember the night that my uncle sat under the table for two hours trying to catch the one who was lifting it with his foot, while the same table bounced up and down merrily above his head. It is sufficient for me to say that as the one who was the most frequent instigator of such activities, I never once indulged in fraud or trickery to raise a table. It was never necessary to do so.

For the first dozen or so times the sight of the table mysteriously rising on two legs was sufficiently exciting. Later, I began to cherish the hope that some day enough power might be generated to raise all four legs off the floor at once. That, however, I never achieved, although I understand that others have. Three legs up was no problem. More than that and gravity took over and the whole thing would come crashing to the floor.

Once we had the table up, it was a simple matter to frame questions which could be answered by "knocking"; the two elevated legs thudding to the floor and bouncing back up again. For example: Will my mother have any more children?—Knock once for yes and twice for no. How many grandchildren will she have?—Knock once for each child. What is the first initial of the person Mary Jones will marry?—Knock once for each letter, beginning with A.

If we ran out of questions we could always ask the table to dance, which it did very proficiently by moving up and down in whatever rhythm we specified.

On occasions the responses were ridiculous. I remember being told that I would marry my high school English teacher and that we would have eight children. Since the lady in question was already in her late fifties and had not shown any inclinations to wedlock for years, the prospect seemed remote. At such times we would sternly admonish the table to stop such nonsense and tell the truth. Sometimes after a prolonged spate of nonsensical replies someone would say in exasperation, "Table, are you tired?" The table would beat out a resounding "yes" and quit for the night.

At other times we would be amazed at the accuracy of its responses. Answers were many times given that later proved to be entirely correct, although we were unaware of it at the time. So we passed many a long winter evening, never suspecting that we were engaging in anything other than harmless entertainment.

People have sometimes asked me about the possibility of securing information regarding profitable financial investments in this way and, of course, there are many who would use the table for this purpose. We never did, for two very good reasons. First of all, my mother strictly forbade any such "serious" questions, and in the second place, we never had any money to invest anyway.

During these years I was introduced to one other occult practice. In my late teens a friend demonstrated to me a "trick" in which he had become proficient. He would take a Bible, insert a large key in its pages, and tie it tightly shut with heavy cord so that the key could not be pulled out. The Bible was then hung on a long string from the hole in the key to the ceiling. When the Bible hung motionless, he would solemnly recite Ruth's words in Ruth 1:16. After pronouncing that solemn vow of commitment he would ask his questions, the suspended Bible revolving to the right for the answer "yes" or to the left for the answer "no." Though at that time I was unconverted, I found this use of the Scriptures frightening and could not bring myself to become involved.

Eventually, our involvement with table raising grew less and less. Some years later while taking a pre-theology course at Waterloo Lutheran University I attended a lecture by a visiting German scholar, Dr. Kurt Koch, whose book, *Between Christ and Satan* (1961), opened to me the true nature of table raising and its attendant dangers. In the meantime, God had effectually called my parents and myself from the kingdom of darkness into the kingdom of his dear Son. Graciously, He has protected us from the ill-effects of what we wickedly did in ignorance, and His Word now assures us that that wicked one now has no power over us. I do not know of anyone still practicing table raising in that little Ontario town where my parents still live. It seems that most of them are content to serve Satan in less spectacular ways.

It remains for me to attempt some analysis of the unscriptural nature and the dangers of this and other manifestly occult pursuits. In the first place, table raising and all such practices represent an illegitimate method of searching for knowledge. That is not to suggest that the quest for knowledge and understanding is anything but good and proper. Indeed, such a quest is not only necessary but commanded by God. "Get wisdom, get understanding," Solomon declares (Prov. 4:5). Even prior to the Fall and his expulsion from Eden, Adam required a knowledge and understanding of his environment in order to fulfill his God-given role of subduing the earth, bringing the facts of his environment into subjection to God his King. The New Testament, no less than the Old, demands the pursuit of knowledge. For example, I John 4:1 lays upon the believer the obligation to test the spirits to see whether they are of God, and such an obligation involves the diligent quest for knowledge and the full use of our intellectual capacities. We are to serve God not just with our souls, but also with our minds, and such service involves a constant quest for factual truth. The establishment of universities by earnest Christians in the past was no accident. It was simply the result of godly men seeking to fulfill their obligation to comprehend, investigate, and subdue the creation to the glory of God.

The pursuit of knowledge is legitimated by the God-given mandate of Genesis 1:28; however, the Bible also recognizes that some of that knowledge necessary for the bringing of the creation into subjection is beyond the natural ability of man to achieve. So God gave to Adam even in Eden what special revelation he required. His own natural powers of observation and analysis could never have informed Adam of the monumental significance of the tree in the midst of the garden. Some of the information necessary for man's obedience must be given supernaturally. Therefore God verbally and propositionally fills in the gaps in man's knowledge to enable him to comprehend and accomplish his task. Later in the history of revelation, the prophetic office was established, in order that man might be instructed and encouraged in his quest for obedience to his Creator. Thus, to man's own inherent abilities for the obtaining of that wisdom requisite for obedience and fruitful service, God adds the necessary provision for special, supernatural revelation. Neither of these sources of understanding, either the natural exercise of man's intellectual capacities or the God-ordained processes of special revelation, is to be despised.

Obviously, gaining information relative to himself and his surroundings by supernatural means is intriguing to man. The Urim and the Thummin must have been as fascinating to young Hebrew boys as table raising was to me. Both are decidedly supernatural. But there is a vastly important difference. The one was God-ordained and therefore legitimate. The other is not.

Nowhere in the Scriptures is there warrant given for the quest for information by supernatural means other than those of God's appointment. Not only is the practice not warranted; it is uncompromisingly condemned. Pagan religion has always abounded in the occult. Divination by various means always played a large part in heathen life and culture. Israel was therefore required to avoid "the wizards that peep and mutter and seek unto her God" (Isa. 8:19, 20). Her supernatural revelation is sufficient in the law and the testimony. That law unhesitatingly condemned all forms of witchcraft (Lev. 20:6). Those who are tempted to indulge in fortune telling, card laying, palm reading, or table raising, and who see no harm in putting a Ouija board under the Christmas tree for Johnny's amusement, would do well to remember this. All such "innocent diversions" are transgressions of God's Word. To have recourse to such sources of information is in reality to despise the God-appointed provisions for our growth in understanding.

But if such intriguingly supernatural means of discerning truth as the Urim and Thummin were legitimate for God's people in the Old Testament, why should similarly supernatural pursuits today be regarded as sinful or dangerous? Hebrews 1:1 provides a clear answer. God did indeed effectively reveal His will unto the fathers by such diverse (and fascinating) means, but now He speaks to us in a different fashion. He now speaks to us in His Son. His revelation of himself and His will has reached its culmination and completion in the One who is himself "the brightness of his Father's glory and the express image of his person." The prophetic office has found its fulfillment in Jesus Christ. We need not, indeed we dare not seek to re-establish it elsewhere. It is *in Christ* that all the treasures of wisdom and knowledge are hid (Col. 2:3). We must not deny that truth by seeking to return to the Urim and Thummin, or indeed to any of the ordinances of that under-aged world. And if we cannot return to biblical ordinances that were once legitimate but are so no longer, by what leaps or rationalization shall we justify turning to means that were *never* biblically legitimate? He who seeks wisdom wisely will seek it in Christ, who gives freely His Spirit to guide men into all truth (John 16:13), not in crystal balls or dancing tables. The Westminster Confession of Faith puts it all very succinctly:

> Although the light of nature, and the works of creation and providence do so far manifest the goodness, wisdom, and power of God, as to leave men inexcusable; yet they are not sufficient to give that knowledge of God, and of his will, which is necessary unto salvation. Therefore it pleased the Lord, at sundry times, and in divers manners, to reveal Himself, and to declare that His will unto His Church; and afterwards, . . . to commit the same wholly unto writing: which maketh the Holy Scripture to be most necessary; those former ways of God's revealing His will unto His people being now ceased.
>
> Westminster Confession, I,1

In the second place, we are confronted not only with the manifestly unbiblical nature of table raising but also with the documented ill-effects of such activities upon those who pursue them. At the time when I became convinced of the demonic nature of table raising, I had little understanding of the theological principles I was violating. What led me to abandon it forever was the documented evidence of mental anguish, spiritual declension, and violent death that are so often the experience of those who practice such pursuits. It was Dr. Kurt Koch who first set these sad facts before me. I read his book, *Between Christ and Satan*, first with utter horror, then with fearful gratitude to a gracious God as I realized what He had done in preserving and protecting us from the power of the great adversary. Dr. Koch has spent much of his ministry in counselling those brought into bondage through the occult. He has documented not a few but hundreds of cases of occult practitioners, including table raisers. Here is the story of a young woman who has lost all sensitivity to divine things, including the ability to pray or read the Scriptures. Here is another who is driven in despair to a violent and tragic suicide. Here is an entire family developing mental problems of fearful proportions. Here are others overwhelmed by sexual aberrancies. The tale goes on and on of lives ruined, human spirits shattered, minds diseased. Such is the price that has been exacted for participation in "harmless amusement." Like a roaring lion, Satan goes about seeking whom he may devour. Foolish sinners, not content with what God has given, seek new thrills, new experiences, novelties and excitements, but the ways of Satan are the ways of death. The road of the occult leads to the pit. May the conquering Christ who has through His finished work cast out the prince of this world (John 12:31) protect His own from the destroyer. Little children, keep yourselves from idols.

APPENDIX C
The Gnostic Tradition
and Renaissance Occultism

Thomas Molnar

Modern scholarship has found that the stereotyped image we used to have of the Renaissance was considerably falsified by the retrospective view that educated Westerners were until recently casting on the fourteenth, fifteenth, and sixteenth centuries. It has become clear, thanks to such scholars as Hans Baron, Frances Yates, Oscar Kristeller, Eugenio Garin, and others that the Renaissance did not only revive the memory and the monuments of Greece and Rome, it also rediscovered the pagan myths which used to shape the inner life of the Hellenistic and Roman citizens. "Pagan myth" is not to be equated with "mythology," but with a plurality of currents of religious, spiritual, and esoteric inspiration whose origin goes back to prehistoric times and which took shape in Egypt, India, Mesopotamia, and Iran. This is not the place to explore their varied history and the combinations in which they entered with one another; we might mention only that singly and in combinations these currents had entered the Mediterranean basin around the beginning of the Hellenistic era, the third century B.C., and overcame easily the half-hearted resistance offered by the Roman pantheon.

It is a great miracle that, after permeating the minds of Greeks and Romans, these doctrines nonetheless yielded pride of place to Christianity. This is the more astonishing as the Christian doctrine, although it has firm roots in Judaism and in Greek speculation, is difficult to bear because it opposes so clearly the spontaneous bent of the archaic mind which predominated in most parts of the world and which threatens to prevail once more in our time. I refer to the Hebrew-Christian concept of separating God and man as Creator and created, of not confusing their natures, their persons, their powers. In practically all other religious and para-religious doctrines and systems, the temptation is not resisted to identify God and self, to recognize in the soul a divine substance, indeed *the* seat of divinity. Man is struck by the duality of body and soul, matter and spirit, and since he is greatly impressed by his own superiority over the rest of the visible and thinkable universe, by the consciousness he alone seems to possess, he easily persuades himself of a radical duality: man is one with the spiritual principle, God, while everything else is below him, immersed in the depth of materiality and existential misery. This central theme has, of course, many varieties, but all of them display the belief that man himself, so vastly different from the surrounding world perceived through the senses, can only be of a divine essence, not a creature himself, first among, but nevertheless only one of, the creatures. What I meant by saying that Christianity is hard to bear, becomes thus clarified: insertion in the hierarchy of creation, acceptance of a role assigned by the Creator, above the rest of other creatures, yet definitively and distinctly not divine.

As said before, the triumph of Christianity had pushed back the Eastern doctrines from the fifth century on, after a gigantic struggle against them, against their formulations in Greek philosophical language. These were the doctrines to which we refer generally as *heresies*. Yet, the church's victory does not mean that these heresies were extirpated, only that they went "underground" and reappeared afterwards in various disguises: incorporated in quasi-official teaching, in marginal propositions, in rejected theses, and, finally, in a *corpus* of esoteric documents passed on by one generation to another. Such a body of teaching was, for example, the Jewish Cabala which claimed a tradition going back to the Jews' captivity in Babylon where they had supposedly studied the Brahmanic texts of India, and, later, the Persian spirituality. Another tradition surfaced much later, in the seventeenth century, known as the Rosicrucian teaching, which claimed a long lineage of sources: Egypt, the Eleusian mysteries, the Persian magi, the Pythagoreans of Graecia Magna, and the wise men of Arabia. A yet later esoteric doctrine, Freemasonry, mentioned as its origin the alleged Egyptian mysteries of Pharaoh Tutmes III, four thousand years before Christ. In addition, there circulated in the Middle Ages a variety of manuscripts on astrology, claiming to have preserved the secret names of gods (spirits) from earliest antiquity. These astrological secrets blended with the work of the alchemists, particularly active in the late Middle Ages and in the Renaissance centuries, and whose tradition is as old as the earliest mining and metallurgical activities of men, whether in Greece, China, or Africa.

These esoteric teachings are intimately related. As late as the eighteenth century, it was known that most free-masons were also alchemists; the works of Swiss psychologist, C. G. Jung, show that alchemical speculation is present in the deepest layers of the human psyche—namely in the form of symbols conveying to man meanings which cut across centuries and civilizations. The Oxford historian of Oriental religions, R. C. Zaehner, showed recently the link between Brahmanic speculation, the practice of Zen, and the beliefs of the "Manson-family" of the famous murder case in California. Another historian of religion, Mircea Eliade, demonstrates in numerous writings that the alchemists' preoccupation with the "life" of metal, its passion, death, and resurrection (transfiguration) parallels the same events in the life of Christ, as we can see when we note in alchemical texts that gold for them is less the metal as we know it, than a symbol, or rather the incarnation of light.

Today we can safely assert that the Renaissance was the time when all these esoteric doctrines first presented themselves to Western man in the daylight of open speculation, that is, without efforts on the part of the church to suppress them. In this sense we may even say that the Renaissance is that period in Western intellectual history when the first serious attempt was conducted against the Christian concept of God, men, and creation, by those doctrines which are incompatible with it, but which had been resisted for more than a millenary, from Clement and Irenaeus, through St. Augustine and Athanasius, to Thomas Aquinas. We must, however, be careful to distinguish among the Renaissance currents. Philosophically speaking, orthodox Christian doctrine, from Augustine to Thomas, represents the victory of rational speculation—a thin and ever-threatened line—over a mostly radical mysticism whose characteristic sign was and is that it denies the distinction of God and man, self and totality, object and subject, conceptual thought and enthusiasm, etc. In the heyday of scholasticism (thirteenth century) the victory of orthodoxy was also that of Aristotle whose balanced rational outlook, integrated (by St. Thomas) with basic Christian doctrine, was able to neutralize the two kinds of assaults directed against scholasticism: the revived later-Greek systems of Stoicism and Epicureanism, on the one hand, and the hermetic-occult teachings, on the other hand. Aristotelianism remained official university teaching even after the Renaissance, not because attacks against it did not multiply and grow, but because Renaissance conceptual turmoil was unable to distill anything systematic and coherent with which to replace it. Only towards the end of the seventeenth century did the scientific view acquire enough authority to penetrate academic life and remove the last remnants of Aristotelian scholasticism.

Underneath the continued Aristotelianism of the universities, the occult systems had a relatively easy way of penetrating the intellectual circles of Renaissance Europe, beginning, of course, with Italy whose south (Sicily included) had been almost uninterruptedly exposed to Byzantine (Greek), Syrian, and Arab influence. Viewed from this angle, the Renaissance appears to us in a new light: as a synthesis of Christian, Hebrew, Greek, and occult doctrines, and some of the Renaissance heroes as rather confused intellects, standing at the crossroads of contradictory idea-systems. Before mentioning some by name—and situating them elsewhere than what is their consecrated place in our textbooks—let us describe the corpus of esoteric doctrines as it was handed down from ancient times to the Renaissance scholar.

The first period of flowering of esoterism can be put to the second and third centuries A.D., when the oriental doctrines penetrated the Roman Empire. By this time, the Augustan "restoration" was exhausted, and from then on the Roman world was to be a battlefield of doctrines and ideologies. From Egypt (?) the teachings of the mythical Hermes Trismegistus (thrice-great) proposed a kind of super-religion, older and truer than that of Moses and Christ, the religion of a god of mysteries. Salvation consisted in the knowledge (gnosis) which recognized the self as a part of the divine intellect, of which not everybody, only an elite, partakes. Thus the true doctrine is the secret of a few initiates—a pattern we find in each of the occult doctrines: the division of men into elect, magi, gnostikoi, alchemists, on the one hand, and masses, profane ones, divided ones, material ones, on the other. The French scholar, A. J. Festugiere, describes the gnostic initiate as attributing his personal suffering ("alienation" according to the contemporary Greek term, *allogenes*, that is, born elsewhere, belonging elsewhere) to the radical evil of the world from which he tries to escape; in contrast, the Greek sage, writes Festugiere, takes pleasure in the world's orderliness (kosmos) and finds his modest place in it even though he too is subject to the human condition.

Thus the first thing about the occult doctrines is that their adepts regard the universe as evil, and they view their own function as refugees from it or destroyers of it. My real self, the esoteric adept holds, is part of God, divine; what remains, my body and its passions, is of no consequence, it can be suppressed, or, on the contrary, it may be given full freedom since in that case *its* evil behavior does not involve *me*, my real self. The adept of occultism is not a human being in the same sense as the others, for he bears a higher element, he is not in a "conditioned state" (writes the contemporary esoteric, Rene Guenon), and he is only that part of himself which is of a divine essence. I am, said the Arab mystic Abu Mansur el-Helladj (tenth century), a divine hypostasis, an incarnation of God. Later, in the sixteenth century, Caspar Schwenckfeldt asserted that Christ is born in every man and that instead of salvation (the soul going to God and contemplating his glory) there is divinization, *theosis*; man becomes God, since the two are anyway indistinguishable.

These are, in the form of an abridged expose, the main tenets of esoterism. An equally important part is the one which describes the *techniques* of escaping from the (material) world, the *art* (magic aʀt) of securing for the spirit its homecoming to God. Esoterism speaks of the spirit (pneuma), not of the soul (psyche); the latter is "soiled" by all the material and passionate things that happen to man while he is immersed in profane existence, whereas the spirit is what is pure and untouched in him, the truly divine part. The esoteric technique is then the art of liberating the spirit from its material and psychic envelopes, the way of ascending to the One, the art of commending to the forces of the universe which is the adept's prerogative.

How does the adept reach perfection? Principally, by abolishing the multiplicity of which the world of appearances consists, and by joining them in a fused unity. Multiplicity itself is reducible to the two opposites of existence: the male and female principles which should be joined in the androgynous figure. These two poles of existence are found in such elements as sulphur and mercury, in the heavenly and the earthly, in the sponsus (Christ) and the sponsa (church). The objective is to restore their unity and thereby abolish contrasts which keep the world going through the instrumentality of struggle and conflict (*conjunctio oppositorum*). Only when the world will cease to be agitated, and finally to exist, when multiplicity will be reabsorbed in the One (a Western version of the Buddhist nirvana?), will the esoteric himself come to rest.

These ideas struck the Renaissance mind with a tremendous impact. These minds, for one thing, were deeply permeated by the age-old symbols inherited from countless generations, symbols which had traditionally found their way into literature, art, science, medicine, religion, and every act of life. The Renaissance man still lived in a sacralized world in which things carried a meaning, were animated by sacred forces, and were equivalently expressed by myth and by science. *Art* itself was not so much an object of enjoyment as a means among many of influencing the world—just as plants, for example, were not grouped in botanical categories but were playing specific roles in a universe of correspondences. The rediscovery of hermetic documents—*Poimander, Picatrix, Adocentyn*, the conversations of Hermes with his son, Tat, the Cabala, the Zohar, the astrological treatises—was as important for the Renaissance mind as the rediscovery of Plato's dialogues and the complete texts of dozens of Greek and Roman writers. At the end of the fifteenth century, Pico della Mirandola explained that the new knowledge obtained from magic, the secret arts, the Cabala, etc., proves the divinity of Christ better than the conventional documents, the Bible, and the Gospels. This statement meant, of course, that the latter needed confirmation from documents still more ancient which dated supposedly from time immemorial, from the "sages of Egypt." What the Renaissance scholar meant by universal knowledge, was, consequently, the mastery of occult art hitherto not available to Christians, an art consisting of knowledge but also of manipulation. The magic art now placed in the hands of the Renaissance scholar was the equivalent of technology placed at the disposal of twentieth-century intellectuals: both thought that the world may be thereby transformed in its substance.

For Cornelius Agrippa of Nettesheim, a German "humanist," magic was the natural consequence of cosmic unity. The *art* permits our ascent to the "original world" because the dogma held that "what is above is equal to what is below" and the two worlds may be reciprocally influenced through the magus. The magus acquires his status by ascending to the celestial sphere so as to be in a position to manipulate, give orders to, the sub-celestial things. For this purpose, the magus possesses talismans, magic objects, statues of spirits and divinities which, when suitably manipulated (like, for example, the Golem in Jewish Renaissance mysticism), confer upon the magus extraordinary powers, ultimately the powers of transforming the world. When this happens, wrote Giordano Bruno, another Renaissance humanist, the Egyptian religion will again prevail (over Christianity).

The nature of the magic object was studied with understandable care. Here the alchemists were in the forefront of the search. All modern students of alchemy (Eliade, Silberer, T. Burckhardt) agree that the objective was not gold but the *prima materia*, the original matter, the Philosopher's Stone which would be a fusion of opposites, able to bring about the "chemical marriage" (of sulphur and mercury) and produce a *substantia coelestis,* a heavenly substance, itself the supreme talisman since it combines the two spheres. The Christ, himself regarded as a fusion of the divine and the human, was merely one of the forms of the Original Man (the Adam Kadmon of the Cabala), a microcosm of creation, symbolized in many ways, among them as a complete sphere or an egg (symmetry), or the *ecclesia spiritualis,* in contrast to the worldly, material church of Rome. The Original Man was, of course, neither male nor female, it was an androgynous figure possessing double sex characteristics and eventually two heads, one male, one female. (The same is true of the tantric symbols, of Tibetan and Chinese symbols, etc.) The Philosopher's Stone, the Original Man, the Androgyne, and the Sphere were expressions of totality, and as such, symbols of a finally abolished multiplicity, symbols of the Whole and at the same time of Nothingness. Another sign, used later, is the perfect square surmounted by a cross, signifying tamed matter, the spiritualized world.

All this was not specifically the product of Renaissance speculation, although, quite understandably, the various currents so far mentioned could not converge before the weakened Christian faith and weakened doctrinal defense allowed them to surface as freely as they now did. It seems that the Renaissance made one important contribution to esoterism, the concept of the community itself as a "talisman," a kind of Philosopher's Stone on a large scale, the *city* regarded as the Original Man of vast proportions. Humanists like Bruno, Campanella, Andreae, and others laid out in their writings the "ideal city"—not as an urban project actually to be built, but as the final symbol for man's divinization. The many "utopias" (not excluding More's own) were subcelestial images of the celestial spheres, with God, "the Great Metaphysician" as king. Within the city, the Rosicrucians asserted, there will be universal harmony, a new language, and spiritual fusion with God. Let us bear in mind that Pico della Mirandola also found the "dignity of man" (in his famous discourse still regarded as the chief document of humanism) in his ability to synthesize heaven and earth so as to control his own destiny. Campanella's *City of the Sun* was to be in contact with the cosmos inasmuch as it was the incarnation of man, an artificial heaven. Paracelsus, another famous magus, promised a "new age of singing, dancing and jubilation" by the year 1600. *Utopia* was the ideal city not on account of its better laws and more durable institutions, but because it was a kind of gigantic *lapis philosophorum,* the juncture of heaven and earth, the place where man becomes divine.

Let us draw a few conclusions from the above discussion. We saw that the terms "renaissance" and "humanism" are not necessarily terms of praise, clarity, and ideality, but much more complex than to be compressible in one—positive —category. "Renaissance" was also the revival of ugly, idolatrous, and often obscene creeds, and "humanism" may mean just what it says: the adoration of man and his occult powers to create the world and himself. Of the magic ascent of Bruno, Agrippa, and others one may say what R. C. Zaehner recently wrote about Charles Manson's "trip": "Where he had been all things were One, and there was no diversity at all. He had passed beyond good and evil. At last he was free."

The second conclusion is that the fashion of the occult is not a mere harmless fad from which merchants of books, movies, songs, and festivals may reap ample profit; it is the sign of cultural confusion, of the distention of social ties, each member of the cult doing his own thing, making his own "ascent" to his own heaven, falling into his own abyss. Thirdly and most importantly, occultism is an unmistakable sign that reason is downgraded, and with it conceptual thinking, logic, rationality. Saying this, I do not mean, in my turn, to downgrade all mental categories other than reason. A civilization would be dreadfully impoverished if it made no room for mysticism, fantasy, imagination, and the irrational. It would not be a civilization at all. But it should be clear from this study that the occult *denies* reason and reason's function to be the ultimate arbiter of all things man strives to comprehend. Occultism does not do this by attacking reason directly, but by resorting to instruments (talismans, magic statues, signs, formulas, utopias, etc.) which, the occult adept holds, will transform man's creaturely state (*status creaturae*) into a divine state. The result will be, as Festugiere remarks, moral aberration (to a divine being all things are possible and permitted) and also intellectual aberration, the loss of proportions in things human, divine, scientific, cultural, social, and political.

In this manner a strange alliance is concluded between the occult and the rationalistic (as opposed to the rational, the reasonable). Since the magus has solved the riddle of the universe, and more, he has changed the universe into what he wanted it to be (abolition of good and evil, fusion of opposites, and so on), he gained a supra-rational power, a vantage point where he usurps the right of deciding the real and the unreal, being and non-being. Clinically, all kinds of diagnoses might apply; less scientifically, let us say only that such attitudes, indeed such ambitions, point to the sickness of the soul which tears itself away from being and its eternal laws.

Notes

INTRODUCTION

The most readily available account of SHC is Vincent H. Gaddis, *Mysterious Fires and Lights* (New York: Dell, 1967), pt. III. The Reeser case is treated in detail in *True Detective* (Dec. 1951). Also important, but less accurate than Gaddis' book, is the article by Allan Eckert, "The Baffling Burning Death," *True* (May 1964). The quote from Krogman appears in Eckert's article.

CHAPTER 1

1. Robert Nisbet, "Radicalism as Therapy," *Encounter* (March 1972).
2. Immanual Kant, *Critique of Pure Reason*, trans. Norman Kemp Smith, section B xxxiv.
3. E. A. Burtt, *The Metaphysical Foundations of Modern Physical Science* (Garden City, New York: Doubleday Anchor, [1926] 1954), pp. 52–56.
4. *Ibid.*, p. 105.
5. Eugene Wigner, "The Unreasonable Effectiveness of Mathematics in the Natural Sciences," *Communications on Pure and Applied Mathematics*, XIII (1960), pp. 1–14.
6. Gordon Leff, *Bradwardine and the Pelagians* (Cambridge University Press, 1957), p. 19.
7. Burtt, *Metaphysical Foundations*, pp. 58, 69n.
8. *Ibid.*, p. 121.
9. Kant, *Pure Reason*, A 761, B 789.

10. *Ibid.*, A 125.
11. *Ibid.*, A 126.
12. *Ibid.*, A 126–27.
13. Cornelius Van Til, *The Defense of the Faith* (rev. ed.; Philadelphia: Presbyterian & Reformed, 1963), pp. 124–26.
14. William Irvine, *Apes, Angels and Victorians* (New York: McGraw-Hill, 1959), p. 113.

CHAPTER 2

1. Karl Marx, "Private Property and Communism," *Economics and Philosophic Manuscripts of 1844* (New York: International Publishers, 1964), pp. 144–45.
2. Hermann Hesse, *Siddhartha* (New York: New Classics, 1951), p. 153.
3. Ed Sanders, *The Family* (New York: Dutton, 1971), p. 106.
4. Gary North, *Marx's Religion of Revolution: The Doctrine of Creative Destruction* (Nutley, New Jersey: Craig Press, 1968).
5. *Meister Eckhart*, trans. Raymond Bernard Blakney (New York: Harper & Row, 1941), pp. 233–34.
6. R. J. Rushdoony, *The Institutes of Biblical Law* (Nutley, New Jersey: Craig Press, 1973), p. 32.
7. *Ibid.*, p. 35.

CHAPTER 3

1. Lyall Watson, *Supernature* (New York: Bantam, 1974), p. viii.
2. *Ibid.*, p. 21.
3. *Ibid.*
4. *Ibid.*, p. 25.
5. *Ibid.*, p. 47.
6. *Ibid.*, p. 50.
7. *Ibid.*, pp. 51–52. Cf. Michel Gauquelin, *Cosmic Influences on Human Behavior* (New York: Stein & Day, 1973).
8. *Ibid.*, p. 288.
9. *Ibid.*, p. 253.
10. *Ibid.*, p. 282.
11. Sheila Ostrander and Lynn Schroeder, *Psychic Discoveries Behind the Iron Curtain* (New York: Bantam, 1970).
12. *Ibid.*, p. 7.
13. *Ibid.*, pp. 67–76.
14. C. S. Lewis, *The Screwtape Letters* (New York: Macmillan, [1943] 1969), Letter VII, pp. 32–33.
15. Ostrander & Schroeder, *Psychic Discoveries*, p. 20.
16. *Ibid.*, pp. 130–34.
17. *Ibid.*, p. 101.
18. *Ibid.*, p. 110.
19. *Ibid.*, p. 115.
20. Riverside, Calif. *Press-Enterprise* (March 29, 1969).
21. Ostrander & Schroeder, *Psychic Discoveries*, ch. 11.
22. *Ibid.*, pp. 156–57.
23. Thelma Moss, *The Probability of the Impossible* (Los Angeles: Tarcher; distributed by Hawthorne Books, New York, 1974), p. 228.
24. *New York Times* (Sept. 12, 1971).
25. Reported by *New York Times'* Hanson W. Baldwin; reprinted in Martin Ebon (ed.), *The Psychic Reader* (New York: New American Library, 1970), pp. 51–53.

26. Kenneth Roberts, *Henry Gross and His Dowsing Rod* (New York: Pyramid Books, [1951] 1969), chs. 13, 18.
27. Ostrander & Schroeder, *Psychic Discoveries*, p. 384.
28. Max Toth and Greg Nelson, *Pyramid Power* (New York: Freeway Press, 1974), ch. 8.
29. Charles F. Pfeiffer and Harold F. Vos, *Wycliffe Historical Geography of Bible Lands* (Chicago: Moody Press, 1967), p. 68.
30. Toth & Nelson, *Pyramid Power*, pp. 97–98.
31. *Ibid.*, pp. 150–52. Cf. Peter Tompkins and Christopher Bird, *The Secret Life of Plants* (New York: Avon, 1974), pp. 310–11.
32. *Ibid.*, pp. 159–60.
33. *Ibid.*, pp. 160–62.
34. Moss, *Probability*, pp. 58–59.
35. Ostrander & Schroeder, *Psychic Discoveries*, pp. 226–31.
36. Tompkins & Bird, *Secret Life*, p. 381.
37. *Ibid.*, p. 382.
38. Orthodox scientists have criticized Backster's experiments for being unrepeatable.
39. Tompkins & Bird, *Secret Life*, ch. 10.
40. *Ibid.*, p. 104.
41. *Ibid.*, p. 108.
42. *Ibid.*, p. 112.
43. *Ibid.*, p. 69.
44. Ostrander & Schroeder, *Psychic Discoveries*, p. 412.
45. Tompkins & Bird, *Secret Life*, pp. 212–13.
46. *Ibid.*, pp. 33–34.
47. *Ibid.*, p. 35.
48. *Ibid.*, pp. 37–38.
49. *Ibid.*, ch. 3.
50. Jule Eisenbud, M.D., *The World of Ted Serios* (New York: Pocket Books, 1968).
51. Ostrander & Schroeder, *Psychic Discoveries*, ch. 15.
52. Eisenbud, *Serios*, ch. 10.
53. *Ibid.*, p. 266.
54. *Ibid.*, p. 334.
55. Moss, *Probability*, p. 239.
56. Eisenbud, *Serios*, p. 313.
57. *Ibid.*, p. 319.
58. *Ibid.*, p. 322.
59. *Ibid.*, p. 323.
60. *Ibid.*, pp. 326, 327.
61. *Ibid.*, p. 329.
62. James ("The Amazing") Randi, a professional magician and full-time debunker of paranormal "frauds," that is, anyone who can perform seemingly impossible feats without sleight of hand, has asserted that he can duplicate all of Serios' "tricks." This is the standard rebuttal of all professional magicians. However, when challenged to match Serios' skills under controlled conditions, Randi has consistently begged off: Curtis Fuller, "Dr. Jule Eisenbud vs. the Amazing Randi," *Fate* (Aug. 1974), pp. 65–74. Randi is the author of a book supposedly debunking all of Uri Geller's key-bending, mind-reading stunts: *The Magic of Uri Geller* (New York: Ballantine, 1975). The book was ecstatically praised by establishment scientists.
63. Ostrander & Schroeder, *Astrological Birth Control* (Englewood Cliffs, New Jersey: Prentice-Hall, 1972).
64. Wayne Sage, "ESP and the Psychology Establishment," *Human Behavior* (Sept./Oct. 1972), p. 58.
65. Watson, *Supernature*, p. 72.
66. Sage, "ESP," p. 57.

67. *Ibid.*, pp. 57–58.
68. *Ibid.*, p. 58.
69. *Ibid.*, p. 57.
70. *Ibid.*, p. 59.
71. *Ibid.*
72. Arthur Koestler, *The Roots of Coincidence* (New York: Vintage, 1973), p. 44.
73. *Ibid.*, p. 45.
74. *Ibid.*, pp. 80–81.

CHAPTER 4

1. Carlos Castaneda, *The Teachings of Don Juan: A Yaqui Way of Knowledge* (New York: Pocket Books, 1974), p. 21. Originally published by the University of California Press, 1968.
2. *Ibid.*, p. 24.
3. C. S. Lewis, *The Abolition of Man* (New York: Macmillan, [1947] 1965), p. 88.
4. *Ibid.*, p. 69.
5. *Ibid.*, p. 68.
6. *Ibid.*, p. 71.
7. *Ibid.*, p. 72.
8. Castaneda, *Journey to Ixtlan* (New York: Pocket Books, [1972] 1974), p. 122.
9. Castaneda, *Tales of Power* (New York: Simon & Schuster, 1974), p. 243.
10. Lewis, *Abolition of Man*, p. 80.
11. *Ibid.*, p. 83.
12. Lynn White, Jr., "The Historical Roots of Our Ecological Crisis," *Science* (March 10, 1967). This widely quoted essay has been ably refuted by R. V. Young, "Christianity and Ecology," *National Review* (Dec. 20, 1974).
13. Castaneda, *Teachings*, p. 69.
14. Thomas Molnar, *God and the Knowledge of Reality* (New York: Basic Books, 1973).
15. Castaneda, *Teachings*, pp. 68–70.
16. *Ibid.*, p. 158.
17. *Ixtlan*, p. 147.
18. *Ibid.*, p. 75.
19. *Ibid.*
20. Castaneda, *A Separate Reality: Further Conversations With Don Juan* (New York: Pocket Books, [1971] 1974), pp. 149–50.
21. *Ibid.*, p. 150.
22. *Ibid.*
23. *Ibid.*, p. 151.
24. *Tales of Power*, pp. 284–85.
25. Anton Szandor LaVey, *The Satanic Bible* (New York: Avon, 1969), p. 33. By late 1972, this book was in its eighth printing.
26. Castaneda, *Tales of Power*, p. 59.
27. *Separate Reality*, p. 77.
28. *Ibid.*, p. 81.
29. *Ibid.*, p. 80.
30. *Ibid.*, p. 181.
31. *Ixtlan*, p. 191.
32. *Separate Reality*, p. 85.
33. *Tales of Power*, pp. 232–33.
34. *Separate Reality*, p. 63; *Ixtlan*, pp. 25, 249.
35. *Separate Reality*, p. 137.
36. *Ixtlan*, p. 34.
37. *Separate Reality*, p. 195.

38. *Ibid.*, p. 199.
39. *Ibid.*, p. 40.
40. *Ibid.*
41. *Teachings*, p. 120.
42. *Separate Reality*, p. 64.
43. *Tales of Power*, p. 280.
44. *Ixtlan*, p. 88.
45. *Separate Reality*, pp. 232–34.
46. *Teachings*, pp. 97–98
47. *Ibid.*, pp. 116–17, 155–57.
48. *Ibid.*, pp. 126–29.
49. *Ibid.*, pp. 140–41; *Separate Reality*, pp. 29–31.
50. *Separate Reality*, p. 240; *Tales of Power*, pp. 147–62.
51. *Tales of Power*, pp. 166, 182, 253, 261.
52. *Teachings*, p. 66.
53. *Tales of Power*, p. 51.
54. *Ixtlan*, p. ix.
55. *Tales of Power*, p. 193.
56. *Ibid.*, p. 249.
57. *Ixtlan*, pp. 135–36.
58. *Separate Reality*, pp. 219–20; cf. 126, 258.
59. *Tales of Power*, p. 27.
60. *Ibid.*, p. 47.
61. *Separate Reality*, p. 260.
62. *Ibid.*, p. 147.
63. *Ibid.*, p. 148.
64. *Ibid.*, p. 218.
65. *Ixtlan*, p. 211.
66. Kant, *Critique of Pure Reason*, Section A 126–27.
67. Castaneda, *Separate Reality*, p. 219.
68. *Tales of Power*, p. 22.
69. *Ibid.*, p. 101.
70. *Ibid.*, p. 13.
71. *Ibid.*, p. 127.
72. *Ibid.*, pp. 182, 252.
73. *Ibid.*, pp. 185, 189.
74. *Ibid.*, p. 178.
75. *Separate Reality*, pp. 23, 148, 197–98, 216–17, 242; *Ixtlan*, p. 161; *Tales of Power*, p. 166.
76. *Tales of Power*, p. 262.
77. *Ibid.*, p. 263.
78. *Ibid.*, p. 266.
79. *Ixtlan*, p. 155.
80. *Ibid.*, p. 183.
81. *Tales of Power*, p. 240.
82. *Ibid.*, p. 125.
83. *Ibid.*, p. 123.
84. *Ixtlan*, p. 91.
85. *Ibid.*, p. 98.
86. *Tales of Power*, p. 67.
87. *Ibid.*, pp. 81–82.
88. *Ixtlan*, p. 143.
89. *Tales of Power*, p. 159.
90. *Ibid.*, p. 174.
91. *Ixtlan*, p. 239.

92. *Tales of Power*, p. 17.
93. *Ibid.*, p. 192.
94. *Ibid.*, p. 206.
95. *Ibid.*, pp. 52–53.
96. *Ixtlan*, p. 11.
97. *Ibid.*, p. 265.
98. *Separate Reality*, p. 82.
99. *Ibid.*, p. 91.
100. Mircea Eliade, *Cosmos and History: The Myth of the Eternal Return* (1959); *The Sacred and the Profane: The Nature of Religion* (1961); *Myths, Dreams, and Mysteries* (1967); *Myth and Reality* (1963); *Rites and Symbols of Initiation: The Mysteries of Birth and Rebirth* (1958): all published by Harper Torchbooks. This is only a small sample of Eliade's voluminous output.
101. Ronald Rose, *Primitive Psychic Power* (New York: Signet, [1956] 1965), p. 192.
102. Castaneda, *Separate Reality*, pp. 216–17.
103. Los Angeles *Times* (June 8, 1975).
104. Castaneda, *Ixtlan*, p. 239.
105. *Ibid.*, p. 155.
106. *Teachings*, p. 129.
107. Rose, *Primitive Psychic Power*, pp. 101–02.
108. Frances Yates, *Giordano Bruno and the Hermetic Tradition* (New York: Vintage, [1964] 1969), p. 454.

CHAPTER 5

1. *Newsweek* (April 8, 1974), p. 61.
2. John Godwin, *Super-Psychic: The Incredible Dr. Hoy* (New York: Pocket Books, 1974), p. 109.
3. *Ibid.*, p. 106.
4. *Ibid.*, p. 21.
5. *Ibid.*, p. 35.
6. *Ibid.*, p. 115.
7. *Ibid.*, p. 101.
8. Bryan R. Wilson, *Magic and the Millennium* (London: Hineman, 1971), pp. 21–26.
9. William C. Martin, "This Man Says He's the Divine Sweetheart of the Universe," *Esquire* (June 1974).
10. Godwin, *Super-Psychic*, p. 100.
11. Charles C. Cochrane, *Christianity and Classical Culture* (New York: Oxford University Press, 1944), p. 159.
12. Jackson Harrison Pollack, *Croiset the Clairvoyant* (London: Quality Book Club, 1965), pp. 47–52.
13. *Ibid.*, p. 165.
14. Norma Lee Browning, *The Psychic World of Peter Hurkos* (Garden City, New York: Doubleday, 1970), pp. 190–91.
15. Pollack, *Croiset*, p. 99.
16. *Ibid.*, p. 36.
17. *Ibid.*, p. 20.
18. *Ibid.*, p. 27.
19. *True* (April 1964), p. 125.
20. Browning, *Hurkos*, p. 48.
21. *Ibid.*, p. viii.
22. *Ibid.*, p. 51.
23. *Ibid.*, p. 54.
24. Vincent Bugliosi, *Helter Skelter* (New York: Norton, 1974), p. 250; Ed Sanders. *The Family* (New York: Dutton, 1971), p. 97.

25. Bugliosi, *Helter Skelter*, pp. 55–56; Browning, *Hurkos*, pp. 253–55.
26. Browning, *Hurkos*, pp. 65, 95, 201, 206.
27. *Ibid.*, pp. 84–85.
28. *Ibid.*, pp. 110–11.
29. *Ibid.*, pp. 235–36.
30. *Ibid.*, p. 241.
31. Castaneda, *Teachings of Don Juan*, pp. 110–17.
32. Browning, *Hurkos*, p. 272.
33. Ostrander & Schroeder, *Psychic Discoveries Behind the Iron Curtain*, ch. 12.
34. *Philadelphia Bulletin* (May 30, 1974).
35. Ruth Montgomery, *A Gift of Prophecy* (New York: William Morrow, 1965), p. 19.
36. *Ibid.*, p. 16.
37. *Ibid.*, p. 111.
38. Donald Hatch Andrews, *The Symphony of Life* (Lee Summit, Mo.: Unity Books, 1966), p. 9.
39. Richard Rhodes, "Heaven on Earth," *Harper's* (May 1970).
40. Montgomery, *Gift*, p. 25.
41. *Ibid.*, p. 26.
42. *Ibid.*, p. 74.
43. *Ibid.*, p. 83.
44. *Ibid.*, p. 26.
45. *Ibid.*, p. 94.
46. R. J. Rushdoony, *This Independent Republic* (Nutley, New Jersey: Craig Press, 1964), p. 142.
47. Montgomery, *Gift*, p. 171.
48. *Ibid.*, p. 182.
49. *Ibid.*, p. 181.

CHAPTER 6

1. Doris Agee, *Edgar Cayce on ESP* (New York: Paperback Library, 1969), p. 14.
2. Thomas Sugrue, *There Is a River* (rev. ed.; New York: Holt & Co., [1943] 1948), pp. 60–61.
3. *Ibid.*, p. 7.
4. *Ibid.*, pp. 23, 45–46.
5. Harmon H. Bro, *Edgar Cayce on Religion and Psychic Experience* (New York: Paperback Library, 1970), p. 24.
6. Hugh Lynn Cayce, "Introduction," H. L. Cayce (ed.), *The Edgar Cayce Reader* (New York: Warner Paperback Library, [1969] 1974), p. 8.
7. Sugrue, *River*, pp. 55–56.
8. Bro, *Religion*, p. 9.; Cayce, (ed.) *Reader*, p. 8.
9. Sugrue, *River*, p. 106.
10. *Ibid.*, p. 121.
11. Hugh Lynn Cayce, *Venture Inward* (New York: Harrow Books, [1964] 1972), p. 51.
12. Jeffrey Furst, *Edgar Cayce's Story of Jesus* (New York: Coward-McCann, 1969), pp. 340–41.
13. Sugrue, *River*, pp. 137, 145–46.
14. *Ibid.*, p. 126.
15. H. L. Cayce, *Venture Inward*, pp. 33–35.
16. Sugrue, *River*, p. 146.
17. Jess Stearn, *Edgar Cayce—The Sleeping Prophet* (New York: Bantam, [1967] 1971), p. 105.
18. Sugrue, *River*, p. 21.
19. H. L. Cayce, *Venture Inward*, pp. 36–39.
20. Sugrue, *River*, p. 237.

21. Bro, *Religion*, p. 264.
22. Agee, *ESP*, p. 31.
23. Sugrue, *River*, p. 147.
24. *Ibid.*, p. 247.
25. Agee, *ESP*, p. 203.
26. Furst, *Jesus*, p. 41.
27. Stearn, *Prophet*, p. 229.
28. *Ibid.*, p. 40.
29. *Ibid.*, p. 77.
30. *Ibid.*, p. 39.
31. *Ibid.*, p. 34.
32. *Ibid.*, p. 35.
33. *Ibid.*, p. 257.
34. Agee, *ESP*, p. 65.
35. *Argosy* (Feb. 1975), p. 75.
36. Sugrue, *River*, p. 351.
37. Mary Ann Woodward, *Edgar Cayce's Story of Karma* (New York: Berkeley Medallion, 1971, p. 46.
38. *Ibid.*, p. 84.
39. H. L. Cayce, *Venture Inward*, p. 112.
40. Furst, *Jesus*, p. 52.
41. H. L. Cayce (ed.), *Reader*, p. 23.
42. *Ibid.*, p. 111.
43. Furst, *Jesus*, p. 232.
44. Agee, *ESP*, p. 77.
45. Furst, *Jesus*, p. 19.
46. H. L. Cayce, *Venture Inward*, pp. 206–07.
47. Furst, *Jesus*, p. 32.
48. *Ibid.*, pp. 32–35, 40–41.
49. *Ibid.*, p. 23.
50. *Ibid.*
51. *Ibid.*, p. 71.
52. *Ibid.*, pp. 78–79.
53. Frances Yates, *Giordano Bruno and the Hermetic Tradition* (New York: Vintage, [1964] 1969), p. 5.
54. Furst, *Jesus*, p. 172.
55. *Ibid.*, p. 173.
56. *Ibid.*, pp. 173–74.
57. *Ibid.*, p. 78.
58. *Ibid.*, p. 26.
59. *Ibid.*, p. 220.
60. *Ibid.*, p. 247.
61. *Ibid.*, p. 284; cf. 270.
62. *Ibid.*, pp. 164–66.
63. *Ibid.*, p. 171.
64. *Ibid.*, p. 314.
65. Woodward, *Karma*, p. 23.
66. *Ibid.*, p. 22.
67. *Ibid.*, p. 21.
68. *Ibid.*
69. *Ibid.*, p. 17.
70. *Ibid.*, p. 255.
71. H. L. Cayce, *Venture Inward*, p. 75.
72. Furst, *Jesus*, p. 308.
73. Gina Cerminara, *Many Mansions* (New York: Signet, [1950] 1967), p. 63.

74. *Ibid.*, pp. 72–73.
75. Ibid., p.75.
76. *Ibid.*, p. 154
77. F. A. Hayek, *The Road to Serfdom* (Chicago: University of Chicago Press, 1944), ch. 10
78. Furst, *Jesus*, p. 333.
79. Stearn, CF88; cf. 363–64
82. Agee, *ESP*, p. 41.
83. Stearn, *Prophet*, p. 163.
84. *Ibid.*, p. 84.
85. Agee, *ESP*, ch. 7; Bro,*Religion*, ch. 5; H. L. Cayce, *Venture Inward*, p. 73.
86. Agee, *ESP*, p. 69.
87. Furst, *Jesus*, p. 57.
88. *Ibid.*
89. Agee, *ESP*, p. 54; cf. Appendix B on astrology in Furst, *Jesus*.
90. H. L. Cayce (ed.), *Reader*, p. 159.
91. Furst, *Jesus*, p. 36.
92. Agee, *ESP*, p. 28.
93. *Ibid.*
94. Max Weber, *Economy and Society* (New York: Bedminster Press, [1924] 1968), p. 241.
95. H. L. Cayce (ed.), *Reader*, pp. 31–32.
96. *Ibid.*, p. 33.
97. *Ibid.*, p. 34.
98. *Ibid.*

CHAPTER 7

1. Max Weber, "Science as a Vocation" (1918), in H. H. Gerth and C. Wright Mills (eds.), *From Max Weber: Essays in Sociology* (New York: Oxford University Press, 1946), pp. 138–39.
2. John G. Fuller, *Arigo: Surgeon of the Rusty Knife* (New York: Pocket Books, 1974), p. 58.
3. *Ibid.*, pp. 58–60.
4. *Ibid.*, p. 64.
5. *Ibid.*, pp. 55–56.
6. *Ibid.*, pp. 66–67.
7. Bryan R. Wilson,*Magic and the Millennium* (London:Hineman, 1971), p. 106.
8. *Ibid.*
9. *Ibid.*, p. 113.
10. Fuller,*Arigo*, pp. 48–49.
11. Hans Holzer, *Beyond Medicine* (New York: Ballantine, 1974), pp. 65–66.
12. Wilson, *Magic*, p. 118.
13. *Ibid.*, p. 118n.
14. Fuller, *Arigo*, p. 200.
15. *Ibid.*, pp. 20–21.
16. *Ibid.*, p. 75.
17. *Ibid.*, p. 125.
18. *Ibid.*, p. 82.
19. *Ibid.*, p. 91
20. *Ibid.*, p. 99.
21. *Ibid.*, p. 19.
22. *Ibid.*, pp. 23–25.
23. *Ibid.*, pp. 35–36, 43.

24. *Ibid.*, p. 45.
25. *Ibid.*, p. 134.
26. *Ibid.*, p. 143.
27. *Ibid.*, p. 145.
28. *Ibid.*
29. *Ibid.*, p. 146.
30. Thomas Kuhn, *The Structure of Scientific Revolutions* (Chicago: University of Chicago Press, 1962), pp. 4–5.
31. Fuller, *Arigo*, p. 162.
32. *Ibid.*, p. 168.
33. *Ibid.*, p. 174.
34. *Ibid.*, p. 195.
35. Kuhn, *Scientific Revolutions*, p. 21.
36. Robert K. Merton, *Science, Technology and Society in Seventeenth Century England* (New York: Harper Torchbook, 1970); Merton, *Social Theory and Social Structure* (New York: The Free Press, 1969), ch. 18.
37. Wilson, *Magic*, p. 119.
38. P. T. Bauer, *Dissent on Development* (Cambridge, Mass.: Harvard University Press, 1972).
39. Wilson, *Magic*, p. 121.
40. Ronald Rose, *Primitive Psychic Power* (New York: Signet, [1956] 1968), p. 87.
41. Harold Sherman, "*Wonder*" *Healers of the Philippines* (Santa Monica, Calif.: De Vorss, [1967] 1974), p. 275.
42. *Ibid.*, pp. 279–80.
43. *Ibid.*, p. 277.
44. *Ibid.*, p. 89.
45. *Ibid.*, p. 125.
46. *Ibid.*, p. 16.
47. *Ibid.*, p. 88.
48. *Ibid.*, pp. 24, 58, 61, 192.
49. *Ibid.*, p. 59.
50. *Ibid.*, p. 163.
51. *Ibid.*, p. 68.
52. *Ibid.*, pp, 54, 288.
53. Tom Valentine, *Psychic Surgery* (New York: Pocket Books, 1975), p. 17.
54. Sherman, "*Wonder*" *Healers*, p. 252.
55. *Ibid.*, pp. 139–40.
56. *Ibid.*, p. 301.
57. Carlos Castaneda, *A Separate Reality*, pp. 217, 219.
58. Valentine, *Psychic Surgery*, p. 160.
59. *Ibid.*, p. 51.
60. *Ibid.*, p. 52.
61. *Ibid.*, pp. 71–72.
62. *Ibid.*, p. 57.
63. Sherman, "*Wonder*" *Healers*, p. 198.
64. *Ibid.*, p. 197.
65. *Ibid.*, p. 199.
66. *Ibid.*, p. 193.
67. On Astara, see David St. Clair, *The Psychic World of California* (New York: Bantam, 1973), pp. 253–56.
68. *Ibid.*, pp. 160–61.
69. Valentine, *Psychic Surgery*, pp. 142–43.
70. Ronald Rose, *Primitive Psychic Power*, pp. 28–35.
71. Kurt Koch, *Occult Bondage and Deliverance* (Grand Rapids, Mich.: Kregel, 1972), pp. 78–79.

72. *Ibid.*, p. 55.
73. *Ibid.*, p. 54.
74. Valentine, *Psychic Surgery*, p. 214.

CHAPTER 8

1. Augustine, *The City of God*, XII:17.
2. *Ibid.*, X:14.
3. Mircea Eliade, *Patterns in Comparative Religion* (New York: Sheed & Ward, 1958), p. 399.
4. Victor Lasky, *The Ugly Russian* (New York: Trident, 1965).
5. P. T. Bauer, *Dissent on Development* (Cambridge, Mass.: Harvard University Press, 1972), pp. 78–79.
6. Helmut Schoeck, *Envy: A Theory of Social Behavior* (New York: Harcourt Brace Jovanovich [1966] 1969), p. 37.
7. *Ibid.*, p. 40.
8. *Ibid.*, p. 47.
9. *Ibid.*, p. 48.
10. *Los Angeles Times* (Oct. 9, 1975).
11. Schoeck, *Envy*, p. 41.
12. *Ibid.*, p. 50.
13. Anton Szandor LaVey, *The Satanic Bible* (New York: Avon, 1972), p. 51.
14. *Ibid.*, pp. 51–52.
15. *Ibid.*, p. 52.
16. *Ibid.*, p. 89.
17. *Ibid.*, p. 41.
18. *Ibid.*, p. 30.
19. *Ibid.*, p. 31.
20. Aleister Crowley, *Magick in Theory and Practice* (New York: Castle, n.d.), pp. 152–53.
21. *Ibid.*, p. 127.
22. *Ibid.*, p. 42.
23. *Ibid.*, pp. 36, 62, 144, 256–57.
24. *Ibid.*, p. 24n.
25. *Ibid.*, p. 193.
26. *Ibid.*, pp. 167–69.
27. *Ibid.*, p. 164.
28. *Ibid.*, p. 65.
29. *Ibid.*, p. 164.
30. *Ibid.*, p. 96.
31. R. J. Rushdoony, *Politics of Guilt and Pity* (Nutley, New Jersey: Craig Press, 1970).

CHAPTER 9

1. C. S. Lewis, *The Screwtape Letters* (New York: Macmillan, [1943] 1969), Letter # 7, p. 33.
2. Colin Wilson, *The Occult: A History* (New York: Random House, 1971), p. 23.
3. *Ibid.*, p. 28.
4. *Ibid.*, p. 39.
5. *Ibid.*, p. 23.
6. *Ibid.*, p. 103.
7. *Ibid.*, pp. 193, 232.
8. Aleister Crowley, *Magick in Theory and Practice* (New York: Castle, n.d.), p. 11.

9. *Ibid.*, p. 17.
10. Robert K. Merton, *Social Theory and Social Structure* (New York: The Free Press, 1969), ch. 18.
11. H. J. Shepard, "Gnosticism and Alchemy," *Ambix*, VI (1958), pp. 140–48; Shepard, "The Redemption Theme in Hellenistic Alchemy," *Ambix*, VII (1959), pp. 42–76.
12. Mircea Eliade, *The Forge and the Crucible: The Origin and Structures of Alchemy* (New York: Harper Torchbook, [1956] 1971), p. 225.
13. *Ibid.*, pp. 109–11.
14. *Ibid.*, pp. 124, 167.
15. *Ibid.*, pp. 174–75.
16. Louis Pauwels and Jacques Bergier, *The Morning of the Magicians* (New York: Avon, [1960] 1973), p. 118.
17. Eliade, *Forge*, pp. 190–91. Eliade relies on the study of Lutheran alchemy written by the Lutheran scholar John Warwick Montgomery: "Cross, Constellation, and Crucible: Lutheran Astrology and Alchemy in the Age of the Reformation," *Transactions of the Royal Society of Canada*, I, Ser. 4 (June 1963), Sect. II, pp. 251–700.
18. It is the thesis of this book that man's self-deification is the very heart of the religion of Satan—the temptation to be as God.
19. Pauwels and Bergier, *Morning*, p. 137.
20. *Ibid.*, pp. 60–61.
21. *Ibid.*, p. 357.
22. *Ibid.*
23. *Ibid.*, pp. xxii-xxiii.
24. *Ibid.*, p. 341.
25. *Ibid.*, p. 416.
26. *Ibid.*, p. 287.
27. Crowley, *Magick*, p. 5.
28. Eliade, *The Two and the One* (New York: Harper Torchbook, [1962] 1969), pp. 11–12.
29. *Ibid.*, p. 12.
30. *Ibid.*, pp. 13–14.
31. Eliade, *Myths, Dreams, and Mysteries* (New York: Harper Torchbook, [1957] 1967), p. 49.
32. *Ibid.*, p. 50. •
33. Eliade, *Rites and Symbols of Initiation: The Mysteries of Birth and Rebirth* (New York: Harper Torchbook, [1958] 1965), p. 107.
34. Eliade, *Myth and Reality* (New York: Harper Torchbook, [1963] 1968), p. 62.
35. *Ibid.*, pp. 157–61.
36. Eliade, *Shamanism* (Princeton: Princeton University Press/Bollingen, [1964] 1974), pp. 127–44.
37. Ludwig von Mises, "Stones into Bread, the Keynesian Miracle," in Henry Hazlitt (ed.), *Critics of Keynesian Economics* (Princeton: Van Nostrand, 1960).
38. Edward Banfield, *The Unheavenly City* (Boston: Little, Brown & Co., 1970), p. 53.
39. *Ibid.*, p. 127.
40. *Ibid.*, p. 222.
41. Aldous Huxley, *The Doors of Perception* (New York: Perennial Library, [1954] 1970), p. 21.
42. *Ibid.*, p. 30.
43. *Ibid.*, p. 53.
44. *Ibid.*, p. 60.
45. *Ibid.*, p. 64.
46. *Ibid.*, p. 65.
47. Paul J. Stern, *In Praise of Madness* (New York: Norton, 1972), p. 86.
48. *Ibid.*
49. R. M. Bucke, *Cosmic Consciousness* (New York: Dover, [1901] 1969), p. 6.
50. *Ibid.*, pp. 4, 22.

51. *Ibid.*, p. 17.
52. *Ibid.*, p. 194.
53. *Ibid.*, pp. 145–46.
54. Cornelius Van Til, *The Psychology of Religion* (Syllabus, Westminster Seminary, Philadelphia, 1961), p. 62.
55. Nandor Fodor, *Freud, Jung, and Occultism* (New Hyde Park, New York: University Books, 1971).
56. R. C. Zaehner, *Zen, Drugs and Mysticism* (New York: Pantheon, 1972), p. 98.
57. *Ibid.*, p. 115.
58. *Ibid.*, p. 108.
59. *Ibid.*, p. 81.
60. *Ibid.*, p. 116.
61. *The Cooperator*, V (Spring-Summer, 1973), p. 2.
62. Thomas Molnar, *God and the Knowledge of Reality* (New York: Basic Books, 1972), pp. 89–90.
63. R. J. Rushdoony, *This Independent Republic* (Nutley, New Jersey: Craig Press, 1964), p. 142.
64. *The Cooperator*, V (Spring-Summer, 1973), p. 14.
65. *Ibid.*, p. 12.
66. *New Consciousness Education*, I (Jan. 1973).
67. Barbara M. Hubbard, "The Politics of Transcendence," *New Worlds Newsletter*, Phase II, Vol. II (Jan. 1974), p. 2.
68. R. J. Rushdoony, "Humanistic Law," introduction to E. L. Hebden Taylor, *The New Legality* (Nutley, New Jersey: Craig Press, 1967), pp. vi-vii. The passage has been corrected and appears in an accurate form in Gary North, *Marx's Religion of Revolution* (Nutley, New Jersey: Craig Press, 1968), pp. 118–19.